# THE MOVEMENT
# AND THE MIDDLE EAST

# THE MOVEMENT AND THE MIDDLE EAST

*How the Arab-Israeli Conflict
Divided the American Left*

Michael R. Fischbach

Stanford University Press
Stanford, California

Stanford University Press
Stanford, California

© 2020 by Michael R. Fischbach. All rights reserved.

No part of this book may be reproduced or transmitted in any form or by any means, electronic or mechanical, including photocopying and recording, or in any information storage or retrieval system without the prior written permission of Stanford University Press.

Printed in the United States of America on acid-free, archival-quality paper

Library of Congress Cataloging-in-Publication Data

Names: Fischbach, Michael R., author.
Title: The Movement and the Middle East : how the Arab-Israeli conflict divided the American Left / Michael R. Fischbach.
Description: Stanford, California : Stanford University Press, 2019. | Includes bibliographical references and index.
Identifiers: LCCN 2019012962 (print) | LCCN 2019013916 (ebook) | ISBN 9781503611078 (ebook) | ISBN 9781503610446 (cloth: alk. paper) | ISBN 9781503611061 (pbk.: alk. paper)
Subjects: LCSH: Arab-Israeli conflict—1967–1973—Foreign public opinion, American. | New Left—United States—History—20th century. | Israel—Foreign public opinion, American.
Classification: LCC DS119.7 (ebook) | LCC DS119.7 .F564 2019 (print) | DDC 956.04/81—dc23
LC record available at https://lccn.loc.gov/2019012962

Jacket design: Kevin Barrett Kane

For Lisa, Tara and Adnan, Grace, and Sophia

# Contents

viii    Contents

# Acronyms

| | |
|---|---|
| AAUG | Association of Arab-American University Graduates |
| AAWO | Alliance Against Women's Oppression |
| AFFP | American Friends of Free Palestine |
| AFSC | American Friends Service Committee |
| ASU | American Servicemen's Union |
| AZYF | American Zionist Youth Foundation |
| BARU | Bay Area Revolutionary Union |
| BDS | Boycott, Divestment, and Sanctions Movement |
| CIA | Central Intelligence Agency |
| CLP | Communist Labor Party |
| CONAME | Committee on New Alternatives in the Middle East |
| CPME | Committee for a Progressive Middle East |
| CPSU | Communist Party of the Soviet Union |
| CPUSA | Communist Party of the United States of America; Communist Party USA |
| CRV | Committee of Returned Volunteers |
| CSMEL | Committee to Support Middle East Liberation |
| DSA | Democratic Socialists of America |
| DSOC | Democratic Socialist Organizing Committee |
| FBI | Federal Bureau of Investigation |
| FOR | Fellowship of Reconciliation |
| FSLN | Frente Sandinista de Liberación Nacional |

| | |
|---|---|
| JA | Jewish Agency |
| JLP | Jewish Liberation Project |
| JPF | Jewish Peace Fellowship |
| JUJ | Jews for Urban Justice |
| LNS | Liberation News Service |
| MERIP | Middle East Research and Information Project |
| MIT | Massachusetts Institute of Technology |
| NAARPR | National Alliance Against Racist and Political Repression |
| NAM | New American Movement |
| NLG | National Lawyers Guild |
| OAS | Organization of Arab Students |
| OL | October League |
| PDFLP | Popular Democratic Front for the Liberation of Palestine |
| PFLP | Popular Front for the Liberation of Palestine |
| PFLP–GC | Popular Front for the Liberation of Palestine—General Command |
| PFOC | Prairie Fire Organizing Committee |
| PHRC | Palestine Human Rights Campaign |
| PLO | Palestine Liberation Organization |
| PSC | Palestine Solidarity Committee |
| RCPUSA | Revolutionary Communist Party USA |
| RZA | Radical Zionist Alliance |
| SANE | National Committee for a Sane Nuclear Policy |
| SCLC | Southern Christian Leadership Conference |
| SDS | Students for a Democratic Society |
| SDUSA | Social Democrats USA |
| SI | Socialist International |
| SNCC | Student Nonviolent Coordinating Committee |
| SPA | Socialist Party of America |
| SUNY | State University of New York |
| SWP | Socialist Workers Party |
| TWWA | Third World Women's Alliance |
| UCLA | University of California at Los Angeles |
| USYC | United States Youth Council |
| UVA | University of Virginia |
| VVAW | Vietnam Veterans Against the War |

| | |
|---|---|
| VVAW/WSO | Vietnam Veterans Against the War/Winter Soldier Organization |
| WAI | Women Against Imperialism |
| WPP | White Panther Party |
| WRL | War Resisters League |
| WSP | Women Strike for Peace |
| WSU | Wayne State University |
| WUO | Weather Underground Organization |
| WWP | Workers World Party |
| YAWF | Youth Against War and Fascism |
| YCPDME | Youth Committee for Peace and Democracy in the Middle East |
| YIPME | Youth Institute for Peace in the Middle East |
| YPSL | Young People's Socialist League |
| YSA | Young Socialist Alliance |

# THE MOVEMENT
# AND THE MIDDLE EAST

# Prologue

THE MIDDLE EAST erupted in violence on June 5, 1967, after weeks of mounting tension ended with a preemptive Israeli attack on Egyptian airfields. Ironically, the hippie counterculture's international "Summer of Love" was launched in San Francisco that same month. Israeli forces quickly followed up on their success in the air by all but destroying the Egyptian, Syrian, and Jordanian armies in six days of fighting, capturing a huge amount of Arab territory in the process. Israelis and their supporters around the world celebrated the Jewish state's victory in what they called the "Six-Day War," rejoicing in what they believed was Israel's salvation from bloodthirsty Arabs bent on its destruction. Polls showed that Americans were virtually unanimous in siding with Israel. Indeed, the percentage expressing sympathy for Israel skyrocketed from about 60 percent in 1966 to 95 percent the following year. Less than 5 percent sympathized with the Arabs and the Palestinians.[1]

By contrast, the Arab world in 1967 mourned what it called "al-Naksa": the Setback. For the Palestinian Arabs in particular this was the second catastrophe they had suffered in under twenty years. The first was when the Arab-Israeli war of 1948 led to the creation of Israel out of 77 percent of British Palestine. No comparable Palestinian state emerged: the remaining 23 percent of the country, the West Bank and Gaza, came under Jordanian and Egyptian control. Wherever they found themselves living after 1948, Palestinians were either stateless or subjects of other peoples and governments. The war was also a socioeconomic and demographic nightmare for the Palestinians; they called it "al-Nakba": the Disaster. In the process of the fighting, nearly three-quarters of a million Palestinians—one-half of Palestine's Arabs—either fled or were expelled from their homes by Israeli forces, ending up as refugees in Arab territory. Israel destroyed their abandoned villages and forbade their return. The 1967 war nineteen years later triggered a second huge exodus of Palestinians in the wake of the fighting and the resultant Israeli military occupation of the West Bank and Gaza.

The pro-Israeli triumphalism that swept over America after the war had its origins in earlier attitudes. Even before the war, some American leftists disagreed with what they considered this uncritical attachment to Israel and concomitant denigration of the Arabs. In November 1966, Daniel Rubin, a Communist Party USA (CPUSA) central committee member, decried American Jews' "upside-down approach to Israel" and support of the Jewish state as a progressive country threatened by ignorant, reactionary Arab aggressors. "By accepting this picture, Jews in the U.S., usually unwittingly, find themselves aiding U.S. monopoly in its all too successful attempt to control the economy and the governmental policies of Israel to the detriment of the Israeli masses," Rubin lamented. "They find themselves on the side of U.S. imperialism in opposition to national liberation movements and on the side of rabid anti-Communist cold-warriors."[2]

This was the CPUSA's party line: what best served the interests of Jews in the United States was not to support Israel blindly but to see that the real question in the Middle East was the struggle to overthrow imperialism, the common enemy of both Jews and Arabs in the region. The Jewish-Arab conflict merely diverted the attention of both peoples from what would lead to their liberation. Rubin also waxed personal in his commentary, stating, "As an American Jewish Communist, I feel ashamed and angry that a Jewish government coming from a people who have known so much oppression should oppress Arabs within Israel and play the U.S. imperialist game of supporting their oppression in neighboring countries."[3]

Immediately after the 1967 war began, the CPUSA leadership also adopted the position that Israel's actions were "aggressive." Rubin's fellow Jewish communist Sid Resnick strongly objected. For him, Israel was merely defending itself against a threatened Arab genocide. "The Arab chauvinist threat to Israel's existence was real in May and June 1967," he asserted. "In fact, 'de-Zionizing' the State of Israel and converting it into an Arab Palestine state is impossible without destroying the people and State of Israel."[4] Pointing beyond the CPUSA to the entire American Left, Resnick intoned: "Within left-wing movements, Jewish and non-Jewish radicals ought to challenge that sham 'internationalism' which glorifies Palestinian Arab terrorists and runs interference for Arab chauvinism. This disgraceful attitude which allows any slander of Israel, of the Jewish people and Jewish history to pass as 'Marxist' interpretation must be challenged both for its falsity and for its compromising of socialist humanism."[5] Resnick left the CPUSA a year after the war, and later recalled, "I thought the party was wrong in completely condemning Israel as the aggressor in the 1967 war."[6]

That two Jewish members of the same left-wing political party held such divergent and mutually antagonistic views on the Arab-Israeli conflict is illustrative of a major problem that bedeviled and ultimately weakened the American Left in the 1960s and 1970s, ironically at a time when it was at its strongest since the 1940s: which side, Israel or the Palestinians, deserved the support of left-wing activists? Almost all white leftists agreed on the need to end the Vietnam War, support the black freedom struggle, and strive for a "new politics" in America. This is broadly what activists meant when they spoke of "the Movement": a large, loosely organized collection of people pushing for an end to the war and radical change in America. And while many black leftists readily supported the Palestinians,[7] their white comrades were deeply and sometimes bitterly divided over how to situate the Arab-Israeli conflict within their respective ideologies and strategies. In part, this conflict was doctrinal; in part, generational and even ethnic. Many scholars have written about the US Left in the 1960s and 1970s and the reasons for its weakening and decline, but none have analyzed the Arab-Israeli conflict's role in this context, or indeed discussed the white Left's grappling with that conflict to any great extent.[8]

The major split in the Left came down to this: how far did left-wing support for revolutionary internationalism and anti-imperialism extend? Did it apply across the board, or was one country, Israel, somehow exempt from scrutiny? Support for global revolution versus "Israel exceptionalism" proved to be a major source of contention and division within the Left in the 1960s and helped weaken it. The disproportionately large Jewish presence within the Left further complicated the question of how to situate Israel and the conflict in the Middle East. Whether to support Israel or the Palestinians sometimes became a particularly and deeply personal decision for many Jews, because the issue often was tied to their identity as members of a global minority that long had struggled against a bitter history of persecution. Should they be part of a broader revolutionary impulse seeking to change the world for all, or make an exception for Israel and exempt it from anti-imperialist, pro–Third World stances adopted by much of the Left?

With so many things already preoccupying the Movement during the 1960s and 1970s, what caused activists to begin grappling with the Arab-Israeli conflict? The main reason was the 1967 war. The Arab defeat provoked an immediate surge in Palestinian nationalism. Many Palestinians believed not only that the Arab states had twice (1948 and 1967) proven incapable of helping them save Palestine, but also that the Arabs never could liberate Palestine for them. This would have to be a struggle they waged themselves, using a different approach. The Arabs' loss in 1967 gave a tremendous boost to the Palestinian guerrilla group al-Fateh, which had emerged in the Arab world in the late 1950s and had been attacking Israeli targets from bases in the Arab frontline states since 1965. Al-Fateh guerrillas were soon joined by fighters from other groups that emerged during and after 1967, including the Popular Front for the Liberation of Palestine. These various *fida'iyyin* (Arabic: those who sacrifice themselves, "fedayeen") soon launched more and more attacks on Israel, claiming they were launching a people's liberation war, much as Algerian, Cuban, and Vietnamese revolutionaries had done and were still doing. The guerrillas drew praise from the Arab world as the only Arabs still brave enough to continue the struggle, against great odds, the powerful Israeli enemy.

Extensive media coverage of the Arab-Israeli conflict during and after 1967 placed the new Palestinian resistance movement squarely in the world's spotlight, which in turn situated it within the overall international revolutionary fervor of the global 1960s. Their faces wrapped in checkered *kufiyya* (keffiyeh) headscarves and their hands gripping AK-47 assault rifles, enthusiastic Palestinian fedayeen impressed both other Third World independence movements and the global media. It was not long before they caught the imagination of the American Left as well, particularly when viewed in relation to what was happening in Vietnam.

This book tells the story of the varying white left-wing American attitudes toward the Arab-Israeli conflict during the 1960s and 1970s, and asks why these had such a tremendous impact on activists' divergent agendas, identities, and understandings of how to effect change in American society and foreign policy. The truth is that intra-Left arguments over whether to support Israel or the Palestinians were not just differences of opinion; they also mirrored much deeper debates about identity and political action in the 1960s and 1970s. Two major rifts can be distinguished.

The first was the split over who in the Middle East deserved the Left's support. This became a marker of whether or not one was committed to a universal restructuring of society, which pro-Palestinian leftists tended to advocate, or wished to make Israel an exception to that restructuring. "It was a major issue," the famous SDS (Students for a Democratic Society) leader Mark Rudd recalled decades later. "It distinguished the true anti-imperialists from the liberals."[9] Pro-Palestinian radicals in New Left groups like SDS and the Yippies quickly began hailing the Palestinians as a Third World people fighting for freedom against an ally of American imperialism in the Middle East. This assessment was shared by Old Left Marxist parties like the Socialist Workers Party and the Workers World Party. As the 1960s faded into the 1970s, post–New Left underground revolutionaries like the bombers of the Weather Underground similarly declared their allegiance to the Palestinian struggle, as did aboveground Marxist parties within the New Communist Movement like the Revolutionary Communist Party USA and the October League.

These and other groups viewed themselves as revolutionaries seeking the fundamental restructuring of capitalist American society and dismantling its imperialist web of control over the Third World. For them, the Palestinian national movement against Israel fitted in perfectly with this worldview. On the other hand, some on the left (and liberal but not quite left-wing allies in the Democratic Party, trade unions, and mainstream anti–Vietnam War activists) lined up solidly behind Israel, even if they agreed with pro-Palestinian radicals on just about everything else. A total revolutionary restructuring of the world was not on their agenda; the restructuring stopped at the borders of the Jewish state. These activists saw Israel as a progressive socialist state seeking to defend its very existence against Arab dictatorships, and accordingly balked at jumping on the anti-Israeli bandwagon.

Among organized political parties, nowhere did this tension over which side to support create more significant intra-party problems than within the Old Left's most venerable organization, the CPUSA, which underwent much conflict inasmuch as many Jewish comrades rebelled against the hostile, anti-Israeli attitude of their party bosses. For the communists' rivals in the Socialist Party of America and its 1970s-era offshoots like the Social Democrats USA and the Democratic Socialist Organizing Committee, the choice generally was even clearer almost from the beginning in 1967: support Israel wholeheartedly.

Other parts of the Movement that were animated by the Left tried not to champion either side but keep the entire issue of the Arab-Israeli conflict at arm's length. This was particularly true of the movement to end the Vietnam War. The large antiwar coalition called "The Mobe" exerted great efforts to focus solely on the war in Vietnam, not war in the Middle East, despite efforts by some, like those in the Workers World Party, to push it into condemning Israel. Antiwar figures like Martin Luther King Jr. similarly faced the dilemma of how to remain morally consistent in their denunciations of war yet not offend important pro-Israeli constituencies. In other instances, antiwar activists openly embraced Israel, which on occasion led to some strange contradictions. For example, some of those who denounced America's use of advanced F-4 Phantom aircraft to drop napalm in Vietnam simultaneously urged American leaders to sell F-4s to Israel so that it could (and did) drop napalm on Arabs. Bitter divisiveness also broke out within the women's movement; pro- and anti-Zionist women clashed viciously.

A second agonizing fault line emerged along questions of Jewish identity. Jews were disproportionately well represented on the American Left in the 1960s and 1970s, as well as among those from across the liberal-left political spectrum in movements like feminism and the campaign to end the Vietnam War. This worsened and often personalized the struggle between left-wing internationalism and Israel exceptionalism. Many Jews in the Movement had been raised to love Israel, but not all Jews on the Left were so moved. Indeed, some of the sharpest denunciations of Israel and expressions of support for the Palestinians came from Jews. The entire Left would feel the impact of this Jewish "civil war."

The impact on the Left of these contending discourses was negative in terms of its longevity: disagreement over the Arab-Israeli conflict contributed to the Left's eventual decline, starting in the 1970s. The CPUSA never recovered from its internal dissension over the issue. The post-1960s Marxist Left continued to champion the Palestinians' armed struggle at a time when even the Palestinians themselves were starting to move in a different direction, further marginalizing these leftists and diminishing their effectiveness in reaching out to other Americans. The divisiveness pushed the democratic socialist Left in particular further and further to the right, with important consequences for future left-wing electoral activity. The emergence of revolutionary expressions of support for the Palestinians also spurred the growth of neoconservatism, particularly when certain erstwhile Jewish leftists abandoned the Left over its treatment of Israel during the 1960s.

Despite these negative consequences for it, the support for the Palestinian cause that the Left disseminated in the 1960s became rooted more widely in American society. In the 1970s, after the Vietnam War and its associated turmoil were over, more and more progressive Americans concerned about US foreign policy, global peace, and human rights began questioning Israeli policy and urging support for the Palestinians. The fact that the Middle East was changing, with more and more attention being paid to the idea of creating a Palestinian state alongside Israel, consolidated this trend. Despite the decline of the Left, pro-Palestinian consciousness had become ensconced permanently within the broader progressive mainstream by the late 1970s and early 1980s. On the other hand, so, too, had strongly pro-Israeli sentiments. Where progressive Americans stand on these issues today thus stems from the events of decades past.

This narrative history is the result of many years of deep research in many states and the District of Columbia, as well as in Israel, Jordan, and Lebanon. In the process I not only examined documents housed in public and university archives, in addition to those available online and on microfilm, but supplemented this with research into printed primary and secondary sources, and also with requests, via the Freedom of Information Act, to view documents from US government agencies such as the Federal Bureau of Investigation and the Central Intelligence Agency. I also interviewed American and other progressives who were active in the 1960s and 1970s, whether in person, by telephone, or by mail and email. These interviews were crucial not only to fill in the historical narrative but also to capture the feelings and words of key players in this drama.[10]

I often quote directly from contemporary activists and the various documents they produced. Why should we be concerned with the feelings and words of those who lived through these events decades ago? Writing in 2006, Bernardine Dohrn, a former member of the militant Weather Underground, commented on the surge in interest in that group in the early twenty-first century. "Hopefully there will be a blizzard of memoirs, films, and historical inquiries into the rainbow of *other* activities of equal or greater importance that were embarked on in that zesty, defiant era known as the sixties," Dohrn observed. "Those stories too deserve loving attention, scrutiny, and lessons learned. Not from a nostalgic longing for past glories, which were never all that, but as segue to the urgent imperatives of today."[11] This book focuses attention on some of those stories and humbly aspires to prompt readers to consider such imperatives.

# 1   The Times They Are a-Changin'

*The New Left and Revolutionary Internationalism*

WHEN WAR ERUPTED in the Middle East on June 5, 1967, Bob Feldman was listening to the radio while recuperating from the measles. Feldman had entered Columbia University in 1965, and in November 1966 had joined its chapter of Students for a Democratic Society (SDS), the most noteworthy student radical group in the nation in the 1960s. In 2009, he recalled having heard on the radio that day in 1967 that Egypt and Syria had attacked Israel, and that the Jewish state's very existence was in peril. "Because the U.S. mass media portrayed Israel as being the victim of Arab military aggression in 1967," Feldman remembered, "I did not get upset when it appeared that the Zionist military machine was rolling over the Egyptian Army and would win the June 1967 War quickly."[1]

A few weeks later, however, a fellow student Feldman bumped into outside Columbia's Butler Library disabused him, saying: "Israel, you know, started the war in order to capture new lands." Stunned, Feldman responded, "I thought the Arabs started the war in order to drive the Jews into the sea?" His friend replied that Israel had in fact struck first. In August that year, the Black Power Student Nonviolent Coordinating Committee (SNCC) issued a newsletter denouncing Israel and hailing the Palestinians.[2] Years later, Feldman recalled: "[My friend's] analysis of the 1967 Mideast War caused me to read more deeply about what had exactly happened. And when SNCC came out in opposition to Israel's seizure of Arab lands and continued refusal to recognize the legitimacy of the claims of the Palestinian refugees and their Palestinian nationalist representatives, I inwardly supported SNCC's position."[3] He was a changed man.

SDS stood at the apex of the New Left, a term that was coined by the sociologist C. Wright Mills.[4] The New Left was a loosely organized collection of young, mostly white leftists who sought structural change in America but who generally eschewed ideological constructions and instead based their activism on moral passion and street-level politics. They looked upon the Old Left—the doctrinaire Marxist and socialist parties like the Socialist Party of America and the Communist Party USA that emerged in the late nineteenth and early twentieth centuries—with disdain. Yet observing the widening conflict in Southeast Asia in the early 1960s and American military interventions elsewhere, as in the Dominican Republic in April 1965, New Leftists began to develop a more sophisticated politics that dovetailed with the growing pro–Third World, anti-imperialism being proclaimed by the Black Power movement. Support for national liberation struggles and guerrilla movements around the world came to be an essential part of New Left ideology by the late 1960s. As one former young leftist noted decades later, "There was a movement to see all peoples' revolutionary struggles as one. Wherever people were adopting armed struggle, people in the New Left and the Marxist Left were thrilled and supported it."[5]

No such overseas struggle animated New Leftists more than the Vietnamese struggle against the United States, but it did not take some of these young people long to offer verbal support for the Palestinian struggle in the wake of the 1967 war in the Middle East.[6] Two events, both spearheaded by black militants, played a particularly crucial role in developing New Left consciousness about Israel and the Palestinians. SNCC's anti-Israeli newsletter article in August 1967 came first. Several weeks later black activists at the National Conference for New Politics successfully demanded that the gathering issue a statement denouncing Israel.[7] The issue of Americans' attitudes toward Israel and the Palestinians was now on newspapers' front pages. The stage was set for SDS and others in the Movement to tackle the Arab-Israeli conflict.[8]

## Students for a Democratic Society and the June 1967 War

Just nine days after the war ended in the Middle East, the June 19, 1967, issue of *New Left Notes*, an SDS publication, carried a motion for adoption at an upcoming national SDS meeting. Roy Dahlberg was just shy of twenty-three years old. He had started out in SDS as a member of the San Francisco chapter and risen to become a member of the group's national interim committee. Dahlberg's motion noted that the recent Arab-Israeli war had "brought about strong reaction from American Jews and confusion on the Left in general." Dahlberg urged Jews to stay focused on an anti-imperialist analysis of the Arab-Israeli conflict: the Arab stance toward Israel as a colonial settler state was the same stance that black Africans maintained toward such states on their continent. From this perspective, settler colonialism was no more justified in Israel than it was in Kenya or Mozambique. "Perhaps most discouraging is the number of American students expressing the desire to fight for Israel," Dahlberg wrote. Not understanding the nature of the conflict, they "let emotion fog their reason entirely."[9]

Most Americans knew little about the Middle East, and reacted differently to the war. Judith Tucker, a Radcliffe student, learned things about the Arab-Israeli conflict that were completely new to her from Radio Havana's coverage of the war, which was "like a totally different story," she remembered. "The narrative was so different from what we were getting from American news. I thought, 'there's a whole other side to this story.' It wasn't a part of any discourse on the Left in '67." She recalled there being "very little talk of Israel-Palestine—virtually none" on campus prior to that.[10] Others reacted more strongly. Dan Siegel was not pleased with Israel's action during the war. During his first term as a law student at the University of California, Berkeley, in the fall of 1967, Dan Siegel discussed what he called Israel's "reckless behavior" with fellow students, and he subsequently became a leader in the SDS chapter there.[11]

As we have seen, Jews were disproportionately numerous in the New Left.[12] Many of them were against the war in Vietnam and against Big Power military intervention in the affairs of Third World countries, yet had been raised to think of Israel as a bastion of socialist progress surrounded by a sea of reactionary Arabs. So how were they to understand Israel's preemptive attack in 1967, its subsequent military occupation of Arab territory, and the armed Palestinian resistance groups that emerged with such force thereafter?[13] Mark Rudd recalled that the war led to much "soul-searching" for him. He had been raised in a "typical American Jewish family" of "moderate Zionists," and "in Hebrew School I was taught to love Israel and buy trees; my parents dutifully gave to the UJA [United Jewish Appeal], which had Israel in the forefront of its causes." The outbreak of the 1967 war prompted him to give a great deal of thought about the Middle East. On the second day of the 1967 war, when a good friend of his whose parents were Holocaust survivors told him that he felt he should be in Israel fighting, Rudd was taken aback: "I realized at the time that nationalism (Jewish in this case), meant a whole lot less to me than internationalism; and that I was thoroughly anti-imperialist."[14]

During his upbringing "the promotion of Zionism wasn't intense" but "it was always there, kind of a given," David Gilbert, also a Jewish SDSer at Columbia, recalled: "In Hebrew school, I learned the prevalent myths: Israel made the desert bloom, was the only democracy in the region, and was surrounded by a hostile Arab population." Although not strongly Zionist, he felt no need to challenge this and saw no contradiction with his involvement in the early 1960s in the civil rights and antiwar movements. However, by 1967, the year after he graduated from Columbia, Gilbert had progressed from involvement in anti–Vietnam War work to supporting Third World liberation struggles in general. The 1967 war led him to see Israel as "an enemy of Third World people" and Zionism as "a form of racism."[15]

Some Jewish SDSers felt that their background predisposed them to an interest in the Arab-Israeli conflict. While an undergraduate at the University of Michigan, Bob Ross became one of the founders of SDS in 1960. He "absolutely" felt his Jewishness was a factor in this regard. "I was always highly conscious of being a Jew, but a secular Jew [and] not a Zionist Jew. My father came from the communist movement. My mother was a [five-time Socialist Party presidential candidate Eugene] Debs socialist. I had a Left, highly-identified-as-Jewish, secular, non-Zionist background."[16] Other Jewish SDS activists agreed, and in fact openly embraced the Palestinian cause precisely because their Jewish background demanded that they do so, they said. Mike Klonsky worked at the SDS regional office in Los Angeles before moving to the group's national offices in Chicago in 1968 to assume a position in the national leadership. Looking back decades later, Klonsky recalled: "A lot of the activists at that time were Jewish, and a lot of us felt we had a special responsibility to speak out on those issues [e.g., the Palestinian cause] because we were Jewish. I interpreted my role as a Jew as someone who needed to support such causes."[17]

Not all left-wing Jews in SDS were quite so sanguine about challenging the positive attitude about Israel of so many American Jews, at least, not at first. Hilton Obenzinger was a student involved in the antiwar movement and other activities at Columbia. "I was raised in a Jewish family, pro-Israel, and edu-cated in a Zionist-oriented Conservative Jewish congregation," he recalled. "Most of my family were murdered by the Nazis, so it was very emotional in a lot of respects. Israel was a form of redemption." Obenzinger remem-bered staying up all night once during the June 1967 war, reading the *New York Times* and worrying about Israel. "Wasn't Israel sort of socialist? Weren't they advanced, democratic and progressive? Why did the Arabs want 'to push the Jews into the sea'?" Yet he also thought "there's something going wrong here." Moreover, he also had to reconcile his warm feelings for Israel with the Israeli government's support for the American war in Vietnam, symbolized by former Israeli general Moshe Dayan's 1966 trip to Vietnam to report on the war for an Israeli newspaper. "This was cognitive dissonance in a big way," Obenzinger noted years later. "I either had to be consistent with my principles or begin fudging them out of some sense of ethnic loyalty."[18]

Naomi Jaffe had become a "passionate Zionist" at the age of five, with the creation of Israel in 1948. Her feelings as a young girl came as a result of "the desperate pride with which my parents and other adult relatives viewed the founding of Israel as a response to our [Jews'] unbearable vulnerability and victimization in the Holocaust." Jaffe felt very conflicted and initially uncom-fortable with those in SDS who embraced the Palestinian cause after 1967. She also found that *not* criticizing Israel would alienate her from her leftist comrades, for whom revolutionary internationalism—support for global rev-olution—was a part of their radical identity. Jaffe "gradually and painfully came to accept it as an inevitable part of the radical ideology and world view that I shared with the other young student radicals with whom I associated."[19] Other Jewish SDS members concurred that the group should come down sol-idly on the side of the Palestinians. One of SDS's national secretaries, Michael Spiegel, said Jewish New Leftists needed to move beyond their upbringing in order to remain true to their internationalism. Although at first "shocked by the prospect of anti-Zionism," they would "come to the inevitable conclusion" that it was correct.[20]

Arab students attending SDS's annual conference in Ann Arbor, Michi-gan, in June 25–30, 1967, soon after the war, took the initiative to discuss some ideas about the Middle East with their American counterparts.[21] SDS seemed receptive. At the convention, the SDS foreign affairs workshop produced a minority report that criticized the American role in the creation of Israel and called Zionism and anti-Semitism two sides of the same coin.[22] In late 1967, the SDS leadership printed *Zionism and the Israeli State: An Analysis in the June War* by Larry Hochman, who knew a thing or two about Zionism, having spent ten years, starting at age eleven, in a socialist Zionist organization, Hashomer Hatzair, and lived on Kibbutz Merhavya in Palestine. Returning to the United States, Hochman eventually taught physics at Eastern Michigan University, by which time he had become an ardent anti-Zionist.

Hochman succinctly stated what he saw as the essence of the Arab-Israeli conflict: the disruptive creation of a Jewish state in an Arab part of the globe in the context of Western imperialism: "To become more fundamental, the central issue in Southwest Asia is the fact that a Jewish state has been established in the midst of the Arab world without the invitation or consent of the indigenous population. The Jewish immigration occurred, and could only have occurred, under the aegis of Western colonial control." He also dismissed a common belief among New Leftists that Israel was a progressive socialist state worthy of their support by arguing that what type of governmental system was in place in Israel was of little consequence when dealing with the central factor in the conflict, namely, that the native Palestinians were displaced by Zionism. "The fact that foreign colonizers established certain domestic structures is completely irrelevant to the question of the indigenous people's rights," he wrote.[23]

Hochman summed up well the feelings of many New Left Jews who began championing the Palestinian cause during and after 1967. They believed that Zionism was a colonial movement that transported outsiders, mostly Europeans, into an area of the developing world already inhabited by other people, and then displaced them to make a state for themselves. This was like what American settlers had done to the Indians. The fact that Israel was Jewish state, or that they themselves were Jewish, was of no consequence to their analysis.

## SDS's Pro-Palestinian Stance

The SDS national leadership's new thinking about the Middle East was not only a result of the war that broke out that year; some SDSers had started rethinking the organization's purpose. Years of political agitation against racism and the Vietnam War had not produced the kind of change in America that many in SDS had hoped for, and some in the leadership began arguing that it should move from being a student protest group to a revolutionary organization dedicated to bringing about structural change in America. Related to this was its leftward move toward Marxism. Earlier SDS activists had eschewed Marxism and derided it as part of the "Victorian" Old Left's ideological fixation on the notion that social change would come through a revolutionary working class—what C. Wright Mills dismissed as the "labor metaphysic."[24] Part of this shift toward Marxism stemmed from SDS leaders' struggle against the influence within the group of the Progressive Labor Party (PL), a communist organization enamored with the People's Republic of China and Mao Zedong.

By late 1968, the national leadership declared that the time was right for SDS to shift its focus from being a student movement to becoming a revolutionary movement for all youth, particularly working-class youth. This was crystalized by a political statement that the SDS national council adopted in December 1968, entitled "Toward a Revolutionary Youth Movement," which had been written by one of the leading anti-PL figures within SDS, Mike Klonsky. In March 1969, national SDS figures Bill Ayers and Jim Mellen discussed support for Third World nationalist struggles as the basis for a Revolutionary Youth Movement faction saying, "all our actions must flow from our identity as part of an international struggle against U.S. imperialism."[25]

Because of this new focus on revolution, anti-imperialism, and support for Third World revolutions, some in SDS had come to the conclusion by late 1968 and early 1969 that the group should take an even more active stance with regard to the Arab-Israeli conflict. By that time the Palestinian guerrilla movement was constantly in the headlines and much more noticeable than in 1967. In Paris in the summer of 1968, Peter Pran, a thirty-two-year-old Norwegian graduate student who was president of the SDS chapter at the Illinois Institute of Technology in Chicago, was asked by Palestinian activists if his group supported their struggle. Pran returned to the United States and published a piece in *New Left Notes* in March 1969 stating that SDS had been remiss in not coming out publicly in support of the Palestinians. Issuing internal education material was one thing; supporting the Palestinians in public was another. "SDS cannot pretend to be a consistent backer of revolutionary struggles around the world without taking a strong stand on the Middle East war, one of the most important battles in the world today," Pran argued. He insisted that SDS' national council or national convention adopt a resolution to that effect.[26]

The SDS national interim committee thereafter decided to begin distributing information on the Middle East to educate the general membership.[27]

SDS's Radical Education Project reprinted a pamphlet issued in mid-1968 by the anti-Zionist Israeli Socialist Organization, Matzpen, entitled *The Other Israel*. The cover of another SDS pamphlet, *The Struggle in the Middle East*, prepared for the spring national council meeting scheduled for March 28–30, 1969, in Austin, Texas, bore the emblem of the Palestinian National Liberation Movement, known as al-Fateh, with the legend: "This symbol means, 'INVADERS! GET OUT OF OCCUPIED LAND!'"[28]

A key figure in SDS in 1969 publicizing the plight of the Palestinians was Susan Eanet. Like Klonsky, whom she married, Eanet was a Jewish SDSer who strongly supported the Palestinians. She dropped out of college, began working at SDS offices, and by 1969 was working as a writer for *New Left Notes*. In the first four months of 1969, Eanet published articles in six issues of *New Left Notes* that championed the Palestinians and their cause, conveying a strong signal about the national leadership's position on the Arab-Israeli conflict.[29] In the first of these articles she claimed that aside from Vietnam the Middle East was perhaps "the leading struggle against US imperialism in the world today." She then went on to offer a detailed history of Zionist immigration to Palestine, arguing that the Zionist displacement of the Palestinians was similar to the conquest of Native American Indians by white settlers. In the case of the Zionists, "they chose to colonize 'the heathen' who occupied the Arab lands in order to create a new Jewish homeland. . . . Thus the so-called birth of Israeli 'socialism' was founded on the complete relocation of thousands of people of color."[30] In another article, Eanet defended SDS against the charge of being anti-Semitic for criticizing Israel by claiming that criticism of racism and imperialism in the Middle East was no more anti-Semitic than agitation against racism in the United States was anti-American.[31]

Eanet's articles aroused immediate controversy in SDS, not all of whose members agreed with the national leadership's new stridently pro-Palestinian focus. A contemporary assessment noted: "It is a very volatile issue, especially at heavily Jewish campuses such as Columbia."[32] *New Left Notes* soon published letters to the editor both praising and criticizing Eanet's pieces. In his letter in the March 20, 1969, issue of *New Left Notes*, Peter Pran asserted: "The State of Israel must be abolished. Its Zionist, racist government and its league with imperialism thoroughly exposed and fought, until the day the land is again taken back by the Palestine refugees to whom it belongs—before it was stolen by the Israeli Jews." Richard Morrock, however, used the same issue of the newspaper to denounce Eanet's February 28, 1969, article for what he considered its factual errors and simplistic analysis. The whole emphasis of the article, Morrock wrote, "was on presenting the Zionists as 'racist' bad guys, and the Arabs as 'anti-imperialist' good guys."[33] There were also reports of a decline in financial support for the group as a result of its public pro-Palestinian tilt.

As planned, the issue came up at the SDS national council meeting in March 28–30, 1969, where Klonsky chaired a workshop on the Middle East. Yet despite the pre-convention publicity about the Palestinians, only seven people reportedly attended the workshop, and it failed to adopt the motion on the Middle East that Klonsky had proposed.[34] The national office's desire to move forward with a clear pro-Palestinian position seemed to gain little traction with the wider membership. The main issue for SDS and the Movement at large was the war in Vietnam, not the Middle East. Those who thought about and discussed the Arab-Israeli conflict did so with great conviction, but the question did not seem to interest a majority of the SDS's 100,000 members. Bob Feldman summed up this feeling: Vietnam was the "issue that most seemed to threaten my life, because of the draft. So, like most other Movement people, I didn't make Palestinian solidarity work any kind of political priority at this time."[35]

Factionalism over ideology and direction led SDS to split apart three months later during its June 1969 national convention in Chicago, and two of the various factions that emerged continued to support the Palestinian cause. The Weatherman faction began publishing a short-lived publication entitled *Fire!* after the Chicago convention, which carried a two-part article on the Palestinians and the Arab world in its November 21 and December 6, 1969, issues. The other pro-Palestinian faction that emerged from the breakup of SDS, the Revolutionary Youth Movement II group, called on SDS members to "support the just struggles of the Palestinian, Congolese, Colombian and all other peoples fighting for national liberation."[36] Although the immediate cause of the factionalism had nothing to do with certain SDS leaders' pro-Palestinian, anti-Israeli stances, the wider dissension within the membership caused by those stances in SDS's last two years of functional existence no doubt further weakened an organization that already was beset with internal problems, and it faded away after 1970–71.

SDS's decline symbolized the wider disintegration of the New Left. Its partial embrace of the Palestinian cause was, however, a major factor in the wider identification of white leftists in the Movement with the Palestinians.

"It was a major issue," Mark Rudd noted decades later. "It distinguished the true anti-imperialists from the liberals." A member of SDS at Queens College, Wayne Price, agreed: "It was something that people had to think about. Anti-imperialism was widespread. It was one of the big disputes, the dividing lines, between those who called themselves revolutionaries and those who were liberals and social democrats."[37] "Almost everybody . . . thought of it as an issue," Bernardine Dohrn concurred.[38] Most SDS members' strategic or tactical goals did not, however, extend to campus protests on behalf of the Palestinians or demonstrating for their cause in other ways. The war in Vietnam, the black freedom struggle, and working against the capitalist system took precedence.

Pro-Palestinian activists within SDS were not, however, the only New Leftists to challenge support for Israel. Members of one particularly famous and widely publicized group—"non-group" might be a more appropriate term—were doing so as well: the Yippies, a loose group of anarchistic young people, led by Jerry Rubin and Abbie Hoffman, both of them Jewish, who self-consciously merged radical New Left political attitudes with countercultural hippie lifestyles.

## "Moses as an Arab Guerrilla"

The Yippies' flamboyant hair styles and clothing, outrageous behavior, opposition to the Vietnam War, hostility to American culture, and wild political and media antics made them the embodiment of the 1960s and the New Left in the eyes of many Americans. What most did not know, however, was that Rubin and Hoffman also strongly supported the Palestinians. "I do not believe in 'freedom' for Jews at the expense of Arabs and black people," Rubin wrote, and Hoffman proclaimed: "I hate Israel and want to see the Palestinians triumph."[39]

Long before he became a Yippie, Rubin knew a great deal about Israel and the Palestinians. Having interacted with Arab students as a youth in Cincinnati, he "felt that their arguments against Israel were right, but that didn't bother me. I'd go to Israel and convince the Israelis of the rightness of the Arab cause. Like Gandhi, I would convince the Israelis to offer love to the Arabs."[40]

Rubin moved to Israel in mid-1961, and his experiences there radicalized him. "Israelis openly described Arabs the way whites talked about blacks in America," he later wrote. "I respected the Israeli people but I felt frustrated whenever politics came up. The very things I was running away from in America I found in Israel. My heart was Jewish but my head leaned toward internationalism. . . . So here I came for idealism and I got—America. I became anti-Israeli and pro-Arab."[41] He regarded himself as an "internationalist," and associating with Palestinians and communists, rather than with mainstream Jews, led to his being put under surveillance by Israeli intelligence.[42]

His Jewishness contributed significantly to his pro-Palestinian views, Rubin believed. "It is the Jew who should always be on the side of the poor, the oppressed, the underdog, the wretched of the earth, because of the Jewish experience," he wrote in July 1970. "And thousands of young ex-Amerikan [sic] ex-Jews are." Connecting this with the Arab-Israeli conflict, he wrote: "If Moses were alive today, he'd be an Arab guerrilla."[43] Years later, Rubin's former wife and Yippie co-founder, Nancy Kurshan, offered her own thoughts on the pro-Palestinian sentiments of Rubin, herself, and other Yippies. Born into a radical Jewish family, Kurshan was studying for her Ph.D. at Berkeley when she met Rubin, after which she dropped out to join him in New York to work on preparations for the march on the Pentagon in October 1967. "Jerry was definitely supportive of the Palestinian struggle as was I," Kurshan recalled. "We had both been interested in Israel, both had visited before we met each other and I think it's fair to say that we were both disappointed [in Israel]."[44]

Abbie Hoffman differed from Rubin in that he rarely expressed himself publicly about Israel and the Palestinians in his writings in the 1960s and early 1970s. Like some other Jewish leftists, he tended to focus on other priorities and kept his attitudes to the Arab-Israeli conflict private. Hoffman's support for the Palestinians was already evident by the time he was tried in 1969 for conspiracy as one of the famous Chicago Seven defendants. He once passed a note to one of his lawyers, Alan Dershowitz, indicating his support for the Palestine Liberation Organization (PLO).[45] One of the few times Hoffman went public was when he signed a document entitled "Liberation of Palestine and Israel" that appeared in the July 1, 1971, issue of the *New York Review*. This scored all sides in the Arab-Israeli conflict for policies that did not contribute to peace, adding, "But the first steps toward change must come from the militarily more powerful partner."[46] One year later, Hoffman again made a public comment when he told a reporter covering the protests at the Democratic Party's 1972 national convention in Miami Beach, Florida, "I am very pro-Jewish, but anti-Zionism."[47]

By the time he went underground in February 1974 to avoid imprison-ment on charges of selling cocaine, Hoffman's private views on Israel and the Palestinians had become quite anti-Israeli. It was only a few months after the October 1973 Arab-Israeli war had broken out, a war that nearly brought the United States and the Soviet Union to blows. Much of what we know of Hoff-man's attitudes about the Arab-Israeli conflict comes from letters between him and his wife, Anita, which the latter published in 1976. The letters indi-cate a hardening of his attitudes toward Israel. In October 1974, he wrote to Anita expressing his concern that the conflict would erupt into open warfare again and that Israel might use nuclear weapons—weapons that the world was coming to believe that Israel possessed, but which it officially denied pos-sessing.[48] Two months later, Hoffman wrote of his strong feelings about the conflict in a letter which reveals the degree to which he hated Israel and now openly championed the Palestinians: "I am violently anti-Israel and no longer believe they have a right to exist. During the past ten years they have forfeited any right they might have 'earned'. . . . Zionism was the cause of the war. The PLO are as guilty of aggressions as were the North Vietnamese!! . . . I hate Israel and want to see the Palestinians triumph."[49]

Hoffman also was concerned that the United States might be dragged into a war in the Middle East because of Israel's close identification with the West and American support for Israel: "their [Israel's] cultural identity with the West and the irrational sympathy and guilt they muster from W.W.II experi-ence, only force me to conclude they are destined to bring the U.S. into war." He feared that the strong pro-Israeli feelings of American liberals would work against efforts to keep the United States out of a Middle Eastern war: "I'm amazed at how venomous hatred for the Arabs is among the liberals. . . . There won't be the base for organizing against such a war [an American war in the Middle East] as in Vietnam, and left protests will be suppressed with a mighty boot." Hoffman rued the fact that he had not agitated more on the issue: "If I were active politically like before, I'd have gone and debated someone like [Meir] Kahane in Jerusalem, gotten kicked out, then gone to Arab countries to learn more, then [returned and done] educational work."[50]

Other Yippies besides Rubin and Hoffman were drawn to the Arab-Israeli conflict. One was Paul Krassner, one of the original Yippies. Born to Jew-ish parents in Brooklyn, Krassner was a writer and comedian who associated with a variety of political and cultural figures in the 1960s, including the noted comedian Lenny Bruce. Prior to that, Krassner began publishing an influential satirical magazine called *The Realist,* starting in mid-1958. While the bulk of his material dealt with other topics, Krassner, too, was conscious of the Arab-Israeli conflict and issues relating to Israel's relations with the Palestinians. In fact, the very first issue of *The Realist* in 1958 contained an article condemning a Jewish religious law in Israel prohibiting Jews from marrying non-Jews ("non-Jews" in the Israeli context chiefly meant Palestinian Arabs). It was entitled "Jewish Aryanism in Israel."[51] Nearly a year after the 1967 war, *The Realist* once again turned its attention to the conflict. It published two articles on the Middle East in its May 1968 issue: a pro-Israeli piece by Henry P. Durkin, of the New York State section of the conservative Young Americans for Freedom group, and a piece by Nat Freedland satirizing the influence of religion in day-to-day Israeli life.

Krassner noted decades later that his "feeling [toward the Arab-Israeli conflict] was based on gut instincts rather than scholarly research" and could be summed up by a comedy bit he used to perform that featured an imaginary conversation he held with God: "Listen, God, when you told the Jews about the promised land and then, after WW II and the US and other countries turned them down they went to Palestine, and you knew what the reaction would be, that the Palestinians wouldn't say, 'Oh, welcome, feel free to take our land.' And God replied, 'I never promised. I just said I'll see what I can do.'"[52]

Like Rubin, other Yippies had a personal interest in the Arab-Israeli conflict. Sharon Krebs helped establish the Free University of New York in 1965, and she and her husband had lived and studied for two years in Lebanon prior to that.[53] It was perhaps this experience that prompted them to lend their names as sponsors of the Ad Hoc Committee on the Middle East, a new group formed in New York in July 1967 to protest Israeli policy and express support for the Palestinians. Other Yippies were conflicted because of their Jewish backgrounds. Stew Albert was the driving force behind a meeting that several Yippies once had with a young Palestinian official who worked at the PLO office in New York City. Albert was one of the original Yippies, and was valued for his intelligence and humor. His romantic partner and eventual wife, Judy Gumbo, was another Yippie who came along to the meeting at the PLO office. Gumbo, Albert, and fellow Yippie Jim Retherford went to the PLO office because, the latter recalled, "Stew was very anguished, and wanted to know about the alleged anti-Semitic nature of the PLO." According to Retherford, Albert "had a compelling personal desire to reconcile contradictory perceptions of Israeli oppression of Palestinians and institutionalized anti-Semitism by the PLO, and I have a recollection of Stew asking the hard questions of the PLO liaison officer who met with us." The young PLO officer claimed to have been born to a Jewish mother. When asked if the PLO were anti-Semitic, he responded, "No; that would be like me hating myself."[54]

Besides personal factors, Yippie interest in the Palestinians stemmed from their anti-imperialist worldviews. Gumbo noted as much: "Our pro-Palestinian sentiments came from the fact that the Yippie core were all pretty much rebellious Jews. . . . We identified with all the liberation movements of the day of which the Palestinians were one. We identified with anything with the word 'liberation' in the title: the National Liberation Front [Viet Cong], black liberation, women's liberation, gay liberation, Chicano liberation, and the PLO."[55] It was precisely the kind of New Left anti-imperialism that had motivated SDS's support of the Palestinians. Nancy Kurshan agreed: "We viewed it as a struggle similar to the Vietnamese or perhaps the American Indian Movement in this country."[56] Jonah Raskin concurred that he and others in the Yippies and other New Left circles in which he moved gave the Middle East a good deal of thought: "Yes I thought about it and talked about it. It was a major topic—along with others. It was a place in the world that I and people I knew paid attention to—along with Ireland and Vietnam." Calling himself an anti-Zionist, Raskin said "Israel and the Palestinians has always been there as an issue for Jews and New Leftists and former New Leftists I knew and know."[57]

On the other hand, Jim Retherford noted that while the Yippies were aware of the issue, it was not something that prompted them to actual action: "We concentrated on Yippie actions. I do not recall any actions on the Palestinian issue. . . . With the U.S. support for Israel, and the development of Israel as sort of the American deputy, or enforcer in the Middle East . . . it wasn't as straightforward as some of the other things [like Vietnam]. This isn't something we marched about. It was something that was there as bedrock as part of the overall political analysis of U.S. imperialism."[58] This attitude in fact reflected the attitudes of many others in the New Left: supporting the Palestinians stemmed from their ideological worldviews, but rarely motivated them to carry out demonstrations or other practical ways of expressing this support given more pressing concerns facing them, like stopping the war in Vietnam.

Another example of how New Leftists allied with the Yippies shared their strong support for the Palestinians, but did not do much publicly about the issue, was the Michigan-based White Panther Party (WPP), which was formed after Eldridge Cleaver of the Black Panther Party suggested that whites sympathetic to the Black Panthers should form their own comparable organization. John Sinclair was one of the moving spirits behind the WPP. A poet, journalist, marijuana advocate, and manager of the proto-punk band MC5, Sinclair formed the WPP in 1968 along with his wife Leni, and Lawrence "Pun" Plamandon.

In early 1970, Rubin and Hoffman met with members of the WPP to discuss merging the two movements. As a result, Sinclair drafted a proposed ten-point program for a unified WPP-Yippie party in April 1970 that specifically mentioned the Palestinians: "We support the national liberation struggles of the black, brown and youth colonies in the United States of Amerika *[sic]*, of the Provisional Revolutionary Government of South Vietnam [Viet Cong], the Pathet Lao movement in Laos, the Khmer Rouge movement in Cambodia, the Palestine Liberation Movement (al-Fatah) in the middle east, all Latin American national liberation movements, and all other peoples and colonies throughout the world who are struggling for their freedom from the forces of modern imperialism."[59] Sinclair and the WPP were also clear about their support for the Palestinians in the July 4, 1970, issue of the party's underground paper, the *Ann Arbor Sun*. It carried an article entitled "Palestine Will Win," which featured a Danish journalist's interviews with members of two Palestinian guerrilla groups in Jordan.

Once again like SDS and the Yippies, however, the WPP never did much publicly on behalf of Palestine solidarity. Plamandon recalled that although he personally had done some reading on the Palestinians in 1967–69, and visited the offices of al-Fateh while briefly living in exile in Algeria in 1970, the WPP as a whole did not focus much on the Middle East: "I must say that the Middle East was not a significant focus of my or other WPP members attention. The war in Vietnam and the threat of American fascism was my/our primary focus. Additionally, as I remember it, there was not so much support for Palestinian liberation in Ann Arbor. Pro-Israeli support was quite strong in Ann Arbor at the time."[60]

As the 1960s progressed, some young New Left activists started embracing liberation movements like those in Vietnam, Africa, the Middle East, and other parts of the underdeveloped world in part because it seemed to them that these Third World peoples were the leading edge of the struggle against global imperialism and the capitalist system that undergirded it.[61] While opposing the war in Vietnam and even openly supporting the National Liberation Front (Viet Cong) in Vietnam was becoming more and more widespread by 1967, supporting the Palestinian cause was another thing altogether. It was a particularly radical stand to take and served as the dividing line between those whom New Leftists considered true revolutionaries and those adopting a stance of Israel exceptionalism. Siding with the Palestinians and attacking Israel broke the taboo against saying anything detrimental about a country that had been a touchstone for many New Left Jews growing up.

New Leftists like those in SDS were especially active on college campuses in the 1960s. It comes as no surprise, then, that during and after 1967, colleges and universities across the United States quickly became the battleground between student groups that gravitated to one side or the other in the Arab-Israeli conflict.

# 2   Conflict in the Ivory Tower

*Campus Activism*

INASMUCH AS THE New Left originated among students, much of its early political activity took place on college campuses. On May 16, 1967, amid the tension in the Middle East that ultimately led to the June War three weeks later, a pro-Arab rally was held in Sproul Plaza, the center of student political life on the campus of the University of California at Berkeley. A leaflet entitled *Zionism, Western Imperialism, and the Liberation of Palestine* was distributed that connected the Arab-Israeli conflict with the civil rights movement, stating that "the Zionist settler state was founded on an exclusivist racial basis," and that this racial discrimination continued to be practiced on the Palestinian citizens who remained in Israel after 1948. Although Zionism constituted a type of apartheid, the broadsheet claimed, it did not generate the same degree of negative criticism in the West that white-minority-ruled Rhodesia and South Africa did.[1] A few months after the war, a group calling itself the Friends of the Tri-Continental Progressive Students held a press conference in late October 1967 at which it gave notice that it would begin a campaign of disseminating the Arab point of view about the Middle East on campus. The Arab-Israeli conflict had come to Berkeley.

In the late 1960s, some of the loudest, most vigorous New Left support for the Palestinian struggle and questioning of American and Israeli policy in the Middle East was on American college campuses. SDS published information about the Arab-Israeli conflict, and Yippies privately discussed it, but campus demonstrations and related events were physical manifestations of the new pro-Palestinian sentiment that emerged within the New Left starting in 1967. Pro-Israeli students and groups were quick to react and begin pushing back.

## The Pro-Palestinian Student Movement

Berkeley was perhaps the American university most associated with campus protest at that time, and witnessed some of the first and the most significant expressions of left-wing support for the Palestinian cause of any American campus starting in the fateful year 1967. Initial pro-Palestinian activities at Berkeley actually came at the initiative of Middle Eastern students, not American New Leftists. The SDS campus leader Dan Siegel recalled that Iranian and, to some degree, Palestinian, students were influential in stimulating campus interest in the Arab-Israeli conflict.[2] The Organization of Arab Students (OAS), a national group with chapters on various campuses, had in fact been organizing actions nationally even before the 1967 war broke out, such as a demonstration in front of the White House on May 31, 1967.[3]

Yet in a pattern that would characterize pro-Palestinian activity on other college campuses as well, it was not until the Palestinian resistance movement in the Middle East figured in headlines in the West in 1968 that activity on behalf of the Palestinians began becoming more common among American students at Berkeley and elsewhere. There were other reasons, too, why the question of Palestine did not really emerge on college campuses until late 1968 and early 1969. By that time, SNCC, the Black Panthers, and other Black Power groups already had brought pro-Palestinian sentiments into public view throughout the country; white students began following their lead.[4] Groups like SDS were also just beginning to widen their anti-imperialist polemics to include issues beyond Vietnam, including the Middle East.

For all these reasons, many pro-Palestinian activities started to occur in early 1969. A pamphlet was circulated issued by the Friends of the Tri-Continental Progressive Students at Berkeley stating that the Palestinians and the National Liberation Front (Viet Cong) in Vietnam had declared mutual support. The group was therefore issuing a call to all those on campus who supported the Vietnamese people, but not the Palestinians, to "draw the parallel" between the two.[5] Berkeley also joined over thirty other campuses in hosting "Palestine Week" in May 1969, and on May 13 of that year, an Arab student organization invited the Marxist scholar Hal Draper and the left-wing writer Paul Jacobs to debate "Zionism and Socialism." In January 1970, the

Arab Students' Association sponsored a lecture featuring the Welsh journalist Colin Edwards, who had just returned from a visit to Palestinian guerrilla areas in the Middle East.

On September 6, 1970, militants from the Popular Front for the Liberation of Palestine (PFLP) hijacked three international aircraft and compelled the pilots to fly them to a desert airfield in Jordan; a PFLP sympathizer hijacked a fourth. The PFLP then blew up the planes, after evacuating the passengers, whom they held hostage. This precipitated a full-fledged attack on armed Palestinian guerrillas in the country by the army of Jordan's King Hussein, a conflict known to Palestinians as Black September. An Old Left Marxist party, the Socialist Workers Party (SWP), subsequently held an event on October 1, 1970, under the rubric "Third World Revolutionaries Speak in Defense of the Palestinian and Arab Revolutions." The "Third World revolutionaries" in question were nonwhite SWP candidates running for California state offices in the November 1970 election: Herman Fagg, who was black; Antonio Camejo (Hispanic); and Patti Iiyama (Asian-American). The October 1973 Arab-Israeli War later led to a teach-in, and flyers appeared on campus that month in support of the Egyptian-Syrian war effort. One entitled *The Real Enemy Is Now at the "Front"*— a reference to the United States, which was sending massive amounts of aid to Israel—solicited funds for the Arab Relief Fund in Berkeley; another advertised blood drives in nearby San Francisco and San Jose to collect blood for Egypt and Syria.[6]

Other branches of the University of California besides Berkeley also held Palestine Weeks and similar activities. As at most universities, little was heard about Arabs or the Middle East at the University of California at Los Angeles (UCLA) before 1967. One student there, Roxanne Dunbar-Ortiz, who was very much aware of the plight of the Palestinians, was "outraged" by this. No one spoke up for the Palestinians partly because most on the Left were focused on the war in Vietnam. "It was like a carnival on the UCLA campus celebrating the [1967] Israeli victory," Dunbar-Ortiz lamented.[7] As it had elsewhere, that had changed by 1969. In May 12–15, 1969, a Palestine Week event sponsored by the OAS in UCLA's "free speech area" drew around three hundred protesters on its final day.

On April 18, 1969, Columbia University in New York hosted a teach-in entitled "Teach-In on the Middle East: Arab Liberation vs. Imperialism-Zionism," organized by the OAS and the youth groups of several Marxist parties. A host of speakers spoke, including George Tomeh, from the Syrian mission to the United Nations; Randa Khalidi al-Fattal, editor of *Arab World,* a publication of the Arab League's Arab Information Center; Rita Freed of the Committee to Support Middle East Liberation; Peter Buch of the SWP; Ibrahim Abu-Lughod, a Palestinian professor teaching at Northwestern University; Hisham Sharabi, another Palestinian, who was at Georgetown University; Elias Shoufani, a Palestinian professor at the University of Maryland; and Larry Hochman, a professor at Eastern Michigan University who had written *Zionism and the Israeli State* for SDS in 1967. At one point the event descended into fistfights between pro and anti-Israeli members of the audience.[8] In the second half of 1970, Columbia seethed with pro-Palestinian events. Several took place during the fall semester shortly after the events of Black September in Jordan. Two SDS members, Stephen S. Cohen and Barry Sautman, debated Stephen W. Cohen, a student from a Zionist group on campus. The SDS's Stephen Cohen argued for replacing Zionism in Israel with a secular, democratic state; the other Stephen Cohen said that he and other Jewish students in his group supported Palestinian nationalism, but also supported Zionism.[9]

Various Midwestern schools were active on the issue as well. A Palestine Week was held at the University of Wisconsin at Madison in May 1969, as it was at many other colleges and universities that month. In the summer of 1970, two students at the University of Wisconsin at Milwaukee, Joseph McCarty and Martha "Marta" Abraham, founded a group called Students for Peace and Justice in the Middle East. The Palestine Solidarity Coalition emerged at Indiana University at Bloomington. The University of Chicago hosted a Palestine Week in May 1969, as well as an event entitled "The Middle East Crisis, Israel, and the Palestinian Revolution" on October 4, 1970. Antioch College, a bastion of liberal and left-wing activity in Yellow Springs, Ohio, hosted a Middle East teach-in that lasted nearly a week in February 1971.

Further east, the American Friends of Free Palestine (AFFP) was founded at the University of Virginia (UVA) in April 1970. It consisted of students and others "interested in the issues and problems of Palestine. It seeks to further discussion inside the University community about both political and humanitarian aspects of these issues. To this end, the organization will distribute literature, sponsor lectures, films, seminars, debates, and undertake similar activities."[10] In an unsubtle swipe at pro-Israeli liberals, a flyer for a Palestine Week sponsored by AFFP at UVA in February 8–14, 1971, denounced "dovish liberals" for supporting certain American wars for imperialism, trumpeting: "Come to PALESTINE WEEK at the University of Virginia. DIG IT!"

## Palestine in the Campus Press

Student journalism dealt with the Arab-Israeli conflict in ways that had a national impact at Wayne State University (WSU), a working-class-oriented university in Detroit that was a natural site of pro-Palestinian activism. Detroit was home to a thriving radical black scene, and also hosted the nation's largest community of Arab immigrants and Arab-Americans. Arab students therefore had a large presence on campus.[11] WSU was therefore one of the campuses where Arab students worked together with white and black Americans in joint actions on behalf of the Palestinians. It was no surprise, then, that students picketed the Israeli ambassador to Washington, Yitzhak Rabin, when he gave a speech at the Sheraton Cadillac Hotel in Detroit on January 23, 1969. Two weeks later, a teach-in on "The Arab Liberation Struggle and Its Relationship to Zionist Israel" was held on the WSU campus, and on February 21–22, 1970, the OAS held a symposium there on "Palestine, the Arabs, and Zionism."

The most controversial and widely reported campus action dealing with Palestine at WSU was an article supportive of the Palestinians that appeared in the student paper *The South End* in January 1969. Starting in the 1968–69 academic year, the paper was edited by John Watson, who had a long history of involvement with black activism and journalism. Working with Watson was Nick Medvecky, the paper's associate editor and, later, managing editor. Medvecky was an army veteran who prior to working on the paper had been involved in the civil rights and anti-war movements as well as the Socialist Workers Party. On January 8, 1969, the front page of *The South End* carried an editorial summarizing a recent al-Fateh press release, with commentary by Medvecky, illustrated with a sketch of a Palestinian guerrilla fighter holding a pen that closely resembled a rocket-propelled grenade.[12]

The response was immediate and vociferously negative. Years later, Medvecky recalled, "We [he and Watson] had no idea that we were then grabbing hold of the third rail in American politics. We were quite literally astonished at the response."[13] Jewish students at WSU wrote indignant letters to the editor and eventually formed a Jewish Action Committee. Louis Panush, president of the Zionist Organization of Detroit, wrote to a noted Jewish advertising executive and fundraiser for WSU, Leonard Simons, on the day the article came out, calling it "a thoroughly misleading, vicious anti-Israel, anti-Jewish propaganda piece." He asked Simons, as a friend of WSU, to contact WSU's president, William Rea Keast, and the university's board of governors and request that they disassociate themselves from *The South End*'s "vicious Arab propaganda," saying that a student newspaper should not "lobby for Al-Fatah and Arab murderers," promoting terrorism as a form of national liberation.[14]

Simons contacted Keast on January 24, 1969, and pressured him and others at the university to do something about the paper. "I frankly can't convince myself that something can't be done to stop the paper from being used as an Arab propaganda tool instead of a student newspaper," he wrote to Keast. He then went for the financial jugular by noting, "Rea—from what I hear among the leaders of the Detroit Jewish Community—WSU is getting 'hurt' and losing many friends." He added that a particular Jewish donor was considering withholding a planned donation to WSU because of the article.[15]

Nor was the hostile reaction to the article restricted simply to those in the Jewish community in Detroit. Some local Jews wrote to national Jewish organizations seeking help and guidance in confronting the article.[16] The uproar even reached Israel. On February 28, 1969, the Israeli evening paper *Ma`ariv* ran an article entitled "The Jews of al-Fateh," blasting Medvecky for "rewriting history" and proposing "extreme" solutions to the Arab-Israeli conflict," illustrated with a photograph of *The South End*'s sketch of a Palestinian guerrilla fighter.[17]

This was not the first time that Watson and *The South End* had angered people in the Detroit community. Under his editorship, the paper had adopted a strident, confrontational tone. Watson intended for the paper to serve a wider audience than just students at WSU. The paper's masthead bore the slogan "One Class-Conscious Worker is Worth 100 Students" and the crouching black panther emblem made famous by the Black Panther Party. "We speak for the revolution," Watson proclaimed in a February 2, 1969, radio interview, adding: "The information which we print about the Arab-Israeli conflict . . . is ignored in the regular establishment press."[18]

*The South End*'s notoriety also prompted attacks on the paper for publishing the al-Fateh article from outside the Jewish community, including politicians, alumni, and the press. Members of the Michigan state legislature threatened to cut $100,000 in aid to WSU unless Watson were fired from his editorial position. State Senator Robert J. Huber indicated that the state senate had authorized an investigation into "subversive groups" on Michigan campuses.[19] Calls were eventually made to the attorney general of Michigan, Frank J. Kelley, to take some kind of action against the WSU board of governors for allowing the university to spend public funds to finance publi-cation of *The South End;* in the end, Kelley refused.[20] The Wayne State Fund, an alumni group, threatened the university with financial retribution. Instead of defending his right of free speech at a public university, the local chap-ter of the American Civil Liberties Union attacked Watson. On February 3, 1969, unknown parties even tried to burn down the paper's offices. According to witnesses, a Molotov cocktail was thrown at the building from a passing police car.[21]

Feeling the pressure from alumni, donors, politicians, and others, Keast struggled with what to do: how to uphold the paper's academic freedom while taking heed of the many complaints and financial threats to the university he was receiving. Detroit was still feeling the effects of violent racial distur-bances in July 1967, and Keast no doubt shrank from the thought of shutting down a paper that was edited by a black student and that served as a voice for the city's black community.[22] While Watson, as editor, drew most of the public condemnation, Keast felt that it was Medvecky who was the driving force behind what he called "the unfortunate fad" of supporting al-Fateh. "Medvecky, however, is responsible—what share in proportion to others who may be influenecing *[sic]* the editorial outlook from behind the scenes—for the current unfortunate fad to find the Israealis *[sic]* culpable of 'oppressor mentality' in their relations with the Arab nations," Keast noted in an internal document.[23]

Finally, after nearly a month of deliberating about what to do, Keast wrote an official letter to Watson on February 4, 1969, saying: "Recently, the *South End* has lent itself to treatment of the Arab-Israeli conflict—one of the most volatile issues of our time, upon which the peace of the world may quite liter-ally depend—in a highly irresponsible and inflammatory manner, and it has printed attacks upon Jews, Poles and other ethnic groups that are disturbingly reminiscent of Hitler's Germany."[24] WSU's board of governors passed a reso-lution endorsing the contents of the letter on February 13, 1969. Despite the dressing down, however, Watson stayed on as editor through the end of the school year.

## New Left and Radical Zionist Student Groups

"The leftist Jewish student is today's Uncle Tom," a Jewish student, M. J. Rosenberg, declared in a *Village Voice* article entitled "To Uncle Tom and

Other Such Jews." Black Power advocates embraced their blackness; why should Jewish leftists not accept their Jewishness? "The Jew must accept his identity, he's not just another white man." Jewish leftists who criticized Israel were denying their Jewishness because they were ashamed of it. Jews like Mark Rudd of SDS had become "Uncle Jakes" fighting on behalf of every people other than their own, he raged. Jews should stand up and admit to being Jews. "Ghetto Jews, you'd better do some fast thinking." As for himself, Rosenberg wrote, if he had to choose between the radical but anti-Israel SDS and a specifically Jewish cause, he would choose the latter. "If the barricades are erected, I will fight as a Jew."[25]

Rosenberg's article drew a considerable amount of attention among Jewish students worried about the rise of pro-Palestinian and anti-Israeli sentiments on American campuses. Pro-Palestinian campus groups and activities began facing a counterattack almost immediately after the 1967 war. Some of this came from traditional Jewish university organizations and from long-standing Zionist groups active on college campuses. In other cases, new groups emerged from within the broader radical environment that parted company with the rest of the New Left over Israel.

Michael Jay Rosenberg was raised in a non-Zionist, socialist Jewish household. During the 1967 war, he recalled that he cared about Israel, not so much because of Zionism as "because Israel was the Jewish State and I was a Jew." When the Palestinian cause started to be discussed at the State University of New York (SUNY) at Albany, where he was a student, he was moved to action. Rosenberg spent the summer of 1968 studying at The Hebrew University of Jerusalem, his first visit to Israel. After his return to Albany for the 1968–69 school year, he went on to establish what he described as a "Jewish militant organization" on campus called Am Yisrael as a direct response to the anti-Israel, pro-Palestinian stances of groups like SDS at SUNY Albany.[26]

Am Yisrael caused an immediate controversy on campus. On the evening of February 12, 1969, the 150 students and a few faculty members who attended the tumultuous opening gathering of the group were treated to an evening of shouting, accusations, and emotion. Charges were leveled against "faculty members on this campus who are anti-semitic," with Rosenberg denouncing what he called the "Nazi type of line right here in the student center at Albany State."[27] The week before the meeting, Rosenberg had published an opinion piece in the February 11, 1969, issue of the student newspaper denouncing members of the SWP on campus as, among other things, "mostly WASPs with a smattering of foot-shufflin' Jews" who "advocate the liquidation of Israel at the hands of the Al Fatah gangster movement."[28] Rosenberg did not mind that his strong words seemed intemperate to some. "In dealing with those who oppose Israel," he later wrote in 1971, "we are not reasonable and we are not rational. Nor should we be." He later claimed that "self-hating" Jews were the very product of the success of Zionism when he wrote "It is a measure of the singularity of the Jewish experience that only the Jews produce self-abnegating youth in the wake of success. The assimilationist Jew has always been with us, but it took the success of the Zionist dream to create in the diaspora a new breed of self-hating Jews."[29]

Rosenberg's feelings were not unique. They coincided with the feelings of other Jewish young people who wanted to retain their leftist idealism but not, as Rosenberg put it, "surrender their identity just so they can be accepted by their 'revolutionary' peers" who denounced Israel." Nor, he continued, would they "give up their radicalism to accommodate the Jewish establishment." "We are radicals," he wrote. "We actively oppose the war in Viet Nam. We support the black liberation movement as we endorse all genuine movements of liberation. And thus, first and foremost, we support our own."[30] However, that support would end the moment that other leftists called for the end of Israel.

Jack Nusan Porter was another pioneer in the movement in Israel's defense among radical Jewish college students. Born Nusia Jakub Puchtik in Rivne (Russian: Rovno), Ukraine, Porter survived the Holocaust and came to Milwaukee as a two year-old in 1946. In 1968, while pursuing graduate studies at Northwestern, where he became involved with SDS, he formed the Jewish Student Movement. "We recognize and actively support the integral role that the State of Israel plays in the life of the Jewish people," he declared. "We will not identify with or join with any groups that argue for the destruction of the State of Israel." One of his group's first activities was to picket the French consulate in Chicago that year to protest what the group perceived as France's tilt toward the Arabs.[31]

Other campus groups emerged that tried to combine Jewish New Left activism with concern for Israel. At Berkeley, Jewish activists from SDS, the Peace and Freedom Party, The Resistance, and other groups with a "deep commitment to Jewish thought" launched a paper called *Jewish Radical* in early 1969. In Seattle, about the same time, the Radical Jewish Student Union was formed at the University of Washington.

The Jewish Liberation Project (JLP), which combined left-wing thinking with open Zionist support for Israel, emerged from a working paper produced in July 1968 by a dozen Jews in New York City, Itzhak Epstein, Ruth Grunzweig, and Aviva Cantor among them. Typifying the "Radical Zionism" movement, the JLP believed that it was in Israel that American Jews truly could contribute to building a just society. It felt its duty was to correct negative views of Israel on the Left by pointing out that Israel was a "great social experiment" that was creating "new forms of socialism." "We are best suited," the group's foundation statement noted, "to communicate a positive position on Israel to the American Left. Our aim is to make the American Left seek the truth about Israel themselves, rather than relying on prejudiced formulas."[32] Jews needed a safe place of refuge; not just a place where there were other Jews, but "a Jewish place."[33]

Another group that emerged among young Jewish leftists in the late 1960s was the Radical Zionist Alliance (RZA), the leaders of which included figures such as Jonathan Brandow and David Twersky. The RZA was formed out of a conference held at Camp Ramah in Palmer, Massachusetts, in February 13–14, 1970. The meeting produced an alliance of groups that called themselves the RZA, as well as a "Radical Zionist Manifesto," dated February 15, 1970, that upheld the twin ideals of socialist Zionism and mutual Israeli-Palestinian recognition. RZA's slogan "Be a Revolutionary in Zion, and a Zionist in the Revolution" was aimed at radical Jews' involvement in both American political groups, as well as, one day, activity in Israel after they had moved there.[34] The RZA held its first national convention in June 1970 in Atlantic City, New Jersey. "Zionism is the national liberation movement of the Jewish people," its constitution proclaimed. "We look toward mutual recognition of the national rights of the Jews and Palestinian Arabs, and the cooperation of all people in the area toward the realization of socialism and justice."[35] The RZA and others later sponsored an event at the Massachusetts Institute of Technology titled "Zionism, the Middle East, and Revolution" on November 9, 1970.

Other pro-Israeli student groups multiplied in the late 1960s. Avraham Shenker, head of the organization and information department of the Jewish Agency (JA) for Israel said that 110 Zionist student groups had been created on campuses in the United States and Canada by mid-1969, as traditional Zionist organizations also focused more on college activities.[36] An example was the American Zionist Youth Foundation (AZYF), which in 1968 established a university service department to provide a "positive Israel presence" on North American campuses. In September of that year, it held a seminar at Highstown, New York, to discuss the effectiveness of efforts to reach "indifferent and alienated Jewish collegians and faculty members" and bring them "closer to the Jewish community through personal contacts with the reality of Israel."[37] Shenker went so far as to encourage Israeli students in the United States to join New Left groups expressly in order to turn them toward Zionism. He contended that 30 percent of the New Left was made up of Jews, and that because they were attracted to anti-Israel stances on a rational level, not an emotional one, it was easier to combat their beliefs and convert them to pro-Israeli thinking.[38]

A few months later, the JA's youth and Hehalutz department joined with the AZYF in hosting a seminar in Jerusalem for thirty-one visiting American and Canadian students from twenty-six different universities on how to counter Arab propaganda. The goal was to help them reach out to radical Jewish students with a pro-Israeli message upon their return to North America. The month-long seminar began on July 17, 1969, and featured study groups on topics such as "Techniques of Mass Communications," "Historical Foundations of the State of Israel," and "The Arab Refugee Problem." Participants in the latter were to be taken on a tour of a Palestinian refugee camp.[39] For its part, the World Zionist Organization's youth department arranged for Amos Kenan, an Israeli leftist who was critical of New Left stances on Israel, to give a lecture tour at American universities.

The Israeli government was also eager to shore up pro-Israeli sentiment on American campuses. Prime Minister Golda Meir complained about Israel's plummeting reputation in the world, once grousing that "all of a sudden, all of the Arabs become poor Arabs. . . . We haven't sinned in any way. What do you expect us to do when we have Fatah and terror?" She argued that Israel need to work harder to acquaint the world with the facts of the Arab-Israeli conflict.[40] Some in the Israeli government were doing just that. In the wake of the 1967 war, Dan Vered, an Israeli student in Florida who was head of the Jewish student organization in Dade County, Florida, as well as leader of the local Israeli student group at the University of Miami at Coral Gables, received a packet of Hebrew-language materials from his government entitled "Know How You Should Respond." It contained publications issued by a range of Israeli political parties, including the Israeli Communist Party (MAKI faction), the leftist MAPAM Party, the center-left MAPAI, and the right-wing nationalist Herut Party. Jewish student leaders should use the pro-Israeli positions found in the different materials and tailor them to fit the American audience they were addressing the instructions said, Vered recalled: "If you speak with Republicans, use what is found in Herut. If you speak with Democrats, use what is found in MAPAI. If you speak with the New Left, use what is found in MAPAM and MAKI."[41]

## An Attempt at Balance

A notable example of activism on campus that tried to strike a balance between New Left concern about the Palestinians and traditional Jewish support for Israel was the Committee for a Progressive Middle East, which emerged at Berkeley in 1969. This was in many ways the brainchild of Michael Lerner, a well-known radical in Berkeley. His father, Joseph H. Lerner, was a strong Zionist who served as vice president of the Zionist Organization of America. As a result, the younger Lerner grew up seeing famous Zionist visitors like David Ben Gurion and Moshe Sharett sitting at the family table. After graduating from Columbia in 1964, where he was the national chair of Atid, the college student organization of the Jewish Theological Seminary, Lerner lived for a while on Kibbutz En ha-Shofet in Israel. Lerner began graduate studies at Berkeley in the fall of 1964, where he was Jerry Rubin's roommate and took part in the Free Speech Movement. He chaired the Berkeley SDS chapter in 1966–68.

During the 1967 war, Lerner found himself defending Israel's actions to some of his friends in the anti–Vietnam War movement. Yet he also maintained frequent contact with Palestinian students, who gave him a "greater sensitivity" to Palestinian problems and concerns. Lerner and the leader of the Berkeley Free Speech Movement, Mario Savio, wrestled over what to do about the Left's attitude toward the Arab-Israeli conflict in the wake of the 1967 war. "We did it," Lerner recalled, "to counter a Left that was totally anti-Israel: 'Israel is nothing but a colonial venture.' We disagreed with that. That's what initially brought us into conversation about it." Lerner and Savio feared that the question of Israel would destroy the Left.[42]

At the same time, the two also were critical of the growing pro-Israeli chauvinism within the organized Jewish community in the United States. "While that was being raised," Lerner remembered, "both of us were encountering the circling of the wagons by the pro-Israeli forces, or shall we say the pro-settlement, pro–right wing forces in Israel." Lerner and Savio started reading and discussing the Middle East with a variety of people, and came to the conclusion that while some in the Left were wrong in their attitudes toward Israel, "the discourse that was prominent in the Jewish world was [also] deeply distorted."[43]

After nearly a year and a half of readings and discussions, Lerner and Savio eventually formed a group at Berkeley in March 1969 called the Committee for a Progressive Middle East (CPME). Trying to straddle the growing campus divide between New Left radicals and those students, mostly Jewish, who still defended Israel, Lerner conceded that while "irrational," the anti-Zionism of many young left-wing Jews was "correct in its fundamental impulses." After all, Israel was supported by such conservative Republican leaders as Senator Barry Goldwater and California Governor Ronald Reagan, he noted, and it did not support the National Liberation Front (Viet Cong). Given this, and given the fact that left-wing Jewish youth perceived establishment Zionist organizations as mere "tools of the American establishment," it made sense to Lerner that Jews in the Movement therefore concluded that Israel was merely a stooge of American imperialism too. Lerner himself agreed: "They [American Zionists] are out-and-out tools of the U.S. State Department, switching their line on almost every question to suit U.S. needs. . . . How convenient for American Zionists that it turns out the best way to help Israel is to support the U.S. government in everything."[44]

The CPME issued a statement that offered balanced criticism of both Israel and the Palestinians. It argued that the two sides should stop fighting each other and instead combat what the committee felt was the real enemy: "capitalist imperialism" and big power politics. Leftists could criticize the capitalist nature of Israeli society, but not the wider right of the Jewish people to national self-determination in that country. The CPME conceded that Zionism should have chosen another, less populated place on earth than Palestine to build a Jewish state, but quickly noted that what now existed was the reality that had to be dealt with. Arab states had turned their masses against the Jews of Palestine when they should have joined them in their national liberation struggle against the British in 1945–47.

The CPME statement also cautioned the Palestinians that no matter what al-Fateh might be accomplishing through its violent actions, it was actually serving the interests of imperialism and the Arab ruling classes, not the Palestinian masses. It was ridiculous for anyone to think that the Arabs were fighting a national liberation struggle in the usual sense. Revolutionary Arab nationalism merely diverted the Arab world's attention away from American imperialism. The statement called on al-Fateh to halt guerrilla warfare against Israel and instead focus on "redirecting that struggle internally in Arab lands."[45]

A few months later, the CPME issued a statement inviting students to attend a meeting on the evening of May 15, 1969, titled "Does Israel Have the Right to Exist?" The statement echoed some of the CPME's positions, particularly in affirming Israel's nationhood and urging the Left not to be a partisan of either side but instead work for the reconciliation of both Israeli and Palestinian rights, not support the defeat of one side or the other. Turning to campus events, the CPME statement then scored the Radical Student Union for endorsing Palestine Week without demanding that Arab students recognize Israel. The statement ended by noting that the Middle East situation was complex and required "study and thought," not "cute" resolutions issued so that students could prove "they're really 'with third worlders.'"[46]

The events that Lerner and the CPME set up for May 15, 1969, unwittingly had something to do with the iconic march that day by Berkeley students to take back People's Park, something Berkeley students, community activists, and hippies had created on university-owned land, but that subsequently was seized by California Highway Patrol and Berkeley police officers. The CPME held a rally in Sproul Plaza on May 15. When news of the police takeover of People's Park reached the campus at noon, the entire dynamic of the CPME meeting immediately changed. Students in the crowd wanted to know what they should do about the seizure of the park, and Dan Siegel, the president-elect of the student body, a law student and SDS member, announced that they should all march down to the park. The CPME's Middle East–oriented rally immediately became a footnote to a student-police clash that left one person dead and led to the occupation of parts of Berkeley by the California National Guard.[47]

The CPME did not survive the momentous events of the spring and summer of 1969 in Berkeley. The student body went home, and the city was preoccupied with returning to normal after its occupation by the National Guard. In the fall, Lerner moved to Seattle to take up a teaching position. However, the CPME was not the only group at Berkeley that offered an alternative to the Left's strong criticism of Israel and that spoke instead of Arab-Jewish cooperation in the Middle East. A leaflet appeared on the Berkeley campus three years later advertising a rally for "self-determination for Palestinians and Jews" to be held on September 29, 1972 in San Francisco by the Committee for Justice and Peace in the Middle East. Adorning the leaflet was a drawing of an Arab wearing a keffiyeh headdress alongside a Jew blowing a ram's-horn shofar, each raising a fist.[48]

Nor was the CPME the only student group that tried to bridge the gap between concern for the Palestinians and concern for Israel. At least one attempt was made by American Jewish students visiting the Middle East to serve as a conduit for dialogue. In 1969, some Jewish students traveled to Jordan and met with members of al-Fateh. They also traveled to Israel and talked with students from the National Union of Israeli Students. Because they could not meet directly with al-Fateh in Jordan, the Israeli students asked the visiting Americans if after their return to America they could contact the Palestinians they had met in Jordan and ask them if they would be willing to discuss a solution to the Arab-Israeli conflict with the Israelis. Each side could then publish its respective statements in the pages of the American Jewish student publication *Ba-Golah—In Exile.*[49]

Student activism was one of the defining characteristics of the New Left, and it is not surprising that Movement activists' divergent views of the Middle East spurred passions on campuses across the country. As a result of their activism, some young Americans broadened their horizons by leaving their colleges and universities and traveling to Cuba, North Vietnam, and various African countries, direct experience that not only taught them but inspired them, they believed. When some young people began hearing about the Arab-Israeli conflict and the Palestinian guerrilla struggle after 1967, they decided to broaden their knowledge beyond pamphlets, policy statements, and demonstrations and actually travel half-way around the world to the Middle East.

# 3 (Fellow) Travelers
## Left-Wing Youth in the Middle East

HEARING SOLDIERS YELLING and chambering rounds into their weapons while he was walking across the bridge over the Jordan River that connects Jordan with the Israeli-occupied West Bank, twenty-seven-year-old Nick Medvecky probably wondered if this trip had been a good idea after all. Medvecky, a left-wing student and journalist, was touring several Middle Eastern countries in the late summer and fall of 1969. Now he was facing the moment of truth when he was walking, literally, across the fault line that separated mortal enemies in the Arab-Israeli conflict. As he made the short walk across the bridge, with armed Jordanian and Israeli soldiers scurrying about, everyone at the scene wondered what would happen next to the hapless American.

Learning about Israel and the Palestinians from the growing number of printed sources or campus events that took place after the 1967 war was not enough for certain young left-wing Americans. Some decided to leave the comfort of their North American homes and travel to the Middle East to see the conflict up close. They were partly motivated by adventure, but the fact that young people felt that they had been lied to about Vietnam propelled some on a mission to discover the truth about the Arab-Israeli conflict on their own. In still other cases, young journalists writing for the underground and alternative press wanted to be able to present their readers with first-hand information, and young Jewish leftists visited Israel and even moved there.

For whatever reason they traveled there, their experiences in the Middle East proved transformative for some of them.

## Solidarity Tours

Medvecky's dramatic walk across the Allenby Bridge originated in the outcry that greeted the article about al-Fateh and the Palestinians that he had written for Wayne State University's student newspaper *The South End* in January 1969 (discussed in chapter 2). Six months after the controversial article appeared, he said, two Israeli military officers who were studying at WSU came to him one day with an interesting offer. Would Medvecky be willing to visit Israel, all expenses paid, courtesy of The Jewish Agency for Israel? He could thus see the country for himself. Medvecky agreed, but then decided to approach Soraya Obaid, a member of the Organization of Arab Students at Wayne State, to inquire about whether or not the group could arrange for a similar expenses-paid trip of some of Israel's surrounding Arab neighbors. Two weeks later, Medvecky had in hand an invitation from none other than Yasir Arafat, chair of both al-Fateh and the Palestine Liberation Organization (PLO), to tour Lebanon, Syria, and Jordan as a guest of al-Fateh.

Paying his airfare out of advances for stories he proposed to write after he returned, Medvecky flew to Beirut in late August 1969. After meeting his al-Fateh contact at the Strand Hotel, he visited several Palestinian refugee camps in the city, including the Shatila and Burj al-Barajneh camps. Medvecky had to visit the camps disguised as a Palestinian (complete with a keffiyeh head-dress) to avoid detection by Lebanese army soldiers guarding the entrances. To ease his back-and-forth travels through three Arab countries and pass through various checkpoints staffed by Palestinian guerrillas and other security personnel, Medvecky carried several documents and passes issued by al-Fateh. From Syria, Medvecky entered Jordan and visited various locations, including refugee camps and an al-Fateh training camp in the mountains outside Amman. He even interviewed Arafat.

True to his journalistic calling, Medvecky sent handwritten dispatches to the Liberation News Service in the United States, among others, the first from Lebanon on August 26, 1969. "My greatest problem is in seeing so much & having so little time to write and rest. I'll try to be as prompt as possible," he wrote to the editors. Medvecky's first dispatch then went on to describe an experience he had at the al-Fateh camp in the hills some fifteen miles outside

Amman. Approximately forty guerrillas were listening to a lecture on "The Strategic Policy of al-Fateh" by Khaled al-Hassan, the head of the PLO's political department, who went by the nom de guerre Abu Sa`id. "I can't overstate the amount of misery and degradation these people [Palestinians] continue to live under," Medvecky wrote. "I also can't overstate the extent these people are rallying behind and joining Al Fatah."[1]

Medvecky decided that instead of traveling back through Syria to Lebanon, whence he would fly to Israel via Cyprus (no direct flights existed between Israel and the Arab world), it would be much simpler, faster, and cheaper just to cross the short bridge spanning the Jordan River. However, that was not an official border crossing point but rather a fortified cease-fire line separating Jordan from the Israeli-occupied West Bank. Although advised that neither side allowed tourists to cross, Medvecky nonetheless asked his al-Fateh escort to drive him from Amman down into the Jordan Valley to the bridge on September 1, 1969. After casually taking photographs on the Jordanian side, he simply decided to start walking across without telling anyone ahead of time, all the time shouting out to the Israeli side, in English, that he was an American journalist. Startled Jordanian and Israeli soldiers began shouting and grabbing their weapons, but Medvecky succeeded in crossing over to the Israeli side safely whereupon he immediately was accosted and thrown to the ground by angry Israeli soldiers. After proving that he was, in fact, an American and not some kind of infiltrator, Medvecky said that the amazed Israelis told him that he was the first foreigner to cross the bridge since the end of the 1967 war and could easily have been shot. After convincing the Israeli soldiers that they ought to call his hosts at the Jewish Agency (JA), Medvecky was picked up by someone from the JA and driven to Jerusalem. He spent several weeks traveling the width and breadth of Israel as a guest of the JA. After flying back to Beirut from Israel via Cyprus, Medvecky returned to the United States after ten eventful weeks in the Middle East.[2]

Several months after returning from his trip, Medvecky said, he was approached by Jean Whilden Townes, who was inquiring about Palestinian contacts for a trip to the Middle East in the summer of 1970 that some people in the Boston area were planning for journalists. Townes had grown up in an apolitical household and served in the Peace Corps in Africa after graduating from Carleton College in 1963. When she returned home in 1967, she stopped off in Israel. She spent some time harvesting apples on a kibbutz, knowing nothing about Middle Eastern politics. Townes recalled that at one point during her stay she was taken to see the ruins of a Palestinian village that had been abandoned by refugees in 1948. "I realized that there was something going on here that I didn't understand," she recalled.[3]

Upon her return, Townes joined a group of former Peace Corps and other international service volunteers called the Committee of Returned Volunteers (CRV). Established formally in December 1966, the CRV grew to be quite critical of American foreign policy, dismissing the Peace Corps as "nothing but a graduate school for imperialism."[4] She also became involved in a Middle Eastern study group in the Boston area. The group decided to set up a trip to the Middle East that would include people associated with underground and left-wing papers. It was in this context that Townes contacted Medvecky, who agreed to help her find some other people for the trip. He in turn contacted some activists with the League of Revolutionary Black Workers in Detroit, as well as a local women's liberation group. The plan was for the group to fly to Lebanon and then travel overland to Jordan through Syria. Once there, the group would attend the Second World Conference on Palestine September 2–6, 1970.

Eventually, seventeen people, eight women and nine men, received visas from the Lebanese consulate in New York to enter Lebanon as part of the group.[5] The group flew to Beirut in late August; while in the Middle East, they were guests of the General Union of Palestine Students. They spent about one week in Lebanon, visiting Palestinian refugee camps in and north of Beirut, the ancient ruins of Ba`labakk (Baalbek), a Palestine Red Crescent Society hospital in eastern Lebanon, and taking an overnight trip to visit refugee camps in southern Lebanon.[6]

Medvecky later recalled that on the eve of their departure to Jordan overland via Syria, al-Fateh officials met the group members at their hotel in Beirut. They had heard that some in the group wished to travel to Israel and, according to group member Sharon Rose, "they freaked out."[7] They also took Medvecky to task for having crossed over to Israel from Jordan the previous summer. The CIA was monitoring the trip as part of its Operation MH/CHAOS. According to information the CIA received, a fellow group member, Peewee "Rufus" Griffin, called Medvecky a "Zionist pig" at the meeting. Other members of the group were suspicious of Medvecky as well, although some had suspicions about Griffin himself. Medvecky said he argued with the al-Fateh officials that the group members were journalists, and journalists should be able to see and report from both sides of the Arab-Israeli divide.

The Palestinians were not convinced, but Medvecky remained firm that the group should visit Israel. As a result, he was expelled from the group, and stayed in Lebanon while the rest traveled to Syria.[8]

With unexpected time on his hands—six weeks until his return flight home from Beirut with the rest of the group after they returned from Jordan—Medvecky had to come up with a new plan. Through a Beirut-based American journalist, Abdallah Schleifer, he met officials from Palestinian factions other than al-Fateh and eventually received sponsorship from the Popular Front for the Liberation of Palestine–General Command (PFLP–GC). Medvecky spent his time traveling throughout Beirut, southern Lebanon, Syria, and Jordan, in the company of PFLP–GC fighters, sometimes armed as they were. Among the PFLP–GC bases Medvecky visited was one specifically for training foreigners.[9]

The rest of the group first spent a week at an international student work camp in southern Jordan working on various projects, including helping build a camp for members of the Ashbal (Arabic: lion cubs), an armed al-Fateh youth brigade. Some of the Americans recall even being given unloaded weapons with which they would go on patrol at night at the camp. They donated blood and were given aluminum necklaces that listed their blood group.[10] After a trip to the ancient city of Petra, some of them visited an al-Fateh medical facility in Shawbak, near al-Karak. After a week, three members of the group stayed behind to work at the clinic, mostly just sorting medicine; the others returned to Amman.[11]

Most of the delegation returned to Amman to attend the Second World Conference on Palestine in Amman September 2–6, 1970. Over a thousand delegates from many countries attended the gathering, which took place despite rising tension and shootouts between Palestinian guerrillas and the Jordanian army. "This experience was like living in a liberated zone," one of the Americans noted. "It was clear that we were having this conference not because of the graciousness of the Jordanian authorities but because the guerrillas were around us with their Kalshinkovs [sic; AK-47s] and their machine guns." Arafat addressed the gathering, as did representatives of other Asian and African liberation movements.[12]

The three Jewish members of the tour group issued a statement on September 2, 1970. When it was published in the United States, their names were "withheld upon request." In the Arabic-language Palestinian newspaper al-Fateh, however, the statement was signed by Sharon Rose, Joseph Center, and

Marilyn Lowen, who used the name Maryam Fletcher while she was in Jordan. The statement began, "As revolutionaries of Jewish heritage in the United States of America, we take this opportunity to wholeheartedly support the Palestinian liberation movement." It went on to say: "We cast our lot with the Palestinian liberation movement which struggles in behalf of our semitic sisters and brothers. . . . As American Jews, we will attempt to combat the Zionist propaganda machine which chokes freedom of thought in the Jewish community and prevents Jewish youth from rejecting Zionism and joining the ranks of anti-imperialist struggle."[13]

The trip was very influential in the lives of several of those who went. Jean Townes's experience affected her for years thereafter. She recalled one incident when group members were being driven through a valley in Amman and shooting broke out between Jordanian troops and Palestinian guerrillas who were on opposite hilltops above the valley. Although they were not in any danger of being hit in the crossfire, it was nonetheless a harrowing experience. "For a significant number of years afterwards, if there was a loud bang or a firecracker, I just hit the ground," Townes said decades later. "It really affected me in ways that surprise me." She also remembered that when some of the group were with al-Fateh in southern Jordan, the Palestinians offered to let the Americans practice shooting some AK-47 assault rifles. "I didn't go. I didn't want to do it," Townes said. "Maybe two of us didn't. But the others went to get the experience of operating a weapon."[14]

Another group member, Susie Teller had joined the Peace Corps after graduating from college and taught in Turkey for two years. After returning to the United States, like Townes, she was active in the CRV. The trip proved to be an eye-opening three weeks for her. "At the time," Teller later recalled, "there was no question that I was pro-Israeli. I thought planting trees in Israel was a wonderful idea." On the other hand, she knew that what the American media reported about other issues was not true, so maybe what she had heard and read all these years about the Arabs was not true either.[15] Teller's time in the Middle East convinced her that this was indeed the case. "I've been misled. I've been taken advantage of," she said in an article she wrote shortly after returning. "I do not believe the liberal rhetoric about Israel. I could not have said that one month ago. Now I know that Israel is not a 'socialist state.' When the native population is forcibly expelled and their towns demolished, the replacement cannot be called socialist or even liberal."[16]

Teller also recalled how the al-Fateh people assisted the group's hasty departure from Jordan. The September 1970 Black September fighting between the Jordanian army and the Palestinians was about to break out, and "the Palestinians told us, 'pack your bags; we're going out in the middle of the night.' We were given fake Syrian passports in a car with tinted windows, and they told us 'don't talk.' We got through. We drove all night."[17] Sharon Rose also remembers their dramatic journey out of Jordan to Syria and eventually back to Beirut. The group was told to "get in the car now" by the Palestinians, and she lay on the floor of the car as it sped through the Jordanian-Syrian border.[18]

Georgia Mattison already had some experience living in the Middle East with the knowledge that her government's policy toward the region was at odds with her own sense of justice. Mattison served in the Peace Corps in Iran after completing college. It was while she was there that she learned for the first time that the United States government had assisted the military coup d'état that overthrew the government of Iranian Prime Minister Mohammad Mossadegh in 1953. "This just floored me," she recalled decades later. "No one had told me this in the Peace Corps. . . . I felt really betrayed by my government. 'We'll just overthrow your government and then we'll throw you a few Peace Corps volunteers.'" Mattison returned to the United States and "felt really betrayed by the Peace Corps and that my country was doing these things in my name."[19] She, too, joined the CRV.

Mattison considered the trip "fantastic; we went over and got an earful. We learned a lot," she recalled. "I came back with a great appreciation for the Palestinian point of view and how wrenching it was for them, or anybody, to be thrown out of their land." At the same time, Mattison probed the Palestinians she met and asked them hard questions. "I asked a lot of sharp questions during the trip: did they really understand that the Zionists and all of these poor refugees from the Holocaust had been set up too, that the British had set up all of these conflicts?" The dangers involved in the trip also impressed her when she reflected back on them. Mattison recalled that when it became clear that the Black September fighting was about to erupt, their Palestinian handlers told group members to write a final letter to friends or loved ones. "They were telling people to write last letters; it was that bad."[20]

Gene Guerrero, too, experienced the angst and frustration of an eye-opening journey that challenged his preconceptions about the Arab-Israeli conflict. "Over and over again while I was there I wondered how I could have been fooled so long," he wrote shortly after returning to Atlanta. "The issue is so simple. A nation of people—brutally expelled from their land by an outside power." Decades later, he still described it as "a very powerful trip."[21] Guerrero was one of those who traveled to southern Jordan and helped with a medical clinic that al-Fateh was constructing near al-Karak. He and others plastered the basement of an old building that was chosen to serve as the clinic, and later helped sort medicine for the Palestinians.[22] Like others on the trip, Guerrero returned home to write and lecture about his experiences.

Joe Stork also felt that the trip was an important step in propelling him further into work on the Middle East. Stork served in the Peace Corps in Turkey before pursuing graduate studies at Columbia University and becoming heavily involved in the CRV.[23] His participation in the 1970 trip to the Middle East stemmed in part from his questioning of the dominant narratives about Israel, the Arabs, and US involvement in the Middle East he had encountered in life to that point, and led him to deepen his commitment to activism by helping to establish the Middle East Information Project (MERIP) in the fall of 1970 after he returned from the trip.

Some of the journalists on the trip dutifully managed to send dispatches back to various newspapers and agencies in the United States describing their travels as they were experiencing them. Orville "Chris" Robinson and Roger Tauss, for example, typed up a story entitled "Palestine: They Say There Is No Resistance" on September 4, 1970, and sent copies to the Liberation News Service, the *Philadelphia Free Press,* and the *Liberated Guardian.* Their dispatch also railed against the governments of Israel, the United States, the Soviet Union, and Arab countries for their respective attempts to throttle the Palestinian revolution, hailing the Palestinians as the "vanguard struggle against Western imperialism in the Middle East."[24] Medvecky also reported back to the radical press in the United States in the course of his trip. In a dispatch from Damascus dated September 12, 1970, he described how he and his PFLP–GC guide managed to leave Jordan and enter Syria just four days before the full-scale Black September fighting broke out in Jordan.[25]

Other progressive Americans traveled to the Middle East as individuals rather than part of organized tours. Judith Tucker, a Radcliffe SDS member, began graduate studies at The American University of Beirut in the fall of 1969. She wanted to study Arabic, and because of the demand there for teachers of English, she could study by day and earn money working at night in Lebanon. Tucker recalls that left-wing foreigners, including Americans, often came through Beirut to meet with the Palestinians. Some Europeans even received guerrilla training. Tucker also recalls that the 5th of June Society in Beirut, a group of Arabs and foreigners in Beirut that sought to provide the Palestinian perspective to Westerners, "was a 'go-to' place for leftists who came from the States." Tucker then studied in Paris in 1971–72 before returning for graduate studies at Harvard.[26] She later became involved with MERIP and began teaching modern Middle Eastern history at Georgetown University.

Ellen Siegel was another member of the New Left generation who traveled to the Middle East and came back changed. Siegel was an activist in the anti–Vietnam War movement, supported the Black Panthers, and was involved with the women's movement. She also used her skills as a nurse to help establish the People's Free Medical Clinic in Baltimore in 1970. Although as a Jew she had been taught growing up that there was no such thing as a distinctive Palestinian people, she kept hearing reports about Palestinian refugees in the years after 1967. Siegel joined with some other Jewish women opposed to the Vietnam War and formed a consciousness-raising group that discussed Zionism, Israel, and the Palestinians.[27]

In the summer of 1972, Siegel traveled abroad with a friend. While in Greece, she decided to visit Beirut in September to learn more about the Palestinians. Siegel visited The American University hospital and met a Palestinian physician. She then took a taxi and asked the driver to take her to a Palestinian refugee camp. He took her to the Burj al-Barajneh camp in southern Beirut, where a Palestinian fighter gave her a tour. Siegel met an elderly refugee patient at Haifa Hospital in the camp who had photographs of his trees and gardens in pre-1948 Palestine next to his bed. "This was my first understanding that there were people who had been living on this land," she recalled.[28]

While there, she also learned about the massacre of Israeli athletes by Palestinian gunmen that had just taken place at the Munich Olympic Games. On September 8, 1972, Israeli planes bombed several Palestinian refugee camps in southern Lebanon in reprisal. Siegel volunteered her services to the Palestine Red Crescent Society, which provided medical services in Palestinian camps, and was sent to the south to assist with victims of the Israeli attacks. After several months in Lebanon, she also traveled to Israel via Cyprus and spent three months there and in the occupied West Bank, where she "was disturbed by the militarism. Repression and denial of rights of the very people who had been born on the country's soil were evident. I wondered, at whose expense had we [Jews] made 'the desert bloom'?"[29]

Siegel returned from her trip to the Middle East a different person. "I saw terrible things [in Burj al-Barajneh]," she recalled. "I believe in my heart that I never really left the camp. The plight of the Palestinians has stayed with me." She became involved in Palestine solidarity work, and briefly returned to Beirut in 1980. Horrified by the destruction wrought by the Israeli invasion of Lebanon in June 1982 and the siege of Beirut that lasted all that summer, Siegel made her way back to Beirut once again in September 1982. She volunteered to work at the Gaza Hospital in the Palestinian refugee camp of Sabra. She was present there during the infamous Sabra-Shatila Massacre, when Lebanese militiamen from the Phalange Party, the Lebanese Forces, and the South Lebanon Army massacred over one thousand unarmed Palestinian refugees while Israeli troops surrounded the camps and fired flares at night to illuminate the scene for their Lebanese allies. Siegel and other foreign medical staff were themselves threatened with execution by the militiamen, but eventually were rescued by the Israeli army and survived.[30]

Another self-described member of the New Left who visited the Middle East also returned with some changed perspectives on the conflict as a result of some extremely unusual and dangerous circumstances: the unfortunate luck of having been both hijacked and then forced to huddle in fear through the vicious Black September fighting in Amman in September 1970. Miriam R. "Mimi" Beeber was a nineteen-year-old Jewish student at George Washington University when, after traveling to Israel in the summer of 1970, her flight home was one of those hijacked on September 7, 1970, by militants of the Popular Front for the Liberation of Palestine (PFLP). Beeber was later moved from the desert airfield where their plane had landed and detained by the PFLP in Amman. They were freed on September 26 after the harrowing experience of surviving the fighting in the company of their captors.

Beeber later conceded that her views of the Palestinians and the Arab-Israeli conflict had changed despite the horrific experiences of being hijacked, held hostage, and surviving a war. She later told reporters that even though she had been threatened several times, the ordeal made her aware of the Palestinians and their side of the conflict. "When I left Israel, I was pro-Zionist," she said. "I still am, but I'm so much aware of the other side of the problem." Beeber also seemed somewhat chastened in her views about the New Left's self-proclaimed militancy. "I feel that I am a part of the New Left, but after seeing the little bit of war I did . . . people don't realize how terrifying it is . . . people die . . . it's nothing like what is going on in the States."[31]

Siegel and Beeber were not the only ones who discovered that traveling to the Middle East could be dangerous. Abdeen Jabara, a young Lebanese American attorney, flew to the Middle East to attend the Second International Symposium on Palestine in Kuwait in February 13–17, 1971. His itinerary included a stopover in Jordan. While traveling to the capital Amman on the night of February 11 with several other passengers in a shared taxi, Jabara was wounded when Jordanian troops staffing a checkpoint along the road opened fire on their car with a machine gun. Two passengers died in the attack; Jabara was among the injured. Before the soldiers could shoot again, he and two uninjured passengers sprang from the cars and ran into a Palestinian refugee camp that abutted the road. They ended up being helped into the home of the camp's mayor, after which some fighters from al-Fateh came and took Jabara to a hospital, where he underwent surgery to remove shrapnel in his body. After being moved to a better hospital and recuperating for two days, Jabara left the country and flew on to Kuwait to attend the conference.[32]

### Dateline Middle East

It was a less-than-ideal time for the left-wing American journalists George Cavalletto and Sheila Ryan to begin arguing. It was mid-September 1970, and the rooftop apartment they were renting in Amman was suddenly on the front lines of the bloody Black September fighting between Jordanian troops and Palestinian guerrillas. Even as the intrepid couple quarreled, the building, which lay across the street from an al-Fateh training camp for paramilitary Ashbal youths, was buffeted by gunfire. Jordanian soldiers were positioned directly in front of the building, and the shooting between them and the Palestinian camp across the street enveloped their apartment building, from which all its inhabitants save the American couple had fled. Ensconced between two mattresses for protection, Cavalletto and Ryan tried to keep low as the battle raged. "I said the only way I can survive," Cavalletto recalled years later, "is to give up and admit that I'm going to die." The young Americans later discovered an unexploded mortar shell right above where they were staying, but they survived to continue their careers as alternative journalists writing about the Palestinian cause.[33]

Cavalletto and Ryan wrote for the Liberation News Service (LNS), formed in the summer of 1967 as a news service that would bring stories and information to underground newspapers that the mainstream media and news agencies ignored. They first visited the Middle East as part of their honeymoon in 1969. They ended up staying about a month in the Jordanian capital, spending time at the PLO office as well as with Palestinians from al-Fateh, the PFLP, and the Popular Democratic Front for the Liberation of Palestine.[34] The pair returned to Jordan in June 1970 and stayed nearly a year until the spring of 1971. They interviewed hundreds of people for LNS, including the PFLP spokesmen Ghassan Kanafani and Bassam Abu Sharif. A piece they wrote entitled "Where is Palestine?" highlighted the Palestinians' objection to Israel as a Zionist state, not to the presence of Jews in the country per se, saying: "It is this exclusive character of the Zionist settler-state which links it inextricably, through dependence and service, to imperialism." Ryan focused attention on Palestinian women in an article entitled "Women: Your Place Is with the Commandos, Not Only with Your Children."[35]

A chance to visit and live in the Middle East also proved transformative for Jeffrey Blankfort, a veteran San Francisco Bay Area photographer who had been born into a family of progressive, non-Zionist Jews. In 1970, Blankfort was approached by LNS's David Fenton, who suggested that he go to Lebanon and Jordan to work with Ryan and Cavalletto. During his four and a half months there in 1970–71, Blankfort spent time with Palestinian guerrillas as well as ordinary Palestinians while taking photographs.[36] "I went there as a journalist," Blankfort recalled years later, "but it turned my life around. I've been actively fighting for Palestinian rights ever since." Blankfort was shocked to discover, for example, why the Palestinians in Lebanon had become refugees in 1948. Years later he recalled his "epiphany" in learning about what had been done to them by his fellow Jews:

> When I went to the refugee camps and saw people living there who had been forced out of their country by people, including relatives of mine, who had never been oppressed a day in their lives, there was something radically wrong. And when I went to the Lebanese/Israel border [on the Lebanese side], and stood there looking down at a town . . . in which, it turned out, my sister and brother-in-law were living . . . standing next to two Palestinians, who were born in Palestine, and here I am, an American, a Jew, an American Jew, and I have a US passport in my pocket, and I have more legitimate rights to

live in that country than these two Palestinians, for me there was something immoral about that. It was immoral then, and it's immoral now.[37]

Some of the pro-Palestinian activists who visited the Middle East felt that a real problem facing the US Left was a dearth of information and critical analysis of the Middle East. To remedy this, one group of activists, calling themselves the Middle East Research and Information Project, or MERIP, decided to create a new left-wing journal, *MERIP Reports*, that would focus exclusively on the Middle East, particularly on the Arab-Israeli conflict and the plight of the Palestinians.

The immediate background for MERIP's formation was the trip to Lebanon, Syria, and Jordan made by seventeen American activists and journalists in August and early September 1970 (see above). Among them were Sharon Rose, Georgia Mattison, Jean Townes, Catherine Tackney, Robert Firth, and Joe Stork. About six weeks after their return to the United States, they met in New Hampshire in late October 1970 to share their frustrations with the lack of reliable news about the Middle East. Another person who had lived in the Middle East, Peter Johnson, joined them. In addition to having traveled to the Middle East, most of those gathered also had been involved with the CRV.

They all agreed that what was needed was good, independent, critical analysis with which to confront the Left about the Palestinians. At that first meeting, the activists therefore decided to produce a publication whose main focus would be analysis of the American role in the Middle East and the wider political economy of the region. They ran MERIP as a collective, and initially maintained offices in Washington and Boston staffed by members. The first issue of *MERIP Reports* came out in May 1971, and was an informal affair geared toward the existing radical/alternative press. It featured only three articles, and consisted of six mimeographed pages stapled together. This format reflected the fact that it did not view itself as a magazine or a journal in its own right but rather a source of information for left-wing publications, much like the LNS.[38]

## Jewish Leftists in Israel

Leftists seeking to meet and understand the Palestinians were not the only young Americans who traveled to the Middle East in the late 1960s and early 1970s. So did left-leaning Jewish youth who not only traveled to Israel—some even moved there permanently—but ended up impacting Israeli political groups in the process. One such American who moved to Israel in 1967 and translated her support for the civil rights movement into action was Naomi Kies. Kies taught sociology at The Hebrew University of Jerusalem, and starting in March 1971 became a close advisor to the Israeli Black Panthers Organization, a group of young activists protesting the low socioeconomic and political status of Mizrahi/Sephardic Jews in Israel. The Israeli Panthers had taken their name from the Black Panther Party in America.[39] Kies was one of several people who worked with them as they cultivated the media and sought to broadcast their message, and even allowed them to use her home as their base of operations after their headquarters burned down.[40]

Other American Jews played roles in the left-wing Israeli group SIAH. SIAH was both a Hebrew-language acronym for Smol Yisra'eli Hadash (New Israeli Left) and the diminutive form of the word "dialogue" in Hebrew, with a meaning approximating "colloquy." The group's origins lay with defectors from the left socialist Zionist party MAPAM who left the party in frustration in 1968 after it joined with the center-left MAPAI party of Prime Minister Levi Eshkol to form what was called the Labor Alignment. SIAH held its first national conference in November 1969. As an Israeli expression of the international New Left, SIAH's new existence benefited from the "crisis immigration" of 1967, which saw many new immigrants come to Israel from North America and Europe after the war. Some of these were young people who had been influenced by New Left youth politics but had broken with their colleagues over the question of Israel and Zionism.[41]

Joel Beinin exemplified the kind of young, left-wing American Jews who were involved with SIAH. He grew up absorbing his parents' strong Zionist convictions and by age ten already was in the senior leadership of the socialist Hashomer Hatzair youth group. Beinin began playing an active part in Hashomer Hatzair's efforts to combat the anti-Zionism of the New Left in the late 1960s as a student at Princeton. "It was important to those of us who saw our Zionism as part of the New Left to be in dialogue with these people," he recalled years later.[42]

A socialist and a self-described member of the American New Left, Beinin began moving away from his Zionist beliefs after the 1967 war. In the summer of 1969, he traveled to Cairo to study Arabic and found himself living in the same dormitory as a number of Palestinian students. Despite Zionist claims he had heard that there was no such thing as a unique Palestinian people, it

became clear to him that these Arabs spoke a different dialect than Egyptian
Arabs, ate different kinds of food, and in fact possessed a distinct national
identity. Confused, he returned to the United States to begin his senior year
at Princeton and confided his new uncertainties to some of his older comrades in Hashomer Hatzair: "I said, 'We have a problem. There are Palestinians.' Prior to that, [saying] that was considered anti-Semitic. They were just
generic Arabs. I said 'these people are real, they have their independent culture, they aren't Egyptians.' I didn't have a political answer to the fact that
there were Palestinians. MAPAM didn't have an answer."[43]

Beinin traveled to Israel in late 1970, stayed for several years on Kibbutz
Lahav, and in 1971 became involved with SIAH. "We were much more of a
direct democracy: direct action, action-by-consensus, very much the spirit
of the New Left," he recalled. However, SIAH did not solidly reject Zionism
and side with the Palestinians uncritically. Its members were not all in agreement about whether to define SIAH as Zionist, anti-Zionist, or non-Zionist.
Instead, they focused on ending the occupation of the West Bank and Gaza.[44]

## Young Americans in the Palestinian Resistance

Other young Americans not only traveled to the Middle East to understand
the conflict, they ended up working with Palestinian guerrillas. On September
4, 1970, the NBC-TV "Nightly News" carried a televised report from Beirut
by the American journalist Marc Schleifer.[45] Schleifer's film footage showed
three white Americans, described as being active in the New Left, training in
a Palestinian refugee camp in Beirut with a local militia unit organized by the
Popular Democratic Front for the Liberation of Palestine (PDFLP). They were
shown taking part in physical training, but not with weapons, and all three
had their faces covered with checkered Arab keffiyeh headscarves:

> Schliefer: These Americans train each day with the militia in this camp,
> armed Palestinian civilians who support the guerrillas and defend the camps.
> They keep their faces covered with Arab headdress in order to preserve ano-
> nymity and avoid what they describe as the possibility of reprisals from the
> CIA and pro-Zionist groups like the Jewish Defense League. And they study
> the tactical and military problems of revolution in the underdeveloped world,
> what they call the Third World. The three Americans are active in the New
> Left. George, where are you from in the States?
>
> George: Well, I'm from Boston, and Bobby and Huey are from Oakland.[46]

Schliefer: And what brought you here into the ranks of the Popular Democratic Front?

George: Well, we figure that any national liberation struggle in the world is really important, and it's important to aid it not only morally and by words but materially. So we came here to materially aid the revolutionary struggle.

Schliefer: Do you intend to go back to the United States?

George: I intend to go back to the United States eventually, with the revolution.

Huey: We came here because the struggle is international—like the Democratic Front says, it's *alami* [Arabic: "international"]—of the world, and whether we fight in Oakland, Chicago, New York, or in Jordan, Lebanon, or Palestine, it's the same struggle.

Bobby: We're here primarily to express the American movement's solidarity and support of the Palestinian liberation struggle, and to pick up whatever skills are necessary for liberation and struggles in America.[47]

Were they alone? Eighteen months earlier, rumors had begun circulating in Washington that al-Fateh agents in the United States were trying to recruit Americans. In response to an inquiry, US Assistant Attorney-General J. Walter Yeagley informed Representative J. Herbert Burke on May 6, 1969, that the FBI would investigate such reports, and that the Department of Justice would deport any foreign students involved in illegal activities of this sort.[48] More stories and reports surfaced that same year about al-Fateh recruiting Western radicals to attend a course in Jordan that summer. The August 18, 1969, issue of *Newsweek* carried a story that 140 students, mostly European but allegedly including four Americans, had attended a five-week al-Fateh course in Amman the month before.[49] Al-Fateh agents had discussed forming an "international brigade" to fight in Jordan in the summer of 1970 with SDS members at an Arab conference in Montreal, according to the FBI,[50] and at least one American was recruited to work against Israeli interests at about that time.[51] The CIA also believed that al-Fateh had been inviting groups of Americans and Europeans "to participate in training and indoctrination courses in the summers of 1968 through 1970."[52]

One US citizen, Patrick Arguello, born Patricio José Arguëllo Ryan in San Francisco to a Nicaraguan father and an American mother, did train with Palestinian guerrillas and would die in one of the PFLP's most notorious operations. At age three, Arguello moved with his family to Nicaragua, where he lived until 1957. He spent his teenage years in Los Angeles, where he earned a BA degree from the University of California at Los Angeles in 1966, then going on to pursue graduate studies in Chile. He then returned to Nicaragua and became involved in the revolutionary Sandinista National Liberation Front (Spanish acronym: FSLN). In August 1969, the Nicaraguan government exiled Arguello for his political activities, whereupon he traveled to Europe and became involved with a FSLN cell there.

As part of its attempts to secure training for its militants, the FSLN— like other revolutionary movements—collaborated with Palestinian guerrilla movements and sought to have its fighters trained in Palestinian camps in the Middle East. The FSLN therefore sent Arguello to Jordan to train with the PDFLP in April–June 1970. Frustrated that the training in an arid Middle Eastern environment was not appropriate for a country like Nicaragua, Arguello returned to Europe and eventually made contact with another group during the summer, the PFLP. It agreed to work with him, but required that he help in one of the group's most spectacular acts.

Arguello was assigned to partner with Leila Khaled in hijacking El Al Israel Airlines Flight 219, flying from Amsterdam to New York, on September 6, 1970—one of several planes the PFLP intended to hijack that day and fly to a desert airfield in Jordan. As the first woman ever to participate in hijacking a plane—TWA Flight 840 from Rome to Athens in August 1969—Khaled was a revolutionary icon. Posters portraying her clutching an AK-47 assault rifle and wearing a black-and-white keffiyeh were displayed widely among leftists around the world. Israeli sky marshals foiled the attempted hijacking of El Al Flight 219, however, overpowering Khaled and shooting and killing Arguello.

After some delay, Arguello's family finally was able to bring his body back to Nicaragua, where he was buried with a photograph of Che Guevara placed on top of his body in the coffin. In the Middle East, Arguello was eulogized as the most famous American citizen to serve in the Palestinian resistance by the PFLP's Ghassan Kanafani: "The martyr Patrick Arguello is a symbol for a just cause and the struggle to achieve it, a struggle without limits. He is a symbol for the oppressed and deprived masses, represented by Oum Saad [Umm Saʿd, a fictional character in one of Kanafani's novels] and many others coming from the camps and from all parts of Lebanon, who marched in his funeral procession."[53] Arguello's mother, Catalina "Kathleen" Ryan, expressed her pride in his support for the Palestinian cause in a statement she issued in October 1970: "My husband and I deny that we are ashamed of Pat. We are proud that he felt so deeply about the Palestinians that he was prepared to die for them."[54]

New Leftists were satisfying their desire to understand the Arab-Israeli conflict more by traveling to the Middle East to see the situation for themselves. A number returned further committed to the Palestinian cause after some underwent life-changing experiences. Back in the United States, other leftists remained deeply sympathetic to Israel and viewed the rise of pro-Palestinian, anti-Israeli sentiment on the Left with great suspicion and displeasure. Nowhere did these feelings erupt with more venom than among liberal and left-wing Jews, who reacted negatively to the anti-Israeli attacks being mounted by their fellow Jews on the Left.

## 4  Israel Exceptionalism

*Jewish Attacks on the New Left*

FOR MENACHEM S. ARNONI, a Holocaust survivor, born in Łódź, Poland, in 1922, the fact that left-wing Jewish youth in the United States would dare to attack Israel after its victory in the 1967 war and support the Palestinian cause could only be explained in psychological terms, as pathology. Surely it was a reflection of their own dysfunction, of their own uniquely Jewish failures, that they could stray from what he considered the obvious and only choice for left-wing American Jews: support Israel, come what may. New Left Jews were those "whose hatred of Israel are expressed psychological complexes stemming from the minority status of American Jewry," he observed. Noting that Jews were prominent in the anti-Israel thrust of the New Left after 1967, he denounced such persons for exhibiting what he called "Jewish self-contempt."[1] Arnoni was not alone. Other Jews used the more familiar term "self-hatred." Clearly, the New Left's attacks on Israel was eliciting a vitriolic response from older progressive Jews whose left-wing sentiments stopped when it came to attacking Israel. It was a case of Israel exceptionalism.

Israel was immensely important to American Jews. It was a symbol of the Jewish people's will and ability to survive in a post-Holocaust world. The horror of the Holocaust and the accompanying sense of abandonment deepened the haunting feeling held by many American Jews in the years thereafter that Jewish survival was always in question. In reflecting on this nagging feeling of dread, the young radical Jewish writer David Horowitz wrote:

There are catastrophes in the life of nations so vast as to disrupt permanently the balance of their social and psychological existence; there are wounds a people can endure which penetrate so deeply into their life structures that the inner being can never be healed. The Nazi Holocaust was such a catastrophe and such a wound for the Jews.[2]

Defending Israel thus became an imperative Jewish obligation. In recalling her youth, the feminist writer Andrea Dworkin expressively wrote, "I could see that if I or anyone made it harder for Israel to exist, Jews might die. . . . Israel was the answer to near extinction in a real world that had been demonstrably indifferent to the mass murder of the Jews. . . . The building of Israel was a bridge over bones; a commitment to life against the suicidal pull of the past. How can I live with having lived? I will make a place for Jews to live."[3]

The Middle Eastern crisis and war of the first half of 1967 therefore had a tremendous impact on all American Jews, not just those that leaned to the left. Many feared that their fellow Jews in Israel were facing literal annihilation by the Arab armies surrounding them in the spring of that fateful year. People stayed glued to the radio; special prayer services were held in synagogues; young people offered to go to Israel to serve in the military or as civilian volunteers. Many contributed money in unprecedented amounts. Just in the two-week period between May 22 and June 10, 1967, American Jews donated $100 million to the United Jewish Appeal.[4] The palpable relief that broke over American Jewry when Israel's army defeated the armies of Egypt, Syria, and Jordan was matched only by the jubilation and renewed sense of Jewish identity felt by many. For some who were not particularly religious, Israel and Zionism became stand-ins for their feeling of Jewish identity, a kind of secular vehicle for identifying with their Jewish roots. Some American Jews even spoke of "we" and "us" when referring to Israelis before and during the war.[5]

For all the demonstrable impact that the events of 1967 had on American Jewry, Israeli generals later denied that Israel and its citizens were actually in danger of physical destruction by Arab armies in 1967. They brushed aside the notion that Israeli Jews were facing another Holocaust. In the spring of 1972, the Israeli press was set ablaze by statements made by several former Israeli generals to the effect that Israel had *not* stood in mortal danger of an imminent invasion by its Arab neighbors in 1967. Major General Mattityahu Peled said that the alleged danger of annihilation was "a tale which was born and elaborated only after the war. . . . The Egyptians concentrated 80,000 soldiers, while we mobilized against them hundreds of thousands of men." Former IDF Chief of General Staff Haim Bar-Lev agreed, saying, "We were not threatened with genocide on the eve of the Six-Day War and we had never thought of such a possibility." A former cabinet member concurred, saying that the "whole story about the threat was totally contrived and then elaborated upon, a posteriori, to justify the annexation of Arab territories." The former Israeli Air Force commander Ezer Weizman went so far as to claim that the famous Zionist dictum of "no alternative" (Hebrew: *ein breira*) was something "endorsed by the Jewry of the Diaspora, which for its purposes wishes to see us heroes standing steadfastly with backs to the sea. The threat of destruction was already removed from Israel during the War of Independence [in 1948]." Non-Israeli Jews liked to believe that Israel had "no alternative" but to strike first in 1967, Weizman continued, because they thought that "Jews were allowed to fight only when they are targets of pogroms."[6]

Official American sources confirmed that both the CIA and the US Department of Defense also felt that Israel was not in peril at the time, and that its armies would prevail in about a week's time—which proved to be quite an accurate prediction. President Lyndon Johnson said as much to Israel's ambassador to the United States, Abba Eban, in the tense weeks before the war. Recent scholarship also demonstrates that Israeli, Arab, American, and other world leaders and analysts all knew that Egyptian forces in the Sinai were occupying defensive positions, and that neither Egypt nor any other Arab state had any intention of attacking Israel, much less wiping it off the map.[7]

Be all that as it may, American Jews felt that Israel had just dodged the bullet of genocide. While relieved at Israel's victory, they continued to worry that it was forever just one defeat away from destruction and its people one miscalculation away from annihilation. Supporting Israel to prevent such an unthinkable thing became a bedrock principle for many, including some Jews on the Left who were aghast at left-wing Jewish attacks on Israel.

## The Attack on "Self-Hating Jews"

Arnoni was one of the first liberal-left Jewish writers publicly to denounce Jewish New Leftists' hostility to Israel as a form of acting out their psychological problems and insecurities about being young Jews in booming postwar

America. His deep anger toward a younger generation of Jews that he felt was irrationally turning its back on the values and identity to which all Jews must cling was emblematic of wider Jewish fear of criticisms of Israel during and after 1967. For many, such attitudes constituted nothing less than an existential threat to Judaism. Jewish fears about Israel's survival therefore prompted deep-set hostility to younger New Left Jews who were perceived as giving aid and comfort to Israel's mortal enemies. This fear was particularly noticeable among Jews older than the New Left generation.

Arnoni survived the infamous Łódź ghetto, established by invading Nazi forces, and later concentration camps such as Auschwitz. After the Holocaust, he moved to Israel for a few years before teaching political science at several universities in the United States. In 1959, Arnoni began editing *The Minority of One,* a progressive publication, whose pages he used to question the war in Vietnam, discuss alternative theories about the assassination of President John F. Kennedy, and other issues that defied mainstream opinion. His publication's masthead declared it to be "dedicated to the eradication of all restrictions on thought."

Yet when it came to Israel, Arnoni was solidly hostile to the thought of left-wing criticism of the Jewish state. In the September 1967 issue of *The Minority of One*, Arnoni wrote a lengthy piece about Israel's virtues and the Arabs' faults, which he entitled "Rights and Wrongs in the Arab-Israeli Conflict (To the Anatomy of the Forces of Progress and Reaction in the Middle East)."[8] Among other things, he excoriated Black Power and New Left advocates of the Palestinians for attaching themselves to external symbols of anti-imperialism rather than substance. For these "inverse racists . . . imperialism being to them white, any non-white movement is ipso facto right"; in any case, they were attracted to anything new and exotic that promised "a world less rotten than one's own," an attitude Arnoni derided as "progressivism-by-keffiyeh."[9]

As a Holocaust survivor, Arnoni believed these attitudes stemmed from the vacuity of such young people's Jewishness. He argued that attacking Israel was merely a vehicle for attacking all that these Jewish young people hated about themselves, their parents, and their lives as minorities in Gentile America. Arnoni described such psychological disorder in expressive if angry terms: "The young bar mitzvah Jew turns against Israel—the Judaism with an address—all the bitterness he has accumulated in his heart against the non-meaning of the Jewishness he has been exposed to. He speaks up against Israel with a vengeance, each time as if laughing at yet another comical guest at his bar mitzvah, each time as if in protest against yet another check received as a gift to drown the hypocrisy of the occasion in an ocean of dollars."[10] Criticism of Israel was another reflection of the New Left's inchoate rebellion against anything considered to be part of the Establishment. Increasingly frustrated with the both the ongoing war in Vietnam and the nature of the New Left, Arnoni left the United States and returned to Israel in 1969.[11]

Other liberal and left-wing Jews echoed the theme that the New Leftists who attacked Israel did so not out of principle and rational thought but rather some kind of psychological disorder. Some claimed that these youths were flagellating themselves for having been born into success. They felt they needed to support the underdogs, the poor and oppressed—the Arabs— whereas Israel represented success. Critics argued that joining the New Left was a way to avoid confronting the significance of their assimilation.[12] Even some Jews from the younger generation agreed. Joshua Muravchik, cofounder of the solidly pro-Israeli social democratic group Youth Committee for Peace and Democracy in the Middle East, noted: "Anti-Israel new leftism has become for many young Jews a modern means of 'passing' in Gentile society."[13] Writing about Jewish radicals who supported the Palestinians, Sheldon Stern interpreted such "passing" bluntly: "They are not truly Jewish if they work toward the destruction of the Jewish state, as they are by supporting the Al Fatah."[14]

Much of the liberal-left Jewish angst about the New Left abandoning Israel was premised on some mistaken analysis. Many who decried attacks on Israel and Zionism did not grasp that these attitudes stemmed from anti-imperialist ideology and a principled sense of Palestinian victimhood, choosing instead to understand them as anti-Semitism, Jewish self-hatred, or romantic identification with Third World revolutionaries.[15] The main issue for these young people was what Israel had done to the Palestinians in the process of creating the Jewish state. Had Zionism created an all-Jewish state in some empty part of the world, perhaps all would have been fine. But it had displaced the indigenous Arab population of Palestine in 1948 and thereafter created a state that only admitted Jewish immigrants while refusing to allow the Palestinian refugees to return—all on the basis of ethnicity and religion. Older Jewish critics of the New Left nonetheless saw youthful hostility to Israel as abstract hatred of it and of Judaism divorced from the historical record; they understood these criticisms as a call for the physical annihilation of Israel and its Jewish inhabitants.

The result of all this was a type of civil war within the Jewish Left between those committed to total worldwide revolution and those who believed in Israel exceptionalism. One of the first manifestations of this came in July 1967, just weeks after the war. *Ramparts,* one of the leading publications of the New Left, printed an article, "Israel Is not Vietnam," in which two Jewish professors at Harvard, Michael Walzer and Martin Peretz, made a case that the Left could not conflate the two and denounce Israel's war in the Middle East in the same terms as it denounced the United States' war in Vietnam. They did not hide the fact that their feelings about Israel were in part driven by a sense of ethnic Jewish loyalty. Walzer and Peretz went on to make several points that constituted an apologetic argument on behalf of Israel and Zionism. First, "Jewish colonization of Palestine" was not an example of exploitative imperialism, because it "differs from other colonizations in Africa and Asia in that the immigrant community was committed to do its own work . . . and not to exploit the Arab population." Furthermore, the men laid the blame for the plight of the Palestinian refugees on the Arab host states for not resettling them rather than on Israel for refusing to allow them to return. Finally, Walzer and Peretz posited that there could be no resolution to the Arab-Israeli conflict until the Arabs recognized Israel's existence.[16]

Four months after the appearance of the article, Peretz published a scorching denunciation of New Left attacks on Israel in *Commentary,* a journal published by the American Jewish Committee,[17] laying the basis in part for future pro-Israeli assaults on New Left thinking about the Arab-Israeli conflict. Peretz blasted what he considered the uncritical, reflexive attachment to Third World revolutionaries by noting, "A certain naiveté about the purity and virtue of the revolutionary world has characterized much Left and anti-war sentiment in America," adding that: "the new left's enchantment with the Third World will prove costly as was its old enchantment with the second [i.e., the Soviet Union and its allies], for the erection of double standards inevitably leads to a corruption of the moral sense no less than the political." Peretz also chided the youthful Left's ignorance of what he considered the real threat to the Middle East, the Soviet Union. Finally, he was dismayed at the innate anti-Americanism he saw in left-wing attacks on Israel: "the orthodox notion of Israel as 'imperialist' or as a neo-imperialist instrument makes sense only to those embittered rank-and-filers for whom the side in a dispute which engages the open and general support of Americans is *ipso facto* bound to be in the wrong."[18]

A major Jewish liberal voice early on against New Left criticism of Israel was that of the political sociologist Seymour Martin Lipset. The son of Jewish immigrants from Russia, Lipset had moved away from socialism toward liberalism by the early 1960s. In December 1969 while teaching at Harvard he published what came to be a classic attack on youthful attitudes to Israel, "'The Socialism of Fools': The Left, the Jews, and Israel."[19] Left-wing antipathy to Israel was rooted, he believed, in the Left's historical belief that "Jewish particularism is somehow reactionary, tribal, traditional, unmodern." This was a belief shared even by Jews. Eastern European Marxist, socialist, and anarchist Jews' opposition to Zionism in the first half of the twentieth century stemmed, he thought, from their psychological need to break with Judaism and assimilate. Lipset also attributed New Left Jewish support for the Arabs in the 1960s to various psychological factors. He agreed with Arnoni that for such young Jews, the Arabs "are weak, underdeveloped, and poor. Anybody defined as an underdog is good, anybody seen as powerful [i.e., Israel] is bad."[20] Moreover, Lipset argued, the New Left "privileged emotion and irrationality over reason; the Arabs represented the former, Israel the latter."[21]

Lipset also reinforced the notion that New Left Jewish hostility to Israel was displaced anger at what young Jews perceived as their parents' hypocrisy. He argued that the real issue was not Israel and its policies vis-à-vis the Palestinians and other Arabs but rather a kind of psychological parental complex: Israel had become a convenient surrogate for expressing New Left Jewish youths' anger at their parents. "Israel, in effect, seems to be behaving like their parents. Israel itself does not really interest them. They are essentially reacting to American Jewish conditions and to the American way of life."[22] He and others simply could not fathom that left-of-center Jews possibly could have a rational, theoretical basis for criticizing Israel and supporting the Palestinians; such stances must stem from some kind of personal failure.

Left-of-center Jews became so concerned about New Left attacks on Israel that they convened an entire conference on the topic of Israel, America, and the New Left on February 21, 1970, at Arden House in Orange County, New York. The gathering met under the auspices of the American Histadrut Cultural Exchange Institute and its executive director, Mordecai S. Chertoff. Some 1,300 attended the conference, "Israel, America, and the New Left." The overall tone of those who made presentations was quite hostile to New Left attacks on Israel. Several of those presentations, along with some additional pieces, were edited and published by Chertoff in 1971 in a volume titled

*The New Left and the Jews*,[23] giving wider exposure to the harsh criticisms of New Left stances on the Arab-Israeli conflict. Lipset included a slightly different version of his "The Socialism of Fools" in the book, while Tom Milstein summed up the view of many who had attended the conference that "the New Left . . . is quite definitely a clear and present danger to the security of the Jewish community in the United States," not just Jews in Israel.[24]

In fact, the New Left and its attitudes to Israel were not quite the existential threat to American Judaism that Milstein claimed. For all the anxiety and fears that large numbers of young Jews were being pulled into a pro-Arab orbit, Jewish young people in fact did not seem to be convinced by left-wing rhetoric about Israel. This was supported a few years later by several studies of Jewish student attitudes. One was based on interviews conducted with forty-eight Jewish students at universities in the northeastern United States in 1973. While the students' American identity outweighed their particular Jewish identity, they also believed that support for Israel was fully compatible with their American identity. The authors of the study therefore concluded that Israel had "become a crucial dimension in the ethnicity of American Jews."[25] The Jewish campus organization Hillel carried out another study about the same time based on a poll of Hillel field directors at 120 major American colleges and universities, which did "not show any significant shift in campus opinion" away from Israel, and observed that the "dire conclusions, already given credence by some spokesmen in the Jewish community are still unwarranted fears."[26]

### The Left-Wing Jewish Rebuttal

Some liberal and left-wing Jews grew tired of being treated as pathological for daring to challenge their elders' uncritical view of Israel. Mike Marqusee recalled the day he was first called a self-hating Jew—and by, of all people, his own father. At the synagogue where his family worshipped, a visiting Israeli had lectured Marqusee's Sunday school class a few months after the June 1967 war on the situation in the Middle East, and Marqusee had publicly criticized him for calling Arabs "primitive." When he told his family about this at the dinner table that evening, however, his father accused him of "Jewish self-hatred."[27]

A few years later at age sixteen, Marqusee wrote an essay objecting to the idea that Jews had to support Israel unquestioningly merely because Israelis were fellow Jews, asking, "What can religious values mean when they include the unquestioning dogmatic support of the militaristic, racist state of Israel simply because its population is primarily Jewish?"[28] Marqusee also referred to how anti-Zionist Jews like some of those in the New Left were being demonized by other Jews who enforced adherence to a consensus about Israel that they themselves had created. In Marqusee's words: "Whenever Jews speak out against Israel, they are met with *ad hominem* criticism. Their motives, their representativeness, their authenticity as Jews are questioned . . . we are pathologized. For only a psychological aberration, a neurotic malaise, could account for our defection from Israel's cause, which is presumed to be—whether we like it or not—our own cause." Marqusee thought this as "fatuous" as anti-Semites' assuming that the behavior of all Jews stemmed from their Jewish identity.[29]

The well-known journalist Paul Jacobs, born to immigrant Jewish parents from Germany, insisted that it was not left-wing Jews who had a psychological problem but rather their middle-class Jewish critics, whose own inner demons aroused irrational Zionist jingoism:

> Ambiguity is the modal tone of Jewish life in America, ambiguity about what it means to be Jewish. . . . The angry lashing-out by many American Jews at anyone who even suggests that perhaps an element of justice can be found in the Arab position is understandable but damned unpleasant for those who get lashed. . . . Even if their Zionism is not deep enough to take them to Israel, it has made them automatic and thoughtless defenders of every position taken by the Israeli government.[30]

Jacobs, who had been a Trotskyist as a youth, was a familiar name in left-wing publications in the 1960s. He covered the trial of the Nazi war criminal Adolph Eichmann in Jerusalem in 1961–62 and ran for senator from California on the Peace and Freedom Party ticket in 1968. Later, in 1976, he helped found the left-wing magazine *Mother Jones*. He returned to Israel shortly after the June 1967 war, and twice again in 1969. He was therefore highly familiar with both the Arab-Israeli conflict and the leftist scene in America.

Jacobs urged both compromise and serious self-reflection on all sides. In the July 1967 issue of *Ramparts*—the same issue that featured Walzer and Peretz's "Israel Is Not Vietnam"—he published an article entitled "A Time to Heal" that asserted that Israel could never secure peace by military force.[31] Writing in the pacifist-oriented *Liberation* in November 1969, Jacobs encouraged the Palestinians to understand the effect that their violent actions and rhetoric had on Israelis.[32] A year later, he co-chaired the Ad Hoc Liberation of Palestine and Israel Committee, which urged new thinking on all sides.[33]

Jacobs's stance earned him a good deal of opprobrium on more than one occasion. "It is a paradox, a twist of bitter irony that the American Jewish community feels threatened at a time when it appears to be more secure than ever in its history," Jacobs wrote. "But they are insecure there, still worried about the gentiles, still uncertain what it is to be a Jew in America." Because of this insecurity, they embraced Israel: "It has become their reserve power; it represents an answer to questions of life in the Diaspora; they are convinced it must be preserved because without it, all Jews in the world will be even more threatened than they are today."[34]

The maverick journalist I. F. Stone was perhaps the first prominent left-wing Jew older than the New Left generation to ask serious questions about Israel publicly in the 1960s and face the consequences for doing so. Born Isidore Feinstein to immigrant parents, Stone became a journalist writing for a number of publications before starting his own *I. F. Stone's Weekly* in 1953. Stone visited Palestine in 1946, and his reporting on his trip with Holocaust survivors as they clandestinely tried to sail there after World War II became a widely acclaimed book, *Underground to Palestine*.[35] He returned to Palestine in 1948, and to the new state of Israel in 1949, 1950, 1951, 1956, and 1964.

In Stone's opinion, the plight of the Palestinian refugees was the central problem that needed to be addressed in order to forge lasting Arab-Israeli peace. "The moral tragedy for world Jewry is that we could not make homes for our postwar refugees without making three quarters of a million kindred people homeless. No solution can be found until we Jews ourselves are willing to face up to the problem in all its terrible three-dimensional human complexity and that means to see it through Arab eyes as well as our own," he averred in the December 5, 1966, issue of *I. F. Stone's Weekly*. "Until their [the Palestinian refugees'] just claims have been met there can be no peace in the area."[36]

After Israel's overwhelmingly victory six months later in the 1967 war, Stone again wrote that "the cornerstone of that [final peace] settlement must be to find some new homes for the Arab refugees, some within Israel, some outside of it, all with compensation for their lost lands and properties." Stone went on to argue that American Jews should now divert their financial contributions away from Israel and toward ensuring a just settlement to the refugee problem. The refugees and their plight should tug at the heartstrings and weigh heavily on the conscience of world Jewry, he maintained: "It was a moral tragedy—to which no Jew worthy of our best Prophetic tradition could be insensitive—that a kindred people was made homeless in the task of making new homes for the remnants of the Hitler holocaust."[37] Stone was quick to point out in the weeks after Israel's victory that lasting peace would come only when it capitalized on that victory and sought a lasting peace settlement with the Arabs—including the Palestinian refugees. "Israel cannot live very long in a hostile Arab sea," he wrote in "The Future of Israel," an article published in *Ramparts* in July 1967.[38]

In the *New York Review* a month later, he dissected the proposition that Israel was a progressive state fighting against reactionary forces bent on its destruction. Stone first discredited the idea that because some Jews had fought against the British for their independence meant that Israel ipso facto could not therefore be a creation of Western imperialism. He pointed out that the same could be said of the American Revolution and Ian Smith's white-dominated Rhodesia. Stone then turned to the charge frequently leveled by partisans of Israel that the Palestinian refugees had run away in 1948; their plight therefore was neither Israel's fault nor its problem to solve. Stone asked, so what if they actually had fled voluntarily? Did that therefore negate their right to repatriation? What about Jews who fled voluntarily from the Nazis, he asked? It was "moral myopia," he continued, for Israelis to dwell on nineteen centuries of Jewish exile and dismiss nineteen years of Palestinian refugee exile. Israel was creating a "moral schizophrenia" in world Jewry, because Jewish existence outside Israel depended upon secular, nonracial, pluralistic societies—but Israel was the exact opposite of that.[39]

Stone was a hero to many liberals and leftists because of his searing journalistic integrity and his speaking truth bravely to power. Thus it was unsettling for some supporters of Israel, particularly fellow Jews, to read his thoughts about the Palestinians and how to resolve the Arab-Israeli conflict. He was not alone. Noam Chomsky, a well-known professor at MIT, was another left-wing Jew who dared to question the dominant discourse on Israel and attacks on radical Jews' criticisms of Israel. Chomsky was born to an immigrant family in Philadelphia, and grew up in a home that was deeply involved with Judaism, Zionism, and Hebrew language culture. As a youth, he had been close to activists from the socialist Zionist groups Avukah and

Hashomer Hatzair. Already proficient in Hebrew, Chomsky began studying Arabic in 1945 during his first year at the University of Pennsylvania. During the summer of 1953, he lived in Israel at Ha-Zore`a, a kibbutz associated with Hashomer Hatzair. One day he saw some stones in a field and asked a veteran member of the kibbutz what they were. The person did not want to talk about it, but later told Chomsky that they were the remains of a Palestinian village that had been depopulated and destroyed in the 1948 war.[40]

Chomsky first became publicly engaged in the question when he was invited to give a talk to the Arab Club at the Massachusetts Institute of Technology in March 1969, an event that was organized by one of his graduate students, Assaf Khoury.[41] By that time he was already famous as an opponent to the Vietnam War. Much had changed since 1967, when Chomsky had wholeheartedly supported Israel in its war with the Arabs. "At the time of the Six Day War in June 1967," he wrote in late 1972, "I personally believed that the threat of genocide was real, and reacted with virtually uncritical support for Israel at what appeared to be a desperate moment. It retrospect, it seems that this assessment of the facts was dubious at best."[42]

In "Nationalism and Conflict in Palestine," a 1968 article that appeared in several publications, including *Liberation* and the left-liberal Israeli *New Outlook*, he laid out his vision of an alternative to the kind of ethnic nationalism that drove the Arab-Israeli conflict: cooperation among people who share common class interests. The shared interests of the Arab and Jewish peoples in Palestine/Israel could be achieved, he argued, through communities in which political and economic institutions were under democratic, popular control and where resources were devoted to satisfying human needs. Chomsky argued that these interests could not be served by either a Jewish state or an Arab state.[43]

Chomsky refused to attack Jewish New Leftists for their stances on the Arab-Israeli conflict; he believed in the free flow of ideas. When he was invited to participate in the February 1970 conference on "Israel, America, and the New Left" held by the American Histadrut Cultural Exchange Institute at Arden House in Orange County, New York, Chomsky became rather like the biblical Daniel in the lions' den. Most of the American and Israeli Jews who spoke at the conference bitterly denounced the New Left for its stances on Israel. Chomsky insisted that in the first place, there was no such thing as a unified New Left stance on Israel, and that it was "demonstrably false" to characterize the New Left as overwhelmingly pro-Arab and anti-Israel.[44]

Chomsky also dismissed the idea that self-hatred and anti-Semitism were what was driving New Left attitudes to Israel, calling this a transparent dodge to avoid dealing with what New Leftists had to say: "First and most important, it is necessary to stop equating criticism of Israeli government policy with anti-Semitism, to put an end to the silly talk about Jewish self-hatred (or else, to provide some evidence to substantiate what have, so far, been simply wild charges), and to pay some attention to what people are actually saying and thinking."[45]

Like Paul Jacobs, Chomsky went beyond just defending the New Left to push Americans (and American Jews in particular) to examine the complexities of the Middle East openly, honestly, and rationally. "Since the Six-Day War, critics of one or another aspect of Israeli policy have been subjected to ridiculous accusations and childish distortion," he wrote. "Surely it is obvious that a critical analysis of Israeli institutions and practices does not in itself imply antagonism to the people of Israel, denial of the national rights of Jews in Israel, or lack of concern for their just aspirations and needs."[46]

He also believed that liberal and left-wing Jews who supported the war in Vietnam and who were moving to the political right—some eventually formed the core of the neoconservative movement—used those who questioned Israeli policies as convenient whipping boys when attacking those, like him, who opposed the war. Years later Chomsky asserted:

> You could use Israel to beat the New Left over the head. It became a convenient weapon to attack the New Left, and they were able to adapt a stance that has enormous appeal to intellectuals: supporting Rambo and appear to be humanitarian. . . . It was very convenient to support Israel because you were supporting the United States. For intellectuals, it was difficult [to advocate patriotism] . . . but on this issue, you could be very passionate.[47]

Chomsky took pains to explain the real reasons he felt that leftists were coming under attack for their stances on the Arab-Israeli conflict. In the era when the Cold War consensus on how the United States should deal with the Soviet Union was coming to an end, it became more and more difficult for liberals to justify a muscular American foreign and military policy abroad and "military state capitalism" at home. Left-wing protests against the Vietnam War specifically, and American imperialism generally, made it more difficult for liberals who were turning into neoconservatives to argue persuasively about issues like building American military strength. The "comfortable world of the intelligentsia" was under assault in the 1960s. They could cheer without guilt as Israel battled "Soviet-backed designs to throw Jews into the sea," however, and "rejoice vicariously" at Israeli power.[48] They could not cheer on the American military in Vietnam, but they could celebrate the 1967 Israeli victory with a clear conscience, simultaneously promoting the "idea that America must be the gendarme of the world [too]."[49]

Some young left-wing Jews agreed with Chomsky's argument about the general conservative thrust of the attack on New Left Jews. Barry M. Rubin enrolled at Georgetown University in 1967 and eventually became a leader in the SDS chapter there. He later worked as foreign editor for the left-wing newspaper *The Guardian* and became involved with the Middle East Research and Information Project (MERIP). "There's been a recent revival of Zionist ideology in the United States, which I think is purposely aimed not only to give aid and support to Israel but also to attempt to make people—especially Jews in this country—accept a racist, reactionary ideology which also will turn them against the American Left," Rubin wrote in 1972.[50]

David Horowitz, a confidant of the Black Panthers and editor at *Ramparts*, was another young Jewish leftist who noted the connection between support for Israel and rising conservative attitudes in the late 1960s, especially among American Jews. Israel and the conflict allowed those Jews who were moving rightward anyway to justify their actions and assuage their guilt, Horowitz asserted. Those who had voted for Richard Nixon for president in 1968 and 1972 could rationalize having done so by claiming that Israel was safer with Nixon in the White House. "The peril of Israel thus becomes a necessarily justifying basis for the conservative shift of America's Jews, much as the creation of Israel and the consequent nationalization of Judaism are organic elements in its cause," he wrote in 1974.[51]

## An Attempt at Reconciliation

A noteworthy 1960s Jewish radical who self-consciously tried to ground the ability to question Israeli policy with loyalty to his Jewish heritage was Arthur Waskow,[52] one of the founders of the National Conference for New Politics in Chicago in August 1967 and a member of the steering committee of the New Mobilization Committee to End the War in Vietnam. The assassination of Martin Luther King Jr. in April 1968 and the black rebellion that swept through Washington, DC, as a result helped transform the hitherto secular activist into one deeply concerned with Judaism and Jewish renewal, which ultimately led to his association with Jews for Urban Justice (JUJ) and the "radical Judaism" movement.

Waskow was concerned about the Arab-Israeli conflict partly because his wife, Irene (née Elkin), had a sister who had been in the Zionist youth group Habonim, and who had moved to Israel to live on a kibbutz in the Negev Desert. Waskow's growing interest in the issue led him to travel to Israel in the spring and summer of 1969, where he met the Israeli peace activist Uri Avnery, the Palestinian mayor of Hebron, Sheikh Muhammad Ali Ja`abari, and others. He returned committed to a peaceful resolution of the conflict.

In "A Draft of a Possible Position for Jewish Radicals in America, on 'The Diaspora, Zionism and Israel,'" published in a new Jewish journal called *Sh'ma* in the fall of 1970, Waskow declared that American Jews had a special responsibility to encourage Israeli Jews to safeguard their freedom by striving for peace and justice in the Middle East. Jewish radicals in America were "distressed" at Israel's internal problems, its alliance with the Great Powers, instead of with the anti-colonial movements sweeping through the Third World, and its failure to "deal justly and face-to-face with the Palestinian people." The piece also supported creation of an independent Palestinian state.[53]

Waskow also no doubt had a role in "For Peace and Justice in the Middle East: A Position Paper of Jews for Urban Justice Adopted November 10, 1970," issued by JUJ in November 1970. Saying that JUJ was "neither anti-Zionist nor 'pro-Fatah,'" this document boldly called on the Israeli government to admit that there was indeed a distinct Palestinian people living in Gaza and on both the East and West Banks of the Jordan River. Israel should declare its willingness to discuss the means for it to achieve independence with Palestinian leaders, including those in the PLO, in return for which they should recognize the existence of an Israeli people that deserved its own full independence within its borders.[54]

The next year Waskow worked with Paul Jacobs as co-chair of the Ad Hoc Liberation of Palestine and Israel Committee, which put together a statement entitled "The Liberation of Palestine and Israel" that appeared in the *New York Review* on July 1, 1971. Among the thirty-three signatories were well-known liberal and left-wing Jews like Chomsky, Todd Gitlin, Abbie Hoffman, Arthur Green, Michael Tabor, Sidney Lens, Michael Lerner, Anatol Rapaport, Arnold Jacob Wolf, and the non-Jewish physician and peace activist Benjamin Spock were among the thirty-three signatories. "We urge that the American

Jewish community and the American anti-war and radical movements take up these issues not by a mindless endorsement of one party orthodoxy or another in the Middle East but with serious study and a sensitive commitment to the liberation of both the Israeli and Palestinian people from militarism and exploitation," the statement declared.[55]

In 1971, Waskow published *The Bush Is Burning! Radical Judaism Faces the Pharaohs of the Modern Superstate,* in which he charged that both the Jewish establishment and the New Left were forcing young American Jews to choose between al-Fateh and ultra-Zionism to the exclusion of other points of view. The Jewish establishment was urging Jews not to oppose the war in Vietnam in order not to upset the US empire and endanger ongoing American support for Israel, he asserted. Waskow condemned this "blind hysterical support" for both the Israeli state and the policies of each and every particular Israeli government.[56]

In this "Jewish civil war," left-wing Jews critical of Israel argued their positions forcefully and defended themselves against fellow Jews who accused them of self-hatred and other psychological maladies. These young Jews were not the only ones on the Left to adopt stances critical of Israel and its preemptive strike in the June War, however. Activists from a variety of Old Left Marxist parties did so too.

# 5    Theory and Praxis

*The Old Left against Israel*

A VITALLY IMPORTANT chapter in the history of how white leftists in the Movement dealt with the Arab-Israeli conflict in the 1960s and 1970s was written by the parties of the Old Left. The Old Left, which had been powerful in the 1930s, was decimated by the anti-communist hysteria that swept the United States during the early Cold War years. Nevertheless, Old Left parties like the Communist Party USA, the Socialist Workers Party, and the Socialist Party of America still existed in the 1960s, and some were quite active in the movement against the Vietnam War and other causes. They also took strong stances on the Arab-Israeli conflict. Jews were prominently represented both among Old Leftists who criticized Israel and those who supported it, thereby deepening the Left's "Jewish civil war."

Although often wrongly conflated with the New Left in the minds of their critics, Old Left parties had long struggled with the doctrinal questions of Zionism, nationalism, and imperialism. Given the disproportionately large number of immigrant and native-born Jews in these organizations, the issue of Zionism in particular had been a focus of theoretical analysis in them long before the 1960s. Most of these Old Left parties experienced the same drift toward the Palestinians that characterized parts of the New Left, and they used their parties' top-down leadership structure and infrastructure to spread their ideas among youth—in contrast to the looser, more chaotic structure of New Left groups like SDS. Old Left student groups and Middle East–themed front groups were particularly active in this regard on college campuses in the 1960s.

It was the 1967 war that most directly reignited Old Left discussion and activism about the Arab-Israeli conflict. Given most Old Left parties' historical opposition to Zionism, it was no surprise that some of them came out swinging at Israel in their ideological statements. Others went further and took to the streets with brash, New Left–style protests and demonstrations against the Jewish state and in support of the Palestinians. No group better epitomized the latter than the neo-Trotskyist Workers World Party (WWP), whose front woman on the Arab-Israeli conflict was herself a member of the New Left generation.

### Action in the Streets

In June 1967, twenty-four-year-old Rita Freed found herself at the forefront of the vocal efforts of the Workers World Party to aid the Palestinians and other Arabs in their struggle against Israel. Freed had been raised in a household with a religious Orthodox Jewish father before she became a Marxist. In 1962, she became a founding member of the WWP's youth group, which came to be called Youth against War and Fascism (YAWF). In June 1967, Freed and an ad-hoc committee she led carried out what was probably the only protest against Israel undertaken by Americans while the 1967 war was still under way. Despite the conflicted attitudes about Israel exhibited elsewhere on the Left, notably by progressive and left-wing Jews, Freed and the WWP left no doubt about where they stood on the Arab-Israeli conflict, and were not at all hesitant about letting the world know.

The WWP emerged in 1959 when Socialist Workers Party national committee member Sam Marcy, who was born Sam Ballan to Jewish parents in Russia before immigrating to the United States after the Russian Revolution and civil war, broke with the party and helped found a new one. It stood apart from some of the hesitancy and debate about the Arab-Israeli conflict that characterized groups like SDS by resolutely supporting the Arabs and denouncing Israel. Several days into the war, on June 9, 1967, the party issued a statement that it published in its newspaper, *Workers World*, under a banner headline that read "U.S. Is the Real Sponsor of Israel's Attack on the Arabs." It claimed that the war in the Middle East was not between Arabs and Israel, but rather between American, British, and French imperialism and the Arab revolution: "It is not 'little' Israel against the manifold Arab peoples, but giant imperialism against the struggling Arabs."[1]

The WWP's editorial revealed other facets of its stance toward the Arab-Israeli conflict. Given its Trotskyist heritage the party was hostile to the Soviet Union and what it considered its revisionist Marxism, so the editorial blasted the Soviet Union for its "sellout" of the Arab revolution. It took aim at the West as well, arguing that it was cynically using its own victims, the Jews, against the oppressed peoples of the Arab world.[2] "The state of Israel is itself a tool of imperialism," the statement continued. This was facilitated by the fact that many people sympathized with Israel because of the historical oppression of the Jews. Resurrecting Old Left theorizing about the Jewish Question—whether Jews could ever fully assimilate into Western society—the WWP editorial noted that the Jewish Question "can never be settled by Israel oppressing other nationalities on behalf of imperialism, but only by a struggle of the Jewish nation *against* the imperialism which subjugates *all* oppressed nationalities." As for the Palestinians, the WWP statement declared that "the Palestinian Arabs should be returned to their homeland on a status quo ante basis."[3] It was noteworthy for using the term "Palestinian" (as opposed to "Arab," as was common on the Left) at this early stage in 1960s pro-Palestinian solidarity work.

Two weeks later, *Workers World* editorialized that Israel had been the aggressor in the 1967 war, that it was the agent for Western imperialism in the Middle East, and that the Arabs were struggling against imperialism, even though some of them were ruled by conservative leaders. "The state of Israel is on the side of the oppressors and against the oppressed," the June 24, 1967, editorial declared. The historical oppression of the Jews might "cloud" this issue, but did not change it.[4] The Jews deserved a homeland, but it should be a state shared with the Palestinians. Party co-founder and editor of *Workers World* Vincent Copeland wrote, "every nation, particularly a persecuted and dispersed nation yearns for a homeland. There should be a homeland, yes. But why in the Arabs' homeland?" The solution to the present conflict would come with the creation of a joint Jewish-Arab, anti-imperialist state.[5]

The WWP did more than just theorize and editorialize about Israel and the Palestinians. Party activists were the only ones on the Left who actually demonstrated against Israel during the 1967 war. Even the New Left had not done as much. On June 10, 1967, the last day of the war, activists from YAWF picketed the US mission to the United Nations in New York City, carrying signs bearing slogans such as "U.S.-Israeli Aggression Against the Arab People" and "U.S. Get Out of the Mideast." Shortly after this demonstration the WWP decided to hold a conference on the Middle East on June 21 in New York, organized by a front group it put together called the Ad Hoc Committee on the Middle East; Freed was the committee's coordinator.[6] According to a notice in the *National Guardian*, the purpose of the gathering was to continue to agitate against Israel by planning another demonstration, as well as other actions "protesting U.S.-Israeli aggression against the Arabs."[7]

Among those listed as sponsors of the upcoming conference was Deirdre Griswold, WWP co-founder Vincent Copeland's stepdaughter. Griswold had just returned from six months in Europe working with Bertrand Russell's International War Crimes Tribunal in Sweden and Denmark investigating alleged American war crimes in the Vietnam War. For her, taking a stance against Israeli actions in the Middle East went hand in hand with protesting American actions in Vietnam. "It really flowed from our worldview," she said years later. "It just flowed from how we saw the role of the U.S. in the post-war period, the drive, the impulse to move in and take over and become dominant in areas where other powers had been the colonial rulers." An additional impetus for her was the fact that "we were living in the country that was the most responsible for what was going on."[8]

On June 21, 1967, the new Ad Hoc Committee on the Middle East held its conference in New York City as planned, with Freed presiding. Approximately a hundred people attended. Freed made it clear that "in opposing the Israeli state, we are not attacking the Jewish people, nor disregarding the rightful desire of this oppressed nation for a homeland." A press release issued just over a week later stated that the purpose of the new committee was "exposing U.S. monopoly interests in the Middle East," showing how Israel was a base for Western domination of the Arabs and revealing how America's anti-Arab and pro-Israeli policy in the Middle East did not really stem from sympathy for the Jewish people.[9] In the first activity of the committee after its founding meeting, committee members handed out anti-Israeli leaflets at a pro-Israeli rally entitled "Vietnam and Israel: There Is a Difference" that was held on June 22, 1967, at the Manhattan Center in New York City, where Senator George McGovern spoke.

The committee used leaflets and an advertisement in the *National Guardian* to promote a demonstration the WWP planned for July 14 at the Israeli mission to the United Nations. It shrewdly aimed to connect American support for the Israeli occupation of Arab territories with the Vietnam War. The official slogan of the protest was "Protest U.S.-Israeli Aggression— Demand Israeli Troops Withdraw from Captured Arab Territory." Others included "Stop U.S.-Israeli Aggression!"; "Withdraw Israeli Troops from Arab Lands!"; and "Get the U.S. Sixth Fleet out of the Mediterranean!" The publicity was openly aimed at the peace movement, and stated inter alia, "Don't Just Oppose *One* Case of U.S. Aggression."[10] In the end, the committee held its planned demonstration in front of Israel's mission to the UN; approximately 135 picketers attended.

Freed and the Ad Hoc Committee on the Middle East continued their activities in the second half of 1967 with the same vigor. In August, one of the committee's original sponsors, a black American convert to Islam named Ali Anwar, introduced a resolution at the National Conference for New Politics in Chicago that included a condemnation of Israel. That was the first time in the 1960s that many white leftists had been part of an activity that included an attack on the Jewish state, and many were shocked.[11]

In the second half of 1967, Freed produced a detailed study of the Arab-Israeli conflict in a pamphlet she wrote for the committee entitled *War in the Mideast, June 1967: What Were the Forces Behind It?* Once again, this argued that "the real reason for the June war was the multi-billion dollar profits of American oil companies. . . . Israel was created for the sake of oil, not for the sake of the Jewish people." Freed pointed out that for nearly nineteen centuries, hardly any Jews talked about establishing a Jewish homeland, and that the emergence of Zionism in Europe precisely at the same time that European imperialism was conquering much of the developing world was no coincidence.[12]

After eighteen months of vocal anti-Israeli activism on behalf of the WWP, the Ad Hoc Committee on the Middle East changed its name in early 1969 to the Committee to Support Middle East Liberation (CSMEL). By then, there was talk on the Left of Palestinian liberation, and the Palestinian guerrilla movement, spearheaded by the Palestine Liberation Organization, was headline news. CSMEL and other WWP-affiliated groups continued to be active on the streets carrying out demonstrations and arranging public events. For example, CSMEL joined with YAWF and the Coalition of Anti-Imperialist Movements on February 15, 1969, in another demonstration in front of the US mission to the UN in New York City; about a hundred people participated. Later in the year, CSMEL picketed outside the Pfister Hotel in Milwaukee,

Wisconsin, on November 13, as Senator Hubert H. Humphrey spoke inside at an Israel Bonds dinner.

The WWP did try on some occasions to move beyond theorizing and demonstrating and actually connect with Middle Easterners. Freed flew to Algeria in May 1971 to attend a Palestine Week conference. Palestinians and Israelis even joined WWP-affiliated groups. A Palestinian who was involved with the party was Ali Kased,[13] a West Banker forced into exile for his political activities by the Jordanian authorities. In the late 1960s, Kased moved to Puerto Rico and then to New York City, where he became involved with YAWF. Kased later was active in the Committee for a Democratic Palestine, and, in 1981, he helped form the November 29 Coalition for Palestine. Michael Rubin was involved in the party's work on the Middle East. Born to a Jewish family in Vienna, he immigrated to the United Kingdom, then to the United States, and then to Palestine in 1947, where he fought with the Jewish Hagana militia during the 1948 Arab-Israeli War. Rubin left Israel in 1967 and came back to the United States, whereupon he became involved with the Ad Hoc Committee on the Middle East. In 1968, the committee published a pamphlet he and Freed had written titled *An Israeli Worker's Answer to M. S. Arnoni*, a response to the harsh criticisms that Arnoni had mounted against leftist attacks on Israel (see chapter 4 above).

CSMEL continued its activist policy of picketing in front of Israeli institutions in the United States and at events at which Israeli or American politicians were speaking. On May 15, 1970, the day after the twenty-second anniversary of Israel's declaration of independence, CSMEL activists demonstrated in front of the Israeli Discount Bank in New York City. On September 16, YAWF picketed the Sheraton Blackstone Hotel in Chicago, where President Richard Nixon was staying, chanting, "Support black and Arab liberation" and "Israel is a death trap for the Jewish people." Four days later, some two hundred activists from YAWF and CSMEL demonstrated outside the Hilton Hotel in New York City, where Israeli Prime Minister Golda Meir was addressing a meeting held by the United Jewish Appeal. They carried the Palestinian flag, and chanted slogans such as "No GIs to the Middle East" and "Free Leila, jail Golda"—a reference to the Palestinian airplane hijacker Leila Khaled.

CSMEL faded away in the early 1970s. Freed left the WWP amid some internal dissension, and YAWF thereafter picked up the WWP's remaining Middle Eastern protest and education efforts. It developed a Middle East committee, which demonstrated outside a United Jewish Appeal dinner on March 5, 1973, at the Hilton Hotel in New York, where Golda Meir made another of her speeches while in the United States. The following month, YAWF's Middle East committee co-sponsored a "Deir Yassin Demonstration" in New York City on April 9, the twenty-fifth anniversary of the killings of Palestinians in the village of Dayr Yasin by Jewish forces during the 1948 war. YAWF also staged what the WWP claimed was the only anti-Israeli protests that took place during the October 1973 Arab-Israeli War, one of which was in Houston; police arrested twelve demonstrators, eight of whom were Mexican-Americans.[14]

The WWP's high level of involvement in the Arab-Israeli conflict was historically significant. The energy and brash demonstrations that the WWP mounted around the issue may or may not have convinced many people who had not already made up their minds about the issue, but its vigorous stance against Israel no doubt helped shape the overall tenor of the Left's response to the 1967 war and Arab-Israeli relations thereafter, which was moving clearly in the direction of supporting the Palestinians. Many 1960s young radicals like those in SDS were moving in a more militant and confrontational direction, and the WWP's in-your-face demonstrations against Israel may have helped radicalize them on this issue.

## The Search for Theoretical Clarity

Even aside from his physical size, the burly Socialist Workers Party (SWP) candidate Fred W. Halstead was unique among those running for president of the United States in the 1968 elections—he traveled to the Arab world during his campaign, and his vice presidential running mate, Paul Boutelle, had organized a rally the year before to present the Arab view of the Arab-Israeli conflict. The SWP also had openly embraced the "Arab Revolution" and denounced Israel as the aggressor in the 1967 war. Its rivals in the WWP harbored no illusions about running candidates in elections, but the SWP was anxious to bring its stance on the Middle East to the ballot box. Yet the party was also different from the WWP in that its members were not united behind a single theoretical understanding of Israel and the Arabs. Indeed, much internal discussion and debate emerged within the party about this question even though most party factions agreed on the need to condemn Israel and support the Arabs. Like New Leftists, some Old Leftists were far from united in their positions on the Arab-Israeli conflict.

Halstead grew up a radical, born in Los Angeles to a socialist Jewish mother and an Irish-American father who had been in the militant anarchosyndicalist Industrial Workers of the World (IWW; Wobblies) labor union. The younger Halstead himself became active in the union and civil rights movements, and was one of the key members of the SWP involved in the anti–Vietnam War movement in the 1960s. Chosen as the SWP's presidential candidate, Halstead embarked on a world tour in the summer of 1968 to meet with American soldiers in Vietnam and visit sympathetic comrades and groups in Asia and Europe on his long way home. He traveled to Egypt as part of his itinerary, and Barry Sheppard, the editor of the SWP's newspaper, *The Militant*, obtained an interview in Cairo with a spokesperson from al-Fateh's information center, Akram Abd al-Majid. The interview appeared in the September 20, 1968 issue of *The Militant*,[15] which probably was the first time that al-Fateh was able to explain its aims directly to the American Left.

The SWP was formed in 1937 by followers of Leon Trotsky who had broken away from the Socialist Party of America. Trotskyists had long offered theoretical analyses of Zionism and the situation facing Jews in the modern world.[16] The party's influence was particularly important in terms of its stance on the Middle East for three reasons. The first was that the SWP was quite active among 1960s youth on college campuses through its youth wing, the Young Socialist Alliance (YSA). Second, the party was heavily invested in lengthy theoretical discussions of Zionism, the role of the Palestinians in the "Arab Revolution" and how to accommodate both Jews and Arabs in the same country. These no doubt contributed to the growing anti-imperialist analyses of the Arab-Israeli conflict being adopted by New Left groups like SDS.[17] Third, despite its own anti-Israeli stance, the SWP played a role in preventing the US antiwar movement from criticizing Israel's role in the 1967 war in the same way that it criticized the US war in Vietnam (see chapter 8 below).

At the time of the June War, the SWP was a member of an association of Trotskyist parties called the Fourth International. Two days after the fighting ended on June 10, 1967, the United Secretariat of the Fourth International issued a statement that was clear in its denunciation of Israel for its "aggression" in having started the war. It was also emphatic in calling upon member parties of the international world to commence action alongside the Arab peoples in combatting Israel and imperialism. It noted: "The State of Israel, inspired by Zionism, has. . . played a reactionary role in the Middle East in the service of imperialism and against the freedom movement of the Arab masses. . . . The Fourth International holds that it is the duty of the international workers movement to reject. . . any equivocal or eclectic position [vis-à-vis the conflict that the Zionists started]." It also called for formation of a "block with the Arab peoples" against Israel and its imperialist masters, and called upon member parties to take concrete action and eschew empty phrases.[18]

The SWP responded accordingly. In fact, it did so even before the war began. The party newspaper, *The Militant,* expounded the party's theoretical understanding of the conflict as war clouds were gathering in the weeks before the hostilities actually began. Published on the day the fighting started, June 5, 1967, an article appeared in *The Militant* asserting that the root of the crisis in the Middle East was Western oil policy. It also stated the party's stance on Zionism, saying that "there was nothing inherently progressive about establishing a tiny all-Jewish state on the Palestinian island of the Arab world."[19]

That marked the beginning of what would be several years of fairly intense intra-party discussion of the Arab-Israeli conflict. A leading figure who articulated the SWP's position on the Middle East after the 1967 war and who was active in explaining it to youth was Peter Buch, a Jewish activist whose immediate family were able to get out of Nazi Germany and immigrate, via Turkey and France, to the United States in 1941. Buch thereafter grew up in the Los Angeles area, received a BS degree from the University of California at Los Angeles, and became an engineer. A member of the socialist Zionist group Hashomer Hatzair as a young man, he went to Israel in 1951 and lived on a kibbutz for six months. Some twenty years later, he recalled that while he enjoyed life on the collective farm, he constantly wondered whether or not Zionism offered the solution to the Jewish problem. "Would the goal of gathering the world's Jews into Palestine solve this problem of the persecution of the Jews?" he asked himself. "Would it really find a safe haven for them?"[20] Buch then came back to the United States and discovered what had happened to the Palestinian refugees in 1948—"how the bulk of them had been expelled"—and broke with Zionism. Far from solving the Jewish problem, he came to believe, "Israel is the most dangerous place in the world for a Jew to be."[21] Buch became a Marxist, and in 1960, he helped form the YSA.

Buch immediately assumed the lead role in the SWP's public attack on Israel and defense of what the party called the "Arab Revolution" after the war. On June 16, 1967, some two hundred people attended the party's Militant Labor Forum in New York, where Buch spoke in front of a large banner reading "Hands Off the Arab Revolution." Two months later, in August 1967, the SWP and the YSA issued a pamphlet entitled *Zionism and the Arab Revolution: The Myth of a Progressive Israel*,[22] which reprinted an article entitled "The Myth of a Progressive Israel" that Buch had written, along with statements issued by the anti-Zionist Israeli group Matzpen.

Despite this, the war prompted considerable intra-party discussion within the SWP, if not always outright dissent, about the proper theoretical stance to take regarding the Arab-Israeli conflict. Debates broke out about how to understand the conflict, and the region generally, in the correct Marxist terms. One theoretical question was whether or not socialists should choose sides or adopt a neutral position toward a capitalist-on-capitalist war. Buch attacked the notion that Israel should be supported because it allegedly was socialist. Just because its governing party was the social democratic MAPAI did not make Israel a socialist country, he argued, any more than England was socialist just because it had a Labour Party government. Israel acted "as a guardian of imperialist interests in the Middle East."[23]

In an August 1967 article in *The Militant*, an SWP staff member, Les Evans, opened the intra-party debate about whether or not to choose sides. Evans had joined the party in 1961 and rose to occupy an important place in its apparatus and publications. He argued that normally socialists should remain neutral in capitalist-on-capitalist wars, but the Arab-Israeli conflict was different. Evans thought along the same lines as Buch: this was a case of a capitalist country, Israel, waging war on a colonial country, represented by the Arabs. The true revolutionary position was to side with the colonized. After all, had not Marxists supported Ethiopia against Italy in 1935–36, even though it was a tribal society, not a socialist one?[24] Evans also explained the origins of the Palestinian refugee problem, writing that they had not fled, as many Americans thought, but were driven out by Israeli forces. "Where did the refugees come from and why?" he asked. "They [Zionists] were opposed *on principle* to anything but a Jewish state, encouraging colonization by Jews from all over the world, which meant in practice that the Arabs must be driven from their homes and land regardless of whether or not they were willing to live in peace with the Jews."[25]

There were other voices, however, that called for a more nuanced SWP approach to the conflict between Israel and the Arabs. In October 1967, the party published a discussion guide in which two SWP members from Boston, Gary Collins and Leonard Gordon, expressed their reservations about how the editors and writers had been writing about the June War in the pages of *The Militant*. It was not that they necessarily opposed the party's pro-Arab, anti-Israeli stance. Rather, they sought greater ideological precision. They took particular issue with the term "the Arab Revolution" that had featured in *The Militant*. Discussing anti-imperialist nationalism in the Arab world was one thing, but talking about the "the Arab Revolution" was quite another. "Hands Off the Arab Revolution" was a misleading slogan, they maintained. They also took issue with *The Militant*'s use of the term "aggressor" with regard to Israel in the recent war, asking whether it was really all that important who had actually fired the first shot in a conflict.[26]

They were not the only ones who objected to the SWP's line in *The Militant*, which published various letters to the editor about the party's stance on the Middle East received since June 1967, both supportive and critical, in the form of a pamphlet.[27] This debate stood in marked contrast to the WWP's unwavering party line. SWP members thereafter continued discussing and debating the party's proper stance toward Israel and the Arabs. Joel Aber, a member of the YSA active in opposition to the Vietnam War, contributed articles to the *SWP Discussion Bulletin* supporting the SWP's backing of what it called the Arab revolution. "Other than Vietnam," Aber wrote, "the Arab world is currently the most active area of the colonial revolution. This fact alone would be reason enough for us to devote increasing attention to the Arab revolution." What was also noteworthy about Aber's logic was that he felt that the SWP, through the YSA, was in a good position to influence the thinking of Arab students in the United States, perhaps leading them to become revolutionary leaders when they returned home.[28]

In addition to paying fastidious attention to theoretical clarity on the issue, the SWP also actively tried to reach American youth with its message about the Middle East. The YSA began discussing the Arab-Israeli conflict on college and university campuses starting in 1969, hosting Middle East events at schools such as Berkeley, Columbia, the University of Pennsylvania, Wayne State University, Indiana University, and schools in the Washington, DC, area. This included reaching out to Arab students. Its December 27–31, 1970 national convention in New York City featured a panel discussion on the Palestinians that included representatives from the Organization of Arab Students and from Palestine House, which had been established in Washington, DC, by George Washington University students.[29] Finally, in an era in which students were fond of posters to adorn the walls of their homes and dormitories, the YSA printed posters in 1970 depicting Palestinian women carrying AK-47 assault rifles with the caption "Revolution until Victory: Defend the Arab Revolution" in English and Arabic.[30]

Peter Buch remained particularly active in reaching out to American youth (and others), traveling to different parts of the United States to speak out on the Middle East. Starting in October 1970, Buch undertook a lengthy six-month tour sponsored by the YSA to more than sixty-eight towns across North America spreading the SWP's message. He also attended a Palestine Week conference in Algeria in May 1971. No doubt because of the harsh criticisms directed against Jewish youth who supported the Arabs, he was careful to argue that Zionism had failed to solve the Jewish Question by setting up a Jewish state. In line with Trotsky's concept of permanent revolution, Buch believed that the Jewish Question was tied up with the wider revolutionary struggle against imperialism. He also denounced Israel's policies toward the Palestinian refugees. "Progress and socialism," he noted, "do not mean the expulsion of a people from their native territory."[31] The refugees had not left Palestine willingly in 1948; their exodus amounted to "the virtual dispossession of an entire people."[32]

After three years of intra-party discussions about what the party's stance toward the Arab-Israeli conflict should be, the SWP adopted a major resolution on the topic at its national convention in Cleveland in August 8–12, 1971. Presented to conference delegates for discussion prior to the convention, this was largely the work of Gus Horowitz, a member of the party's national committee. Horowitz had grown up an observant Jewish family and was pro-Zionist before joining the SWP. Years later he recalled, "despite not being particularly expert on the Middle East, I was responsible for drafting our position." The 1967 war led Horowitz to start thinking differently about Israel and the Arabs. "I started to read a lot of stuff and became clearly aware of the injustice of the situation under which the Palestinian people lived," he remembered. "The socialist ideas that I had thought of as 'Israeli ideals' seemed false."[33]

Horowitz's resolution, entitled "Israel and the Arab Revolution," exemplified the SWP's search for ideological precision on the Arab-Israeli conflict. It was a deeply theoretical analysis of the conflict that vigorously supported the Palestinian people, which it described as "an oppressed nationality, a people who are oppressed not simply as Arabs in general, but also specifically as Palestinians." He argued that the Palestinian cause was a purer liberation struggle than that waged by the "bourgeois" Arab regimes supported by the Soviet Union, because the Palestinian struggle was not seeking accommodation. His resolution also insisted that it was the basic duty of the SWP to support the Palestinian struggle for self-determination and to replace the Israeli state with a democratic, secular one.[34]

Given the SWP's concern for adopting the correct theory, the resolution also analyzed Israel and Zionism. Israel was defined in the resolution as a "settler-colonialist and expansionist capitalist state maintained principally by American imperialism, hostile to the surrounding Arab peoples." It argued a particularly important point regarding whether or not Israeli Jews had the right of self-determination, just like other peoples. The resolution stated that the SWP in fact was "opposed to the Israeli state and the concept of self-determination for oppressor nationalities." Just because there now were Jews in what had been Arab Palestine did not mean that the party had to concede them the right of self-determination. To the contrary, it asserted that the party rejected the abstract moral right of self-determination for all nationalities at all times and under all circumstances. For example, Horowitz noted that the party did not support a separate white state in South Africa and Rhodesia just because there were whites living there. Rather, the SWP raised its demand for self-determination for oppressed nationalities, not because of an abstract moral idea that all nationalities have a right to self-determination, but because self-determination was a means for the oppressed to rise up against their oppressors.[35] Despite a minority position proposed at the SWP's convention,[36] Horowitz's resolution won the day and was adopted.

Moving beyond mere theorizing about the Middle East, the SWP also tried to reach out to fellow radicals in the region. Horowitz followed up on his success getting the party to adopt his resolution on the Middle East by traveling to Lebanon in September 1973 and on other occasions, at one point discovering that an SWP article about self-determination co-written by himself and Barry Sheppard had been translated into Arabic there. Lebanese Trotskyists were also reading the SWP's Middle East discussion bulletin. Horowitz corresponded with a Lebanese Trotskyist named "Jaber," pointing out to him that one could not issue a blanket condemnation of Arab nationalism for oppressing the Kurds (especially in Iraq) without also considering the progressive role played by Arab nationalism in other situations, such as the struggle against Zionism and imperialism. He also met the Palestinian

Trotskyist leader Jabra Nicola in London and shared some SWP documents about the Middle East with him.[37]

The outbreak of the October 1973 Arab-Israeli war saw the SWP once again wrestling with the question about which side to support. Some party members questioned why the party supported the Arabs versus Israel, given that both sides were capitalist. The SWP writer Tony Thomas noted that such questions confused the SWP's stance on capitalist-versus-capitalist wars with its stance on imperialist-versus-imperialist wars. In an article he wrote for *The Militant* in November 1973, Thomas wrote that the 1973 war was not a question of two imperialist sides in conflict; rather, it was an example of a nationally oppressed people (the Arabs) struggling against colonial oppressors (the Israelis). Socialists ought to "take the side of the oppressed despite our differences with their leadership . . . in the current war with Israel, the difference Marxists have with the Arab rulers is over *how* and for what to wage this struggle, not whether to wage it."[38] For his part, Horowitz waxed confident that this new war would help the SWP's efforts. "In addition to all the other myths that were exploded by this latest war," he wrote to a Lebanese Trotskyist, "we have seen many signs of the increased possibilities for winning people over to an anti-Zionist position in the USA."[39]

## In the Margins

In searching in the late 1960s and early 1970s for a correct party line on Zionism, Israel, and the Arabs, the WWP and SWP were not alone on the Old Left, just particularly visible. Other Marxist groups also showed growing interest in the Israeli-Palestinian conflict and, despite their relatively small numbers, had an impact on leftist opinion in the United States. These included the Progressive Labor Party (PL), which had arisen out of a split in the Communist Party USA when disagreements about Soviet policy led to an exodus of pro-Chinese members, who then formed the first openly Maoist group in the United States in July 1962. PL was quite influential among young leftists in the 1960s and had some success in infiltrating SDS. It was largely because of its Marxist-Leninist stance that SDS and others in the New Left shed their aversion to Old Left ideology and increasingly turned to Marxism in the late 1960s.

PL confronted the 1967 war in two ways that mirrored the stances of the WWP and SWP: condemning Israel and attacking the Soviet Union's policy toward the Middle East. Where it differed from them was that it offered no comments supportive of the Palestinians as such. The party ran an article in the July 1967 issue of its newspaper, *Challenge,* which blamed Israel for forcing the Palestinian refugees from their homes during the 1948 war, saying, "The Jews were doing to the Arabs what had been done to them by the Nazis, if not in quantity, certainly in quality. . . . To make the Arab population of Palestine pay for the sins of Hitler is a greater sin than Hitler's." The same issue of the paper devoted a good deal of space to what PL viewed as Soviet perfidy toward to the Arabs.[40]

What set PL apart from other Marxist parties and New Leftists was its hostility to Palestinian nationalism, or indeed any other kind of nationalism. It not only attacked Israel and Zionist nationalism, but criticized the Palestinians as well. It was not enamored with Palestinian guerrillas and warned these groups that ultimate liberation would come through Marxist class struggle, not nationalism.[41] PL urged the Palestinians and other Arabs to eschew groups like al-Fateh and pursue a class struggle led by a vanguard Marxist-Leninist party instead. "Without Marxist-Leninist leadership the heroism of the Arab guerrillas will fail, in the long run, to serve the people," *Challenge* asserted in August 1969.[42]

Another Marxist voice on the Arab-Israeli conflict that was raised frequently in the 1960s despite his relatively marginal position as a librarian at the University of California at Berkeley was that of Hal Draper. Born Harold Dubinsky, the son of a family of immigrant Jews, Draper wrote hard-hitting, deeply theoretical Marxist analyses of Zionism and the Jewish Problem throughout a long career. He had helped form the Socialist Workers Party in 1937–38 but soon left it to help establish the Workers Party, led by the prominent theoretician Max Shachtman, which changed its name in 1949 to the Independent Socialist League (ISL). The ISL later merged with the Socialist Party of America (SPA) in 1958, prompting Draper to leave in 1962, whereupon he and some others in Berkeley formed the Independent Socialist Club. A New York chapter was soon developed as well, and in 1967, a number of such clubs formed an association, the Independent Socialist Clubs of America. Within two years the clubs joined with some ex-members of SDS and created the International Socialists.

Aside from his other writings, Draper's major contributions to discussion of the Arab-Israeli conflict in the 1960s were two "clipping books" he edited in 1967, which reprinted articles he and others had written: *The First*

*Arab-Israeli War 1948–49*, and *Zionism, Israel, & the Arabs: The Historical Background of the Middle East Tragedy*.[43] These were published and circulated in Berkeley, home to many left-wing activists. Draper harshly attacked Zionism, writing, "For Zionism is, first of all, a doctrine about a tribal blood-mystique which makes all Jews a single nation no matter where they live or how." All that Zionism had done, he argued, was create a new ghetto for Jews, a state ghetto in the Middle East. This was not the new life Zionism promised to Jews; it was merely more of the old life.[44] One young man who read Draper's clipping books and came away changed was Wayne Price, a Jewish student who had joined SDS while at Queens College. "I was very much shook up, when I first read Hal Draper's clipping book," he recalled years later, "to see the history of how the Israelis had chased out the Palestinians and taken their land. I no longer could accept Israel as a legitimate enterprise."[45] Draper and his followers in the International Socialists instead advocated a secular, binational state for both Jews and Arabs created by what Price called in an August 1969 position paper an "internationalist, working class–led socialist revolution."[46]

The Spartacist League, another tiny Marxist group, had a slightly different vision, arguing that as long as Arabs and Israelis looked on one another as their chief enemies, the Middle East would be unable to defeat the real enemy, imperialism. The group believed that the solution to the Arab-Israeli conflict would lie in Marxists rising above parochial Jewish and Arab nationalism and embracing and deepening class struggle instead, under the slogan "TURN THE NATIONAL WAR INTO A CLASS WAR—THE MAIN ENEMY IS AT HOME!" It advocated creation of a "bi-national Palestinian state, federated into a pan-Arab workers state, itself stripped of reactionary nationalist features," along with a "Hebrew nation" that would guarantee the continued right of Israeli Jews to self-determination.[47]

Old Left Marxists played important roles bringing awareness of the Arab-Israeli conflict to the Left, whether through theory or praxis. While the New Left *raised the question* of the Palestinians for a new generation of radicals, groups like the SWP and the WWP actually *did something* about it immediately in 1967 and thereafter. The SWP in particular injected theoretical rigor into left-wing debates about Israel and the Arabs, as did independent Marxists like Hal Draper. The WWP was important because it operationalized its stances through street-level activities that attracted young radicals seeking action, not just speeches and theoretical discussions. Yet others in the Old Left were much more conflicted about what stance to adopt vis-à-vis Israel during and after 1967. Sometimes internal conflicts resulted in major intra-party dissension. Nowhere did this create as much damage as within the Communist Party USA.

# 6  Ghost of Revolution Past

*Conflicted Communists*

ON JUNE 6, 1967, one day into the war that had broken out in the Middle East, Paul Novick, a longtime Communist Party USA (CPUSA) member, published an editorial in the left-wing Yiddish newspaper he edited, *Morgen Freiheit,* entitled "Save Israel," asserting that "all states in the Middle East have a right to exist." This included Israel, he maintained, which had been recognized for decades by the CPUSA and the Communist Party of the Soviet Union, from which it took its lead. He argued that because Jews supported Israel did not mean they were Zionists, and those on the Left who conflated Jews' support for Israel with Zionism were making a mistake. Just because Israeli policy did not always seem correct, Novick continued, was no basis for calling for the dismantling of Israel, any more than the imperialist policies of the US government were justification for destroying the United States of America. The revolutionary internationalist support for the Palestinians and other Arabs voiced by other left-wing groups was not shared by communists like Novick, for whom Israel represented an exception to leftists' denunciations of imperialism.

Novick was speaking for Jewish comrades in the CPUSA who stood with Israel during the war and felt that Israel was a Jewish and socialist state eminently worthy of their assistance. These Marxists felt that their fellow Jews in the Middle East deserved their support in the face of threatened annihilation by reactionary Arab states—even though the Soviet Union was an ally of some of those very states. The problem was that the CPUSA's leadership followed the position of the Communist Party of the Soviet Union (CPSU): it condemned Israel for having committed "aggression" in the June War because it had struck first. Coming on the heels of a decade of dissatisfaction with Soviet stances toward Jews and other grievances of some American Jewish communists, the intra-communist rift engendered by the 1967 war created another war of sorts, this time within the ranks of the CPUSA. If other Old Left parties like the Workers World Party and the Socialist Workers Party were fairly clear about who was to blame for starting the war and how their members should think about Israel, the CPUSA membership was deeply divided. A number of party comrades were Jewish and solidly pro-Israeli, even if they were not themselves Zionists, and they balked at accepting the official party line condemning Israel as the aggressor. The Israel exceptionalism of those liberal and left-wing Jews who attacked pro-Arab New Left positions was being replicated to some degree within the ranks of the Old Left's historically most significant party.

## Communist Party Orthodoxy and the 1967 War

The events of 1967 took place against a lengthy background of ideological discussions of Zionism and the Jewish Question in the CPUSA, going back decades.[1] When the war broke out, the party's leadership seemed somewhat unsure of itself, and issued a statement that was even-handed in calling for all parties to withdraw their military forces. Party General Secretary Gus Hall issued it to the news media on June 5, asserting, inter alia: "Whatever may be one's views on the crisis in the mid-East, there can be only one conclusion regarding the military struggle which has erupted between Israel and the Arab states. It is a wrong war. It is a war that benefits only the American and British oil monopolies and no one else. The problems of the Middle East cannot be solved through armed conflict. In the interests of all the peoples of the Middle East, Arabs and Jews alike, the armed forces of all countries should withdraw into the confines of their borders."[2] However, the CPUSA's national leadership quickly fell in line with the CPSU, agreeing that the war was an act of aggression on the part of Israel.

The party's problem was that many Jewish comrades—who according to some estimates, made up at least one-half of all party members—felt that Israel had been surrounded by hostile Arab enemies bent on its annihilation in the weeks prior to Israel's preemptive strike, and subsequently rejoiced at

Israel's ultimate victory.[3] Israel for them was an expression of the Jewish people's national identity and will to live in a post-Holocaust world, even if they rejected the Zionist claims that the creation of Israel and its Hebraic culture was the sole, valid response to the Jewish Question.[4] Moreover, they believed that Israel was a socialist state committed to progressive values. Not surprisingly, therefore, these Jewish comrades balked at the CPUSA's official stance and a serious intra-party controversy quickly broke out.

Addressing a June 10, 1967, meeting of the CPUSA's national committee, Hall tried to uphold the official stance but still took pains to criticize both Israel and the Arabs. A stalwart veteran of the party and faithful follower of the Soviet line, who was born Arvo Kustaa Halberg in Minnesota to Finnish immigrants, Hall was recruited to the Communist Party of America (CPA) in 1927 and rose to be general secretary of the successor CPUSA in 1959. In his speech, he was careful to state that the war was an "act of aggression on the part of the Israeli rulers," not its people. He denounced the "criminal behavior of Israel," which had "acted as a tool of U.S. monopolies." Hall did not omit the Arabs in his criticism either, saying, "Israel is today a hard fact of this world's reality," and the Arab states had to accept this fact.[5]

No doubt attuned to Jewish party members' feelings about Israel, Hall also stressed that Israel was a country close to the hearts of millions of Jews and non-Jews around the world. "The continued existence of the State of Israel must be the concern of all peoples," he intoned. Israel had "deep meaning for the entire world," especially for the Jewish people. Yet he cautioned that Jews must not allow reactionary forces to exploit these emotions to cover up Israel's actions in support of Western oil monopolies.[6] Finally, he argued that peace should now be Israel's top priority, and the chief requirement for a peaceful resolution of the conflict should be solving the problem of the Palestinian refugees. "Israel should recognize its moral obligation to repatriate and compensate the Arab refugees," Hall said, using the term "Arab" rather than "Palestinian," as most Americans did at that time.[7]

Jewish CPUSA members found themselves on both sides of the divide. According to a document produced by the FBI, communists in Chicago donated blood and collected money and supplies for Israel and condemned the Soviet Union for its pro-Arab stance. Comrades in New York City met to call on the party to support Israel. On the other hand, Hyman Lumer, a high-ranking Jewish party member, one of the CPUSA's main spokespersons, stood by the party's official Middle East position. Lumer sat on the CPUSA's national executive committee, served as the party's education director, and edited the party's publications *Political Affairs* and *Jewish Affairs*. As an old party hand, he was well qualified to speak on matters of communist doctrine and quickly set out to publicize the CPUSA leadership's position on Israel to maintain party discipline.

In July 1967, Lumer published a pamphlet entitled *The Middle East Crisis* detailing the CPUSA leadership's stance on the Arab-Israeli conflict. In it, he appealed to his Jewish comrades to set aside parochial emotionalism and adopt a dispassionate, Marxist approach to the war, which he argued had given rise to intense Jewish nationalism and "anti-Arab chauvinism" among American Jews. "As communists," he wrote, "we must judge events not emotionally but in the light of sober reality." Working-class internationalism, not nationalism, was the standard by which communists should judge events. Lumer further argued that the real conflict in the Middle East was not one between Jews and Arabs, but between Anglo-American imperialism and all of the region's people. On the emotional subject of Israel, Lumer wrote, the Palestinian refugees paid the unfortunate cost of the establishment of Israel, inasmuch as the Jewish state was "based on displacement of Arabs to make room for Jews." This allowed the country to become even more wedded to the "racist concept of a purely Jewish state." As Gus Hall had done, Lumer also condemned Arab calls for Israel's destruction and the notion that all the Arabs' problems would disappear if Israel were wiped off the map.[8]

## Pro-Israel, Non-Zionist

If Hyman Lumer and other CPUSA leaders thought that the explanations offered in his pamphlet *The Middle East Crisis* would heal the rift within the party over the Israeli-Palestinian conflict, they were badly mistaken. The conflict among Jewish members of the CPUSA continued, and official CPUSA statements like Lumer's were countered in Jewish publications associated with the party, such as *Morgen Freiheit*. Established in April 1922 as *Freiheit* ("Freedom"), it changed its name to *Morgen Freiheit* ("Morning Freedom") in June 1929 and became the Jewish paper most aligned with the communists.[9] It distanced itself publicly from the CPUSA in the 1950s, and thereafter presented itself as a "progressive" rather than a "communist" paper.[10] During and after the 1967 war, *Morgen Freiheit* rejected the CPUSA line that Israel had waged an aggressive war. How, the paper asked, in a July 9, 1967, editorial, "Time to

Stop Calling 'Nazis,'" could representatives of the Soviet Union call the Israelis "Nazis" simply for rising up to stop armies that were poised to throw them into the sea?[11]

The leading voice within the *Morgen Freiheit* circle that challenged CPUSA orthodoxy on the Middle East was that of Paul Novick, the paper's co-founder and longtime editor. Born Pesah Novick to a Jewish family in Brest-Litovsk in Russian-controlled Byelorussia (now Belarus), Novick immigrated to the United States in early 1913. He helped found *Morgen Freiheit* in 1922 and became its editor in 1939. When the 1967 war broke out, Novick had risen in the CPUSA's ranks and was a member of its national committee. His June 6, 1967, editorial "Save Israel" was the first major shot across the bow of CPUSA orthodoxy. The second came when the party's national committee issued a statement shortly thereafter condemning Israeli aggression in the war, and Novick was the only committee member to vote against it.[12]

The CPUSA political committee then met with him on June 7 and offered him the choice of resigning from the party or being expelled for his independent stance.[13] He refused to resign, and defiantly ran an editorial in *Morgen Freiheit* on June 22, 1967, entitled "The Soviet Union and Israel." In it, he rhetorically asked why the Soviets called Israel the aggressor when it was merely defending itself, much as the Soviet Union had done in the face of the Nazi German invasion of June 1941. "We are for the fact that Israel should live," he wrote. "We are for the entirety of the whole State of Israel. We are for the territorial integrity of Israel and for recognition of Israel by her neighbors. The Socialist lands must support the right of Israel to live and must oppose the incitements to anti-Semitism through the attacks against Israel at the United Nations."[14]

The conflict between the CPUSA and *Morgen Freiheit* only worsened as the months wore on. By early 1969, party leaders not only felt that Novick and his paper were too supportive of Israel, they also insisted that he was supportive of the wrong communist party in Israel. The CPSU declared that the only communist party in Israel worthy of official recognition was the largely Arab party, RAKAH, not the Jewish party, MAKI, because the former was officially anti-Zionist and supported wider Soviet stances and allies in the region (like Egypt), whereas the latter was more critical of them.[15] On February 23, 1969, the CPUSA's national committee sent out a letter under the signature of its national organizational secretary, Daniel Rubin, to local party chapters around the country, which accused *Morgen Freiheit* of heading into "a blind alley of Jewish nationalism," of backing MAKI, and of supporting Israeli aggression.[16]

On April 6, 1969, Novick fired back with a speech at the Town Hall in New York City. Among other things he reported on his October–November 1967 trip to Israel, but also addressed the ongoing controversy within the CPUSA. He sought to downplay the argument over whether Israel was at fault for launching an aggressive war two years earlier by claiming that the character of the war "has long since been removed from our agenda." Not only that, but he said, "our slogan over the years has been, 'Israel is here to stay.'" Arab terrorists who attacked Israel were therefore not national liberation fighters. What communist activists needed now, he suggested, was a "people's front" that would call on Israel to withdraw from the territories it occupied during the war, call on the Arabs to recognize Israel, and support UN Security Council Resolution 242 of November 1967.[17]

Another Jewish publication associated with the party, *Jewish Currents*, also refused to espouse the CPUSA stance on Israel. In some ways, it had started out as the English-language offshoot of *Morgen Freiheit*, first emerging in the late 1940s as *Jewish Life*. In late 1957, the publication decided to adopt an editorial policy independent of the CPUSA, and it changed its name to *Jewish Currents* in January 1958. The 1967 war saw *Jewish Currents* support Israel, and, much like *Morgen Freiheit*, come under attack by the CPUSA national committee as a result. Several significant voices challenged CPUSA positions in the pages of *Jewish Currents*. One belonged to Morris U. Schappes, born Moishe ben Haim Shapshilevich in Kamianets-Podilskyi, Russia (now Ukraine), who had joined the communist party in 1934, joined the editorial board in 1946, and become its long-standing editor beginning in 1958. He came to describe the paper as "pro-Israel, non-Zionist."[18]

Disturbed by the harsh stances on Israel spilling out of the CPUSA and other left-wing parties after the 1967 war, Schappes published detailed exegeses of what he perceived as the root causes for such hostility: the Left's failure to understand both the Marxist position on nationalism generally and the Jewish Question in particular. In 1970, to outline his opinion, Schappes published a pamphlet titled *The Jewish Question and the Left—Old and New: A Challenge to the Left*.[19] He began by noting that Leninists long had criticized national differences as "obstacles to social progress." Yet this had been interpreted wrongly, Schappes argued, with the result that what he called "national nihilism" had infected the New Left with regard to both America and the different ethnicities residing within its borders—with the notable exception of blacks. The New Left assumed that this negative attitude to ethnic identity was consistent with "internationalism," when in fact it reflected a "political sickness": acting today as if one were living in the world of tomorrow. In a takeoff of the famous dictum that "anti-Semitism is the socialism of fools," Schappes opined that "national nihilism may be said to be the internationalism of fools."[20] Schappes also dared to claim that another problem with the Left's confused attitude to Jews and the Jewish Question was the CPSU's attitude. Drawing on the writings of Lenin and Stalin, the Soviet Union had affirmed the concept of nationhood, particularly with regard to the nationalism of colonized peoples, but the CPSU did not extend that status to the Jewish people.[21]

For all his defense of Israel in the face of communist attacks, Schappes was also aware that many American Jews were far *too* supportive of Israel. In an editorial entitled "Israel, What Now?" that appeared in the May 1971 issue of *Jewish Currents*, he lamented "the fact that there is more hawkish than dovish sentiment in the American Jewish community than in Israel itself," something that "constitutes a grave danger for progressive Jews here."[22] In the end, however, his balancing act—his attempt to be "pro-Israel but non-Zionist"— did not fit in with CPUSA orthodoxy.

Sid Resnick, who worked with Schappes on *Jewish Currents*'s editorial advisory committee, also criticized CPUSA policy on Israel in a way that left little room for nuance. "This irrational, unjust and dangerous [Arab] outlook [vis-à-vis Israel] is the hub of the Palestine Arab terrorist position from which all else flows." He was also strident in his condemnation of the party's position that Israel's actions in 1967 were "aggressive." On the contrary: for Resnick, Israel was merely defending itself against a threatened Arab genocide. "The Arab chauvinist threat to Israel's existence was real in May and June 1967. . . . In fact, 'de-Zionizing' the State of Israel and converting it into an Arab Palestine state is impossible without destroying the people and State of Israel," he claimed.[23]

Resnick also vociferously attacked leftists who supported the "irrational and unyielding hostility of Israel's Arab neighbors." He asked why Marxists questioned the very nature and character of Israel but did not do this for any other country. He conceded that there were indeed problems in Israel, but blamed the rise of right-wing movements in the country on the "chauvinist demagogy of the Palestinian terrorists." According to Resnick, one of the mistakes that led leftists to attack Israel and call its existence into question was their improper understanding of nationalism and national identity—particularly in the Jewish context. He argued that leftists derided Jews for being "parochial and nationalist" just for wanting to live as a sovereign people in their own state, whereas they themselves were "smitten by what they imagine is a more universal or cosmopolitan outlook."[24]

A particularly detailed rejection of orthodox communist thinking was offered in the pages of *Jewish Currents* by Louis Harap. Like Schappes and Resnick, Harap not only wrote for the journal but was a member of its editorial board. From 1948 to 1957, he was *Jewish Life's* managing editor, and he continued to serve on its editorial board after it became *Jewish Currents* in 1958. Harap wrote that the only really important question for Marxists as regards Zionism and the Jewish Question was whether or not the "struggle for a Jewish territorial entity" was compatible with the Marxist belief that class identity trumped national or ethnic identity. In this regard, he noted that the Holocaust drastically changed the question of the Jewish presence in Palestine. Allowing Jewish immigration to Palestine after 1945 and eventually creating a Jewish state there no longer were simply Zionist goals but rather a global humanitarian priority. Those Jews were seeking admittance into Palestine not because they were Zionists but rather simply because they had no other place to go. Harap insisted that those in the party or the Left more broadly must support the existence of the state of Israel regardless of what they thought about Zionism: "But on one issue, Left non-Zionists [must] unreservedly agree with Zionists: Israel now has an inalienable right to exist," he wrote. As for the leftist predilection to criticize Israel in the late 1960s, Harap concluded that the "anti-Israelism" of the global Left approached and sometimes even verged on outright anti-Semitism.[25]

Harap was not blind to what the creation of Israel had done to the Palestinians. Here he waxed blunt: he conceded that Israel was guilty of "serious errors" in relation to the Palestinians in its midst and throughout the Arab world. "Whatever else may be said about Zionism, it would be rash to deny that it scanted the interests of that other nationality in Palestine, the Arabs," he opined. "There is little dispute that the sad history of Jewish-Arab relations reveals that the Zionist movement as a whole, with a few honorable exceptions, showed a virtually total lack of awareness of the existence or importance of the Arab presence in Palestine."[26] Harap took particular aim at the socialist Zionist concept of the "conquest of labor," by which Jews were implored to hire only fellow Jews and not Palestinians. This, he claimed, worked directly against principles of class solidarity between Jewish and Arab workers.[27]

Party orthodoxy knew it had a serious problem on its hands. In 1968, Lumer wrote a report on the CPUSA's work among Jews in which he summed up the issue:

> Among American Jews the Middle East war of last year gave rise to an up-surge of intense, emotional, unreasoning Jewish nationalism, coupled with an alarming outburst of anti-Arab chauvinism. This is a most dangerous de-velopment, stimulating the growth of every form of extreme nationalism and chauvinism. . . . It views all opposition to the policies of the Israeli government as either anti-Semitism or betrayal of the interests of the Jewish people.[28]

The CPUSA's public response to this problem was to strike back hard at the dissidents in its ranks. At the CPUSA national convention in May 1969, Novick was not renominated to serve on the party's national committee. A few months later, he responded by adding his signature to a September 29, 1969, statement titled "For the Security of the State of Israel! For Peace in the Middle East!" by "Leaders of Progressive Jewish Organizations," which he published in *Jewish Currents*. Schappes signed it as well. Affirming Israel's right of existence within secure borders, the statement urged that the great powers work to implement UN Security Council Resolution 242 of November 1967 as the basis of Arab-Israeli peace.[29]

The CPUSA's leaders realized now that they were facing a serious rebel-lion against party discipline over the Israeli-Palestinian conflict. On April 14, 1970, the party's political committee publicly addressed the growing split. It issued a statement on the Middle East that directly and candidly spoke to the problems within the CPUSA, particularly party leaders' problems with *Morgen Freiheit* and *Jewish Currents*. It stated frankly that it expected CPUSA comrades to observe party discipline in this matter:

> In recent years we have had to fight for our position against powerful pres-sures of bourgeois nationalism. Some in our ranks, however, have been guilty of opportunist capitulation to such pressures and have taken a line in direct opposition to that of the Party. The National Committee took note of this in its [February 23, 1969] letter to the Party clubs of a year ago. It is now neces-sary to place the matter much more sharply. . . . Under these circumstances,

looseness with regard to following Party policy can no longer be permitted. It is incumbent on every Party member to fight for the Party's policy in this area and to work to carry it out to the best of his or her ability. The Party can demand nothing less.[30]

The struggle between the orthodox CPUSA stalwarts and pro-Israel dissidents intensified, a struggle that a June 1970 report by the ever-watchful FBI described as "a crisis of the first order of magnitude" within the party.[31] The FBI had every reason to believe this. First, it claimed it had over 250 informants within the CPUSA who could report on intra-party squabbles.[32] Second, the bureau's secret COINTELPRO program had itself been responsible for magnifying dissension about Israel within the party. That program developed a system for spreading mischief within the party by sending counterfeit letters, written in a contrived Jewish "dialect" and signed "Irving," to a journalist at the New York Times. In the letters, "Irving" claimed to be a disgruntled Jewish member of the CPUSA passing along information about intra-party problems. This actually ended up being used by the journalist in stories about matters relating to Jews and Israel within the party, according to a FBI memorandum, which noted that the Irving letters "have proven to be embarrassing and injurious to the CPUSA."[33]

By mid-1971, the increasingly bitter conflict between the CPUSA leadership and dissidents like Novick had reached a crisis point. Novick wrote to the party's political committee on June 22, 1971, outlining the pressures faced by Morgen Freiheit in trying to maintain its presence in an American Jewish community strongly attached to Israel during and after the 1967 war. This did not mollify party leaders, who established a subcommittee to decide whether or not Novick should be allowed to remain in the party. Novick was found guilty of "opportunist capitulation to the pressures of Jewish nationalism and Zionism, which has led him to depart more and more from a Marxist-Leninist position and to move increasingly in the direction of Jewish nationalism," and the subcommittee recommended that his party membership be terminated. Novick responded by resubmitting his June 22 letter on November 10, 1971.[34] Party officialdom was not convinced. Hyman Lumer and Daniel Rubin wrote that a party like the CPUSA could "operate effectively only on the basis of strict, disciplined adherence to its decisions by all members." Acting on the basis of the subcommittee's report, the CPUSA's national committee then established a trial committee of nine party members to decide Novick's fate.

Based on their recommendations, the CPUSA's national committee decided on February 16, 1972, to expel Novick from the party if he did not change his ways within six months. On April 13, 1973, the party announced his formal expulsion.[35]

The CPUSA survived the controversy over Israel, but the entire episode took its toll and weakened it. Party bosses knew they needed to work hard to regain its strength. As far back as 1968, some, such as Lumer, argued that the party needed to bring more Jewish members over to the party's line on Israel by increasing its activities among Jews, rather than simply continue trying to enforce party discipline. Lumer took care to note that this meant reaching younger Jews. He noted that much of the CPUSA's existing work on Jewish issues had been restricted largely to the older, Yiddish-speaking, New York City–based Jewish community. Greater efforts to reach younger, English-speaking Jews across the country were needed, Lumer argued. After all, the New Left had engaged a whole new generation of left-wing students; so, too, should the CPUSA.[36] Perhaps to deal with the need to reach younger Jewish leftists, the party launched a new English-language publication in June 1970 entitled *Jewish Affairs* to compete with the opposition voices that found expression in *Jewish Currents* and *Morgen Freiheit*. Not surprisingly, Lumer was a major contributor to it. *Jewish Affairs* quickly began criticizing the stances toward the Middle East adopted by *Morgen Freiheit*, *Jewish Currents*, and the MAKI faction of Israeli communists.[37]

In early 1971, the CPUSA broadened its Middle East work beyond simply shoring up support among its Jews by establishing a front group called the Committee for a Just Peace in the Middle East, co-chaired by Alex Kolkin and Sam Weintraub. Beyond trying to articulate its position on the Arab-Israeli Conflict to the left-leaning public, the party was no doubt also motivated to create the committee because rival Old Left parties like the Workers World Party also had set up Middle East–oriented front groups. One of the committee's star speakers and writers was Herb Aptheker, who by the early 1970s was emerging as the CPUSA's main mouthpiece on Israel and Jewish affairs. An academic, he had edited the party's theoretical publication *Political Affairs* as well as its Jewish organ, *Jewish Affairs*. Aptheker also had ties with the younger New Left generation. His daughter, Bettina, was an important figure in the Free Speech Movement at the University of California at Berkeley in 1964, and he himself went on a fact-finding trip to North Vietnam in January 1966, along with the peace activist Staughton Lynd and the New Left leader Tom Hayden.

Aptheker quickly began making the rounds of speaking and publishing on behalf of the committee, always ensuring that the CPUSA's official line on the Arab-Israeli conflict was articulated. One of the first was a public meeting held at Hotel Piccadilly in New York City on July 30, 1971. Aptheker stressed that the conflict was not at heart a question of Arab versus Jew, but rather of imperialism/colonialism/racism versus national liberation/self-determination/social progress. Israel's right to exist was not in question, he proclaimed, emphasizing the party's long-standing position.[38] On October 29, 1971, Aptheker spoke at a rally at New York's Diplomat Hotel along with Lumer and Jarvis Tyner, a young black comrade who served as national chair of the party's Young Workers Liberation League and who was its vice presidential candidate in the elections the following year.

The Committee for a Just Peace in the Middle East continued its work into the 1970s by issuing statements and taking part in demonstrations much as rival Old Left front groups were doing. Committee activists took part in a demonstration at the Israeli mission to the UN in New York on November 23, 1971, and distributed a leaflet reading in part "Stop the War in Vietnam! Prevent Nuclear War in the Mid-East! End Israeli Aggression!" Connecting the Middle East and Vietnam, committee members held a rally at the Marc Ballroom in New York City on April 21 1972, at which they condemned the American bombing of Hanoi and Haiphong in North Vietnam. "The struggle to end the Vietnam war and the fight for peace in the Middle East are indivisible parts of one battle," a leaflet printed for the occasion read.

As part of efforts to recoup its membership losses and bring attention to its stance on the Middle East, the CPUSA also decided to court black Americans. Party Chairman Henry M. Winston, himself black, published an article in November 1970 entitled "Black Americans and the Middle East Conflict," in which he wrote: "The struggle of the Arab people is an inseparable part of the fight of all peoples for liberation from imperialism. And this is indissolubly linked to the struggle of Black people in the U.S."[39] Three years later, the CPUSA established another front organization that addressed the Arab-Israeli conflict, as well as issues of interest to blacks: the National Alliance against Racist and Political Repression (NAARPR). The alliance grew out of the National Committee to Free Angela Davis, formed in about 1971 when the noted CPUSA member Angela Davis was arrested and tried for murder. The first conference of the NAARPR was held in Chicago in May 1973; Davis became NAARPR's co-chair, and fellow black party member, Charlene Mitch-ell, served as its executive-secretary.

Beyond its attempts to recruit militant blacks into party activity, the NAARPR was also significant in that its emergence marked the beginning of a new era in which the CPUSA began specifically addressing the issue of the Palestinians and championing their cause—as opposed simply to criticizing Israel and supporting a peaceful solution to the Arab-Israeli conflict. Davis traveled to communist East Berlin for the Tenth World Festival of Youth and Students in July and August 1973, and reportedly met Palestine Liberation Organization (PLO) Chair Yasir Arafat there. A year later, in August 1974, she and the NAARPR issued a statement in support of the PLO and against Israeli jailing of Palestinians in the Occupied Territories.[40]

### The Debate in Marxist Journals

The debilitating dissention among communists and other Marxists about just how to understand the Arab-Israeli war of 1967 was also fought in left-wing political journals that lay outside the CPUSA's orbit. One of the most signifi-cant of these was *The National Guardian,* an independent newspaper estab-lished in 1948, which later changed its name to *The Guardian* and became a major voice on the left in the 1960s. It was conscious of the rising tensions in the Middle East in the spring of 1967, and on the eve of the June War, it pub-lished two stories on the crisis in an effort to be evenhanded. One was written by Abdallah Schleifer, a pro-Palestinian American living in East Jerusalem, while the other was by the socialist Zionist journalist Richard Yaffe. When the war came to an end a week later, the *National Guardian* laid out its thoughts about the Israeli victory in a less even-handed way in its "Viewpoint" section: it wrote that Israel was in alliance with imperialism in its struggle against the Arabs. The piece also decried Israel's Law of Return for allowing only Jews to immigrate to Israel, not the Palestinian refugees, displaced since 1948.[41]

Irving Beinin was a major figure at the *National Guardian,* serving on its coordinating committee. Although he came from a family of Zionist Jews, he later moved toward Marxism. Beinin played an important role in its editorial stance on the Middle East, and in a piece titled "The Mideast War Solves No Problems," he argued on June 17, 1967, that Israel had faced two choices in the late spring of that year: peace with the Arabs at any cost, or, as it ultimately chose, "escalation of the nationalist, anti-Arab sentiment, glorification of the Jewish military and reliance on might to establish Jewish hegemony." Israel's rejection of cooperation with the Arabs thus left alliance with American and British imperialism as its only option.[42]

Beinin's criticism of Israel engendered a fierce response. In the first few weeks after the war, the *National Guardian* exploded with a lively exchange of letters to the editor about the conflict from readers. It was clearly the first time some of them had seen such strong opinions about Israel since the war had ended. According to Beinin, most of the letters he received criticized the newspaper's coverage and editorial stance on the June War.[43]

In an article in response, Beinin noted, inter alia, first, that prewar Egyptian threats to destroy Israel had been empty bombast; second, it remained unclear whether or not Egypt's closing of the Straits of Tiran, between the Gulf of Aqaba and the Red Sea, to Israeli shipping was as significant as it had been made out to be; third, Israel had supported imperialism, even if it was not an imperialist state; fourth, peace was impossible unless Israel, and not the Arab states, dealt effectively with the 1948 Palestinian refugees; and fifth, it was Israel that had demonstrated that it did not want peace, so why did people keep asking why the Arabs were not making peace?[44]

One letter actually charged that the newspaper was being anti-Semitic.[45] Another felt the opposite: that the *National Guardian* long had covered up what really had been going on in the Middle East. Believing that he now understood the true nature of what Israel was doing to the Palestinians, its author wrote that the newspaper:

> had successfully kept me in the dark about the real nature of what has been happening in Israel by feeding me a steady diet of cozy little stories about the brave people of Israel tending their "socialist" collective farms with the submachine guns strapped to their backs—thus conjuring in my mind the picture of vicious Arabs attempting to undo these brave people's "socialist" work—the GUARDIAN (on which, unfortunately, I depended for all my news) prevented me learning the truth of the matter.

He only had recently discovered the "real nature of Zionism—namely, that the Israelis had gotten their 'homeland,' as they call it, by stealing it from the Arabs."[46]

In keeping with the rising criticism of Israel and support for the Palestinian guerrilla movement that was emerging on the Left, the *National Guardian* thereafter began devoting more coverage to the Israeli occupation of the West Bank and Gaza and the Palestinian resistance in the months and years after the 1967 war. The articles all were solidly behind the Palestinian guerrillas. As part of an article in the November 4, 1967, issue entitled "Israeli Gains Spur Arab Resistance," Abdallah Schleifer wrote that "Israel no longer enjoys 'underdog' status in the eyes of a considerable portion of world opinion."[47] Another American journalist in the Middle East, Tabitha Petran, later described the armed struggle against Israel and its occupation, including an enumeration of al-Fateh and other guerrilla groups, like the Popular Front for the Liberation of Palestine, in an article that appeared in July 1968.[48]

Coverage of the Palestinian guerrilla movement continued a few months later in a September 1968 piece entitled "Arabs Resist Israel's Occupation" that discussed the Palestinian refugees and the Israeli occupation. That article also quoted an Israeli soldier who hoped that the November 1968 presidential elections would lead to an American withdrawal from Vietnam so that the United States could shift its forces to help the Israelis. "We are protecting their oil interests here; there's no reason why they shouldn't shoulder some of the burden," the soldier argued.[49] Such comments unwittingly served the growing New and Old Left discourse to that effect. As for a resolution to the Arab-Israeli conflict, the *Guardian* argued in February 1969 that "real peace in the Mideast will come from the revolutionary struggle to oust imperialism and its allies."[50]

In October 1967, *Monthly Review*, an independent socialist journal established in 1949, published competing editorials on the subject—something it had done on only two previous occasions—with its longtime co-founding editors, Paul Sweezy and Leo Huberman, offering readers their own rival assessments of the conflict. Huberman wrote "Israel Is Not the Main Enemy," conceding frankly that being Jewish affected his thinking about the Arab-Israeli conflict. Israel was "a lackey of imperialism," he wrote—and the Arabs had a "just case" against the Jewish state. However, the main enemy of the Arab masses was "not Israel, but their own feudal, reactionary, bureaucratic governments which exploit them, and Western imperialism which robs them of their wealth." A true Arab liberation struggle therefore would go after the master, the West, and not the lackey, Israel.[51]

Oil was the key to understanding the importance of the Arab world, which was the "field of operation *par excellence* of Western oil imperialism," Sweezy wrote for his part. Israel and Western imperialist interests were "essentially parallel and often identical," which explained the ongoing flow of capital into Israel. Imperialism, "in tacit alliance with Israel," was the main enemy of the Arabs, but Israel's "very existence as a colonizing state rests on the expropriation of lands from the Palestinian Arabs, and in keeping with its Zionist exclusionary character it practices systematic, principled discrimination against all Arabs." Arab enmity to Israel was "of the same kind and as natural as black hostility to white settler states in Africa."[52]

The Old Left was as conflicted as the New Left in terms of what it thought about the Arab-Israeli conflict, a problem exacerbated by the disproportionately large Jewish presence in its constituent parties. Sometimes party leaders said one thing about the conflict while the rank and file felt something else. Such divisions in the CPUSA, the Old Left's historically most significant party, had a lasting impact on one of its major demographic groups, older Jewish communists in the New York area, from which it never completely recovered. Moreover, its adherence to Soviet policy on the Middle East opened the CPUSA to continued attack, not only from the New Left, but from other Old Left parties as well, making it impossible to create a united pro-Palestinian front. Meanwhile, members of another Old Left party, the Socialist Party of America, were moving in a decidedly pro-Israeli direction.

# 7 We're Not Gonna Take It

*The Socialist Lurch toward Israel*

WRITING IN 1971, Carl Gershman, a twenty-eight-year-old leader of the Socialist Party of America's youth group, the Young People's Socialist League (YPSL), and also of the SPA's crusade against left-wing criticism of Israel in the 1960s, blasted it as "an absurd and frightening state of affairs when people use the criterion of hostility to Israel to determine whether someone is anti-imperialist and 'revolutionary.'"[1] Who better to combat youthful attacks on the Jewish state than a left-leaning member of the 1960s generation itself?

Gershman went on to become a key player in the efforts of the SPA to defend Israel against attacks by fellow leftists during and after 1967. He was also instrumental in moving the SPA itself further and further toward a pro-Israeli stance. Significantly, it was he who helped promote a new rationale for why liberal and left-leaning Americans should support Israel that had nothing to do with socialism or even with Jews and Zionism: American support for Israel, he argued, was a crucial way to prevent the Middle East from falling under the influence of the Soviet Union and totalitarian communism. It was the same kind of Cold War rhetoric offered up by one administration after another in explaining why America had intervened in Vietnam. "While the moral issue of our obligation to support a tiny democracy against its massive anti-democratic opposition may be compelling to some," Gershman wrote, "the issue should also be posed in terms of preserving the balance of power in the area."[2]

## The Socialist Party of America

The SPA, established in 1901 out of a merger of socialists from various other groups, stood out among Old Left parties in the 1960s in that it moved further and further away from a somewhat balanced position on the Arab-Israeli conflict eventually becoming strongly supportive of the Jewish state.[3] It was one of the most stalwart opponents of the pro-Palestinian tilt of the more radical Left. Over the decades, it had also become strongly hostile to communism, the Soviet-dominated Third International (Comintern), and the CPUSA—a hostility that was mutual. In 1958, an important development occurred in the history of the SPA that influenced the party's stance on the Arab-Israeli conflict tremendously. The party had merged with the Social Democratic Federation in January 1957 to become the Socialist Party–Social Democratic Federation, which was joined in 1958 by Max Shachtman's Independent Socialist League (ISL). By that point, Shachtman had moved away from revolutionary Marxism toward social democratic politics; he also had become quite anti-Soviet. Under Shachtman's influence, the newly revitalized and renamed SPA would begin to change toward a vigorously pro-Israeli attitude.

Shachtman was born in Warsaw (then in the Russian Empire), but was brought to the United States with his family at one year of age. He had a long history of involvement with some of the most important Marxist parties in the United States, including the CPUSA and the SWP. An early member of the Communist Party of America, he became a Trotskyist after he and others in the party grew critical of Soviet leader Joseph Stalin, eventually broke with Trotsky over the latter's critical defense of the Soviet Union, and ended up a nonrevolutionary social democrat. Shachtman's embrace of democratic socialism led to his entrance into the SPA, where his influence on the party's stance on Israel ultimately was profound—although not always because of his feelings about Jews and Zionism. He himself was Jewish, but came of political age in Old Left parties hostile to Zionism.

The 1967 war helped trigger the SPA's eventual strong support of Israel in its conflict with the Palestinians. At the time, SPA activists were still somewhat split about what position to take. The party developed a statement that took both sides to task, saying, inter alia, "Zionist nationalism on the one hand, and Arab nationalism and reaction on the other hand, each in its own way and fashion, prevent the establishment of peaceful cooperation between Jews and Arabs." The statement also called on Israel to recognize the rights of the Palestinian refugees, including the right to repatriation, and noted that both the United States and the Soviet Union should be condemned for their arms shipments to the region.[4]

However, at least some young people affiliated with the party took a very different stance in the final days before the war broke out, one that was much more sharply pro-Israel and anti-Arab. At the University of California at Berkeley, activists in the Norman Thomas Chapter of the SPA's youth group, the YPSL, distributed a vigorously pro-Israeli, anti-Soviet, and anti–peace movement leaflet on Sproul Plaza on May 25, 1967. Entitled "The *Middle East*—What *Democratic Socialists* Say," the YPSL pamphlet asserted socialist principles of solidarity with the embattled Jewish state and laid out some key themes about the Middle East that would begin to appear time and time again in future socialist publications.

The leaflet started by asserting support for what it called the only democratic socialist state in the Middle East, Israel: "Israel is a democracy under the leadership of a democratic socialist party—MAPAI, the Israeli Labor Party." Egypt, in contrast, was "an authoritarian state, seeking to disguise itself in 'socialist' phrases as do all too many anti-democratic and hence anti-socialist regimes." The leaflet also brought in views of the Cold War and the Soviet-American rivalry, while at the same time denouncing the worldview of some in the American peace movement:

> The present crisis shows the limitations of the simplistic "theory" held by part of the peace movement in the US. According to this "theory" US intervention is "bad"—period. Now we see that the real question is *how* the US will intervene. In Vietnam, where the intervention supports military dictatorship, we *oppose* it and call for stopping the bombing, negotiations and free elections. In the Middle East, if intervention defends a progressive and democratic state, we *support* it. . . . This crisis also undermines another notion common in some "peace" circles—that because the US is often the "bad guy" in the world, the Communists must be the "good guys."[5]

Some older socialists eschewed this unequivocally pro-Israeli response to the war, including David McReynolds. McReynolds, a party member since 1951, had played an important role in the SPA's merger with Shachtman's Independent Socialist League in 1958. Soon after the war, on June 29, 1967, he published a piece in the *Village Voice* that observed, inter alia, that "Israel is less of a democracy than its defenders insist, less progressive than we like to believe."

There was some truth to the charge that Israel was a tool of Western imperialist interests in the Middle East. McReynolds also wrote sympathetically about the Palestinians, and argued that the Arab view that the very creation of Israel in 1948 was an act of aggression was "not illogical." Criticizing US media's reflexively pro-Israeli stance, he insisted that "if Americans continue to mock the Arabs and automatically take Israel's side," peace would remain elusive. "Such an attitude inflames the Arab states and supports the worst and most inflexible element in Israeli political life."[6]

Despite McReynolds's hopes, the SPA began to shift more and more in a strongly pro-Israeli direction in the weeks and months following the war. One reason was the SPA's moving into accord with the position on the Arab-Israeli conflict that was adopted by the Socialist International (SI), the international grouping of social democratic parties to which the SPA belonged. On June 19, 1967, the SI's bureau issued a statement that minced no words in expressing its "full solidarity with the people of Israel who are defending their existence and their liberty against agression [sic]." At an October 10–13, 1967, council conference in Zurich, the SI issued another solidly pro-Israeli statement, affirming its earlier statement but also pointedly condemning the Soviet Union for its "war propaganda and the resumption of large scale arms" shipments to the region. In the United States, the SPA's national committee endorsed the SI statements and began altering its earlier stance that had criticized both the United States and the Soviet Union for their respective arms shipments.[7]

Another reason why the SPA began embracing Israel more and more after 1967 was the party's overall shift rightward away from its past, which was partly the result of Shachtman's presence. Shachtman and his followers—"Shachtmanites" as they were called—emerged as vigorous Cold Warriors who denounced the Soviet Union and who viewed foreign policy from that perspective. Shachtman also argued that because socialists placed their ultimate hopes for transforming the world on the working class, American socialists must "go to where the working class is": this meant the "realignment" of the Left toward big unions like the AFL-CIO and with the Democratic Party, both long known for their strongly pro-Israeli positions and militant anticommunism. Some of Shachtman's followers, particularly youthful socialists, began achieving positions of influence within the party, its youth organization, and related socialist groups by the late 1960s.

As a result, the SPA differed from the rest of the Left in embracing Israel more and more after the 1967 war, although not without internal debate. The

SPA had not, after all, been known to embrace Israel warmly under its long-time leader Norman Thomas. In 1968, however, the original draft of a new SPA resolution on the Middle East clearly left open the possibility of Israel keeping some of the territories it had conquered from the Arabs in the 1967 war, rather than withdrawing to its prewar borders. Although this wording was not adopted, Israeli sympathizers in the SPA managed to kill a statement that would have put the party on record as opposing any Israeli attempt to annex or settle the occupied territories.[8]

One party member who did not want the SPA's policy to tilt so far toward Israel was Bogdan Denitch, a Yugoslav of Serbian descent born in Sofia, Bulgaria, who had immigrated to the United States in 1946 and joined YPSL the following year. Denitch composed a document entitled "Notes on a Socialist Foreign Policy" that asserted the importance of upholding Israel's right to exist, but not to the point of accepting its territorial expansion or abandoning concern for the Palestinians. He wrote: "We should of course defend the right of Israel to exist as a state, with secure international guarantees. This does *not* mean support for territorial expansion at the expense of the Palestinian people. This does not mean unconditional support for peace agreements at the expense of the Arabs living in what was Palestine. At the very least we should insist on the right of the Arab inhabitants of Israel for *[sic]* full civil and civic rights and some settlement of the refugee problem."[9]

Others agreed that the party should acknowledge the Palestinians' importance in a peaceful resolution of the Arab-Israeli conflict. At the SPA's national convention in June 1970, the party adopted a resolution on the Middle East that included "recognition of the rights of the Palestinian Arabs to a voice on the future of the Middle East." On the other hand, the resolution also diminished the legitimacy of the Palestinian national movement by, saying, "Palestinian nationalism is a post-1948 phenomenon (in the past, the Arabs generally regarded Palestine as part of Southern Syria)."[10]

Starting in 1970, the SPA's rhetoric on the Arab-Israeli conflict hardened. It not only strongly championed Israel and denigrated the Palestinian national movement and its left-wing supporters but also situated its pro-Israeli stance squarely within the context of the Cold War. In November of that year, the SPA helped sponsor a "Rally for Israel." The party also adopted a resolution about that time stridently condemning the Arabs, particularly the armed actions perpetrated against Israel by al-Fateh and other "terroristic guerilla organizations," even when such actions were directed against Israeli military targets in the Occupied Territories. The resolution also derided Arab feelings and called on the Arabs to "end the irrational and anti-social state of belligerence between their countries and Israel," condemning the "obscurantist policy of encouraging attacks on Israel."[11]

The party's anti-Soviet tendencies continued to affect its view of the Middle East. Some party members felt that the United States needed to be firmer in its support of Israel in order to show the Soviet Union that America would not stand idly by while it made strategic gains in the Middle East via its client states. As a result the SPA attacked the administration of President Richard Nixon in a resolution adopted by the SPA's national committee in 1971: "The Arab governments are aware that the United States' commitment to Israel is less firm than the Soviet commitment to the Arabs," it maintained. The statement criticized Nixon as lukewarm in his commitment to Israel, stemming from American oil companies' interests and because "growing isolationist sentiment" was gripping the country due to the traumatic experience of Vietnam.[12]

## The Shachtmanite Tilt

One youthful, energetic voice that articulated the SPA's increasingly pro-Israeli slant in 1970 and thereafter was that of Carl Gershman (see above), who in 1968 began working in the research department of the Anti-Defamation League (ADL) of B'nai B'rith "covering the left" for the ADL's intelligence chief, Irwin Suall. Besides working for the ADL, Suall had been the national secretary of the SPA from 1957 to 1968.[13] Gershman also worked for two prominent black pro-Israeli socialists, A. Philip Randolph and Bayard Rustin—whom some blacks called "Israel's man in Harlem"—when he was a staff member at the A. Philip Randolph Institute from 1969–71.[14] As a result of these connections, Gershman became involved with YPSL, which was headed by another youthful Jewish activist in the socialist movement, Joshua Muravchik. Gershman soon rose to become vice-chair of YPSL, and lent his voice to the vigorous defense of Israel being mounted by other socialists.

Max Shachtman's anti-Soviet feelings influenced Gershman as they had other SPA and YPSL members. Gershman began stressing the idea that supporting Israel was a way that America could deflect Soviet ambitions in the Middle East. Israel, he argued, was a beleaguered socialist democracy with a strong labor movement that was under threat from Soviet-backed Arab reactionaries and terrorists. The Jewish state therefore stood in need of the support of Americans from whatever ethno-religious background, not simply support from Jews because it was a Jewish state. In addition to what other pro-Israeli writers were saying, he asserted that the real enemy of Israel was not the New Left, but rather the Soviet Union.[15] "Israel, a small democracy ruled by a Socialist government and strengthened by a vigorous labor movement, is menaced by an alliance of terrorists and backward Arab dictatorships which together received massive military and political support from the Soviet Union," he wrote. "We urge support for Israel on moral grounds, and also because such a policy contributes to peace in the Middle East by obstructing Arab adventurism and Soviet expansionism. . . . the Soviet drive for hegemony is the central problem in the Middle East today."[16]

Gershman also began asserting that another danger to Israel was what he called the "neo-isolationism"—the "widespread loss of faith that the United States can or even should play a constructive role in the world"[17]—that was growing in American politics as a reaction to the debacle in Vietnam. If not checked, these changing attitudes could herald "a shift in our [America's] world posture [that] would present an immensely greater danger to Israel's security than the antics of the New Left ever did."[18]

These concepts—that Israel's greatest danger stemmed from the Soviet Union, and that an American withdrawal from its pre-Vietnam global vigilance would only worsen this threat—were not unique to Gershman or even to the SPA. Various mainstream Jews and Jewish organizations that were not at all part of the Left were arguing the same points in 1970. In so doing, they often used language virtually identical to that of the SPA. When reacting to Secretary of State George Rogers's peacemaking efforts in the Middle East, which were seen by some partisans of Israel as unfavorable to the Jewish state, Jacques Torczyner of the Zionist Organization of America (ZOA) stated that "The new isolationism of the New Left is at least as dangerous as the isolationism of the far right before the Second World War . . . [Israelis are] convinced that their main adversary is the Soviet Union."[19]

Gershman's vigorous defense of Israel in 1970 was therefore part of a wider pro-Israeli effort to convince the American public that the country's involvement in the Middle East aimed to defend democracy and halt the spread of Soviet influence. Despite socialists' disagreements with the Nixon administration about specific aspects of American policy vis-à-vis Israel, Nixon echoed their sentiments about Israel. The president wrote a memorandum to National Security Advisor Henry Kissinger that year in which he indicated that American strategic interests dovetailed perfectly with Israel's, because the United States was "basically pro-freedom and not just pro-Israel because of the Jewish vote. We are *for* Israel because Israel in our view is the only state in the Mideast which is *pro*-freedom and an effective opponent to Soviet expansion."[20]

As a corollary to his concern about isolationist American reluctance to become involved in foreign affairs, something else concerned Gershman: the possibility that American military weakness would make it difficult for the country to assist Israel in the event of an emergency. As a result of Vietnam, many leftists and mainstream liberals were arguing for cuts in American military spending by the mid-1970s. Not so Gershman. Like others in the SPA, he was enamored with the militantly anti-Soviet, pro-Israeli hawk in the Democratic Party, Senator Henry M. "Scoop" Jackson, who argued for a strong American military posture. An America that was militarily weaker was an America that was less prepared to defend Israel, Gershman maintained. To those Americans, particularly liberal Jews, who supported cuts in military spending, Gershman retorted that being for or against Israel was no longer the problem; the problem was whether or not one supported an American defense policy that enabled the United States to guarantee Israel's security.[21]

Beyond Cold War arguments, Gershman played a role in raising within the SPA and its youth groups the argument that Israel fully deserved the support of socialists because it was the world's best example of how egalitarian socialism should be.[22] He therefore scorned those on the Left who viewed Zionism as some kind of imperialist plot against the Arabs. This type of analysis, he acerbically claimed, was offered only by "slogan-mongers and pseudo-universalists who have a warm spot in their heart for every form of nationalism but the Jewish variety."[23] He also denounced leftists who embraced the Palestinians as revolutionaries because they advocated replacing a Zionist Israel with a secular, democratic state for both Arabs and Jews: "So they coined the slogan of 'the democratic secular Palestinian state' and, with the help of Trotskyites, Guevarists, Maoists or what have you, they publicize it at college forums and similar gatherings."[24]

The SPA's chair, Michael Harrington, probably the most significant socialist intellectual of the 1960s, also began to speak up for Israel in response to pro-Palestinian leftists' attacks on Israel. Harrington's famous 1962 book, *The Other America: Poverty in America*, had influenced mainstream politicians like John F. Kennedy and Lyndon B. Johnson. Born in St. Louis to an Irish-American Roman Catholic family, Harrington went on to teach political science at Queens University beginning in 1972. In the 1950s, Harrington joined the Independent Socialist League and became a protégé of Max Shachtman's, following his mentor into the SPA. He became a member of the SPA's national executive board beginning in 1960 and served as chair from 1968 to 1972. Initially sharply critical of the New Left—he attended the first SDS convention in 1962 and reproached the group for not being sufficiently anti-communist—Harrington later become associated with some of the more leftist and anti–Vietnam War trends in the SPA.

Harrington's stance was more nuanced than Gershman's, but he certainly sided with Israel. During the 1967 war, he lent his name to an advertisement entitled "'To Uphold Our Own Honor . . . ' Leading Americans Speak Out Against Arab Threat to Destroy Israel" that ran in the *New York Times* on June 7. Three years later he wrote an article that laid out some of his own thinking about the Arab-Israeli conflict. Taking aim at New Left critics of Israel, he asked the rhetorical question, Who said that Israel served American imperialism? Answering his own question, Harrington wrote that they were "activists who were so isolated in their homeland that they could not change the course of events romanticized a distant, noble Third World which was to save them from their own irrelevance." In a swipe at the New Left's allies in the Black Power movement, he argued that viewing all Third World people as constituting one people of color was a racist concept. He also scored New Leftists for carelessly thinking that the Palestine Liberation Organization (PLO) was simply another Third World liberation movement that all progressives should support on anti-imperialist grounds, as well as the corollary that because the PLO was struggling against Israel, the Jewish state must be part of the global imperialist system.[25]

Despite all this, Harrington nevertheless evinced a measure of understanding of the Palestinian experience. "For the Palestinians to whom the guerrilla leaders appeal have real grievances," he wrote in 1970. He even argued that peace and democracy could spread to the Middle East if Israel helped the Palestinians create a state of their own.[26] Harrington also understood to some degree that creation of Israel was part of the wider European colonialization of the developing world in the late nineteenth and early twentieth centuries. In 1972, he wrote a lengthy book on the history of socialism in which he observed that "Israel was, in a sense, the last country created by

Europe."[27] Harrington unwittingly seemed to be in agreement with left-wing critiques of Israel that understood Israel as a colonially created state.

## Divisions among SPA Successor Groups

Intense internal strife within the SPA came to a head at its December 1972 convention, which led to its demise. The factionalism had to do with the party's stance on the Vietnam War, the social base of its activity, and whom in the Democratic Party the different factions had supported earlier in that year's presidential elections. In the end, the disagreements over all these issues led the majority to vote to change the party's name to the Social Democrats USA (SDUSA) to reflect the fact that it no longer really was a "party" in an electoral sense. With the tumult of the 1960s winding down and the conservative backlash under way, some also wanted to avoid using the word "socialist" any longer. Significantly, another important factor in the name change had to do with the party's stance on Israel. Those who voted to change the SPA's name to SDUSA felt that the new name would "distinguish the organization from its Communist opponents and from the Socialist Labor Party and the Socialist Workers Party . . . a Trotskyist Communist organization hostile toward Israel."[28] Carl Gershman stayed with SDUSA after the split and emerged as the party's executive director beginning in 1975.

For his part, Harrington left SDUSA soon after the 1972 convention and worked with Bogdan Denitch, Irving Howe, and others to form a new democratic socialist organization in October 1973 called the Democratic Socialist Organizing Committee (DSOC). DSOC continued the old SPA's strong backing for Israel. One of the first resolutions adopted by DSOC at its founding convention called for strong American support for embattled Israel, then in the midst of the October 1973 Arab-Israeli War. "Support for Israel runs deep in the organization," a DSOC publication later reported.[29] Howe himself wrote that "when the Yom Kippur war broke out . . . my reactions were astonishingly intense."[30]

However, for some in DSOC these stances were softening. One reason was the growing global acceptance in the 1970s of the idea of a two-state solution to the Arab-Israeli conflict based on the "land for peace" formula laid out in UN Security Council Resolution 242 of November 1967: Israeli withdrawal from Arab territories it occupied in the 1967 war in return for peace with the Arab world. Harrington, who rose to become DSOC's new national chair, gave an expansive interview to a Jewish publication in November 1975 in which he set forth his thoughts on Zionism, Israel, the Palestinians, and the American role in the Middle East. He used the interview both to castigate the now-defunct New Left for the hostile stances it had adopted toward Israel in the 1960s and to reassert that the Israeli cause was something that the Left could and should embrace in the 1970s. To be sure, he stated, Israel's "intransigence" and suppression of Palestinian rights were problematic, but he hoped that the Left could end up supporting Israel because, in a dig at his rivals in the increasingly rightward-moving SDUSA, "it would be a tragedy if the cause of Israel is identified with anti-detente and Scoop [Senator Henry] Jackson."[31] Harrington also argued that the best long-range solution to the Arab-Israeli conflict was the two-state solution. Israel should have defensible borders, not necessarily the borders left by the 1948 and 1967 wars.

Yet he felt that on their part the Palestinians had a legitimate right to self-determination, because "no matter how you look at past history . . . there is a Palestinian identity." While he argued that "the natural Palestinian state is in Jordan," he nonetheless felt that the best solution for the Palestinians would involve both Jordan and the West Bank.[32] Harrington was not alone in DSOC in coming to see that the Palestinians were a political force in the Middle East that socialists needed to recognize. When DSOC held its 1977 national convention in Chicago, it adopted a resolution calling for self-determination for both Palestinians and Jews, although it did not explicitly call for a two-state solution.[33]

If Harrington and DSOC saw themselves as pro-Israel, but not as militantly so as their former colleagues in SDUSA, they faced a challenge from another group of democratic socialists whose politics lay further to DSOC's left on the Arab-Israeli conflict: the New American Movement (NAM). NAM was different from DSOC in that it formed, not out of the breakup of the SPA, but out the collapse of the New Left and particularly SDS. Among others, NAM was formed by James Weinstein, Staughton Lynd, and the former SDS leaders Michael Lerner and Dan Siegel. They wanted to form a new left-wing socialist organization outside the existing socialist parties that were willing to work with the Democratic Party. Activists circulated a proposal to form NAM in June 1971 that was entitled "The New American Movement: A Way to Overcome the Errors of the Past." NAM chapters started forming that year, and its first national convention took place in June 1971.[34]

NAM took a position on Israel and the Palestinians that was quite supportive of the Palestinian national movement and critical of Israel and Zionism, revealing its differences not only with SDUSA but even with DSOC's more flexible stance. NAM's national council in early 1974 issued a statement firmly proclaiming, "We support the dezionization of the state of Israel," and "We support the right of the Palestinian people to national self-determination in Palestine." The resolution called for recognition of the right of all peoples in the Middle East to establish sovereign states of their own, including both the Palestinians and Israeli Jews. In the case of the former, NAM called for creation of a democratic Palestinian state on the West Bank. Turning its attention to the form and shape of a resolution to the conflict, the statement called for a United Nations peace conference that would include the PLO. However, NAM proclaimed that "the only way the above goals can be achieved is through their [Israel and a Palestinian state's] integration with a struggle for a socialist Middle East."[35]

Five years later, at its August 1979 national convention, NAM adopted another resolution on the Arab-Israeli conflict, which blamed the United States for the lack of progress toward peace in the Middle East, and for opposing Middle Eastern anti-imperialist movements—a reference to the US refusal to recognize or even speak with the PLO. NAM recognized the PLO and called on the US government to do the same, although it added that its own recognition of the PLO did not imply approval of the PLO's stances or tactics.[36]

Given that both were social democratic organizations committed to many of the same ideals, DSOC and NAM began exploring the idea of merging. However, the two groups' different stances on the Arab-Israeli conflict proved to be one of the most difficult points of disagreement during the merger talks and indicated the ongoing dissension within the Left over this issue. NAM believed that the PLO was the "only effective representative of the Palestinian people" and should play a central role in peace negotiations, which the United States should ensure by recognizing the PLO and including it in such talks.[37] Because of this, there was outright hostility within DSOC to merging with NAM. At a June 21, 1980, meeting in New York City of DSOC activists opposed to the merger idea, more than seventy DSOC members signed a statement opposing joining with NAM. One of the group's main objections to NAM was its stance on Israel and the Palestinians. "NAM's position is explicitly pro-PLO," the statement proclaimed.[38] The signers included ten members of DSOC's national board, among them Irving Howe, a key figure agitating against the merger with NAM and a veteran voice on the moderate Left. A much younger activist within DSOC who also opposed the merger was Eric Lee, who worked on DSOC's national staff and who had spent nearly a year living on Kibbutz Bet ha-Shita in Israel.

Both DSOC and NAM pushed ahead with unity talks and established merger committees. At an April 1981 joint meeting of the committees, they dealt with the question of the two groups' divergent positions on the Middle East. The bases for their discussions were ideas that were derived from NAM statements and the stance that the DSOC national executive committee had adopted on the question on March 22, 1981.[39] The compromise unity position on the Middle East finally ended up saying, "We support the right to self-determination expressed in the Jewish state of Israel—and the right of self-determination of the Palestinian people," a statement that pointedly referred to a "state" for the Israelis but mere "self-determination" for the Palestinians. The compromise also asserted that there could be no peace in the Middle East if Israel's neighbors did not recognize its right to exist, or if the Palestinians' right to self-determination was not guaranteed. Also, both sides agreed to language opposing Israel's long-term settlement building policy in the Occupied Territories.[40]

The two groups finally merged and formed the Democratic Socialists of America (DSA) in 1982, with Harrington as one of its two co-chairs. He had predicted that the Arab-Israeli conflict would be the toughest issue that the two groups would have to wrestle with during their long merger talks, and he was right. "We eventually worked out a 'two-state' position in which every word and comma was subjected to careful scrutiny," he later noted in his autobiography.[41] Two of the four democratic socialist groups in America in 1982 (DSOC, NAM, SDUSA, and the Socialist Party of the United States) had merged, but the politics of the Arab-Israeli conflict had proven to be a tough nut to crack to achieve that unity.

Although the Left continued to be hobbled by disagreement over the Arab-Israeli conflict, socialist stances on it were important in both intra-Left debates and public discourse on the topic in the United States. While some socialists moved closer and closer to a strongly pro-Israeli position, the views of others had become more nuanced, or even openly pro-Palestinian, by the 1970s. Such disunity was not unique. In the 1960s and early 1970s, the anti–Vietnam War movement feared precisely this type of dissension and the negative impact it might have.

# 8   Give Peace a Chance?

*The Ambivalent Anti–Vietnam War Movement*

ASKING THE COUNTRY'S most significant anti–Vietnam War coalition to denounce the June 1967 war was a task that fell on the broad shoulders of twenty-nine-year-old Dave Axel, aka Dave Axelrod. On June 17, 1967, the administrative committee of the Spring Mobilization Committee to End the War in Vietnam (the Mobe), of which he was a member, met in New York to plan a protest at the Pentagon in Washington, DC, that fall. Axel raised the question of the Israeli-Arab war, which had ended just a week earlier, and tried to have it put on the agenda. He wanted the Mobe, although focused on the war in Vietnam, to "denounce the U.S.-sponsored Israeli invasion as an aggression against the Arab people." The first line of the resolution he proposed argued: "the war in the Middle East is fundamentally the same as the war in Vietnam, differing only in form but not in essence."[1] The response was not encouraging.

The pacifist, leftist, and other groups and individuals that made up the anti–Vietnam War movement changed the face of the 1960s. While not strictly speaking part of either the New or the Old Left, antiwar activists operated within the same overall movement for change as the Left, and found themselves confronting what to do about the Arab-Israeli conflict almost immediately after the guns fell silent in early June 1967. Everyone in the Movement could agree on the need to end the American war in Vietnam. What to do about the Arab-Israeli conflict once again proved far more divisive, however.

Should the antiwar movement speak out against the fact that Israel launched the 1967 war just as it was demanding that the United States stop the escalating war in Southeast Asia? Some said yes. Some in the Movement supported Israel, and saw the 1967 war as a defensive war forced on the Jewish state. Others blamed Israel for starting the war but nonetheless wanted to keep the Middle East off the Movement's agenda for the sake of unity.

The anti–Vietnam War movement's experience with the conflict reveals much about the continued ambivalence within the Movement about just how to situate Israel and the Palestinians within its worldviews and actions. Sharon Rose, an activist, wrote of the problem of pushing the Left and the peace movement to examine the Middle East conflict:

> To many who have tried to raise the issue of the Middle East for serious discussion among leftists, it has been clear that the inability to deal with the struggle for Palestine has been the main impediment preventing wide discussion of and opposition to US political, military, and economic policies in the Middle East as a whole. Over and over we have heard prospective discussion nipped in the bud with the assertion that the Middle East is not like Southeast Asia or Latin America, and that any attempt to deal with it as such would be mistaken, or at least divisive against the united front against the war in Southeast Asia. For too long the simplistic statement that Israel is not South Vietnam has been allowed to obscure exactly what Israel's role *is* in the Middle East.[2]

How divisions over the Arab-Israeli conflict affected the anti–Vietnam War movement has escaped the attention of scholars.[3] Yet the record shows that these divisions proved nettlesome indeed, enough to affect the actual work of the Movement.

## Controversy among National Coalitions

Dave Axel was a member of Youth against War and Fascism, part of the Workers World Party, which wanted the antiwar movement to condemn all forms of what it viewed as American and American-supported imperialist aggression, whether in Vietnam or elsewhere. Sam Marcy, chair of the WWP and another member of the Mobe's administrative committee, stated this succinctly at the June 17 Mobe meeting: "Failure even to put [the 1967 Israeli-Arab war] on the agenda would completely discredit the Spring Mobilization as an anti-war group and imply that it is opposed to only one of imperialism's wars, while it closes its eyes to another one."[4]

Yet Axel's proposal was opposed vigorously by representatives of several other organizations on the Mobe's administrative committee. The Mobe was a loose grouping of over 200 local and national organizations and had struggled to maintain consensus on everything from the goals of the protests to the tactics used in seeking to end the war in Vietnam. Some groups in the coalition, like the Socialist Workers Party, had long tried to keep the focus of antiwar activities solely on calling for an immediate American withdrawal from Vietnam, rather than broaden it to include wider demands or other causes. Louis Proyect was in the SWP at the time, and recalled later that "the whole point of the single issue was to build a united front between people on the hard Left and on the soft Left. [The issue of the Israeli-Arab war] would split the movement."[5] SWP members on the Mobe's administrative committee therefore moved to quash Axel's proposal. The SWP's Harry Ring called it divisive, noting that the committee had been formed to plan solely for anti–Vietnam War demonstrations. Representatives of the National Committee for a Sane Nuclear Policy (SANE), Trade Unionists for Peace, and other groups on the committee agreed.

The proposal to place Axel's resolution on the agenda thus failed, but it was decided nonetheless to bring the issue up under new business. However, owing to lack of time, Sidney Peck, who chaired the committee, deferred it until the next meeting in July. The YAWF proposal was distributed along with the minutes of the meeting so that members of the committee could study it.[6]

A month later at the Mobe's administrative committee meeting in New York on July 8, 1967, Axel and Deirdre Griswold, representing YAWF, introduced the proposed resolution as planned. Linda Dannenberg, the executive secretary of the Student Mobilization Committee to End the War in Vietnam, reportedly proposed tabling the motion (i.e., removing it from being considered at the meeting) immediately after Axel and Griswold introduced it.[7] Harry Ring asked that the issue at least be discussed, which led Abner Grunauer of SANE and Abe Weisburd of Trade Unionists for Peace to offer an amendment to the motion to table that would allow only opponents of the YAWF resolution to speak. That motion was passed. After discussion, the committee tabled the YAWF resolution because "the consensus was that the subject was an important one and needed to be more fully discussed but that the YAWF resolution was not acceptable to many and that the matter could not be resolved at this meeting."[8]

Such hesitancy by the Mobe and the large and diverse anti–Vietnam War movement more generally to confront the June 1967 war and the Arab-Israeli conflict was not uncommon. Even groups like the SWP that condemned Israel for starting the 1967 war nonetheless felt that it was difficult enough to keep together broad antiwar coalitions like the Mobe just on the basis of opposition to the war in Vietnam, and that to bring in other issues would jeopardize that unity. In addition to Ring, the SWP was represented in the Spring Mobilization by Fred Halstead, a member of the Fifth Avenue Vietnam Peace Parade Committee since its formation in 1965, and the two worked to enforce the Mobe's one-issue focus on Vietnam.

The SWP's Old Left rivals in the WWP vehemently disagreed with the policy of avoiding the Arab-Israeli conflict. Like the SWP, it strongly criticized what it termed Israeli aggression in 1967. Where it differed was that it also felt that the duty of the Left was to combat capitalism and imperialism in all their forms wherever they were to be found. The Ad Hoc Committee on the Middle East, established by the WWP in June 1967, published "A Call to the Anti-War Movement" the following month that urged support for a planned anti-Israel demonstration in New York City on July 14. "Don't oppose just *one* case of U.S. aggression," the advertisement in the *National Guardian* urged. "The anti-war movement cannot be silent on this latest of U.S. imperialism's maneuvers to keep the super-exploited of the earth in bondage. . . . We call on the anti-war movement to support this demonstration against U.S.-sponsored Israeli aggression. DON'T LET THE MIDDLE EAST BECOME ANOTHER VIETNAM!"[9] The party's Rita Freed took a swipe at the SWP, saying: "The so-called radical parties which dominate the anti-war movement have consistently abdicated leadership to the liberal politicians. They have refused to take up the Mideast liberation struggle as an anti-war issue, as they had long excluded the question of Black self-determination: they fail, in short, to expose the class nature of imperialist society and its wars."[10]

Efforts to prod the antiwar movement into addressing Israel's military actions in 1967 and thereafter occasionally met with success by the late 1960s and early 1970s. A group called Arabs and Jews for a Democratic Palestine printed an undated leaflet entitled "From Vietnam to Palestine" around 1969 or 1970 illustrated with a sketch of a National Liberation Front (Viet Cong) fighter wearing a camouflaged sun helmet and a Palestinian guerrilla wearing a checkered keffiyeh headscarf, each armed with an AK-47 assault rifle. "From Vietnam to Palestine: One Struggle, Many Fronts," it read: "Over the past decade the world began to recognize the significance of the Vietnamese struggle against U.S. imperialism. Today we all demand an end to U.S. aggression in South East Asia. . . . We feel that it should not take another decade to see that Palestine is another Vietnam. Like the Vietnamese, the Palestinians are being denied their right to self-determination. . . . As we struggle to get the U.S. out of South East Asia, we must struggle to keep the U.S. out of the Middle East."[11]

Other examples included when the Mobe organized a series of "anti-inaugural" protest events in Washington beginning on January 18, 1969, in conjunction with the inauguration of President Richard Nixon. Some of the protest activities were conferences on various topics, including one entitled "Middle East—New War Already in Progress: Possibilities for Liberation Struggle."[12] Ten months later, a "National New Left Conference on the Middle East" was held in Washington in conjunction with the November 15 Moratorium March there. A demonstration in New York City in September 1970 organized by the Fifth Avenue Vietnam Peace Parade Committee included signs reading "Palestine Will Win."[13] Even the SWP, which initially tried to preserve antiwar unity by keeping the Middle East off limits to discussion in the antiwar movement, decided to include a "Palestinian contingent" in antiwar marches in Los Angeles in May 1970 and Washington, DC, in April 1971.[14]

James Lafferty, an attorney specializing in military draft law, nonetheless found that the Middle East was still a touchy subject among antiwar activists in late 1971. Lafferty was a founder and leading member of NPAC, the National Peace Action Coalition, one of the most important organizations in the third generation of national anti–Vietnam War coalitions, created in mid-1970 after the collapse of the New Mobilization Committee to End the War in Vietnam, which itself had succeeded the original Mobe in July 1969.

In August 1971, Lafferty unwittingly stirred up a hornets' nest when he published an article in a newspaper called *Free Palestine* entitled "The Anti-War Movement and the Struggle for Palestine." In it, he laid out the lessons of the antiwar movement for activists working on behalf of the Palestinian cause, arguing that the Movement against the war in Vietnam was a good model for pro-Palestine activism.[15] Lafferty's article soon prompted a fierce and negative reaction among some national Jewish organizations, which sought to use it to tar NPAC with the brush of anti-Israel bias.

In late October 1971, Phil Baum, an official of the American Jewish Congress (AJCongress), wrote an internal memorandum pointing out what Lafferty had written and connecting the issue with the AJCongress' support for the November 6, 1971, antiwar demonstration that NPAC was planning. Three days later, on October 29, 1971, AJCongress President Arthur J. Lelyveld issued a statement saying that Lafferty's article "now confirms our suspicion that the leadership of the National Peace Action Coalition has had more in mind than the single purpose of ending the war in Vietnam. . . . It now becomes crystal-clear that the next target of the movement under its slogan "NO MORE VIETNAMS" will be the ending of American support for Israel." AJCongress would not participate in the planned November 6 demonstration, Lelyveld said. Others quickly weighed in as well. Joachim Prinz, a prominent rabbi and former AJCongress president, issued a statement on the same day. Three weeks later, a November 23, 1971, in a press release issued by the Anti-Defamation League (ADL), David A. Rose, chairman of the ADL's national executive committee, speculated that "as American involvement in Southeast Asia winds down, some leaders of anti-war efforts in the U.S. are attempting to turn the anti-Vietnam movement into an anti-Israel campaign."[16]

As rumors began spreading about it while it was busy planning simultaneous demonstrations in New York and Los Angeles on April 22, 1972, NPAC felt obliged to issue a "Dear Friend" letter in late March addressing the controversy and seeking to "clarify" misconceptions. NPAC "does *not* [emphasis in the original] take a position on the Mideast or any other subject . . . not directly related to the war in Southeast Asia," the letter stated categorically. The origin of the "confusion" about NPAC, it continued, seemed to lie with Lafferty's article. The coalition took pains to state that Lafferty's article expressed his own opinion, not that of the coalition. It also pointed out that NPAC did not grill its members about their personal viewpoints that were unrelated to the war in Southeast Asia, and furthermore encouraged Jewish groups to participate in the forthcoming April demonstrations against the war in Vietnam.[17]

## Martin Luther King Jr. and Others on the Fence

It was not just the national antiwar coalitions that were hesitant to deal with the Arab-Israeli conflict and that were rent with dissension when they tried. Others in the Movement were also quite careful in what they said about the Middle East war of 1967. The most famous such person was Martin Luther King Jr.,[18] who had come out against the Vietnam War publicly in April 1967. So when war broke out in the Middle East two months later, he struggled to maintain his reputation as a peacemaker without damaging his credentials with his Jewish political allies. King lent his signature to a pro-Israeli advertisement in the *New York Times* on June 4, 1967, the day before Israel attacked, subsequently admitting to his aide Stanley Levison that he had not seen the text before doing so, but felt that it would help his standing in the Jewish community. After actually reading what was published, he felt that the advertisement tilted too much toward Israel; it made him and the other signatories seem like hawks on the Middle East and doves on Vietnam.[19]

Beyond his own image King also was deeply concerned that the June War was sidetracking the antiwar movement, and felt it gave President Lyndon Johnson some breathing room, inasmuch as public attention was focused on the Middle East. As early as June 6, 1967, the second day of the war, King confided to Levison, "I am certainly sorry it happened because it has gotten Johnson the little respite he wanted from Viet Nam." He also worried that the big peace march he was planning for August of that year would need to be postponed or cancelled "until this situation is cleared up," a situation that had "confused it [the march] a great deal." His aides opined that the Movement was "suffering badly" because Jews, who were prominently represented in it, had become hawks when it came to the Middle East. Levison, Jewish himself, agreed that the war was a "real monkey wrench" in the Movement's activities, saying that King's hopes of a big march were now unlikely to be realized. King cancelled the proposed march a few days later.[20]

King ended up developing a strategy he hoped would help him appear balanced and not negatively affect his reputation: offer total support for Israel's right to exist but at the same time explain that peace could only come through economic development in the Arab world. King articulated this approach when interviewed on the ABC television program "Issues and Answers" on June 18, 1967, a week after the war ended, saying that peace required security for Israel, but that continued Arab impoverishment was "going to keep the war psychosis alive."[21]

King took care to restate this in the months after the war. Black Power statements against Israel like the Student Nonviolent Coordinating Committee's August 1967 anti-Israeli newsletter article and the National Conference for New Politics' final statement in September of that year that denounced Israel prompted Jewish organizations to ask King where he stood on Israel and anti-Semitism.[22] His Southern Christian Leadership Conference (SCLC) therefore issued a statement in the fall of 1967 entitled "Anti-Semitism, Israel, and SCLC: A Statement on Press Distortions." It noted: "SCLC and Dr. King have repeatedly stated that the Middle East peace embodies the related problems of security and development. *Israel's right to exist as a state in security is incontestable. At the same time, the great powers have the obligation to recognize that the Arab world is in a state of imposed poverty and backwardness that must threaten peace and harmony.* Until a concerted and democratic program of assistance is effected, tensions cannot be relieved. Neither Israel nor its neighbors can live in peace without an underlying basis of social and economic development." It also was careful to note that ultimate peace required action and vision on both sides: "The solution will have to be found in statesmanship by Israel and progressive Arab forces who in concert with the great powers recognize that fair and peaceful solutions are the concern of all humanity and must be found. . . . Neither military measures nor a stubborn effort to reverse history can provide a permanent solution for peoples who need and deserve both development and security."[23]

Other peace activists followed suit in trying to speak out about war in the Middle East but not to champion either side. A group of mostly Jewish liberals and radicals issued a statement called the "Liberation of Palestine and Israel" in the July 1, 1971, issue of the *New York Review.* Signed by figures such as Noam Chomsky, Sidney Lens, Benjamin Spock, Arthur Waskow, Paul Jacobs, and Arnold Jacob Wolf, the statement concluded: "We urge that the American Jewish community and the American anti-war and radical movements take up these issues not [with] a mindless endorsement of one party orthodoxy or another in the Middle East, but with serious study and a sensitive commitment to the liberation of both the Israeli and Palestinian people from militarism and exploitation."[24]

The group Women Strike for Peace (WSP) emerged from a large women's march against nuclear weapons in 1961 and remained an important voice in the peace movement thereafter. In 1967, WSP also chose to stress a peaceful resolution of the Arab-Israeli conflict rather than publicly take sides. Each WSP chapter maintained considerable autonomy, and issued its own statements about the 1967 war. On June 6, 1967, the Southern California Council of WSP issued a simple statement in reaction to the war that hinted at the confusion about the issue within the peace movement but nonetheless stressed the need for a UN-sponsored cease fire. One day later, the New York City chapter issued a statement that argued for much the same, although it tilted toward Israeli concerns, saying: "We believe that the answer to the Israel-Arab conflict does not lie in the use of military force, but rather in a United Nations settlement that would guarantee the political and territorial integrity of all of the States of The Middle East, reaffirm the right of access of all nations to international waters, and secure an agreement from both sides to negotiate all outstanding differences."[25]

WSP activists around the country continued to be interested in the Arab-Israeli conflict and how to resolve it peacefully in the years after the 1967 war. They often disagreed in private, reflecting the antiwar movement's confused approach as a whole to the conflict. Barbara Bick, an important WSP activist in Washington, DC, spelled out some of the reasons why she felt the Movement was so reticent to take on the Arab-Israeli conflict in a paper titled "Toward Peace in the Middle East." One reason Bick cited was the tendency of young peace activists who adopted a "world outlook" to label Israel as an imperialist ally of the United States. Another reason was "the excessive intensity of emotional support for one or the other side, especially the feeling of Jews for Israel and 'militant' leftists and blacks for the Arabs." Antiwar groups should support neither side but instead firmly apply the Movement's fundamental principles to the situation in the Middle East. Bick ended with a proposal she said was being discussed by "a number of Jewish radicals," calling on Israel to support the Palestinians' right to their own state, withdraw from almost all of the Occupied Territories, and negotiate with the PLO, which in turn was called upon to accept Israel's right to self-determination.[26]

Gladys Knobel of North Shore Women for Peace, a WSP chapter in the north suburban Chicago area, also submitted a proposal for a policy statement on the Middle East in December 1970, which proclaimed: "Women for Peace . . . is neither pro-Israeli or [sic] anti-Israeli, neither pro-Arab, or [sic] anti-Arab, but consistently pro-peace." Knobel's proposal also asserted that "Women for Peace believes that ultimately, these two peoples, Israel, a nation by virtue of a vote of the United Nations in 1948 *[sic]*, and the Palestinians, *a nation struggling to be born*, must live side by side in peace and friendship."[27]

## Doves on Vietnam, Hawks on the Middle East

Yippie Abbie Hoffman joked soon after the 1967 war ended that the Movement "lost a lot of Jewish pacifists in the last few weeks"—they were pacifists when it came to Vietnam but not when it came to Israel.[28] The folk singer Phil Ochs, also Jewish, likewise mocked such people, modifying his famous song "Love Me, I'm a Liberal" at a 1971 concert to include the lines,

> I read underground papers and *Newsweek*, I've learned to take every
> view,
> Ah, the war in Vietnam is atrocious, I wish to God that the fighting
> was through,
> But when it comes to the arming of Israel, there's no one more red,
> white and blue,
> So love me, love me, love me, I'm a liberal.[29]

Indeed, some pro-Israeli liberals and left-wing peace activists felt that it was perfectly consistent to oppose America's war in Indochina while simultaneously championing Israel during its war in the Middle East. Members of the SPA's Young People's Socialist League certainly felt that way. They handed out leaflets on Berkeley's Sproul Plaza on May 25, 1967, entitled "The Middle East—What Democratic Socialists Say." The Movement was wrong to oppose *all* American interventions and assistance to countries overseas, the leaflets contended, because the case of Israel was much different from that of South Vietnam.[30] Walzer and Peretz agreed in their July 1967 article "Israel Is not Vietnam."[31] A few months later Peretz in fact predicted that hostility toward Israel on the part of some in the Left threatened to split the Movement: "It is precisely because so many of the Left rank-and-file feel both existential and rational ties to the people of Israel, while the radical ideologues at the top are in almost complete sympathy with the politics of Israel's enemies, that there have developed within every part of the peace and rights constituency fissures shattering the fragile unities cemented by the war in Vietnam."[32]

A famous dove who also agreed that the situation in the Middle East was totally different from that in Vietnam was Senator Robert F. Kennedy, a partisan of the Jewish state ever since reporting on Palestine during the 1948

Arab-Israeli war as a *Boston Post* journalist. As senator from New York, Kennedy continued to be solidly pro-Israel. He joined 20,000 others at the "Stars for Israel" fundraising rally staged by the United Jewish Appeal in New York on June 11, 1967, just as the June War was winding down. Despite what his own country was doing with F-4 Phantom jets in Southeast Asia, Kennedy publicly supported Israel's request for fifty Phantoms. On May 26, 1968, he made the distinction between Vietnam and Israel quite clear in a speech at a synagogue in Portland, Oregon. Wearing a Jewish skullcap as he spoke, Kennedy stated, "Our obligations to Israel, unlike our obligations toward other countries, are clear and imperative. Israel is the very opposite of Vietnam."[33]

Public stances such as these soon led to some discomfort within the Movement. People began deriding those who opposed the war in Vietnam yet championed Israel's preemptive attack in June 1967 as "doves for war."[34] Approximately a thousand people responded by attending the "Vietnam and Israel: There is a Difference" rally held on June 22, 1967, at the Manhattan Center in New York City. The rally was an attempt to deal publicly with the perceived problem that some antiwar activists faced: how as doves they could justify military action in one place while denouncing it in another. Peter Weiss of the Foreign Policy Council of New York Democrats spoke at the rally and argued that there *was* a fundamental difference between the Middle East and Southeast Asia. Weiss criticized the Johnson administration, saying, "We are concerned about the good guys–bad guys lenses through which our policymakers in Washington view the world, often with disastrous results." Yet when it came to Israel and the Middle East, Weiss did not seem to mind adopting precisely such a good guys–bad guys approach. "In Vietnam, aggression [by North Vietnam] is a fiction," he said. "In the Middle East, [Arab] aggression is a fact." He insisted that "the preponderance of right and justice in the Middle East is with the Israelis, who are entitled to our support, not our mentality."[35]

Another prominent antiwar liberal who sided with Israel and who spoke at the rally was Kennedy's senate colleague George McGovern. He, too, saw no contradiction between opposing the American policy in Vietnam and encouraging greater American involvement with Israel. Three years later, McGovern summed up his logic, saying, "there are fundamental differences between the situation in Indo-China and the situation in Israel."[36] He continued to express support for Israel during his presidential campaign in 1972. In an August 1971 interview, he suggested that he would not be averse to using military force in defense of Israel: "The Middle East is more important than Viet Nam in terms of both our security and our traditions. . . . I would be prepared to take whatever steps are necessary to ensure its survival. . . . we must leave no doubt that we are committing ourselves to Israel's survival."[37]

Nor were Kennedy and McGovern alone among Democratic presidential candidates in the 1960s who were famous for their opposition to the Vietnam War but yet who supported the idea of American military defense of Israel and weapons sales to the Jewish state. Another was Senator Eugene McCarthy, who told a Jewish gathering in Washington in late May 1967 that "if military action is necessary to obtain order and quiet in the Middle East, that action should be taken by the U.S. in concert with other nations. Yet there remains, if these efforts fail, a clear obligation for us to fulfill our own commitments."[38] McCarthy's stance on Israel was so supportive that the month the 1967 war broke out, the national board of the Mizrachi Women's Organization of America voted to bestow the 1967 America-Israel Friendship Award on him.

In a televised debate with Robert Kennedy on June 1, 1968, McCarthy was asked if he agreed with Kennedy's support for supplying fifty F-4 Phantom jets to the Israeli air force. In affirming what he called America's "clear moral and legal responsibilities in the Middle East and Israel," McCarthy agreed with Kennedy on the question of the Phantom jets, despite earlier having supported the idea of an arms embargo against both the Arab states and Israel. "Well, I've said we should work toward it [an arms moratorium]," McCarthy conceded. "But I've said we had to maintain the military strength of Israel against the Arab nations and I've said that we at least have to rebuild the strength that they lost in the recent war. If that means 50 jets, then it's 50 jets."[39]

While running for the Democratic nomination for president four years later in the 1972 elections, McCarthy once again made clear that Israel was an exception to his overall opposition to a foreign policy driven by military action. His campaign literature asserted: "The dominance of the military in our foreign policy has lead [sic] America into major misjudgments. It has furthered neither peace, prosperity, nor freedom. . . . McCarthy favors a total restructuring of policy, concentrating on more productive forms of foreign aid. He would make exceptions only in exceptional circumstances—such as Israel."[40]

All the major Democratic Party presidential candidates in 1968 who opposed the war in Vietnam sided strongly with Israel. However, the small

Peace and Freedom Party, which opposed the war in Vietnam in 1968 and ran candidates for president in several states in the election that year, did question Israeli policy. In Michigan, where the Peace and Freedom Party ran as the New Politics Party, Eldridge Cleaver, the Black Panther Party's minister of information, was its candidate for president, and his vice presidential running mate was Larry Hochman, a professor of physics at Eastern Michigan University and outspoken critic of Israel, who had written a pamphlet on the Arab-Israeli conflict for Students for a Democratic Society in 1967. In Utah, the Peace and Freedom Party adopted a 1968 electoral platform proclaiming that American policy was increasing, not decreasing, tensions in the Middle East, and called on the US government to halt all American military aid to the region. It also faulted the government for adopting "policy largely determined by extra-governmental organizations"—a clear jab at pro-Israeli groups— and called for an end to "private organizational control" of American Middle East policy.[41]

## Vietnam Veterans' Groups

Another segment of the anti–Vietnam War movement was less reticent to take a stand on the Arab-Israeli conflict in the early 1970s: Vietnam veterans groups. Vietnam Veterans against the War (VVAW), an anti–Vietnam War organization whose members had actually fought in that war, was established in April 1967. Starting in the early 1970s, however, it began to admit members who were not military veterans of the Vietnam War, and changed its name to the Vietnam Veterans against the War/Winter Soldier Organization (VVAW/ WSO). It too embraced one side in the Arab-Israeli conflict, but it was not Israel, and it was not until after the Vietnam War was over. Infiltration into the VVAW by Marxist groups like the Revolutionary Union, which brought with it its own pro-Palestinian slant, was another factor in the VVAW's position on the Middle East. It was at this point that VVAW/WSO began expanding its growing anti-imperialist critique to reflect the Revolutionary Union's stance against Israel and in favor of the Palestinians.

One factor in this move was the October 1973 Arab-Israeli war and the possibility of American intervention in the Middle East. The October 1973 issue of the VVAW/WSO *Newsletter* reported that many people were calling the group's national office asking what the group's position was on the war. The organization had no official stance at that point, but called on members to follow the position spelled out in the group's objectives, noting, inter alia: "Basically, the objectives say that we are opposed to any and all intervention of the US military in the internal affairs of other countries. We are opposed to the sending of any US military personnel and materiel to the Middle East to participate in that war. We have seen how the war in Indochina started with just economic military [sic] aid and blossomed into a full-scale war by the US government. We see a similar danger in the Middle East." At some point, the VVAW/WSO also adopted a "Statement on Imperialism" that asserted, inter alia: "The people of Vietnam, Cambodia, Palestine, Angola and Mozambique are some of the leading examples of this fight [against imperialism]," and "We support the struggles for national liberation and self-determination as shown by the struggles of the Vietnamese, Cambodian and Palestinian people."[42]

The VVAW/WSO leadership soon showed itself unafraid to condemn Israel and champion the Arabs. "Another aspect of the [1973] war is that it is being fought over territories that are (or were) controlled by Israel that really belong to the nations of Egypt and Syria and Jordon [sic]. The Arab countries are fighting to liberate those territories and return them to their control. The National Office believes that Israel must give up those territories if there is to be a just settlement."[43]

The 1973 war also prompted the American Servicemen's Union (ASU), another GI organization, to branch out from its earlier anti–Vietnam War activism and take a pro-Palestinian position on the Arab-Israeli conflict. Formed in December 1967, the ASU was the brainchild of Andrew Stapp, then an army private. Stapp had actually visited the Middle East, working at an archeological dig in Luxor, Egypt, in 1964–65. Rather than flee military service, Stapp had dropped out of college in 1966 and joined the army to take the antiwar struggle into the military itself. In the spring of 1967, when he refused to turn over antiwar and socialist literature in his possession, the army court-martialed him. It was after this that he decided to unionize the military by creating the ASU in 1967. An anti-imperialist, Stapp was assisted in his antiwar and unionization efforts within the military by YAWF.

The ASU also was worried about possible American intervention in the Middle East in 1973, as reflected in the banner headline carried on the October 21 edition of the group's newspaper, *The Bond*: "GIs: We must not fight in Mideast!" The article started out by making a clear link between Vietnam and the Middle East: "GIs have no business intervening in the Middle East. We stand nothing to gain, and our lives to lose. Shall we die for 'freedom and

democracy' again? No—because it's only been a few months since our brothers were dying in Vietnam to 'defend' that; we are not fools, we are not blind.
This war is not about lofty ideals; it is about OIL." The article continued by
describing the background to the current war, noting that Arab independence
after the Second World War prompted Western oil companies to seek a new
client to protect their economic interests, leading them to establish the state
of Israel: "The native Palestinians were forced from their land into 'refugee'
(concentration) camps and the US started building up the Israeli military to
threaten the oil-producing nations. . . . the very existence of the state of Israel
represents aggression against the Arab nations." The article ended by calling
on American service personnel to disobey illegal orders, including "orders to
fight in an imperialist war—a war fought in the interest of the billionaire few,
having nothing to do with 'national defense'—just like Vietnam."[44]

The October 1973 Arab-Israeli war jolted not only Vietnam veterans' groups
but a number of active duty military personnel into action as well. The specter
of another overseas commitment of American troops seemed a distinct possibility just months after the last troops had returned from Vietnam. Activists within the military immediately responded. Twenty active-duty military
personnel and civilian activists demonstrated in Jacksonville, North Carolina,
against any proposed American intervention in the Arab-Israeli war. They circulated a petition that they intended to send to the dovish Senator J. William
Fulbright calling on him "to immediately introduce legislation forbidding the
introduction of U.S. forces into the current Mideast hostilities." Nearly three
hundred military personnel and civilians signed the petition before police
arrested three of the servicemen involved. Their arrests represented only a tem-
porary halt to the petition drive; eventually, activists delivered the petition,
signed by some 3,000 people, to Fulbright on November 2.[45]

The reluctance of much of the Movement to take a solid stand one way or the
other on the Arab-Israeli conflict spoke volumes about the continuing controversy about how left-wing forces and their liberal allies should deal with the
question of Israel's preemptive military action in 1967 and subsequent occupation of Arab lands. The antiwar movement not only faced the opposition of
those who actively supported Israel but also the stubborn insistence even of
pro-Palestinian parties like the SWP in keeping the Arab-Israeli conflict off
the Movement's agenda lest it fragment the antiwar coalition they had pains-
takingly assembled.

The last American troops left Vietnam in the spring of 1973, and President Richard Nixon resigned amid scandal in August 1974. The long 1960s gave way to a new period of American history, in which the strength of the Left began to dissipate. Among leftists who continued their struggle in various ways in the 1970s, however, the intra-Left conflict over how to understand and react to the Arab-Israeli conflict nonetheless continued.

# 9   After the Storm

*Divergent Left-Wing Paths*

THE WEATHER UNDERGROUND Organization (WUO), a group of former Students for a Democratic Society members who had gone underground in early 1970 to wage war against the United States through high-profile bombings, decided to augment their armed activities by issuing a manifesto explaining their politics to aboveground activists. The first draft of the document was written in 1972 by Bill Ayers, one of the group's leaders. Ayers had joined SDS at the University of Michigan in 1965, and later became a member of the group's Weatherman faction during the friction that divided SDS starting in 1968. Now over two years underground, he was writing the basis of the WUO's manifesto.

By early 1973, a collective writing process had begun among underground WUO members and associates in which various people offered their thoughts about Ayers's draft document. Part of it detailed the WUO's support for the Palestinian cause. Aware of the sensitivities that some left-wing Jews had about Israel, Bernadine Dohrn, another WUO leader and Ayers's romantic partner, added some comments to the effect that despite the Holocaust, Jews must understand the Palestinians' suffering. Annie Stein, aged sixty, objected and insisted that the much younger activists in the room hear her out. Mother of WUO figure Eleanor Stein Raskin, she knew a thing or two about politics, Jews, and Zionism. Her older sister had moved to Palestine when they were young, but Annie had stayed in New York, joined the Communist Party, and eventually became a labor organizer and civil rights activist. She demanded that Dohrn's language about the Holocaust be changed: it was not *despite* the Holocaust that Jews should understand the Palestinians, she insisted, but precisely *because* of the Holocaust that they had an obligation to do so.[1]

The document—eventually entitled *Prairie Fire: The Politics of Revolutionary Anti-Imperialism—Political Statement of the Weather Underground*—was to be the WUO's major statement of its political line. It included a lengthy section on the Palestinian national struggle. The most famous American left-wing bombers of the 1970s had come down solidly on the side of the Palestinians, showing that the Palestinian cause still animated some radicals, both underground and aboveground, in the years after the storm of the 1960s had broken.

## The Defiance of the Weather Underground

The WUO emerged out of frustration.[2] When it went underground and commenced its bombing campaign in early 1970, the New Left was disintegrating. Nothing illustrated this more than the breakup of SDS the previous year. Yet other factors played a role as well. The Nixon administration's policy of withdrawing American troops from Vietnam starting in 1969 began to lessen the momentum of the Movement, temporarily at least. The killing of four students at Kent State University and two others at Jackson State University in May 1970 put a further chill on campus protests against the war. Eighteen-year-olds were given the vote in 1971, and military conscription ended two years later, taking much of the wind out of the sails of youth discontent. The final withdrawal of all American forces from Vietnam in March 1973 signaled the end of an era, inasmuch as opposition to the war had been the central motivating factor for so much of the Movement. Disillusionment, burnout, and the rising popularity among young people of new issues and causes associated with identity politics, like the women's movement and the gay rights movement, took their toll on the Left as the 1970s progressed. So, too, did continued infighting about Israel and the Palestinians.

Some militants refused to give up their struggle, however. They decided to go underground, hide "in the belly of the beast," and carry on the fight for revolutionary change in the United States in the Nixon and post-Nixon years through bombings and urban guerrilla warfare against the capitalist system and the state that protected it.[3] Newspaper headlines carried stories in the

early and mid-1970s of bombings, bank robberies, kidnappings, and dramatic
shootouts between militant groups and the police. Groups like the WUO also
continued their earlier left-wing support of Palestinian revolutionaries as
well. This was one of the tangible ways in which the radicalism of the 1960s
lived on in the 1970s Left and thereafter: the seeds of a new discourse on the
Arab-Israeli conflict that saw Israel as the oppressor of the Palestinians continued to grow, even as other dimensions of 1960s radical politics fell by the
wayside. No group better epitomized the path taken by these underground
American supporters of the Palestinians than the Marxists of the Weather
Underground.

On July 15, 1970, just shy of two months after publishing its "Declaration
of a State of War" between it and the United States government, the WUO
published a letter in the underground New York newspaper *Rat: Subterranean
News* that repeated the group's revolutionary strategy: initiate underground
guerrilla warfare against the American government at home in conjunction
with the struggles of Third World revolutionaries. Significantly, the WUO
mentioned the Palestinian liberation struggle on that early occasion as one
of the important anti-imperialist struggles with which the group identified:
"Our task is to join the people of the world in destroying U.S. imperialism
and building a socialist society. . . . We must learn from the Viet Cong, the
Latin American revolutionaries, and the Palestine Liberation Front *[sic]*. We
must all begin to think of ourselves as urban guerrillas and attack the enemy
wherever we can."[4]

From the beginning, WUO militants clearly saw the Palestinian struggle
as one of the leading fronts in the battle against imperialism, and they set
out to join in by fighting on this side of the Atlantic Ocean. The revolutionary anti-imperialism they had absorbed from their days in SDS had stayed
with them. In fact, the group's orientation toward the Palestinians can be seen
in the fact that discussion of the Palestinian guerrilla movement emerged
even before that, at the last aboveground activity undertaken by the group,
the National War Council held in Flint, Michigan, in late December 1969. A
document entitled "Everyone Talks About the Weather" was distributed that
mentioned the Palestinian struggle, elevating it to the level of the struggles
in Southeast Asia. It also reflected both the group's anti-imperialism and its
use of New Left language in describing the Palestinians' struggle: "There is
no mystical oppressor creating the misery in the world today. The cause is
Imperialism—Pig Amerika—a system of economic, political, and cultural

exploitation which respects no national boundaries in its hungry expansionism. The people of Cuba and Vietnam, Laos and Palestine, and of the United
States are bound together by this common enemy."[5]

Like other groups from the New Left or that grew out of the New Left,
Jews were well represented in the WUO. That the Holocaust demanded Jews
to stand with victims of oppression like the Palestinians struck a responsive
chord with more people associated with the group than just Annie Stein.
David Gilbert felt similarly. An SDS stalwart at Columbia University who
later joined the WUO, Gilbert's internationalism was not the only factor in
his support for Palestinian liberation. "For myself and many other Jews in the
movement, the bedrock lesson from the Holocaust was to passionately oppose
all forms of racism; we could never join in the oppression of another people,"
he recalled years later. As he prepared to go underground in early 1970, Gilbert decided to cash in his Zionist upbringing—literally. Friends and family
had given him over $2,000 in Israel Bonds for his bar mitzvah ceremony in
1957. He had saved the bonds but decided to cash them in and give half of
the money to the Black Panther Party's bail fund and the other half to the
WUO collective in the Park Slope section of Brooklyn, New York, to which he
belonged. He then slipped into the netherworld of underground life.[6]

Global anti-imperialism and Third World national liberation struggles
were central to the WUO's worldview, which also helps explain why the group
identified its own struggle with those being waged by Palestinians, Vietnamese, and others around the world. Supporting the Palestinians was a "logical
correlation to what we thought about national liberation," Bernardine Dohrn
recalled. She was born Bernardine Rae Ohrnstein to an apolitical family with
a Jewish father and a Gentile mother. Dohrn was in law school when the 1967
war broke out, and remembered the controversy within the National Lawyers Guild, where she worked, over whether or not to support Israel's actions.
Looking back decades later, she said, the pro-Palestinian beliefs that she and
other younger guild members shared pitted them against the pro-Israeli feelings of older members. "Many members were older and Jewish. For my generation, it was obvious. National liberation was on the agenda."[7]

Other Jewish WUO activists agreed. Mark Rudd had been a leader of SDS
at Columbia before going underground. Anti-imperialism and internationalism were strong motivators for him and other WUO members in championing the cause of the Palestinians: "My friends in SDS taught me, quite cor-
rectly, that the world was in revolt against U.S. domination. That was why the

Vietnamese were fighting so hard. I learned to admire the Vietnamese and the Cubans and the Chinese and the Russian peasants who had stood up to make a new society."[8] Howard Machtinger remembers spending many months reading about the Palestinians and the Arab-Israeli conflict while he was living underground. "As a Jew, I wanted to be extra-sure of my footing," he noted years later, adding: "I also recall much discussion of which groups the WUO was sympathetic to: [George] Habash, [Nayif] Hawatma, etc. We talked about Black September, 1970, as well as the attack at the Munich Olympic Games. So it's safe to say that Palestine was much discussed in the WUO, which had a pro-Palestinian perspective."[9]

Yet for other Jews in the WUO, the realization that their firm commitments to anti-imperialism meant abandoning their earlier support for Zionism was a painful experience. It certainly was for Naomi Jaffe. A former "passionate Zionist" who once had lived for six months in Israel, Jaffe's beliefs began to change as a result of joining SDS and seeing the world through its members' eyes. "It little by little became clear that Zionism was an untenable position because it was morally incompatible with everything else I believed; and because it was socially unacceptable in the circles in which I traveled," she recalled. "Logically, there was just no way I could defend Israel in light of our understanding of imperialism as the leading enemy of humankind, Israel's alliance with U.S. imperialism, and Palestinian resistance fitting pretty clearly into what we then called Third World national liberation struggles."[10]

Regardless of how they arrived at their pro-Palestinian convictions, the militants in the WUO certainly saw their own armed opposition to the US government as part-and-parcel of a global anti-imperialist struggle that the Palestinians and others were waging. "Overall, for the WUO, solidarity with Palestine was completely consistent with our general anti-imperialism," Gilbert felt.[11]

Despite supporting the Palestinian guerrilla movement, however, the focus of the WUO's activities in the early 1970s was America: its government, its capitalist structure, and its impact on people around the world. In this regard, WUO militants were repeating the pattern that characterized much of the 1960s Left: they discussed the Arab-Israeli conflict and spoke admiringly of the Palestinian struggle, but did little in practical terms beyond offering such verbal support. In the 1970s, the WUO occasionally mentioned Israeli interests and institutions but did not actually attack them as they did American targets. Although he had been imprisoned prior to the

WUO going underground, SDS-Weatherman faction member Eric Mann, for example, wrote from prison in the October 17, 1970, issue of the *Guardian* to urge that the WUO and other leftists "show concrete solidarity with our courageous sisters and brothers of Al Fatah and Popular Front for the Liberation of Palestine" by organizing demonstrations. Among the possible sites for such demonstrations, he mentioned "Israeli embassies, tourist offices, airlines and Zionist fundraising and social affairs" as "important targets for whatever action is decided to be appropriate."[12] Yet as WUO member Laura Whitehorn recalled years later, Palestine "was in our literature, but there was very little operational stuff we did in terms of it."[13]

The WUO's major statement on the Palestinians and the Arab-Israeli conflict came in 1974 with the publication of *Prairie Fire*. The manifesto, which had been the subject of much group discussion and revision, was intended as a definitive program of action. The WUO was particularly interested in explaining itself in the new, post–New Left, post–Vietnam War era, when its bombing campaign was increasingly seen as anachronistic and ineffective.

That *Prairie Fire* was a significant indication of how the group felt about the Palestinians is indicated by the fact that it contained an entire section entitled "The Palestinian Movement" in its chapter on imperialism and the Third World. That section of *Prairie Fire* started right off by emphasizing the key point that the Palestinian struggle resembled other anti-imperialist struggles in which people were fighting for their freedom from outside colonization—including the American Indians. "There is a sobering similarity," *Prairie Fire* began, "between the situation of the Palestinians and the history of the Native American people. The reality is that Israel is an expansionist power, based on zionist colonization."[14] It continued by stating that Israel was a settler colony, an expansionist country, and a society with a weak, nonsocialist economy.

It then offered a stinging rebuke of what it felt was the failure of the white Left in the United States to adequately support the Palestinians, saying, "The white movement in the US has failed to give clear and open support to the Palestinian struggle. We have not taken on the necessary task of exposing the myths about Israel which cloak the true situation and disarm many people. . . . we cannot escape the responsibility of opposing the crimes of the Israeli government and the consequences of zionist ideology." Despite New Left and Old Left public support for the Palestinians in the late 1960s and early 1970s, the authors of *Prairie Fire* clearly believed that such expressions had not gone far enough. *Prairie Fire* called for educating the American public about the true facts of the Palestinians and Israel. Otherwise, "our silence or acceptance of pro-zionist policy is a form of complicity with US-backed aggression and terror, and a betrayal of internationalism."[15]

The WUO's frustration was no doubt magnified by the realization of how hopeless its own armed struggle had become. A bigger problem it faced was that the Palestinian resistance movement itself was moderating in the 1970s. After a decade of armed struggle, the guerrillas' pin-prick attacks on Israel clearly were neither sparking the Palestinians in the occupied West Bank and Gaza to revolt nor bringing the PLO any closer to conquering Israel itself. Palestinian airplane hijackings and violence against Israelis both in Israel and at venues like the 1972 Olympic Games in Munich were also creating considerable negative publicity for the Palestinian cause. After the Jordanian army mauled PLO forces in 1970 and 1971, Palestinian resistance groups realized that their bases in the surrounding Arab countries were enmeshing them in serious intra-Arab problems. Moreover, a US-led peace process, starting in early 1974, was making slow progress in mitigating Arab-Israeli fighting in the Sinai Peninsula and the Golan Heights. Diplomacy, not continued warfare, seemed to be how the Arabs were trying to wind down their conflict with Israel after 1973.

Accordingly, the Palestinian national movement slowly began adopting a new strategic vision in the mid-1970s. Led by new thinking introduced by the Popular Democratic Front for the Liberation of Palestine and al-Fateh, the PLO began shifting away from its original goal of defeating Israel through a guerrilla warfare and establishing in its place a secular, democratic state for both Jews and Arabs. There was a new goal: using diplomacy alongside armed struggle to bring about an Israeli withdrawal from the Occupied Territories and create a Palestinian state there. This new approach was formalized when the PLO adopted its "Ten Point Program" in June 1974. A few months later, the UN General Assembly invited Arafat to address it in November 1974 and subsequently granted observer status within the UN to the PLO. As Arafat stated in his speech, the Palestinians were not yet dropping "the freedom fighter's gun" but it was clear that the days of hoping that a people's war of liberation alone would succeed were over. Isolated as they were in their underground existence, WUO militants do not seem to have picked up on this, or did not care. They continued to support Palestinian groups like the PFLP that rejected Arafat's new "surrenderist" approach and clung to the 1960s vision of total liberation through armed struggle alone. But the political facts on the ground in the Middle East were changing in the 1970s, just as they were in the United States.

## Weather Underground Spinoffs

In 1975, in an attempt to mobilize public support, the Weather Underground Organization created an aboveground offshoot called the Prairie Fire Organizing Committee (PFOC). Members read Popular Front for the Liberation of Palestine literature, and there was even a Palestine interest group— "Palestine was always part of our politics," Diana Block later recalled. As a member of New York Radical Feminists, Block came to regard Zionism as part of an overall imperialist strategy for domination. For her, the turning point—the moment when she said, "Aha!! That's how all these issues were connected"—was when she read *Prairie Fire*. She became involved in anti-imperialist politics, attended the PFOC's first conference, and eventually became a member of its national committee.[16]

Starting in March 1977, the PFOC produced a journal called *Breakthrough*, which discussed the Palestinian issue. In a 1978 article, the PFOC condemned Zionism as "a version of white supremacy which offers power and privilege to Jews through the power of an Israeli settler-state built on the backs of the nations indigenous to the region, in particular the Palestinians."[17] Yet what was most interesting about the article was its criticism of the American Left's failure to support the Palestinians by the late 1970s, including even the PFOC itself. For all that the Left had done to raise awareness of the Palestinians in the late 1960s, PFOC agreed with the WUO that it by and large had not made pro-Palestinian activism a practical priority in the 1970s. It laid this failure at the feet of racist white privilege and what it termed the "opportunist left," a reference no doubt to groupings like Social Democrats USA and the Democratic Socialist Organizing Committee.[18] PFOC's solution was to build a solidarity movement "based on active, militant support for the armed struggle of the Palestinian people for complete self-determination in a democratic secular Palestine."[19]

Meanwhile, the PLO had moved toward a two-state solution, seeking the creation of a Palestinian state alongside Israel through a combination of armed struggle and diplomacy. The theoretical Marxist understandings of the Arab-Israeli conflict of the WUO and PFOC might have become more sophisticated by late 1970s, but they also were out of touch with mainstream PLO (and global) thinking, aligning themselves with Palestinian rejectionist groups like the PFLP.[20]

Rent by disagreements and defections, the WUO effectively ceased functioning within a year or two after formation of the PFOC. Several of its leaders surrendered to authorities or otherwise emerged from underground life. A few still faced various charges. Mark Rudd was one of the first to give himself up, surrendering to authorities in New York in September 1977. Other militants stayed out of sight, living their new, post-WUO lives. Bernardine Dohrn's surrender in Chicago in December 1980 symbolized the end of an era. In a written statement to the press, Dohrn remained defiant, however, saying that "the nature of the system has not changed," and that she still feared that the United States might soon intervene in Africa and the Middle East, despite the lessons of Vietnam.[21]

Disagreements led to a split within the PFOC as well. The West Coast branch retained the group's name and continued to take aim at parts of American Left for failing to support the Palestinians. It scored leftists for accepting Zionist claims and promoting Israel exceptionalism. "Advocates of this position are 'left' Zionists who accept the basic premise of Zionism (that Jews have the right to the land of Palestine) while mouthing support for Palestinian human rights. They argue that Israel has the right to exist in Palestine because of the murder of 6 million Jews by the Nazis. Israel is a 'special case' in which colonial conquest is justified."[22] In the New York City area, the other faction that broke away from the PFOC, the May 19th Communist Organization, similarly remained committed to 1960s-style anti-imperialism and supporting the Palestinians' original vision. Yet as with the case of PFOC, May 19 did not seem to grasp that, by the mid-1970s, the Palestinian national struggle it was supporting was moving away from total reliance on revolutionary violence to achieve its goals.

Undeterred, some Marxists who had been involved or at least associated with the WUO, the PFOC, and/or the May 19th group in the 1970s went on to become involved in armed radical groups in the early 1980s, at least one of which actually included Israeli targets in its bombing campaign. Laura Whitehorn was one of those militants. Born into a Jewish family that was neither religious nor Zionist, Whitehorn became a part of SDS's Weatherman faction in 1969, and later joined the WUO, PFOC, and, eventually, May 19th.[23] When asked later in life about the violence employed by left-wing groups like the WUO, she stated the case she and others felt:

It is only in this country that the word "violence" stops all discussion cold—at least, when violence seems to be practiced by forces of left opposition. The basic morality of Weather [the WUO] and the Catholic Left, etc., was this: If you live in a country whose government is breaking international law and causing irreparable harm to oppressed people, you have a responsibility to try to stop that. To fail to act in some active manner because of respect for the laws of an illegal regime, we reasoned, is in itself immoral. We also asked, why is violence OK when used excessively by the police or the military, but somehow off limits for the victims of that state violence?[24]

Whitehorn joined one such armed group in the early 1980s: the Armed Resistance Unit, which also called itself the Red Guerrilla Resistance and the Revolutionary Fighting Group. It bombed various government and private buildings in response to American actions overseas, including the US capitol in Washington in November 1983. The Armed Resistance Unit did carry out actions against at least one Israeli target when it bombed the offices of the Israel Aircraft Industries building in New York City in the early morning hours of April 5, 1984. Someone speaking in the name of Red Guerrilla Resistance called the offices of United Press International and stated, "Tonight we struck against the . . . Israeli war makers. This country will no longer be a safe haven for Israeli war makers. Victory to the PLO. Death to Zionism and Imperialism."[25]

## Ideological Purity in the New Communist Movement

In 1968, a Maoist group calling itself the Bay Area Revolutionary Union (BARU; later just RU) emerged in the San Francisco–Oakland–Berkeley area in Northern California, masterminded by Robert Bruce "Bob" Avakian. As a student at Berkeley, where he grew up, Avakian, the son of an Alameda County superior court judge and civil rights activist, had been involved in the Free Speech Movement, SDS, and the Peace and Freedom Party. In 1969, BARU began publishing a series of papers, collectively entitled *The Red Papers*, that were very influential among former New Leftists who felt that what the Left needed at the dawn of the 1970s was a new Marxist-Leninist party to lead a proletarian revolution in the United States, given the decline of the New Left and what they considered the deficiencies of existing Old Left communist parties. In the very first issue of *The Red Papers*, BARU analyzed American imperialism and noted that the present historical epoch of the late 1960s was characterized by anti-imperialist struggles around the world. "Today," it asserted, "Vietnam is the focal point of these struggles. Tomorrow it will be Brazil or Thailand, southern Africa or the Middle East." BARU was predicting that the Palestinians might become the new Viet Cong of the 1970s, and proclaiming that American revolutionaries should accept the responsibility of doing "whatever we can accomplish to weaken our ruling class" alongside these struggles.[26]

BARU was indicative of a wider trend among dedicated aboveground Marxist-Leninists in the 1970s who continued to take a pro-Palestinian stand on the American Left in the new decade, albeit more and more out of touch both with where the Palestinians themselves were going and where mainstream Americans who were starting to align themselves with the Palestinians were moving. This served to weaken the Left even further as it struggled to remain relevant.

Marxist organizations like BARU that emerged out of the collapse of the New Left are sometimes called "the New Communist Movement."[27] They eschewed the adventurism of armed underground groups like the WUO and threw themselves instead into patient party building and theoretical formulation in the hope of creating a viable Marxist-Leninist vanguard party in the 1970s. Believing that the CPUSA was unequal to that task, and hostile to that party's Soviet patrons, most of the small groups in the New Communist Movement adopted positions close to those of the Chinese Communist Party and its leader, Mao Zedong.[28] Something that distinguished it from the New Left and even the Old Left was the virtual unanimity of support for the Palestinians and condemnation of Israel among its constituent groups. As the WUO and its spinoff groups were doing, the Marxists of the New Communist Movement developed increasingly more sophisticated theoretical understandings of the Arab-Israeli conflict during the 1970s, even though these ideological visions of the Palestinian struggle did not correspond to changing realities on the ground in the Middle East.

In December 1969, two of BARU's members, Leibel Bergman and Davida Fineman, traveled to Algeria to meet with Palestinian revolutionaries at the Congress of Palestine Support Committees in Algiers. Fineman had graduated from Cornell in 1965. Bergman was older than the other BARU activists, having been a longtime communist activist involved with the CPUSA and the Progressive Labor Party before working with Avakian and others to establish

BARU. Fineman later toured al-Fateh camps in Jordan as well.[29] It was not her first time in the Middle East. Her parents were ardent American Zionists; her mother had lived in Palestine before the establishment of Israel and later became an official in the State of Israel Bond Organization, and her father was involved in Zionist gun-running. Fineman herself lived in Israel for a time as a young girl and visited Israel several times thereafter. After attending the conference in Algeria, she spent several weeks in Jordan in early 1970 touring refugee camps and meeting Palestinians, including senior al-Fateh figures Yasir Arafat and Salah Khalaf (Abu Iyad). Visiting a school for the daughters of Palestinian fighters who had been killed, Fineman discovered that the girls were being given classes in Hebrew. "They made a big deal of my being Jewish and my solidarity [with the Palestinians]," she recalled decades later.[30]

On April 25, 1970, BARU was instrumental in the formation of something called the Palestine Solidarity Committee in San Francisco; Bergman attended the organizational meeting and Fineman ended up becoming a member. Six BARU members eventually sat on the group's steering committee, along with four Arab members, two of whom were college students. Among its various activities the committee organized screenings of the film "Revolution until Victory" (also called "We Are the Palestinian People"), a 52-minute black and white film that came out in 1973 thanks to the efforts of four people formerly with the New Left film production body known as Newsreel. After their expulsion from Newsreel, the four formed Single Spark Films, which was associated with BARU.[31]

In October 1975, BARU reorganized itself as the Revolutionary Communist Party, USA (RCPUSA), which shortly thereafter took up the issue of Zionism, doubtless motivated in part by the UN General Assembly's vote in November 1975 to condemn it as a form of racism and by articles in BARU's publication *Revolution* around that time. The anonymous author of an internal RCPUSA document—perhaps Avakian—stated that the party's task was to wean the American masses away from Zionism and toward support for Palestinian self-determination under the slogans "Support the Palestinian People's Right to Self-Determination" and "Oppose Zionism as a Tool of Imperialism." To combat Zionism, it was very important to characterize it accurately; mischaracterization that minimized "the real oppression suffered by the Jewish masses in Europe" only helped those who said that communists hated Jews and equated anti-Zionism with anti-Semitism. Dealing forthrightly with anti-Semitism was one of the ways that the RCPUSA would win Jewish Americans to its program, "one of our tasks in making revolution in this country."[32] The RCPUSA did little to actualize its support for the Palestinians, however, and focused on party building.[33]

Another pioneering group within the New Communist Movement that similarly championed the Palestinian cause with sophisticated ideological formulations was the October League (OL). The OL emerged in early 1972, growing out of the October League Collective, formed in Los Angeles in 1969 by a former SDS activist, Mike Klonsky. The OL's May 1972 "Statement of the Political Unity of the October League" declared: "The U.S. and their [South Vietnamese] puppet troops have been dealt a stunning defeat. Similarly, all over the world national liberation is on the upsurge. The armed struggles of the Palestinian and other Arab peoples against U.S.-Israeli aggression have greatly weakened imperialism."[34] The OL later melded itself into the Communist Party (Marxist-Leninist). At the founding congress of the new party in June 1977, Klonsky once again affirmed support for the Palestinians, saying, "Our party will also heighten its support for the Palestinian and other Arab peoples against imperialism and Zionism."[35]

The origins of the Communist Labor Party of the United States of North America extended back to 1968–69 and the formation of the California Communist League. Like the RCPUSA and the October League/Communist Party (Marxist-Leninist), early members of the California Communist League included former members of SDS. They linked up with a veteran black Marxist named Nelson Peery, who had a long and eventful history in communist activism. The CLP was also noteworthy for its strong support for the Palestinians. At its founding party Congress in September 1974, a resolution on the Middle East was submitted by the Progressive Arab Students in North America that criticized the Soviet Union and the United States for starting the October 1973 Arab-Israeli war in order to crush popular liberation struggles. The resolution accused the two superpowers of shifting the focus of the Arab-Israeli conflict from a "direct colonial question" to a "neo-colonial question of a 'mini-Palestinian state'" under the tutelage of petty bourgeois elements of the Palestinian resistance movement—a sharp denunciation of the PLO's new embrace of the concept of a truncated Palestinian state in the West Bank and Gaza.[36]

A split later occurred in the CLP and a faction in the San Francisco area formed the Marxist-Leninist Collective in 1975. Three years later, this group, which by then was espousing a pro-Albanian political line, published a lengthy article analyzing the Middle East and pointing out the doctrinal errors of its pro-Chinese rivals within the New Communist Movement. The article also denounced the concept of a two-state solution to the Palestinian-Israeli conflict. Describing a West Bank Palestinian state as an "apartheid-like bantustan" and a "dirt cage," the collective supported the "long term demand of the Palestinian and Arab peoples for the liberation of the whole of Palestine and the establishment of a democratic, secular state."[37]

The small parties of the New Communist Movement adhered to the PLO's original strategy of total liberation through armed struggle and rejected the Palestinian mainstream's movement toward creation of a rump Palestinian state. They clung to visions of guerrilla armies waging anticolonial struggles from the jungles. The Middle East had no jungles, however, and Palestinian guerrillas could not use neighboring Arab states as sanctuaries and count on their support. There also was an American-led peace process under way. Yet the parties in the New Communist Movement were too busy fighting with one another over the correct party line to notice or to care about the new realities in the Middle East. Despite this, and despite these parties' growing irrelevancy, other liberal-left activists continued to uphold the Palestinian cause in the mid-1970s.

## Palestine Solidarity Groups

Although the temperature stayed below freezing the entire day of January 20, 1976, over six hundred people gathered in a theater at Columbia University in New York City for an event held in solidarity with the Palestinian people—a crowd that dwarfed the few dozen activists who typically had showed up to pro-Palestinian demonstrations in the 1960s. Addressing the crowd were several important PLO figures: Shafiq al-Hut, a member of the PLO executive committee and its official representative in Lebanon; Yasser Abed Rabbo, a high-ranking official from the Democratic Front for the Liberation of Palestine[38] who also sat on the PLO executive committee and headed the PLO's information department; and two officials from the PLO's delegation to the UN, Basil Aql and Hasan Rahman.[39] The event was hosted by a new group, the Palestine Solidarity Committee (PSC).

Instead of retreating underground to wage urban warfare like the WUO, fading into political irrelevancy like the small, deeply divided parties of the New Communist Movement, or assimilating to the left wing of the

Democratic Party, as some socialists were doing, the PSC continued to practice street-level politics. In so doing, it constituted a bridge between 1960s
activism on behalf of Palestine and the new political scene in America in the
late 1970s, when pro-Palestinian sentiments were becoming more accepted.
The Left of the 1960s might have been withering away, but many progressive Americans continued to support the Palestinian cause, and the PSC har-
nessed this sentiment more successfully than either the WUO or the parties of
the New Communist Movement. Its first event, in January 1976, seemed the
auspicious beginning of a new phase of pro-Palestinian activism.

The Palestine Solidarity Committee was the brainchild of Sheila Ryan and
George Cavalletto (see chapter 3 above), inspired by a group in the New York
City area who had held an "Evening of Solidarity" a few months earlier, as
part of an International Day of Solidarity with the Palestinian People, May
15, 1975. That November some of these activists formed a permanent group,
the PSC, dedicated to "supporting the Palestinian national struggle," "exposing the fallacies of Zionism," and opposing "reprehensible" American policy
toward the Palestinians. They and others like them were part of a trend in
the 1970s by which activists formed solidarity committees to support various
national liberation struggles around the world.[40]

The PSC was an example of how concern for the Palestinians was moving
into the 1970s progressive mainstream. There was probably more talk about
the Palestinian problem in America at that point than ever before. A poll
commissioned in November 1978 showed that Americans ranked the Middle
East as the most important foreign policy problem facing the country, even
more than relations with the Soviet Union.[41] The first oil shock of the winter
of 1974, prompted by a reduction in petroleum pumping by Arab oil produc-
ers angry at Western support for Israel during the 1973 Arab-Israeli war, was
one factor in raising Americans' awareness of the conflict. So were American-
led peace efforts in the Middle East after the 1973 war. The PLO's entrance
into the world community, as symbolized by Yasir Arafat's November 1974
speech at the UN and the PLO's move toward diplomacy, brought the Palestinian problem to the attention of Americans in a new way.

Capitalizing on this, the PSC came out swinging in its first full year of
operation. In addition to the forum it hosted at Columbia in January, it began
issuing a publication entitled *Palestine!* starting in April. By that same month,
three additional chapters had been established besides the main one in New
York, in Albany, California; Youngstown, Ohio, and Denver, Colorado. On

May 15, 1976, a number of events were held around the country to commemorate the International Day of Solidarity with the Palestinian People,[42] and nearly a thousand people gathered at a PSC-sponsored event in Brooklyn on the following day. Less than one month later, on June 13, the PSC joined with others in what was called the Palestine Action Coalition to hold a "Salute to Palestine" march in New York City as a counterdemonstration to the annual "Salute to Israel" parade, a pro-Israel event that had taken place every year starting in 1964. By the end of 1976, the PSC had held a total of three demonstrations, in addition to the January 20 meeting addressed by the PLO representatives and a fundraiser for medical aid to Lebanon.[43]

The PSC continued to provide street-level support for the Palestinians throughout the late 1970s. On June 5, 1977, it once again worked with the Palestine Action Coalition to hold another demonstration in opposition to the annual Salute to Israel Parade in New York. When President Jimmy Carter brokered peace talks between Egyptian President Anwar al-Sadat and Israeli Prime Minister Menachem Begin at Camp David, Maryland, in September 1978, Ryan joined about two hundred others to protest the talks in front of the UN building in New York on September 23. She spoke at the event, saying, "Carter is a false prophet of peace. This is not a peace but a pact for a new kind of war against the Palestinian people."[44] Continuing its annual tradition, the PSC again staged a counterdemonstration to the June 3, 1979, Salute to Israel Parade, expressing the group's opposition to the Egyptian-Israeli peace treaty signed that March. The Palestinian people were the "first victims" of the peace treaty, Ryan said, because it denied their right to self-determination.[45]

The PSC ran out of steam in the early 1980s, but its brief history was an important turning point in pro-Palestinian activism. It was an important bridge between support for the Palestinians by the Left in the 1960s and by a new generation of activists in the 1970s. By returning to the active, street-level politics of protest characteristic of that earlier period, PSC paved the way for the emergence of more of that type of political expression in the 1980s, especially after Israel's 1982 war in Lebanon gave rise to a new period of solidarity activism. It also broke with the New Left and Old Left tradition of mobilizing for Palestine in relative isolation from the Arab and Arab American communities, because it consciously worked with Arab Americans.

In the 1970s, the pro-Palestinian leftists of the previous decade moved in different directions. Both the underground Marxists of the WUO and its spinoffs and the aboveground parties in the New Communist Movement continued to press for a global anti-imperialist revolution, but they virtually all clung to the PLO's 1960s vision of a people's war revolutionizing the Middle East, dismantling the Zionist state, and creating a secular, democratic state for both Jews and Palestinians in its place. The changing nature of liberation movements, both successful ones and those still struggling, either escaped their analysis or led them to cling to their ideals anyway. China's rapprochement with the United States and its bitter hostility to the Soviet Union were just two of the reasons why Third World liberation movements failed to threaten capitalist imperialism as some Marxists had hoped they would.[46] Moreover, the Egyptian-Israeli peace process that began soon after the 1973 war ended and culminated in the signing of the first treaty between Israel and an Arab state in March 1979 was a game changer for the Arab-Israeli conflict. If the experience of the PSC showed that pro-Palestinian activists could still inspire Americans, many others on the Left, notably socialists, remained unshaken in their support of Israel.

# 10 The Shadow of the Cold War

## Continued Pro-Israeli Pushback

NOT ALL REMNANTS of the 1960s Left supported the Palestinian struggle in the 1970s. Pro-Israeli socialists in particular continued their earlier battle against the attacks on Israel mounted by other leftists. As far back as 1969, concerned activists from the Socialist Party of America (SPA) formed a youth group that had become the focal point in the socialists' drive to generate support for Israel among America's youth in the 1970s. They called it the Youth Committee for Peace and Democracy in the Middle East (YCPDME), and its leaders hoped to offset the perceived erosion in support for Israel by stressing Israel's progressive, democratic virtues to young Americans of all ethno-religious backgrounds. Joshua Muravchik, a leading figure in the SPA's youth group, Young People's Socialist League (YPSL), summed up the socialists' mission: "In the student world of that era, groups reflecting mainstream America held the allegiance of few. As a result, we YPSL's, although earnestly regarding ourselves not only as socialists but even as Marxists of a sort, and thus to the Left of 99 percent of Americans, spent the largest portion of our energies battling student groups even farther to our Left. Sometimes this allowed us to capture the ostensible middle ground."[1]

However, the "Marxists of a sort" in YPSL were beginning to change in the 1970s, along with their elders in the SPA. Their militantly anti-Soviet and strongly pro-Israeli stances were moving them further to the right and away from others in the Left who either embraced the Palestinians or were more conflicted about the Middle East. This rightward shift in the 1970s was important, not only for maintaining the SPA's pushback against the pro-Palestinianism of other parts of the Left, but also because it illustrated the socialists' importance in the weakening of the Left when some of them embraced what came to be called neoconservatism.

## Zealous Socialist Youth Organizations

Carl Gershman (see chapter 7 above) was a major figure in the Youth Committee for Peace and Democracy in the Middle East. A few years after its establishment, Gershman described the group's aims as trying to combat Arab propaganda by educating American youth about the "true history" of the Arab-Israeli conflict, as well as stressing the need to support Israel as the Middle East's only democracy.[2] This last point was indicated by the use of the term "democracy" in the group's name. For YCPDME members, support for democracy and peace in the Middle East meant support for Israel. Sponsors of YCPDME included the SPA leader Michael Harrington, but also people outside the party like Allard Lowenstein, Hans Morgenthau, Irving Howe, and Martin Peretz. Still, it was clear that the young socialists from YPSL and other groups constituted the leading force in YCPDME. Gershman became the group's director of research, and soon rose to co-chair and, in 1971, to executive director. YPSL's Joshua Muravchik and Richard "Penn" Kemble were YCPDME co-chairs, while Helen Kerszencwejg eventually served as executive director too.

So intertwined were the various YPSL/SPA-associated groups headed by young party members that Democratic Party insider and neoconservative figure Ben Wattenberg once commented wittily on how this situation served the young socialists in their crusade against communism: "I used to kid Tom [Kahn] that he and his activist friends were a cabal, ingeniously trying to bury the Soviet Union in a blizzard of letterheads. It seemed that each of Tom's colleagues—Penn Kemble, Carl Gershman, Josh Muravchik and many more—ran a little organization, each with the same interlocking directorate listed on the stationery. . . . I never did quite get all the organizational acronyms straight—YPSL, LID, SP, SDA, ISL—but the key words were 'democratic,' 'labor,' 'young' and until events redefined it away from their understanding, 'socialist.'"[3]

The YCPDME was moving rightward, as illustrated by its association with moderate and even conservative groups like the National Association for the

Advancement of Colored People, the Catholic Youth Organization, the New Democratic Coalition, the Young Men's Christian Association, the National Conference of Christians and Jews, and, significantly, the United States Youth Council (USYC). Two years before it helped establish the YCPDME, the press revealed that the CIA provided most of the USYC's funding, and it was funded instead thereafter by the Department of State. A YCPDME staff member later wrote that the organization had been "initially formed as an ad hoc committee of the United States Youth Council. . . . The United States Youth Council has remained vital to [it] as a vehicle for obtaining support for Israel among youth leaders."[4]

The YCPDME began its public activities in late 1969, and started publishing a newsletter entitled *Crossroads* in April 1970. That first issue carried an appropriate article for the group's founding purpose: Harrington's "Left's Anti-Israel Stand Challenged." The YCPDME did more than just challenge leftist groups in the 1970s; it also began spying on them and passing the information to the Anti-Defamation League (ADL). The ADL's intelligence efforts—what it called its "information-gathering operation"—in fact extended as far back as 1948, and included monitoring of Arab countries' consulates and United Nations delegation offices, offices of the Arab Information Center and the Palestine Arab Refugee Office, and the various branches of the Organization of Arab Students. As the years went by, the ADL ended up creating files not just on Arab propaganda/public relations offices but also on a huge variety of domestic American groups and individuals that it felt might remotely pose a threat to Jews or Israel. This included everything from right-wing anti-Semitic groups to left-wing groups to black organizations.[5] The ADL's intelligence czar was Irwin Suall, a stalwart member of the SPA who rose to become its national secretary in 1957 and served thereafter in the post until 1968. Initially not a Zionist, Suall visited Israel shortly after the 1967 war and returned greatly changed in his views. Thereafter deeply committed to Israel, he began work for the ADL that year as its national director of fact finding. He amassed files on any and all groups that he and the ADL considered potential threats to Jews and Israel.

Beginning in 1973, the ADL paid YCPDME to provide it with reports on what it considered anti-Israeli groups both on and off college campuses. Left-wing groups that YCPDME monitored included the Young Socialist Alliance, Students for a Democratic Society, Youth against War and Fascism, the Spartacist League, the Revolutionary Student Brigade, the Young

Workers Liberation League, as well as other groups like the Association of Arab-American University Graduates. YCPDME also provided information on what mainstream youth groups like the College Democrats, College Republicans, and the United States Youth Council thought about Israel. In 1975, YCPDME's David J. Kopilow wrote to the ADL and reported, "Working with Irwin Suall, we have monitored and provided reports on anti-Israel activities at many college campuses."[6] In return for these and other services in defense of Israel, the ADL paid YCPDME $5,000 per annum starting in 1973.[7]

In 1974, YCPDME changed its name and became the Youth Institute for Peace in the Middle East (YIPME). A major factor in this was that the group managed to secure federal tax exempt status by altering its name and structure. The renamed group become particularly active that year, when the UN General Assembly invited Yasir Arafat to address it and the Palestine Liberation Organization (PLO) was basking in increased international legitimacy. Like other pro-Israeli organizations, YIPME set in motion a flurry of activities. It immediately denounced Arafat's planned visit, trying to balance its professed humanitarian concern for Palestinian refugees with its castigation of the PLO: "We believe the P.L.O. to be a blood-stained terrorist group whose leaders should not be granted the privilege of addressing the U.N. We deeply sympathize with the plight of the Palestinian refugees but we know very well that the P.L.O. does not represent the Palestinians."[8] That sentiment was strongly at odds with the fact that the PLO enjoyed widespread legitimacy among Palestinians.

YIPME's efforts—articulating the social democratic vision of supporting Israel as the Middle East's only democracy, demonizing the PLO, and stressing the need for American support to Israel to thwart Soviet intentions in the region—were hindered by financial and other problems. At a meeting in New York City in November 1974, the YIPME board of directors discussed the twin problems of being understaffed and existing more on paper than in reality. The group wrestled with the problem of how to move the New York City chapter of YIPME in particular "off paper and on to the campus."[9] Four years later Suall expressed his concern about the lack of pro-Israel groups on college campuses. Perhaps an even bleaker assessment was offered by the socialist leader Bayard Rustin, who opined in a September 1978 letter to fellow neoconservative Daniel P. Moynihan that the country had actually witnessed a decline in support for Israel among youth.[10]

YIPME continued to function for a few more years as it built up coalitions such as what it called the "Democracy Issue Coalition." This included the

Young Social Democrats; the A. Philip Randolph Institute; the Abdala Cuban Movement; the Committee in Support of Solidarity; and Youth for Energy Independence. Cooperation with these groups once again signaled YIPME's growing tilt toward neoconservatism. The Abdala Cuban Movement, for example, was vehemently hostile to the communist regime of Cuban leader Fidel Castro, while the Committee in Support of Solidarity was formed in December 1981 to support the Polish Solidarity trade union movement. Several founders of that anti-communist committee were either sponsors or participants in YIPME and its activities, including neoconservative figures like Rustin, Moynihan, Midge Decter, Lane Kirkland, Albert Shanker, and Ben Wattenberg.[11]

Another socialist group that expressed its concern about the attitudes of youth toward Israel in the 1970s was the League for Industrial Democracy (LID), a socialist organization dating back to the early 1900s. The LID was noteworthy for having given birth to SDS in 1960 (disagreements between the two led to a formal separation in 1965, however). In 1964, its executive directorship passed to a young socialist activist, Tom Kahn. Kahn was well connected among socialist activists despite his youth. He joined Max Shachtman's Independent Socialist League in 1956, and followed Shachtman when the league merged with the SPA in 1958. Kahn was closely connected with Rustin, was greatly influenced by Harrington, and became active in LID and YPSL along with Gershman and Muravchik.

Several years before YIPME activists worried about the level of student support for Israel, the LID had carried out a survey of student attitudes in the spring of 1970 through its Youth Project on Democratic Change. Muravchik and Richard "Penn" Kemble worked on the survey. Among the questions it posed to the student leaders who took part was one that asked what country came closest to their ideals. Israel came in third, following Sweden and the United States. On the other hand, when asked about the Arab-Israeli conflict, only 36 percent of students described themselves as pro-Israeli, compared to 10 percent who favored the Arabs. Disturbingly for the LID, 54 percent were neutral. "Support for Israel among student leaders seems to be eroding under the impact of neo-isolationism and pro-Arab propaganda," the report lamented. It asserted that the generation of the Peace Corps was turning its back on a small, democratic country that had given "life back to a barren land." The report's authors opined that it was troubling that campus leaders were unwilling to support Israel when it was "clearly in the right" in the conflict.[12]

## SDUSA's Move Rightward

At their divisive December 1972 convention, members of the Socialist Party of America, renamed Social Democrats USA (SDUSA), issued a ringing endorsement of Israel restating points the party had been arguing for several years: Israel was a democracy, it had a strong labor movement, and it helped check Soviet ambitions in the world: "Israel, a small democracy ruled by a Socialist government based on a vigorous labor movement, is menaced by an alliance of terrorists and backward Arab dictatorships which together receive massive military and political support from the Soviet Union. We urge support for Israel on moral grounds, and also because such a policy contributes to peace in the Middle East by obstructing Arab adventurism and Soviet expansionism."[13]

The October 1973 Arab-Israeli war ten months later prompted SDUSA to action, stressing its familiar themes once again. It sent a telegram to Secretary of State Henry Kissinger urging American support for Israel, and encouraged its members to contact President Richard Nixon and ask that he provide additional military aid to the embattled Jewish state. After the fighting stopped, SDUSA sent out an "Appeal to World Socialists: Support Israel" on November 10, 1973. It called for fellow democratic socialists to support the "beleaguered people of Israel," reminding them that "on the side of the enemies of Israel there is ranged a vast and powerful conglomeration of totalitarian Communists, reactionaries and anti-Semites." The statement also made clear that the Soviet Union was responsible for starting the 1973 war.[14] SDUSA also organized pro-Israel rallies in New York and Los Angeles.

The "Appeal to World Socialists: Support Israel" urged socialists around the world not to adopt a neutral stance in the war. "Neutrality can only convince the Soviet Union that its arming and backing of aggression in the Middle East and elsewhere will be tolerated by the democratic forces and even rewarded at the conference table."[15] SDUSA also railed against the world's tepid response to Israel's crisis during the 1973 war. "It is difficult to believe the international reaction to this latest outrageous attack on the small democratic state of Israel. It is as though '1984' language were already being imposed on us. . . . it has an Orwellian nightmarish flavor to it—war is peace, lies are truth, hate is love." SDUSA's leaders expressed their "indignation at Communist propaganda and the lack of objectivity by the world at large."[16]

SDUSA was particularly concerned about the possibility of the Senate amending the Emergency Aid Bill for Israel, then before Congress, along the lines of a 1970 amendment proposed by Senators George McGovern and Mark O. Hatfield requiring prior congressional approval of funding military operations in Vietnam. It feared that a war-weary Congress might place similar limits on American military action in the Middle East, calling anything of the sort "not only a threat to Israel's existence, but to world peace" and demanding, "Can we forget the lessons of [the British and French leaders giving in to Hitler in] Munich [in 1938]?"[17] Continuing on the theme of Munich, Bayard Rustin and another leading socialist figure, Charles S. Zimmerman, blasted Senators McGovern and Hatfield, calling them "Congress's [Neville] Chamberlains who would create a Munich in the Middle East."[18]

Gershman, who became SDUSA's executive director in 1975, remained persistently antagonistic to the PLO and denounced efforts by other social democratic parties around to the world to develop relationships with it. In conjunction with a Socialist International (SI) meeting in Madrid in October 14–15, 1977, Gershman made pointedly hostile comments about Bruno Kreisky, the Austrian prime minister, who was the SI's vice president and a known gadfly with respect to Arab-Israeli politics. Kreisky had told the assembled delegates that the position of the Israeli Labor Party, as expressed over the years by Golda Meir, was well known to the SI, but other points of view about the Arab-Israeli conflict were not. Accordingly, Kreisky suggested that in the event that the Arab-Israeli peace process that started with the 1973 Geneva talks failed, the SI should convene a roundtable discussion in the spring of 1978 so that it could discuss the issue and hear new perspectives. His proposal was adopted.

What particularly annoyed Gershman was the so-called Kreisky Report, issued by the SI in October 1977, which called for recognition of Palestinian national rights and argued that Israel would be able to achieve Arab recognition and live at peace if it moved more toward understanding Arab needs and concerns.[19] The New Left and the Marxist Old Left supporting the Palestinians was bad enough, but the social democratic parties of the SI expressing sympathy for the Palestinian national struggle—and the PLO in particular— was much worse for Gershman, especially since Kreisky was a fellow Jew.

"The [Kreisky] report is politically biased and factually distorted to a degree that is quite extraordinary," Gershman wrote in a confidential memorandum. "In addition to its distortion of the truth," he continued, it was "pervaded by a shameless venality, openly referred to as a desire for Arab investments in Europe." Bitterly resurrecting a favorite SDUSA analogy, he asserted: "Even more pervasive is the spirit of Munich, i.e., if only Israel would give in and 'adjust.' Indeed, there is an uncanny parallel that can be drawn between Kreisky's attitude toward Israel and the attitude in the West toward Czechoslovakia in 1938."[20]

The divisions over the Arab-Israeli conflict further weakened the Left in the 1970s. Indeed, some SDUSA activists drifted rightward into the ranks of neoconservatism. Their passionate support for Israel was a major factor in this development.

## The Neoconservative Backlash

A year before he died in 1988, Michael Harrington published *The Long-Distance Runner: An Autobiography,* and one of the many topics he examined in which was the growth of the phenomenon called neoconservatism. In trying to explain why some of the architects of the broad movement known as neoconservatism were Jews who had started their political careers as socialists and even Marxists before moving rightward, Harrington argued that the Left's attacks on Israel in the 1960s were a major factor in the development of the neocons, as they often are called. "There was, after all, a general tendency within the Jewish Left to turn from socialism or liberalism to neo-conservatism," Harrington wrote, "because the issue of Israel played an important role . . . for a whole stratum of Jews."[21]

The negative Jewish reaction to the anti-Israeli, pro-Palestinian sentiments of the Left in the 1960s and 1970s was indeed an important factor in the development and articulation of neoconservatism. Many of the leading lights in the neoconservative movement admitted the prominent role of Jewish intellectuals in their ranks.[22] In offering his own definition of neoconservatism, Norman Podhoretz, noted neocon, wrote that the neocons were "an initially small group of intellectuals—many but by no means all of them Jewish—who began their political lives somewhere on the Left and who, in the closing years of the 1960s, began moving toward a conservative position."[23]

Podhoretz argued that these intellectuals moved rightward because they were defending "the values and institutions of the liberal democratic order." Being conservative in this sense meant conserving what was good about America. Who was threatening the liberal order in the United States in the

1960s? For Podhoretz and his cohorts, the answer was clear: the Left and Black Power advocates. In reacting against the New Left and other radical forces in America, the neocons believed they were fighting to uphold a worldview that in the final analysis was good for America. In fighting to save a noble, liberal democratic order from what they perceived as irrational, illiberal, and uncultured assaults on the very Western values that had served Jews so well in America, they were not just upholding what was good about America but what also was good for the Jews. "Those of us who have fought the Left have done so in the name of liberal values, not in the name of Judaism," Podhoretz wrote in 1971, "but we have been fighting the fight for Judaism in America all the same."[24]

Irving Kristol was a key figure in the development of neoconservatism and a good example of the importance of Israel to its worldview. The son of immigrant Jews and a Trotskyist as a youth, Kristol went on to become a writer and publisher whose views helped set the tone for the neoconservatives' strong embrace of Israel, even though his overall foreign policy arguments were essentially based on the cold logic of what served American national interests. "The 'new thinking' Kristol called for excluded overriding moral commitments, but his own passionate commitment to the survival and well-being of Israel revealed a concern for something more than America national interests," Gary Dorrien writes.[25] During the October 1973 Arab-Israeli War, Kristol confirmed this, saying, "I am not a Zionist. . . . Still, I care desperately."[26] Kristol once summed up how his views had moved away from Trotskyist Marxism toward a more conservative view of society at an American Jewish Congress conference in Israel in 1972, where he stated that both Jews and Israel were politically conservative and should not be afraid to admit it.[27]

Harkening back to the polemics hurled at one another by socialists and communists decades earlier, members of SDUSA were bitter foes of the Soviet Union, and opposing it and supporting Israel were two sides of the same coin for neoconservatives. SDUSA was thus a spawning ground for anti-Soviet, pro-Israeli neocons in the 1970s. "Israel, the only democratic nation in the Middle East, is under attack from military dictatorships and feudal oilogarchies, backed by Soviet totalitarianism whose propaganda apparatus around the world is distorting the issues,"[28] Bayard Rustin and his fellow SDUSA leaders declared during the 1973 Arab-Israeli War. Rustin's swing toward neoconservatism can also be seen in his support for the reconstitution of the anti-Soviet Committee on the Present Danger in early 1976.

Neoconservatives' negative reactions to the criticisms of Israel were also central to their abandonment of the Left and their rightward move. Just as leftists positioned Israel within their theoretical frameworks, so too did neoconservatives, who placed Israel alongside the United States as a paragon of democratic, civilized virtue. "It is not technology for which the Jewish state has served as vanguard in the Middle East, but the sheer, unswerving, uncalculating, incalculable force of human will," Podhoretz's neoconservative wife Midge Decter wrote. "And it is undoubtedly also for this that the Jewish state is most roundly feared and hated by its neighbors; for there is a truly terrible, and permanently disquieting, message in it. 'If you will it, it is not a dream.' If you do not will it, all the science of the Western world will not help you."[29] Decter was on the board of the Youth Institute for Peace in the Middle East, along with Gershman, Rustin, Muravchik, and Richard Perle, all of whom eventually shifted toward neoconservatism.[30]

Another central factor in the neocons' rightward movement was their belief that the Democratic Party through which some had worked was turning pacifist, thereby hindering American ability to respond to Soviet adventurism and defend Israel. The fact that the party nominated the liberal George McGovern for president in 1972 mortified them. Neoconservatives believed that McGovern's nomination represented the hijacking of the party by the remnants of the New Left to the detriment of both America and Israel. For them McGovern and the Democrats' "New Politics" were the quintessential representation of the post-Vietnam, defeatist malaise in America that was leading to isolationism and an unwillingness to confront Soviet-supported adventures around the globe.

Neoconservatives therefore feared that McGovern's stated desire to reduce American military expenditures would hinder the country's ability to assist Israel militarily during a future crisis. Their disgust with the Democratic Party's failure of nerve extended to the presidency of Jimmy Carter, whom they also blamed for not acting decisively to support American allies. In 1977, during the Carter administration, Gershman told an interviewer, "you cannot be for the United States defending Israel if you [are] also for the United States being a very second rate military power in the world. You can't have it both ways."[31]

Gershman was one of those particularly concerned about how a weak American military would affect Israel. He felt that socialists' best opportunity for influence was to work within the Democratic Party. Yet like many who drifted into neoconservatism in the 1970s, he disliked McGovern and was enamored with the Democratic Party's militantly anti-Soviet, pro-Israeli hawk, Senator Henry M. "Scoop" Jackson. To those Americans, particularly liberal Jews, who supported cuts in military spending, Gershman retorted that being for or against Israel was no longer the problem; the problem was whether or not one supported an American defense policy that enabled the United States to guarantee Israel's security.[32]

Podhoretz agreed, and in 1977 pointedly recalled it was the Republican administration of Richard Nixon, not that of a Democrat like Carter, that used America's military strength to come to Israel's aid in a crisis: "What saved Israel from being overrun by the Arab armies [in 1973] was an airlift of American arms; and what had prevented the Russians from intervening when they threatened to do so at a certain point was the American nuclear deterrent. Nothing could have more vividly demonstrated the inextricable connection between the survival of Israel and the military adequacy of the United States."[33] At the same time, neoconservatives recognized that Israel's military prowess conversely bolstered American efforts to contain the Soviet Union. During the 1973 war in the Middle East, SDUSA urged members to write to President Nixon asking him to provide Israel with additional military assistance. One of the things the party asked its members to point out was that such aid would not only help Israel but was important "particularly in view of Israel's critical role in the Mediterranean defense posture of the U.S."[34]

Israel's security was clearly an important factor in the neoconservatives' abandonment of the Left and their Marxist and socialist pasts. Neocons like Nathan Glazer were quick to admit this point: the fate of Israel was not only a central concern for neoconservatives but for all Jews. Writing in 1972, Glazer even stated that support for Israel trumped all other factors involved in Jewish political attitudes and decisions: "For Jews . . . the survival of Israel is a transcendent interest. If the survival of Israel coincides with the larger American public interest, well and good. If it does not—well, the United States is a big and rich country, and the reduction of its influence in the Middle East, or the loss of a point to Russia, should not outweigh this transcendent Jewish interest."[35]

Decter went so far as to write in 1971 that Jews were born with an almost mystical connection to Israel that was part of their identity, something predetermined for them before birth. Any Jew visiting Israel was liable to have the experience "distorted" by preordained connections to the land: "Another trouble to the visitor's ordinary experience, at least if that visitor should be a Jew, is the recognition that his historic relations with the place—again ancient as well as modern—have already and without his participation been fixed. His private responses, being admittedly so irrelevant to the issue of his connection with what they are responses to, are bound themselves to get distorted."[36]

The sense of a deep, existential connection with Israel was expressed by other Jewish intellectuals who were moving to the right as well. Writing shortly after the 1967 war, Martin Peretz declared that Israel was a non-negotiable issue for Jews on the Left: "Those of us in the radical community, then, for whom Israel's rights are on the same moral plane as the rights of the Vietnamese, have drawn a kind of moral cut-off line on this issue; other radicals cannot deny or reasonably plead against it in the name of unity."[37]

Nor were these the only reasons that drew neoconservatives to Israel in the 1970s. Israel also represented for them all the virtues that they saw withering away in America as a result of Black Power, the New Left, the hippie counterculture, and the entire 1960s experience. Israel, they believed, was a vibrant society, united in purpose, and Israelis were ready to fight and die for the good of the nation. Their Israel was a democratic, egalitarian society whose citizens did not hesitate to put aside political differences for the sake of national defense. There were no draft dodgers in Israel, they claimed, no antiwar parades, uncouth New Left protesters, weak-kneed internationalists, or hippie drug addicts. Virtually every Israeli Jew was conscripted into the military and had to perform annual reserve duties. And when duty called, the Israeli military acted decisively and without hesitation. It was precisely the type of muscular military posture the neocons saw lacking in their own country.

The neoconservative Seymour Martin Lipset argued that even non-Jewish conservatives felt this way: "Many non-Jewish conservatives see in Israel's successful military resistance to the Arab world, and its defiance of United Nations resolutions, an example of the way in which a nation which has self-pride—and which is not 'corrupted by the virus of internationalism and pacifism'—can defend its national self-interests. Some see in the Israeli defeat of the Arabs, the one example of an American ally which has decisively defeated Communist allies in battle." He felt that the result would be a rightward shift in traditional Jewish political attitudes.[38] A few years later, two writers associated with the liberal-left political magazine *Dissent*, Irving Howe and Bernard

Rosenberg, seemed to agree. "That significant trends within American Jewish life bespeak a conservative turn seems indisputable," they declared. The impact on American Jews of Israel's need to act in its own best interests "is—perhaps must be—conservative."[39]

To what extent were writers like Lipset, Howe, and Rosenberg correct? Were Jews becoming more conservative in the 1970s, were they abandoning the Democratic Party, and did their attitudes toward Israel have something to do with this? Statistics from the 1972 presidential election reveal that the growing neoconservative trend among certain Jewish intellectuals seemed in fact to reflect a wider change in Jewish political attitudes. There was a significant Jewish shift away from liberals and the Democratic Party and toward the Republican Party in the four years since 1968, when the New Left was at its height. Nixon received 35 percent of the Jewish vote in 1972, nearly triple the amount he got in 1968. Observers were quick to note that some of this Jewish support for Nixon was not the result of their feelings toward Israel but rather reflected racial tensions: Nixon secured a particularly high level of Jewish support in cities and neighborhoods that had witnessed significant black-white racial tensions in the years after 1968. These included Cleveland, where 48 percent of Jews supported Nixon, and Canarsie in Brooklyn, New York, where he received 54 percent of the Jewish vote. Yet others noted that Jews associated Democratic candidate George McGovern with the New Left and its anti-Israel stance, and felt conversely that Nixon had proven himself to be a trustworthy ally of Israel since becoming president in 1969.[40]

The conservative slide continued: in the 1976 presidential elections, Gerald R. Ford captured 27 percent of the Jewish vote, and Ronald Reagan received 39 percent of the Jewish vote in 1980—the highest percentage of Jews voting Republican since 1956, and the second highest in any election since 1920.[41] Podhoretz believed that pro-Israel sentiment motivated the rightward movement of Jewish voters who agreed with Reagan on the need to revive American power vis-à-vis the Soviet Union.

Beyond elections, the rightward drift among some American Jews was also seen in the pages of *Commentary* magazine, one of the leading venues in which the early neocons wrestled with the issues raised by left-wing attacks on Israel and Zionism in the 1970s. Established by the American Jewish Committee in 1945, and already an established journal of Jewish opinion by the 1960s, *Commentary*'s pages were home to the various currents sweeping through the intellectual side of American Jewish life.[42] Various writers in

*Commentary* expressed their disdain toward the Left for what they perceived as its anti-intellectualism, anti-Americanism, and boorishness. *Commentary* became the neoconservative Bible, and featured a number of authors who wrote in defense of Israel such as Gershman, Glazer, Decter, and Peretz.

Peretz was one of the most famous examples of a left-wing Jew whose faith in the Left was shattered by its hostility toward Israel. In "The American Left and Israel," an article in the November 1967 issue of *Commentary,* he blasted the Left's "new heights of righteous arrogance and absurdity" in denouncing Israel after the 1967 war, notably at the National Conference for New Politics, which he himself had helped put together in Chicago. Peretz's piece also laid out what came to be some of the central themes of neoconservatism, particularly as it related to Israel. He railed that "what became increasingly clear was that many of the Left had swallowed an ill-digested, even a thoughtless, pacifism" and that the "Left is still reluctant to face up to Russian mischief in the world." Peretz insisted that "internal democracy is as secure there [in Israel] now as ever before in the country's history" and dourly predicted further defections from the Left, saying, "it is not likely that the Left will soon recover from the malaise of lost confidence which, exemplified by bitter acrimony or nervous silence, now afflicts it."[43] He was so angry with an editorial about the Arab-Israeli conflict in the July 1967 issue of the left-wing magazine *Ramparts*, of which he was a major shareholder, that he sold his shares in disgust.[44]

The most prolific of all the neocons writing on Israel's behalf in *Commentary* was Podhoretz, the magazine's legendary editor. With the greater focus on Israel and Zionism that characterized American Jewry after 1967, Podhoretz featured more and more articles on Israel. He bitterly excoriated its detractors for what he felt were their double standards, and his spirited defense of Israel is a testament to the centrality of Israel in the neoconservative imagination by the late 1970s. Nor did Podhoretz merely restrict himself to literary warfare on behalf of Israel. When the US representative on the UN's Human Rights Commission, Leonard Garment, needed talking points for trying to stop the UN from adopting its resolution equating Zionism with racism, Podhoretz wrote a statement for Garment, which the latter delivered to the UN on October 17, 1975, castigating the resolution as, inter alia, "a supreme act of deceit . . . a massive attack on the moral realities of the world."[45] Podhoretz also wrote much of the speech delivered on the same subject by the US ambassador to the UN Daniel Patrick Moynihan, in which he denounced the world body for eventually adopting the resolution.[46]

The legacy of SDUSA's pro-Israeli pushback and rise of the neoconservatives in the 1970s was significant, and revealed the continued weakening of the Left because of the Arab-Israeli conflict. The neocons' central focus on Israel was part and parcel of their promotion of American military and moral power in the world, and in their steely determination to deter the Soviet Union and other global tyrants by promoting capitalist democracy, they proved enormously influential in American politics beginning from the 1970s on. Of all the issues about which they cared, it was the neocons' virtual obsession with Israel and how the world, including other Americans, treated it that animated many of their leading thinkers. Nevertheless, in the 1970s, Americans who were not part of the 1960s Left continued to question Israel's policies and express concern about the Palestinians. The new thinking about the Arab-Israeli conflict first expressed in the 1960s was moving into the 1970s mainstream.

# 11  Taking Root

*The New Thinking Goes Mainstream*

CONCERN ABOUT THE plight of the Palestinians and willingness to
challenge Israel was moving out of the Left and into spaces in wider mainstream, liberal society in the 1970s. Just under a year after the last American
troops left Vietnam, the pacifists of the War Resisters League (WRL), the oldest secular pacifist organization in the United States, dating from 1923, issued
a formal policy statement on the Arab-Israeli conflict. For some in the peace
movement who long had been concerned about armed conflict in the Middle
East, it was about time.

The WRL's March 1974 statement on the Arab-Israeli conflict was bold.
"We actively oppose any US shipment of arms to any nation, anywhere,
including the Middle East," they declared. Nonetheless, regardless of how it
had come into being, Israel now existed as a state and had to be recognized
by the Arab world. At the same time, a Palestinian state must be created, and
Israel should compensate Palestinian refugees for their property and allow
some of them to return home. Israel should withdraw to the 1967 borders and
stop settlement building in the Arab territories occupied in 1967; Jerusalem
should be subject to internationalization or shared sovereignty; and the UN
should establish a civilian presence in a buffer zone between Israeli and Arab
forces. The pacifists even called for international volunteers who would be
willing to participate in this unarmed presence.[1]

The socialist David McReynolds, a noted protester against the Vietnam
War, played an important role in moving the WRL toward taking a stand on

the Arab-Israeli conflict. McReynolds had been a "peace movement bureau-crat" for decades. He began working on the staff of the pacifist-oriented pub-lication *Liberation* in 1957 and on the WRL's staff in 1960. His was a well-respected voice among peace activists.

On June 29, 1967, the *Village Voice* published an article by McReynolds that laid out some of his thinking. "The goal of the Israeli hawks is 'com-plete military security' for the state of Israel, proving Israeli hawks fully as mad as our own," he wrote. McReynolds contended, too, that there was some truth to the charge that Israel was a tool of Western imperialist interests in the Middle East.[2] Yet he was conflicted about what pacifists' proper stance toward the recent war should be. He believed strongly in nonviolence, but felt that Israel had been in an extremely difficult position in May and June of 1967. He expressed his personal distress in trying to come to a pacifist stance on the war in an astonishingly honest admission to *Village Voice* editor Dan Wolf in late June 1967: "There are a lot of problems involved which leave me not only uneasy but completely baffled. How, for example, can Israel survive—given the tensions that exist—without force of arms. That is, how valid, really, is the pacifist case in that situation? On the other hand, since Israel is, or should be, thinking of the 'long run,' how valid is a military approach 'in the long run.'"[3] In another letter that month, he wrote that pacifists should not try to cham-pion one side or the other, but seek to bridge tension-filled gaps.[4]

McReynolds's personal feelings aside, it would not be until the 1970s that the WRL as an organization finally issued a major public statement on the Middle East. Several things in the intervening years helped spur the WRL to action. The first was Black September in Jordan in 1970, when many feared US military intervention in support of the Jordanian army. Another was the October 1973 war fought by Israel against both Egypt and Syria, which nearly brought the United States and the Soviet Union to blows. That war also prompted more direct peace-making by the Nixon administration on the basis of the land-for-peace formula. Speaking publicly about a peaceful solu-tion to the Arab-Israeli conflict that involved Israeli concessions was no lon-ger novel and beyond the pale of acceptable thought by the 1970s.[5]

On January 16, 1974, a meeting of the WRL's executive committee dis-cussed the idea of issuing a formal statement on the conflict. Committee members noted that the WRL had paid insufficient attention to the Pales-tinian problem in the past, and decided to create a special subcommittee to craft a Middle East policy statement. In February, the subcommittee held an extended, five-hour meeting to parse the wording of the statement.[6] An expanded meeting of the WRL executive committee that met on March 2–3, 1974, then adopted the "Statement on the Middle East."[7]

The WRL's "Statement on the Middle East," which was printed and distributed widely, asserted: "We are partisans of neither side . . . " However, it was clear that the WRL believed that the United States and Israel were ultimately responsible for the ongoing conflict: "We must face with frankness that within the United States the greatest barrier to open discussion has come from the organized forces of Zionism which have sought to equate any criticism of Israeli policy with anti-Semitism." The statement described the first Arab-Israeli war of 1948 as a reaction by the Arabs to what they understood as "an invasion of historically Arab territory."[8]

The statement was timely, because the Palestinian issue erupted on the international scene with renewed force in 1974. The Arab League recognized the PLO as the "sole legitimate representative of the Palestinian people" at its summit meeting in Rabat, Morocco, in October 1974. That same month, the UN General Assembly invited Yasir Arafat to address it, which he did on November 13, 1974. Allan Solomonow, a member of the WRL's executive committee, suggested when it met on December 4, 1974, that the Middle East subcommittee that had drawn up the "Statement on the Middle East" should develop ideas for further WRL action on the issue.

Solomonow was a man deeply committed to bringing about Middle Eastern peace. As a youth, he had been active in Aleph Zadik Aleph, a fraternal organization for Jewish young people associated with B'nai B'rith, and he was later involved with the Jewish Peace Fellowship. At the February 15–16, 1975, meeting of the WRL executive committee, Solomonow suggested that two additional points be added to the 1974 statement: first, that the WRL supported any peace arrangement that considered the "rights and aspirations of both Israelis and Palestinians," whether that be in the form of a two-state solution, a one-state solution, or whatever, and that the PLO somehow be included in any future negotiations. The executive committee agreed.[9]

The WRL was actually not the first pacifist group to tackle the question of peace in the Middle East. The American Friends Service Committee (AFSC), a Quaker pacifist organization, had begun investigating the Arab-Israeli conflict a few years earlier in 1968, and issued a report on peace in the Middle East in May 1970. In September and October of that year, AFSC joined with the Fellowship of Reconciliation (FOR), another religious pacifist organization, to sponsor a tour of the United States by Uri Avnery, an Israeli peace activist and member of the Israeli Knesset. The two peace groups arranged for Avnery to speak at thirty American college campuses, including those of Harvard, Yale, and Princeton, under the auspices of the rabbis who headed the local Hillel Jewish student organizations on each campus. The specific purpose of the tour was to reach out to the Jewish community and present it with the kind of alternative views on the Arab-Israeli conflict for which Avnery was famous, even though FOR admitted that Avnery was not a pacifist, and that hosting him as such was an unusual step for the group to take.[10]

When Avnery arrived in the United States, however, he was met at the airport by a tour organizer who informed him of some startling news: twenty-nine of the thirty Hillel rabbis had decided not to host Avnery after all. The one rabbi who still agreed to host him, Balfour Brickner, later told Avnery what had happened: the national office of the Anti-Defamation League (ADL) had sent around a memorandum to its regional offices urging them to take steps to prevent Avnery from speaking in their areas. The reason? According to the memorandum, dated September 18, 1970 and written by the ADL's Abraham H. Foxman, Avnery was "an opponent of the traditional concepts of Zionism and Judaism" who might "say things which will trouble and even embarrass the Jewish community." Foxman instructed regional ADL offices to recommend that local Jewish groups not sponsor or co-sponsor Avnery's appearances, publicly debate him, or even have any contact with him.[11] Nevertheless, Avnery managed to speak at over twenty colleges and universities during his month touring in the United States and to make appearances at community forums and media events.

Clearly, not everyone in the peace movement was yet open to challenging Israel in the early 1970s. FOR was involved in another controversy just two months later, when it tried to co-sponsor a tour by the Israeli pacifist Uri Davis, who was well known in Israel for his activism on behalf of peace and Palestinian rights. FOR agreed to sponsor his visit along with the Jewish Peace Fellowship (JPF), a pacifist organization with which it was affiliated. However, the JPF eventually balked at co-sponsoring Davis's visit because several members of its board felt that the tour would be too divisive for the Jewish community. Rabbi Everett Gendler, a JPF executive committee member, worked with the FOR to make the Davis tour a reality, however.[12]

## Daniel in the Lions' Den

Daniel Berrigan, a Roman Catholic Jesuit priest who had been prominent in the 1960s anti–Vietnam War movement, laid into Israel at the sixth annual convention of the Association of Arab-American University Graduates in Washington, DC, on October 19, 1973, in a speech on "Responses to Settler Regimes." Berrigan began by telling his audience: "I do not wish to begin by 'taking sides.' . . . If I seem to concentrate upon the conduct of Israel, it is for reasons which to me at least, are profound, of long pondering and finally inescapable." He then laid out those reasons:

> It is not merely because my government, which has brought endless suffering to the world, is supporting Israel. It is not merely because American Jews, as well as Israelis, have in the main given their acquiescence or their support to the Nixon ethos. The reasons go deeper, and strike harder; they are lodged in my soul, in my conception of faith and the transcendent, in the vision Jews have taught me, of human conduct in a human community. . . . I am paying an old debt tonight. It is a debt of love; more properly, a debt of outraged love.

Berrigan accused Israel, a nation of refugees, of creating "huge numbers of refugees" itself, and denounced Israeli militarism and its impact on the Palestinians in stark language: "The Jews arose from the holocaust, a cause of universal joy; but the Jews arose like warriors, armed to the teeth. They took possession of a land, they exiled and destroyed old Arab communities, they (a minority) made outsiders of those who were in fact, the majority of citizens. . . . Israel entered the imperial adventure. She took up the imperial weapons, she spread abroad the imperial deceptions." In his anger, he spoke of "blood myths of divine election," calling Israel "an imperial entity" and "an Orwellian nightmare of double talk [and] racism . . . aimed at proving its racial superiority to the people it has crushed."[13]

When Berrigan entered into the foray over the Arab-Israeli conflict so publicly, some of his erstwhile supporters in the antiwar movement were stunned. The 1973 Arab-Israeli war was winding down when Berrigan gave his speech on "Responses to Settler Regimes." As if he had a premonition of the furor his speech would arouse, he told the audience, "It is of course scarcely possible to open the moral question of Israeli or Arab conduct today, without exciting the most lively passion, and risking the most serious charges." Berrigan began with a harsh attack on the Arab states, then denounced Israeli militarism. He did not spare American Jews, either, expressing deep, even bitter, disappointment in their leaders, who, in his view, had supported Nixon and turned their backs on the antiwar movement in the name of supporting Israel.[14]

Nearly two months passed after Berrigan's speech with little public response. After a bulletin called *Mid-East Probe* eventually reported what he had said, however, Berrigan was transformed from saint to sinner, particularly in the eyes of pro-Israeli supporters of the 1960s antiwar movement. Arthur Hertzberg, president of the American Jewish Congress, accused Berrigan of anti-Semitism in no uncertain terms.[15] Marc Tanenbaum of the American Jewish Committee opined that Berrigan's comments stemmed from his ignorance about Israel. Balfour Brickner of the Union of American Hebrew Congregations also addressed the issue, not just as a Jew and a rabbi, but as a former activist in the Movement, saying: "If once we were allies in the antiwar movement, the continuance of that alliance cannot be assumed, particularly if the glasses used to examine the Middle East are clouded over by inapplicable 'third world' preconceptions, impossibly pacifist postures or unreal universalistic aspirations."[16]

Some quickly leapt to Berrigan's defense. Noam Chomsky noted that Berrigan in fact had strongly criticized both sides in the Arab-Israeli conflict, yet the deafening silence that greeted his attacks on the Arab states was matched only by the vitriol that attended his remarks about Israel. Berrigan's comments were "a model of historical accuracy and balanced judgment as compared with those of many of his detractors," Chomsky said.[17] The veteran peace activist David Dellinger agreed, saying that the sharp nature of Berrigan's comments was a reaction against those ("of us," he noted) who have not broken the "taboo against publicly applying to Israel and Zionism the same standards which we have applied to other countries, and institutions."[18]

Paul Rogat Loeb, a youthful member of the collective that published the pacifist-oriented publication *Liberation*, also weighed in, arguing that the attacks levied on Berrigan by his (Loeb's) fellow Jews essentially stemmed from something else. Berrigan had exposed "this tension between real life and mythic projection which prevents Israel from being rationally and critically dealt with by American Jews." This mythic projection onto Israel embodied the experiences, hopes, and fears felt by Jews in the United States. It was "a projection point for needs denied by American society."[19]

The furor widened when a group called Promoting Enduring Peace, which earlier had intended to bestow its Gandhi Peace Award on Berrigan at an event to be held at the Community Church in New York City on January 9, 1974, started to reconsider its decision. The church's minister, Reverend Donald S. Harrington, demanded that he be able to make a statement disassociating himself from Berrigan as the price for going ahead with the award ceremony at his church. Moreover, the American Jewish Congress and others began complaining about the award. Promoting Enduring Peace then decided to poll its leadership about whether or not to go forward with giving the award to the embattled priest. Berrigan stepped in to end the matter by announcing in late December 1973 that he declined the award in order to avoid becoming a "bystander in a degrading consensus game."[20] The WRL came to Berrigan's rescue. At its January 16, 1974, meeting, its executive committee decided to present its annual Peace Award to Berrigan instead of to Dellinger, as originally planned; it gave the award to Berrigan on March 15, 1974.

## CONAME

In a "Dear Peace People" letter he wrote to introduce the Committee on New Alternatives in the Middle East (CONAME)—the first American peace group focused solely on resolution of the Arab-Israeli conflict—to mainstream peace groups, Allan Solomonow referred to the major difficulty peace activists had in discussing the Arab-Israeli conflict. "Raising the question of 'the Middle East' at peace meetings," Solomonow wrote, "seems to lead to a most disconcerting silence. Some of us would like to change all of that." Our commitment as peace activists, he said, "does not end where the Middle East begins."[21]

CONAME's origins went back the interest shown in the Israeli-Arab conflict by the Socialist Workers Party. In 1969, the SWP decided to sponsor a tour of the United States by an anti-Zionist Israeli and assigned the task of arranging this to two party members, Berta and Bob Langston. The Langstons spent ten days in Israel in the summer of 1969 meeting members of the anti-Zionist Israeli socialist organization called Matzpen (Compass). After their return, they began working with Emmanuel Dror Farjoun, a young doctoral student at the Massachusetts Institute of Technology (MIT) who had joined Matzpen while at The Hebrew University of Jerusalem, to arrange for someone from Matzpen to tour the United States. At Farjoun's suggestion, the Langstons decided to invite Arieh Bober, a leading Matzpen member.[22] Bober gave his first speech in Philadelphia in early March 1970,[23] and CONAME was born.

Berta Langston was the moving spirit behind the formation of CONAME, becoming its secretary and also seeking to broaden the group's agenda beyond just sponsoring the Bober tour. Through Farjoun, they approached Noam Chomsky for assistance. Chomsky agreed to become involved and wrote to some of his associates asking them to become sponsors of the new group. The letter stated that CONAME was not going to take an official stance on the Middle East conflict, but rather would seek to stimulate discussion and "introduce left-wing voices that are rarely heard in the United States." Soon the sponsors included writers, academics, lawyers, singers, and peace activists such as Eric Fromm, William Kunstler, Sidney Lens, Staughton Lynd, Igal Roodenko, Robert Scheer, Pete Seeger, I. F. Stone, and Howard Zinn.

Almost immediately, however, trouble emerged in the new peace group that led to a rupture and the Langstons' departure. It had to do with whether or not CONAME was going to be purely an educational group or an activist one. Minus the Langstons, CONAME rebounded and introduced itself to antiwar groups as a fellow organization, not an advocacy group. Solomonow took the lead in reaching out to the peace community. CONAME representatives met with almost all the major peace organizations—a total of ten groups—during the second week of January 1971 to explain CONAME and its vision to them. Four of the groups contacted committed to becoming a "cooperating" organizations and to donate to CONAME.

Wishing to focus exclusively on peace groups, CONAME decided not to seek the participation of Jewish, Arab, or civil rights organizations.[24] It stressed that it sought "reconciliation, peace and justice in the Middle East," not by passing moral judgments or taking partisan stands on the Arab-Israeli conflict, but rather by encouraging open discussion in which a variety of different narratives—particularly ones not widely disseminated in the United States—could be expressed. "In our country an uneasy silence has confronted the call for earnest dialogue on peace in the Middle East," one CONAME pamphlet asserted. "It is time to shatter that silence."[25] CONAME sought to have peace groups apply the same concern for peace they displayed elsewhere in the world, notably Southeast Asia, to the Middle East as well. Financial and administrative troubles soon led to CONAME's demise, however. In April 1976, Solomonow formally announced that CONAME was merging with FOR, and he began a new endeavor within FOR called the Middle East Peace Project. Thus ended the short life of the first group within the peace movement to deal specifically with the Middle East.[26]

CONAME had lasted less than five years, but its legacy was longer lasting. Seeking Arab-Israeli peace, calling for a Palestinian state, and even holding Israel and the United States accountable for the lion's share of the problems facing a peaceful resolution of the conflict were becoming mainstream ideas by the mid-1970s, in part thanks to the efforts of groups like the WRL and CONAME. What would have been unthinkable just ten years earlier was now clearly on the radar screen of liberal and left-wing peace activists. The earlier hesitancy of anti–Vietnam War groups to embrace the cause of Middle East peace during the era when the Vietnam War still raged, with its concomitant need to keep large antiwar coalitions intact, had seemingly been replaced with a new awareness of the Arab-Israeli conflict by the mid-1970s.

## The Discourse of Human Rights

When Jimmy Carter assumed the presidency in January 1977, speaking of American support for global human rights, media coverage of the issue accordingly skyrocketed. Whereas the New York Times ran 221 stories on human rights, political prisoners, torture, and related issues in 1976, this figure jumped to 536 stories in 1977. Coverage also went up in the Washington Post from 160 stories in 1976 to 540 in 1977.[27] Carter also became the first president to mention the Palestinians by name in the context of legitimate rights. By that time Israel's occupation of the West Bank and Gaza was entering its second decade, and its military rule over more than one million Palestinians was beginning to be a new game changer in the way that the 1967 war had been. The sight of Israel, which many Americans considered the "only democracy in the Middle East," using its armed forces to maintain martial law over a civilian population was becoming the cause for unease among supporters of Israel and others. A 1977 poll revealed that only 13 percent of Americans approved of a country abusing human rights even where there was terrorist activity, compared to 54 percent who felt that there were no conditions that justified curtailing human rights.[28] The time therefore seemed right for supporters of the Palestinians in the United States to begin reaching out to Americans concerned about human rights.

There were other reasons why talk of the Palestinians and their rights was in the air in the late 1970s. Arab Americans had been organizing to enlist public support for the Palestinian cause since 1967. Arab students had long been involved in campus actions and coalition building with American youth, notably African Americans.[29] Some of their elders decided to take the struggle to the broader American public. In mid-August 1967, several Arab academics met at the Ann Arbor, Michigan, home of Rashid Bashshur, a Syrian-born professor teaching at the University of Michigan. The Lebanese American lawyer and activist Abdeen M. Jabara attended as well. The men discussed forming an organization of Arab and Arab American scholars and professionals that would combat Zionist "distortions and misinformation" in the wake of the 1967 war, provide a model of pan-Arabism, improve US-Arab relations, and reduce the feeling of isolation and hostility felt by Arabs and Arab Americans. The group they envisioned would not be a lobby or campus group, but would use the collective talents and prestige of its members as university graduates and professors to accomplish its goals through the dissemination of information. With that, the Association of Arab-American University Graduates (AAUG) was born.[30]

Formally founded in October 1967, AAUG's founding idea was that "if Americans only knew" about what really was happening in the Middle East, they could affect foreign policy decisions for the better. Years later, Jabara summed up this raison d'être as follows: "There was a resolve among this small group that Americans were basically fair minded people, who, if they only knew the true facts about what had happened to the Palestinians, would not support Israel's continuing displacement and occupation of Palestinians and aggression against the Arab countries."[31] Fauzi Najjar became AAUG's first president, with Jabara as the group's first executive secretary. Another early leader in AAUG was Ibrahim Abu-Lughod. Born in Palestine, Abu-Lughod became a refugee in 1948 and ended up in the United States, where he taught political science at Northwestern University. It was Abu-Lughod who in turn invited Columbia University's Edward Said, a young academic who later became one of the most articulate Palestinian voices in the United States, to join the new group. AAUG maintained an ambitious publishing agenda, including the scholarly journal *Arab Studies Quarterly,* starting in 1978. Its annual conferences became major public events.

The 1970s also witnessed the creation of Palestinian groups in the United States as opposed to pan-Arab associations like AAUG. At AAUG's annual convention in New York in 1976, some members began discussing formation of a uniquely Palestinian organization that could bring together Palestinians from different groups and factions. Conversations continued, culminating in an All-Palestine Congress in New York in December 1978 that decided to form a new group, and elections were held around the country in July 1979 for the first meeting of what came to be called the Palestine Congress of North America in Washington, DC, in August 17–19, 1979. Notable leaders in the congress included Naseer Aruri, Samih Farsoun, and Jawad George.[32]

In this atmosphere of greater public discussion of the plight of the Palestinians in the late 1970s, the National Lawyers Guild (NLG) became the first liberal-left American organization to focus attention specifically on Israeli human rights abuses. No one was more responsible for this than Jabara, a law clerk of the Detroit lawyer Ernest Goodman, who helped found the NLG and served as its president during the 1960s. Jabara eventually became the secretary of the NLG chapter in Detroit, and in addition to his interest in constitutional freedoms and civil liberties, he produced some of the first writings calling attention to the American Left's position on the Arab-Israeli conflict.[33]

Jabara tried to submit a resolution dealing with Israeli treatment of Palestinians in the Occupied Territories at the NLG's 1969 convention in Washington, DC. He did not get far. Members of the NLG's resolutions committee told him that they did not know enough about the issue to put it to a vote. They recommended instead that Jabara write an article for the NLG publication *Guild Practitioner* to educate the membership, and he published "Israel and Human Rights" in that the journal the following year.[34] However, it was not until four years later, after the renewed fighting of the 1973 Arab-Israeli war, that the NLG finally acted on the issue. Its convention in Minneapolis in August 1974 created a Middle Eastern subcommittee headed by Jabara and Richard A. Soble. The NLG national executive board then decided in San Francisco in February 1975 that the entire membership needed to engage in formal study of the Arab-Israeli conflict.[35]

As part of the study, the NLG sent a ten-person delegation to the Middle East in July 11–28, 1977, which visited Lebanon, Jordan, and both Israel and the Occupied Territories.[36] The team interviewed people from a variety of backgrounds, including PLO officials in Beirut. For their part, Israeli authorities strip-searched and questioned Jabara and three other delegation members (all of them Jewish). The group had just returned to the United States when the NLG held its convention in Seattle in August 1977. The delegation offered up two resolutions, one calling for recognition of the PLO as the sole legitimate representative of the Palestinian people and a political solution to the conflict based on mutual recognition, and the other criticizing Israeli violations of Palestinian human rights. Both generated considerable acrimonious debate. Eventually, a compromise was reached whereby one resolution was adopted, recognizing the PLO and calling on it to commit itself to a political solution to the conflict based on mutual recognition. The more contentious question of condemning Israel for human rights abuses in the Occupied Territories was shelved for the time being.[37]

The Middle East delegation worked to write up its formal report on the trip, and in February 1978, the NLG national executive board finally took up the human rights question. Guild members from the New York City chapter were particularly upset with the language developed for the national executive board's resolution by the delegation members. They were concerned about the NLG maintaining its good relationship with progressive Jewish organizations and took issue with the delegation's wording to the effect that Israel was guilty of systematic use of torture in the Occupied Territories.[38] Discord continued when the draft report on the Middle East trip was made public that May. Morton Stavis, one of the founders of the NLG and the Center for Constitutional Rights, wrote publicly that he and like-minded NLG members would "continue to resist turning the Guild into a propaganda organ for those who would destroy that State [Israel]."[39] Harvard law school's Alan Dershowitz similarly blasted the NLG for what he considered its turning into a propaganda agent for the PLO.[40]

At the end of 1978, the NLG published a final report, *Treatment of Palestinians in Israeli-Occupied West Bank and Gaza: Report of the National Lawyers Guild 1977 Middle East Delegation,* which supplied numerous details about Israeli human rights abuses in the Occupied Territories. The report also stated that the authors recognized the PLO as the sole legitimate representatives of the Palestinian people and supported UN General Assembly Resolution 194 calling, inter alia, for the return of Palestinian refugees to their homes. "The guild's report had a major impact on left groups in the country," Jabara later recalled. "It was a marker for the Left."[41] Even then, the controversy within the NLG continued, literally up to the day the report was issued. On November 28, 1978, Jabara and several others held a press conference at the National Press Club in Washington to discuss the NLG trip and report. NLG President Henry diSuvero issued a statement to coincide with the release of the report, calling it "a significant breakthrough in the curtain of silence which has been draped on the American legal community by . . . powerful Zionist forces."[42]

Jabara and his colleagues discovered, however, that the American Jewish Congress had learned about the contents of their report and decided to hold its own press conference that very day down the hall of the very same building, at which the NLG's Howard L. Dickstein, a thirty-four-year-old lawyer who had traveled with the NLG delegation, and who disagreed strongly with its conclusions, issued his own seventeen-page "minority report" in opposition to the NLG report.[43] According to Jabara, Dickstein had shown the delegation's draft report to representatives of the Israeli government, who then wrote a detailed rebuttal.[44] Dickstein not only criticized the findings of the majority report, he also included a section denouncing the political stances he found implicit in it. The majority report was "distorted, inaccurate and designed to bring about the liquidation of the Jewish state," Dickstein said.[45]

Lawyers like Jabara opened up a new front in the war for the hearts and minds of the American public. They helped shift the discourse about the Palestinians among liberals and leftists away from an exclusive focus on the PLO and the politics of the Arab-Israeli conflict and toward the growing interest in global human rights, playing a key role in moving the focus of pro-Palestinian activism in a direction that not only fitted in well with the post-1960s era, but that liberal-minded Americans outside the Left could embrace.

In this spirit Jabara also co-founded a group to focus specifically on Palestinian human rights, the Palestine Human Rights Campaign (PHRC). What was also important about PHRC was that while other Palestine support groups in the 1970s like the Palestine Solidarity Committee were either overtly left-wing or were groups formed by Palestinian exiles for their own political purposes, PHRC tried instead to appeal to religious organizations, peace groups, human rights advocates, and other more mainstream Americans. Its early slogan was "Palestinians Have Human Rights Too."

Formed in mid-1977 by Jabara and his fellow Lebanese American James J. Zogby, PHRC began issuing the *Palestine Human Rights Bulletin* in July of that year and held its first major meeting, titled "Palestinian Human Rights and Peace," in Washington, DC, in May 20–21, 1978, which drew over two hundred attendees from twenty-one different states. Within three months of the conference, PHRC had established twelve chapters. It also opened an office in Washington, with Zogby as its first national director.[46] PHRC early on tried to reach out to include a diverse American constituency by forming coalitions with a wide variety of organizations. By 1980, it had formed the Middle East Peace Action Coalition, an interracial coalition made up of the Southern Christian Leadership Conference, Operation PUSH, the La Raza Unida Party, the National Association of Arab Americans, the Methodist Federation for Social Action, the New American Movement, and the Black United Front. "The continuing Middle East conflict is a costly one for the people of the U.S.," the coalition stated. "The continuing Middle East conflict is a dangerous one for the people of the U.S. The continuing Middle East conflict is economically and politically harmful to the people of the U.S."[47]

Zogby soon left PHRC to help establish the American-Arab Anti-Discrimination Committee in Washington in 1980. Replacing him as head of PHRC was Donald E. Wagner, an energetic Presbyterian minister living in Evanston, Illinois, who set up a new national headquarters for PHRC in Chicago, which already had an active chapter. Wagner was a leader of the second generation of pro-Palestinian activists in the United States, who emerged in the 1970s. His first pastoral position was on the west side of the blighted city of Newark, New Jersey, a city hard hit by the violent black rebellion of July 1967. It was the beginning of a change for Wagner, for whom the anti–Vietnam War and Black Power movements began what was to be a lifelong commitment to peace and justice.

PHRC worked hard in the early 1980s under Wagner's leadership. It had established twenty chapters around the country by 1982, and its national office created the Palestine Education Project earlier in September 1981 under the PHRC's educational director, David L. Williams. One of the project's ideas was to offer adult education classes at night in the Chicago area in conjunction with the local Chicago chapter of PHRC. In its first season, nine presentations on the history of the Arab-Israeli conflict were made at Lincoln Park Presbyterian Church in Chicago from September 1981 to July 1982. The project also regularly sent speakers around the country to address various Middle East–oriented events, particularly Arab student presentations held at universities like the University of Iowa, Marquette University, Louisiana State University, Northern Illinois University, and the State University of New York at Buffalo.[48]

Showing people the realities of the Arab-Israeli conflict firsthand was another priority, and Wagner himself led three different delegations to the Middle East in the year 1982 alone. He was in fact in Beirut when the Israeli invasion started that June. He and his tour group managed to fly out of Lebanon on the last two flights that left Beirut International Airport before it closed in the face of the Israeli assault, but Wagner slipped back into Beirut that September at the time of the Sabra and Shatila massacre and was witness to its gruesome aftermath.[49]

PHRC counted Palestinians among its members in line with the trend, started by the Palestine Solidarity Committee in the mid-1970s, of including Arabs, Arab Americans, people of color, as well as Americans of other backgrounds in Palestine solidarity groups. Given the many universities in the Chicago area, PHRC worked closely with several notable scholars in its efforts, including the Palestinians Ibrahim Abu-Lughod and Ghada Hashem Talhami and the exiled South African poet and activist Dennis Brutus; Talhami in fact became PHRC's national chair. PHRC also maintained close relationships with students from the General Union of Palestine Students both in Chicago and in other cities.

As a clergyman, Wagner was particularly interested in making connections between PHRC and religious groups. This represented a new constituency of Americans supporting the Palestinians. Some Christian sects were already taking an interest in the Arab-Israeli conflict, notably pacifists like the Mennonites and Friends (Quakers). Wagner tried to widen the net by including Roman Catholics and mainstream Protestant denominations as well. Sometimes this was a hard sell inasmuch as many Protestants, notably evangelicals, tended to be solidly pro-Israeli and quite unsympathetic to the Palestinians, despite the fact that Palestinian Christians were descendants of the oldest Christian communities in the world.

As such Wagner was the driving force behind two national conferences convened early on by PHRC that were aimed at Christian audiences. The first was the La Grange Conference, held in the Chicago suburb of La Grange, Illinois, in May 18–20, 1979. A draft of the call for the conference laid out the mission of Wagner and the other organizers: "One of the major issues at the heart of this prolonged conflict is the question of the human rights of the Palestinian people—for too long they have been ignored. . . . We the undersigned acknowledge God's concern for all people and our accountability for all of our sisters and brothers whose rights are violated. To remove the distrust and fear of war and to create the conditions for peace are the goals to which we as a Christian people must dedicate ourselves."[50]

In May 7–9, 1981, Wagner organized the La Grange II Conference as a follow up in conjunction with Pax Christi, a Roman Catholic peace group, and the Sojourner's Community, a liberal evangelical Protestant group in Washington, DC. He also brought PHRC into collaboration with Christians in the Middle East by, among other things, forging links with the Middle East Council of Churches and helping to bring Palestinian religious leaders to speak in the United States. Among these was the Palestinian clergyman Elias Chacour, a Melkite (Greek) Catholic priest from the Galilee region of northern Israel.

PHRC continued its work into the 1980s. Americans were more and more concerned about the Middle East conflict. Polls in both 1978 and 1982 showed that they identified it as the biggest foreign policy problem facing the United States, more even than the Soviet Union or the nuclear arms race.[51] Surveys also revealed a marked increase in Americans sympathizing with the Arabs and the Palestinians in the years 1977–79, when such sympathy rose from about 10 percent of the population to close to 25 percent.[52] Activists continued, however, to grapple, sometimes intensely, with how to fit the Arab-Israeli conflict into their worldviews. This gave rise to ferocious conflict in the women's movement.

## 12   Identity Politics and Intersectionality

*Feminism and Zionism*

LETTY COTTIN POGREBIN pulled no punches. Writing in 1982 in the influential feminist magazine *Ms.*, which she and Gloria Steinem had co-founded in 1971, Pogrebin minced no words in her defense of Jewish identity, Zionism, and her belief that the women's movement suffered from the moral rot of anti-Semitism. Pogrebin grew up in a religious Jewish family with a strongly Zionist father whose Russian-born parents moved to Palestine after living in the United States. She became a writer and notable feminist figure whose voice resonated in the Movement. People therefore noticed when she published an article entitled "Anti-Semitism in the Women's Movement" in *Ms.* in June 1982, coincidentally the month that Israel invaded Lebanon in a drive to expel Palestine Liberation Organization (PLO) fighters there. "Anti-Semitism remains the hidden disease of the Movement," Pogrebin asserted. Jewish women were expected to "universalize themselves" and deny their own heritage, she claimed, "so that Palestinian women can have an identity." What, she demanded, was wrong with Jewish pride, with Israel, and with Zionism? Other women were celebrating their ethnic heritage. "*To me,*" Pogrebin wrote, "*Zionism is simply an affirmative action plan on a national scale.*"[1]

The reaction was swift and vociferous, perhaps because Israel's invasion had quickly turned into a lengthy siege and deadly bombardment of West Beirut that shocked the world. Women against Imperialism published a forceful statement in the feminist journal *off our backs* entitled "Taking Our Stand against Zionism and White Supremacy." After noting that many women in the group were themselves Jewish, the statement asserted that the members of Women against Imperialism were disturbed that the charge of anti-Semitism was being used to justify Zionism and the oppression of the Palestinians. "We think the women's movement must take a stand in solidarity with the Palestinian revolution and with the national liberation struggles of colonized third world peoples inside the United States," the writers stated. It was time, the statement continued, to realize that "Zionist 'Israel' was carved in blood from the homeland of the Palestinian people."[2]

Despite moving into the 1970s mainstream, American pro-Palestinian and anti-Zionist sentiments still generated controversy in the sociopolitical and intellectual spaces created by the 1960s Left. The women's movement offered a good example of this.

## Early Palestine Consciousness among Feminists

Feminist interest in the Middle East conflict can be seen early in the women's movement, when the anti-imperialist Left was still strong and American involvement in the Vietnam War still prompted anti-imperialist critiques.[3] Women's revolutionary solidarity with Third World women was manifested in two Indochinese Women's Conferences that were held in Vancouver and Toronto, Canada, in 1971, meetings that allowed American women to meet with female activists from North Vietnam, South Vietnam, and Laos.[4] Such activity was not restricted to concern for Southeast Asia. The year before, in October 1970, Sharon Rose and Cathy Tackney, two American women who had spent time with Palestinians in Lebanon and Jordan in the company of over a dozen other Americans (see chapter 3 above), wrote about their experiences in *off our backs,* providing a detailed and sympathetic discussion of the Palestinian national movement. Palestinian women were able up to a point to achieve social liberation and empowerment as a result of their active participation in the struggle, including in the role of armed combatants, Rose and Tackney believed.[5]

On June 10, 1973, the Women's Educational Center in Boston held a workshop entitled "Middle East: Women's Perspective" in Cambridge, Massachusetts, that featured films and speakers about the Middle East in general and the Arab-Israeli situation in particular. "We want to share with other women what we are learning about U.S. imperialism in the Middle East, the Palestinian resistance, and Middle Eastern women," a flyer advertising the event stated. The socialist feminist Women's School in Cambridge, Massachusetts, later offered a course on the Middle East in the summer of 1974.[6]

The Women's Middle East Committee to Support the Palestinians was yet another group from the early 1970s that was active on the issue. It issued a flyer in the midst of the October 1973 Arab-Israeli war entitled "Self-Determination for the Palestinian People. Solidarity with the Arab Masses." For the committee, "The real issue behind the continuing war in the Middle East is the role of U.S. imperialism and its efforts to liquidate the Palestinian people and to oppress the struggle of the revolutionary Arabs masses." It also denounced "settler colonialism in Israel."[7]

One reason why feminists in the early 1970s spoke out on the Arab-Israeli conflict is because women of color linked to the Black Power movement helped raise the profile of pro-Palestinian and other anti-imperialist politics. An important expression of this was the Third World Women's Alliance (TWWA). TWWA emerged as a women's caucus within the Student Nonviolent Coordinating Committee (SNCC) in 1968 and eventually changed its name to the Black Women's Liberation Committee. Joining with some Puerto Rican women, this New York City–based group of black women changed its name again to the TWWA in 1970–71. The activists within it were trying to address the racism and class nature of the mainstream women's movement, and turn it instead into a revolutionary, anti-capitalist force to confront the triple threat of racism, classism, and sexism.

One of the TWWA's main leaders was Frances M. Beal, born to a black father and a Jewish mother, who had worked with the National Association for the Advancement of Colored People in college before marrying and moving to France, where she was influenced by the Algerian struggle for independence. She met Malcolm X in Paris during one of his visits to Europe. Back in the United States, Beal worked with SNCC, co-founded SNCC's Black Women's Liberation Committee in 1968, and the following year wrote a seminal essay entitled "Black Women's Manifesto: Double Jeopardy: To be Black and Female."[8] She also signed "An Appeal by Black Americans against United States Support of the Zionist Government of Israel," an advertisement placed in the *New York Times* in November 1970 by the Committee of Black Americans for Truth about the Middle East.[9] The TWWA's Maxine Williams signed as well. So did the famous black feminist Florynce "Flo" Kennedy, a noted New York Civil Rights lawyer and member of the women's group called The Feminists, who also had been a sponsor of a June 21, 1967, conference on the

Arab-Israeli conflict held in the city by the Ad Hoc Committee on the Middle East.

Despite these examples, however, there was little discussion in the mid-1970s of Israel, the Palestinians, and the Arab-Israeli conflict in other parts of the women's movement. Some white feminists' view of what constituted "women's issues" did not extend very far beyond male chauvinism, reproductive rights, workplace equality, and battling against social attitudes that limited women's progress. Internationalist stances like anti-imperialism were not "women's issues" in their opinion. The end of the Vietnam War and the decline of the overall impact of the Left by the mid-1970s further weakened anti-imperialist voices among leading feminists.

## International Women's Conferences

The Arab-Israeli conflict nonetheless increasingly impinged on the women's movement starting in the mid-1970s, notably because of the pro-Palestinian attitudes and statements that emerged from two high-profile international conferences on women convened under the auspices of the UN, one in 1975 and the other in 1980. Some American feminists who attended the conferences were surprised and angered to see Third World women embrace Palestinian liberation as a woman's issue.[10]

The first of these meetings was the World Conference of the International Women's Year, held in Mexico City from June 19 through July 2, 1975. Some 7,000 people attended the conference and its associated activities, including 1,300 delegates from 133 nations, seven intergovernmental organizations, and twenty-one UN bodies and specialized agencies. Also included in the tally were delegates from 114 non-governmental organizations with consultative status in the UN Economic and Social Council, as well as eight liberation movements—including the PLO, flushed with its success in acquiring observer status in the UN General Assembly eight months earlier. The PLO's delegation in Mexico City included four women, among them Isam Abd al-Hadi and Jihan Helou. Abd al-Hadi was a veteran activist. She helped form the General Union of Palestinian Women (GUPW) in Jerusalem in July 1965. In 1974, she was appointed to the PLO's central committee, and she remained an important figure in the GUPW. Helou was the chair of the GUPW's external relations committee.

For many women in the developing world, the plight of the Palestinians was part and parcel of the wider structural forces that negatively affected their lives as women. The final "Declaration of Mexico on the Equality of Women and Their Contribution to Development and Peace, 1975" stated a number of things about women and the obstacles they faced,

> *Taking into account* the role played by women in the history of humanity, especially in the struggle for national liberation, the strengthening of international peace, and the elimination of imperialism, colonialism, neo-colonialism, foreign occupation, zionism *[sic]*, alien domination, racism and *apartheid*.

> *Recognizing* that women . . . will become natural allies in the struggle against any form of oppression, such as is practised under colonialism, neo-colonialism, zionism *[sic]*, racial discrimination and *apartheid*, thereby constituting an enormous revolutionary potential for economic and social change in the world today.[11]

While most delegations supported the resolutions criticizing Zionism, some members of the American delegation were aghast. Pogrebin was one. She felt that the conference should have been about dealing with "the monumental problems of female infanticide, illiteracy, high mortality rates, abject poverty, involuntary pregnancies, domestic violence, and so on." Instead, women's real agenda had been "hijacked on behalf of this unspeakable PLO slogan"—Zionism is racism.[12]

Congresswoman Bella Abzug, who served as a congressional advisor to the American delegation, also was angry. Abzug believed that Zionism was the national liberation movement of the Jewish people and deserved the same respect and support as other national liberation movements that were grabbing the headlines in the 1970s. She admitted Zionism had problems. "For Christ sake, it [Zionism] started out as a national liberation movement like every other national liberation movement but it kind of has gone—you know—bad," the noted feminist Robin Morgan recalled her once saying.[13] Nonetheless, Abzug strongly opposed the final declaration of the Mexico City conference. "The attack on Israel was not what we women came to Mexico for," she said. "The anti-Israeli bloc manipulated the women [at the conference], utilizing the women's conference for political purposes."[14]

Betty Friedan, whose 1963 book *The Feminine Mystique* was considered by many to be the opening shot in the women's movement of the 1960s, also came away from the Mexico City conference bitter about the attacks on Zionism. In 1966, Friedan had co-founded the National Organization for Women, the most nationally visible feminist organization to emerge from the women's movement in the 1960s and 1970s. Like her fellow Jewish feminists Progrebin and Abzug, she identified with many progressive causes—but not with the anti-Zionist wave of the 1960s. Friedan was outraged when many conference delegations staged a walkout when Leah Rabin, the wife of Israeli Prime Minister Yitzhak Rabin, rose to speak at the podium of the plenary session. Friedan proceeded to walk the length of the hall to shake Rabin's hand in solidarity with the embattled Israeli and later commented that the anti-Zionism plank in the final declaration was not just wrong but "clearly anti-woman."[15] In her memoirs, she later wrote: "Why should 'Zionism is racism' be a major order of business for the women's movement? It had nothing to do with the women's movement one way or the other. We were resentful that the women's conference was being used for others' nefarious purposes."[16]

The July 14–30, 1980, World Conference of the United Nations Decade for Women: Equality, Development and Peace, and the associated Forum of Non-Governmental Organizations, held in Copenhagen, also brought the Arab-Israeli conflict to the attention of many American feminists. Delegations representing 145 countries and other groups were in attendance, including one from the PLO.[17] One delegate was the general secretary of the GUPW, May Sayigh. Jihan Helou, who had been part of the PLO delegation in Mexico City, was also at Copenhagen. This time the PLO also chose to include the PFLP airplane hijacker Leila Khaled, who was world famous in the late 1960s and early 1970s and infinitely better known than its other delegates. Khaled had literally become the poster girl for Third World guerrillas in the eyes of many American radicals, women included.

Recalling what had transpired in 1975, and knowing that the subject of Palestinian women already was on the conference agenda, the American delegation came prepared to do battle. The Americans had drawn up position papers and contingency papers in advance, mostly written by the Department of State, to deal with the anticipated debates about the Arab-Israeli conflict. Two Jewish women, Esther Landa and Sana Shtasel, served as advisors on the specific subject of Palestinian women, even though one of the US delegation's two congressional advisors was Representative Mary Rose Oakar, herself an Arab American who may have had something to contribute to the topic.[18]

The UN General Assembly's Resolution 34/160 of December 17, 1979, stipulated that the situation faced by Palestinian women as a result of Israeli policies in the Occupied Territories should be on the conference's agenda.

Accordingly, the discussions at Copenhagen tackled the question of the thirteen-year-old Israeli occupation of the West Bank and Gaza. Most delegations believed that it was impossible to separate the social and economic needs of Palestinian women from "the wider context of the struggle of the Palestinian people for self-determination." They "affirmed that a political settlement in the Middle East was a precondition of an improvement in the situation of Palestinian women and that such a settlement could only be achieved with the full realization of the rights of the Palestinian people under the leadership of the Palestine Liberation Organization."[19]

The PLO delegation agreed: it "was idle," a Palestinian delegate said, "to discuss the rights of Palestinian women while the entire Palestinian people was denied basic human rights," and "the struggle of Palestinian women for their own liberation was inextricably linked with the struggle for the liberation of their homeland." A PLO delegate also observed that "improvements in the status of Arab women in the occupied territories were not a substitute for self-determination." In the end, the conference adopted a statement entitled "Special Measures of Assistance to Palestinian Women inside and outside the Occupied Territories" that wound up being part of the final "Program of Action for the Second Half of the United Nations Decade for Women" adopted at Copenhagen.[20]

Once again there was much complaining among American women about what they claimed was the conference's "political" agendas to the detriment of "women's issues." Yet other women agreed with the Palestinian delegation's logic that fundamental political structures needed to be examined if one wanted to understand women's burdens in specific regions of the world. "Clearly, women's oppression cannot be abstracted from the politics, economics, and histories of the societies in which women live," Nilüfer Çağatay and Ursula Funk commented, adding that US participants in the 1980 conference "who ignored this fact. . . . set up a false dichotomy between 'women's issues' and 'politics,' failing to see that a concern for women's issues is itself political."[21]

### The Anti-Semitism Debate

One American attending the Copenhagen conference was Pogrebin, who felt the experience was even worse than Mexico City. She decided to investigate the phenomenon of anti-Israeli feeling among feminists as a result. In between the two conferences she had traveled to Israel twice, once in December 1976 and a second time in March 1978. In the two years after Copenhagen, she followed up with much thinking and sending out surveys to Jewish women. Eventually, she published the influential article "Anti-Semitism in the Women's Movement" in *Ms.* in June 1982, expressing her belief that anti-Zionist, pro-Palestinian sentiments at the two international conferences, as well as certain festering, divisive issues within the women's movement at home in the United States, really amounted to anti-Semitism. Pogrebin's argument mirrored that leveled by critics of the New Left back in the 1960s.

She was not alone. Other Jews in the women's movement were concerned as well. Some felt alienated by the strident Black Power and other nationalist rhetoric among black and Hispanic women in the Movement in the 1970s. Beyond the TWWO, notable black feminist groups had emerged, such as the National Black Feminist Organization and the Combahee River Collective. These Jewish women's alienation was deepened by the open embrace of the Palestinians by some of those espousing international solidarity with other women of color. They believed that elevating black, Hispanic, and Palestinian women but not embracing Jewish women who chose to celebrate their own ethnicity, or who supported Zionism as a Jewish liberation movement, amounted to anti-Semitism. Some therefore demanded inclusion in the politics of ethnic identity as well, a feeling that led to the National Jewish Women's Conference in early 1973 and the Jewish feminist magazine *Lilith*, founded by Susan Weidman Schneider and Aviva Cantor, in 1976. Arlene Raven, who helped found the feminist journal *Chrysalis* and the Women's Building in Los Angeles, said: "I feel reborn as a Jew in the Women's Movement." For some, it worked the opposite way: it was because of the anti-Zionism they encountered in the Movement that they first came to embrace their own Jewishness. "By making Israel a macho imperialist stand-in for all the world's male supremacy, the Women's Movement threw me into the arms of Judaism," *Jewish Week*'s arts editor Elenore Lester wrote.[22]

"It's not cool to be a Zionist. It makes you a pariah in radical feminist circles," the entrepreneur Judy Dlugacz wrote, and the New York psychotherapist Phyllis Chesler observed, "I am saddened and angered by feminists who would never call a [lesbian] separatist coffeehouse or women's center sexist, but who are quick to call the [Israeli] Law of Return racist." Some went on the offensive to affirm, as Abzug had done, that in an era when radical feminists were supporting national liberation movements around the world, Zionism was the national liberation movement of the Jewish people. "In the world I'm working for, nation states will not exist. But in the world I live in, I want there to be an Israel," Andrea Dworkin agreed.[23]

According to other Jewish feminists, however, all this talk of Jewish identity and anti-Semitism had a chilling effect on criticism of Israel in the women's movement. Laura Whitehorn was a Jewish feminist with a long political history in left-wing groups like Students for a Democratic Society, the Weather Underground Organization, the Prairie Fire Organizing Committee, and the May 19th Communist Organization. Reflecting back on the era decades later, she observed, "There was a huge reluctance to take this [the Palestinian question] on among women's movement people because they were afraid of offending Jews." In her experience, "in the women's movement there was a huge fear of being anti-Jewish."[24] The Boston-based journalist Ellen Cantarow noted that "among feminists there was a snail's-horn sensitivity about matters Jewish. The constant assumption was that criticizing Israel meant being anti-Semitic."[25]

Still other women felt that the Jewish identity movement and the growing discussions about anti-Semitism within the women's movement betrayed a deeper need on the part of certain Jewish women to be seen as nonwhite, as victims themselves of ethnic prejudice, much as blacks were. Some radical women objected to this "Jews as fellow sufferers" attitude, arguing that it was allowing Jewish women to escape the reality of being white by posing as victims: not really white, subject to racism, and therefore justified in rallying around their own political movement, Zionism.

The problem with that idea, these radical women argued, was twofold. First, Jews were so used to being persecuted and outside the mainstream in the European context that they could not realize that in the American context, that was no longer true. Jews had effectively become white, they argued. Second, such attitudes were examples of white privilege: using the privilege and security of being white and therefore, however unwittingly, part of the white power structure, to deny belonging to that very power structure. To its critics, this attitude itself smacked of racism. The PFOC's Diana Block—herself from a Jewish background—observed "that there wasn't a lot of self-reflection about whiteness, racism, etc." among Jewish feminists.[26] The PFOC's Judith Mirkinson also noticed this. "There *was* a rise in [an] 'I'm not white, I'm Jewish' victim complex," she noted years later.[27]

For one Jewish woman who had been involved in the Weather Underground, what she called "born-again Jews" in the women's movement were using the perception of belonging to "some other group seen to be less saddled with class/race privilege" than whites in order for them to feel less like a white oppressor. Looking back years later, she said such women "never felt Jewish until it allowed them to be part of a group that experienced discrimination— and thus feel less like a member of an oppressing group and more like an oppressed group."[28] The novelist Toni Morrison had noted much the same thing for the women's movement as a whole as far back as 1971: "There is also a contention among some black women that Women's Lib is nothing more than an attempt on the part of whites to become black without the responsibilities of being black."[29]

The critique of this trend emerged as soon as Pogrebin's article appeared in 1982. In the February 1983 issue of *Ms.*, the editors decided to run a sample of the various letters to the editor the magazine had received in response to her article. One was signed by ten women. It commented on the "disproportionate" attention that the question of anti-Semitism was receiving in the feminist movement, and offered one answer as to why this was the case: "Many white feminists, defensive about constant charges of racism from Third World and white women alike, may be seeking to restore their sense of political rectitude by identifying an oppression of their own. . . . An assertion of Jewish identity and a focus on anti-Semitism allows many Jewish feminists to participate in the politics of the oppressed." The ten signers were distressed that a "politics of *identity*" appeared to be "superseding a politics of issues."[30]

The ten women who wrote the letter also believed that an unfortunate side effect of the Jewish identity movement and the high-profile discussion of anti-Semitism in the women's movement was the tendency to "psychologize dissent that inhibits the process of rational discourse crucial to democratic political deliberations." This came through the labeling of women who opposed Israel's actions as either anti-Semitic or, in the case of Jewish women, "self-hating." The signers of the letter went on to note:

> If ever there was a time when it was urgent for Jews and others to feel free to criticize Israeli politics, that time is now. Such criticism from Jews need not be self-hating, nor from non-Jews, anti-Semitic. Rather it may be the most morally and politically defensible appraisal of the Middle Eastern dilemma possible. These distinctions are easier to comprehend in the current context of the appalling, we believe genocidal invasion of Lebanon by Israel. . . . There is a long, honorable tradition of Jewish opposition to the Zionist vision and

Zionist politics. We hope that charges like Pogrebin's will not contribute to
the decline of that tradition nor silence the open expression of controversial
views in the Women's Movement.[31]

In August 1980, the Alliance against Women's Oppression (AAWO), whose
roots were in the Third World Women's Alliance, which survived until about
1978, and adhered to the latter group's goal of a revolutionary, anti-capitalist, anti-sexist, and anti-racist women's movement, started to include white
women as well, but repudiated Zionism.[32] The AAWO included both lesbians
and heterosexuals and focused on the oppression of lesbian women of color,
attacking gender, racial, and class-based sexism in the United States and other
developed countries from a Marxist perspective.[33]

In October 1983, AAWO published a discussion paper entitled "Zionism
in the Women's Movement—Anti-Imperialist Politics Derailed." The paper
accused the anti-Semitism debate within the Movement of trying to defuse a
radical feminist critique of capitalism and imperialism. It noted that women
in the early 1980s were involved with El Salvador and the war there, but had
"waffled" on the Arab-Israeli conflict. The reason women were not denouncing Israel, AAWO argued, was that the women's movement had become "con-
sumed" with Jewish identity questions and the struggle against anti-Semitism
to the detriment of other pressing issues. "Among radical feminists in particular, there is a powerful temptation to shut out world events and become
immersed in seeking the essence of ever-more narrowly defined personal
identity," the paper declared. It went on to say that left-wing forces within the
women's movement must insist on a debate about Zionism in the face of the
charges of anti-Semitism raised by some Jewish feminists and in the face of "a
retreat into apolitical cultural identity."[34]

AAWO also asserted that women who supported anti-imperialist justice
yet also supported the "legitimacy of the Zionist state" were being inconsis-
tent. It was another example of the struggle between those pushing for revolutionary internationalism and those on the Left who practiced Israel exceptionalism. "Zionist feminists view Israel as the sole guarantor of the survival
of the Jewish people," the group wrote, and they equated anti-Zionism with
the physical destruction of all Jews, so that anti-Zionists appear like "moral
degenerates" who do not appreciate Jewish suffering. Taking the argument
one step further, AAWO stated that because of these relatively successful
efforts to equate Jewish identity with the defense of Israel and Zionism, "the

celebration of Jewish history and tradition becomes a political statement—whether one wishes it to be so or not."[35] In the words used by many in the various identity politics movements, the personal had become political.

Another radical women's group that weighed in on the controversy about anti-Semitism in the women's movement and that supported the Palestinian cause was Women against Imperialism (WAI).[36] Formed in San Francisco in 1981 where some of its founders had been involved in the women's caucus of the Bay Area chapter of the PFOC, it was not long until WAI took up the question of Zionism in the feminist movement. In April 1982, the group produced a pamphlet entitled *The Issue of Zionism in the Women's Movement* that took issue with the slogan heard within the women's movement, mostly famously stated by Bella Abzug, that Zionism was the national liberation movement of the Jewish people. The pamphlet also criticized the growing tendency to say that Jews were part of an oppressed and threatened nationality, that they were "Third World," or at least not white. In fact, WAI argued, Jews were part of a "white supremacist social order" in the United States. "The US, like South Africa and Israel, is a white settler colony."[37]

WAI did not deny concerns about anti-Semitism, but refused to accept that American Jews were therefore on the same level as oppressed people at home and abroad. Quite the opposite: white women needed to struggle against the white supremacy into which they were born. "It is the height of white supremacy to use the holocaust to claim Palestine for the Jews," the pamphlet declared. "Equating anti-semitism with the oppression of colonized people lets white women evade our responsibility to oppose white supremacy."[38] It argued that the women's movement needed to take a stand alongside the Palestinians without allowing charges of anti-Semitism to cloud its judgment about Zionism and without humanizing Zionism by retreating into passivity and saying that Palestinians and Israelis should just work out their own problems on their own. Quite the opposite: women must support the Palestinian struggle alongside all national liberation struggles that were leading the fight against the American empire.[39]

The debate about anti-Semitism in the women's movement and Israel's invasion of Lebanon in June 1982 galvanized the new group to further action. Judith Mirkinson recalled that when the war broke out, "we were appalled. We got involved." WAI women took part in demonstrations against the war, some carrying posters emblazoned with the portrait of Leila Khaled. Even though many in WAI were Jewish, they were accused of various masochistic pathologies. "We were 'anti-Semitic,' we had 'internal anti-Semitism.' It was ridiculous," Mirkinson recalled.[40] A month into the war, WAI published an article entitled "Taking Our Stand against Zionism and White Supremacy" in the July 1982 issue of *off our backs*. In it, the group mentioned that many of its members were Jewish, but once again attacked what WAI saw as the growing tendency within the women's movement to say that Jewish women were "'Third World' or at least not white." This ignored the fact that Jews were part of a "white supremacist social order," whether they liked it or not.

WAI argued that the way to fight American society's rightward movement was not for progressive Jewish women to pretend they were Third World people, but to fight the white supremacist structure of American society. Focusing on anti-Semitism as a form of white racism, holding conferences on anti-Semitism, and so forth, they argued, merely drew attention away from women's support work for Third World struggles. WAI also was disturbed that the question of anti-Semitism was being used to justify Zionism and its oppression of the Palestinians. "Zionist 'Israel' was carved in blood," it said, "from the homeland of the Palestinian people." The WAI article also boldly asserted, "we think the women's movement must take a stand in solidarity with the Palestinian revolution and with the national liberation struggles of colonized third world people inside the United States."[41]

The battle that had been brewing was joined with a vengeance. A Jewish lesbian feminist collective called Di Vilde Chayes[42] fired back at WAI in the same issue of *off our backs,* calling the group anti-Semites. "We are outraged at WAI's insinuation that to fight for Jewish survival is antithetical to working against racism and for Third World liberation," Di Vilde Chayes said in "An Open Letter to the Women's Movement," stressing that *"Zionism is one strategy against anti-Semitism and for Jewish survival."* Moreover, *"Anti-Zionism is anti-Semitism,"* given that it implied the destruction of Israel and the physical annihilation of its people. "Any anti-Zionist position is, therefore, anti-Semitic."[43]

Other pro-Israeli Jewish feminists fought back as well. Nine Jewish women in the San Francisco area issued a statement entitled "Jewish Women on Zionism," saying that they were committed to fighting anti-Semitism, affirming Jewish identities, and living as Zionists, which to them meant that they were committed to the existence of Israel and the right of self-determination for the Jewish people. The women added that they strongly supported self-determination and a homeland for the Palestinian people. However, they were alarmed at the rise of anti-Israel sentiment within the Left and the women's movement since the Lebanon War began in June 1982. "The scapegoating of Israel alone is not a coincidence; it is blatant anti-Semitism," they declared. The women called on everyone, especially non-Jews, to look to see if his or her anti-Zionism was "a veneer for anti-Semitism."[44]

Other lesbians in the feminist movement beyond Di Vilde Chayes joined the debate. Some had long been dealing with Zionism, Israel, and the Palestinians. As far back as September 1970, an issue of *Gay Flames* contained a poem entitled "We are Lesbians" that included an early statement of solidarity with the Palestinian struggle: "We want to see the power of the U.S. Government destroyed. We want to see the N.L.F. [National Liberation Front, or Viet Cong] win. We want to see spring come to Vietnam, and Laos, and Cambodia. We want to see spring come to Palestine, and Pakistan, and Mozambique."[45]

Lesbian publications also were some of the very first, years before Pogrebin's 1982 article, to discuss Jewish concerns about anti-Semitism in the women's movement. The fall 1977 issue of *Dyke,* edited by two young Jewish lesbian separatists, Penny House and Liza Cowan, was devoted to "ethnic lesbians" and included three articles dealing with Zionism and/or allegations of anti-Semitism within the women's movement. Alice Block's "Scenes from the Life of a Jewish Lesbian" spoke of the double oppression of being Jewish and a woman. "Diaspora Takes a Queer Turn," by Janet Meyers, noted that Zionism and lesbian separatism shared certain similarities for the author: "The correlations between the anger and hysteria [on the Left] provoked by the psychic and territorial claims being made by Lesbians and Jews is another in a long series of parallel experiences which, though sometimes painful, have welded together my Jewish-Lesbian identity." Finally, *Dyke*'s editors, House and Cowan, themselves contributed the piece, "Anti-Semitism in the Lesbian Movement."[46]

So it was no surprise that the debate about Palestinians, Israel, and anti-Semitism in the women's movement raged in the pages of gay publications. Di Vilde Chayes published their same attack on WAI in the May 29, 1982, issue of *Gay Community News.* On the other hand, Janet M. Gottler, identifying herself as a progressive Jew, wrote in the June 19, 1982, issue of the same publication that she was increasingly disturbed by such articles, as well as the belief in the wider lesbian movement that anti-Zionism was anti-Semitic. She argued that it was difficult for Jews to examine Zionism critically because of the way they were raised. She would know: Gottler, whose understanding of racism in America made her "very open to looking at a very different perspective about Israel and the Middle East," recalled "having these crying arguments" with her parents over such issues. "To embark on a critical study is a painful, often agonizing experience, for most of us have emotional ties to Israel, ties of blood, family, friends," she wrote. Yet despite all that, Gottler maintained that Jews could not accept a strategy for Jewish survival that involved one group dominating another, "even if it is the supremacy of our own people." Those who questioned Zionism did not want to single out Israel as the worst example in the world; they just wanted to be consistent about race and class across the board. How could we condemn what happened to the Indians to make room for white settlers, yet accept colonization on behalf of Jews in Israel, she asked? How could we struggle against racism and white supremacy in America, yet accept a state that is based on Jewish supremacy? Gottler urged that progressive Jews in the gay and lesbian community, as well as the wider heterosexual Jewish community, educate the Jewish community about Palestinian rights.[47]

Israel's 1982 invasion of Lebanon ushered in a new era for lesbian and heterosexual feminists of all backgrounds in terms of grappling with the Arab-Israeli conflict, which lasted into the 1980s. Some started dialogue groups aiming to heal the divisions brought on by years of partisanship related to Zionism, Jews, women of color, and the Arab-Israeli conflict. One such group of about ten Jewish and Arab women began meeting in Washington, DC, in the second half of 1982.[48] The Lesbian activists (from different ethno-religious backgrounds) Barbara Smith, Elly Bulkin, and Minnie Bruce Pratt produced a book in 1984 based on their grappling with issues of anti-Semitism and racism.[49] In other cases, feminists continued to take impassioned stances. Betty Friedan still battled against mentioning Palestine at international women's conferences, once telling the Egyptian feminist Nawal El Saadawi at the World Conference on Women in Nairobi in July 1985, "Please do not bring up Palestine . . . this is a women's conference, not a political conference."[50] Susan "Suzie" Nelson, who had been active in Students for a Democratic Society and the anti–Vietnam War movement at the University of California at Berkeley, decided to support the Palestinian cause with proceeds from a restaurant she ran.[51] The Caribbean American poet June Jordan wrote in 1982:

> I was born a Black women
> And now
> I am become a Palestinian[52]

Andrew Dworkin reconsidered her earlier views (see above), declaring, "[We Jews have] been blinded, not just by our need for Israel, or our loyalty to Jews but by a deep and real prejudice against Palestinians that amounts to race-hate. . . . Taking the country and turning it into Israel, the Jewish state, was an imperialist act. . . . Jews, nearly annihilated, took the land and forced a very hostile world to legitimize the theft."[53]

The experience of the women's movement in dealing with the Arab-Israeli conflict showed that the intra-left controversies over what stance to adopt toward Israel and the Palestinians clearly had outlived the tumult of the 1960s and early 1970s and were manifesting themselves in part of the identity movement by the early 1980s. It illustrated that yet another sector within white progressive American politics was unable to reach a unanimous position on the Middle East by the early 1980s, as opposed to issues such as the American role in Central America or the black freedom movement in South Africa. Still, anti-imperialist politics was firmly entrenched within some movements that had spun off from the 1960s Left. The pro-Palestinian discourse of the 1960s had clearly come to stay.

# Epilogue

ERIC LEE JOINED the Young Peoples Socialist League as a teenager in 1971 and became a member of the Democratic Socialist Organizing Committee (DSOC) in 1975. He spent most of the following year living in Israel, and five years later, he decided to immigrate permanently to the Jewish state. The US presidential bid in 2016 of Senator Bernie Sanders—a fellow democratic socialist—nonetheless prompted Lee, who was then living in Britain, to join Democratic Socialists of America (DSA). On August 6, 2017, he resigned from DSA, however, to protest its support of the Palestinian Boycott, Divestment, and Sanctions (BDS) campaign "to end international support for Israel's oppression of Palestinians and pressure Israel to comply with international law."[1] He believed that supporting Israel, not boycotting it, was the proper stance for American leftists in the twenty-first century.

Lee wrote online: "I cannot in good conscience be a member of an organization which promotes a boycott of the Jewish state. I consider the BDS campaign to be antisemitic and racist. I oppose it as a socialist and as a Jew. I am appalled that DSA would take such a position. For that reason, despite more than 40 years supporting DSA and its predecessor, I now wish to resign my membership."[2] Lee's anger at socialists who adopted pro-Palestinian stances on the Arab-Israeli conflict went back many years. He had been outspoken in his defense of Israel back when he was in DSOC in the 1970s. When DSOC and another democratic socialist organization, the New American Movement (NAM), held unity discussions in the late 1970s, their divergent positions on the conflict nearly scuttled the talks. Some in DSOC, including both the young Lee and veteran socialists like Irving Howe, tried to thwart the merger, because NAM criticized Israel and supported the Palestinians, whereas DSOC aligned solidly with Israel. NAM and DSOC reached a compromise over the question of the Arab-Israeli conflict, however, and merged to form the DSA.

When DSA embraced the Palestinians wholeheartedly thirty-five years later, only one socialist group remained in the United States that still unabashedly supported Israel, the DSA's old rival, Social Democrats USA. Yet even that tiny group had hedged its stance to include criticism of Israeli government policies.[3] For all intents and purposes, the American socialist and Marxist organizations that were still around virtually all supported the Palestinian cause by the second decade of the twenty-first century. The Left—the true Left, as opposed to liberals—was united on this point, which had been the cause of so much rancor and division decades earlier. However, the US Left was miniscule in 2017. In no way was it as significant a public presence as it had been in the late 1960s. Internal conflict about how to understand the Arab-Israeli conflict during that time created much discord on the Left, and helped weaken what already was a fractious collection of groups and parties when the long Sixties ended.

Americans heard serious anti-Israeli and pro-Palestinian viewpoints in public for the first time in the tumultuous 1960s. These stances stemmed from the radical politics and anti-imperialist worldview of the American Left and the Black Power movement at the time. The impact of this development was significant, both in the short and long terms. The debates about the Arab-Israeli conflict within the Left occurred at a time when it was in its strongest position in decades. The Palestinian issue therefore achieved even greater visibility with the American body politic than it otherwise might have done, becoming a marker of the revolutionary Left: those committed to what they viewed as real revolutionary change both at home and abroad saw supporting the Palestinians in their struggle against Israel and Zionism as a litmus test of true radicalism. It also linked the US Left with one of the most notable Third World struggles. Yet others drew the line at abandoning Israel in favor of the Palestinians, sometimes motivated by a sense of ethnic solidarity. This divisiveness hurt the Left, particularly the Old Left. It split the Communist Party USA and hastened the departure of democratic socialists from the Left, either to pursue electoral work on behalf of the Democratic Party or into the arms of neoconservatism.

The more open way in which pro-Palestinian viewpoints can be discussed publicly today is a direct result of what transpired in the 1960s and 1970s. Support for the Palestinians has moved into the liberal-left mainstream. Since the launching of the November 29th Coalition in 1981, campus groups like Students for Justice in Palestine in 1993, and the BDS movement starting in 2005, advocacy of Palestinian rights has become a permanent part of the progressive American political landscape. In much the same way that left-wing radicals derided those who espoused Israel exceptionalism in the 1960s for not being true revolutionaries, pro-Palestinian activists today sometimes dismiss those left-of-center who defend every conceivable cause except that of the Palestinians as hypocritical and "PEP": "progressive except for Palestine." In late 2015, the Palestinian American historian Rashid Khalidi noted:

> There is a much higher level of discussion of matters related to Palestine than ever before, especially in the field of Middle East Studies and among students on many campuses. This is truer of younger academics than of older ones, and of those in fields related to the study of the Middle East, such as history, literature and languages, and many of the social sciences and humanities. One can today discuss topics on campuses, in the classroom and outside, at a reasonably high level and without overt friction, that would have been completely off limits 20 years ago.[4]

On the other hand, pro-Israeli forces have symbiotically become more organized and powerful over the decades in their attempts to combat pro-Palestinian perspectives at colleges and universities. Khalidi may be correct that Palestine can be discussed more openly on campuses today, but Israel's partisans around the country have set up elaborate mechanisms for limiting such discussions. The Jewish United Fund/Jewish Federation of Metropolitan Chicago published an online document in early 2012 entitled "The Playbook—Tackling the Delegitimization of Israel on Campus," which encouraged students to photograph pro-Palestinian student activities and contact campus officials if "any school 'values' were violated" by them.[5] Internet sites designed to monitor, expose, and counteract pro-Palestinian professors, students, and campus activities have emerged, including Campus Watch and Canary Mission, a site which "documents people and groups that promote hatred of the USA, Israel and Jews on North American college campuses." Scholars for Peace in the Middle East has a page on its website where students can report on BDS activities on their campuses, activities the group describes as part of "a political-warfare campaign conducted by rejectionist Palestinian groups in cooperation with radical left-wing groups in the West . . . [that] seeks the dismantling of Israel and its replacement with another Arab-majority state."[6] Books published recently call Students for Justice in Palestine, which now has chapters on approximately two hundred campuses in the United States, a "well-financed festering hate group" and a "terror-supporting anti-Semitic network."[7] Efforts have been made to equate anti-Zionism with anti-Semitism, making it a form of hate speech when expressed on college campuses.

In presenting the story of the 1960s and 1970s Left, *The Movement and the Middle East* has shown that left-wing identity and action were thrown into sharp relief by responses to the Arab-Israeli conflict. The battle lines usually were drawn between those whose internationalist solidarity with anti-imperialist movements throughout the world led them to support the Palestinians versus those whose global visions of change were tempered by belief in Israel exceptionalism. Although what remains of the American Left today is mostly united behind one point of view, the Arab-Israeli conflict is still divisive among liberal-to-progressive Americans in the neoliberal era, just as it was among leftists back in the 1960s. Nowhere has this become clearer than within the Democratic Party. When the 2018 elections brought into the House of Representatives three Democratic women who publicly expressed support for the Palestinians—Ilhan Omar, Alexandria Ocasio-Cortez, and the US Congress's first Palestinian American female member, Rashida Tlaib— some high-level Democrats were concerned. Just days after the three were sworn into Congress in January 2019, a new organization, the Democratic Majority for Israel, was established to shore up support for Israel within the party—support that was once taken for granted. Clearly liberals and progressives were worried about the growing pro-Palestinian voices, not just in what remained of the Left (Ocasio-Cortez and Tlaib are both members of DSA), but also within the Democratic Party.

They have reason to be worried. According to a 2018 poll carried out by the Pew Research Center, the number of self-described liberal Democrats who sympathized with the Palestinians was nearly twice the number of those who were sympathetic to Israel. A senior staff member working for a Democrat on Capitol Hill was quoted the following year, "People like Ilhlan Omar, Rashida Tlaib and Bernie Sanders have opened the floodgates on this issue. It may be painful for the party as we move in a more progressive direction, But we'll come out in a better place—a more moral and evenhanded place—in the end."[8]

Progressives fighting back against the agenda of President Donald Trump and his allies would do well to consider the weakening of the Left in the 1960s and 1970s due to its infighting about Israel/Palestine as a cautionary tale if they seek to create a united front against America's twenty-first century reactionaries. With Trump so deeply connected with the right-wing policies and visions of Israeli prime minister Binyamin Netanyahu, and with the Left both within and outside the United States virtually unanimous in support of the Palestinians, making common cause with pro-Palestinian activists in any type of anti-Trump coalition may be exceedingly difficult for strongly pro-Israeli progressives. Like American politics, Middle Eastern politics are in turmoil, and they present progressive Americans with the same kinds of challenges they did in the 1960s.

# Acknowledgments

I AM INDEBTED to those who assisted me over the course of years of researching and writing this book. I am especially grateful to the many I interviewed. Some of them, notably Abdeen Jabara and Nick Medvecky, went particularly out of their way to help me by providing me with photographs, documents, and additional contacts, in addition to their detailed recollections. Many thanks go out to the various librarians and archival staff members who worked with me in institutions in this country and abroad.

I particularly would like to acknowledge the hard-working staff of Randolph-Macon College, who do so much for the professors here for so little reward and acknowledgment in return. This includes the wonderful staff of the McGraw-Page Library, under the leadership of Library Director Virginia Young and, later, Nancy Falciani-White, who helped me obtain books and microfilms via interlibrary loan and otherwise assisted me over the years, including Emily Bourne, Megan Hodge, James Murray, Scarlett Mustain, Laurie Preston, Kelli Salmon, Judee Showalter, Lynda Wright, and Lily Zhang. Outside the library I wish to thank Mimi Carter, for her administrative help, as well as history department student assistants Shuyan Zhan, Paige Weaver, Tori Santiago Troutman, and Michael Warren for their help with various research assignments. Special thanks go to Brenda Woody and Princess Tunstall, who kept the history department's building in order, notably my sometimes cluttered office.

Off campus I benefitted immensely from the keen editorial talents of Kate Wahl and Leah Pennywark at Stanford University Press. Others at the press helped me as well, including Stephanie Adams, Tim Roberts, Kendra Schynert, and Kate Templar. I also greatly appreciated the comments of the anonymous peer reviewers and the copy editor, Peter Dreyer, and, as always, remain grateful to various friends and family members for their hospitality, love, and support.

Finally, I gratefully acknowledge the financial support of the Walter Williams Craigie Teaching Fund and the Rashkind Family Endowment, both at Randolph-Macon College, and the Maurice Mednick Memorial Fellowship of the Virginia Foundation for Independent Colleges.

# Notes

Acronyms Used in the Notes

| | |
|---|---|
| AGP | Albert Glotzer Papers |
| AJHSPS | American Jewish Historical Society, Philip Slomovitz South End Collection |
| AJP | Abdeen Jabara Papers |
| BGLP | Berta Green Langston Papers |
| CGP | Carl Gershman Papers |
| CONAMER | Committee on New Alternatives in the Middle East Records |
| CPUSAR | Communist Party USA Records |
| DSAC | Democratic Socialists of American Collection |
| FORR | Fellowship of Reconciliation Records |
| FSP | Fayez A. Sayegh Papers |
| JLCP | Jewish Labor Committee Papers |
| JSOC | Jewish Student Organizations Collection |
| LNSR | Liberation News Service Records |
| MOBER | National Mobilization Committee to End the War in Vietnam (MOBE) Records |
| SDSP | Students for a Democratic Society Papers |
| SDUSAR | Social Democrats USA Records |
| SPAP | Socialist Party of America Papers |
| SPC | Social Protest Collection |
| SWPR | Socialist Workers Party Records |

WRKC        William Rea Keast Collection

WRLR        War Resisters League Records

YULL        Yale University, Leon Litwack Collection

## Prologue

1. Amnon Cavari, "Six Decades of Public Affection: Trends in American Public Attitudes Toward Israel," in *Israel and the United States: Six Decades of US-Israeli Relations*, ed. Robert O. Freedman (Boulder, CO: Westview Press, 2012), 110. For more on contemporary public opinion about the war, see *American Jewish Yearbook*, vol. 69 (New York: American Jewish Committee; Philadelphia: American Jewish Publication Society, 1968), 198–200.

2. New York University, Elmer Holmes Bobst Library, Tamiment Library and Robert F. Wagner Labor Archives, Communist Party of the United States of America Records, ser. II: State and District Records, 1925–2003. subser. B: New York State Records, 1938–2003, box 227, folder 30, *Jewish Affairs*, 1966–71, Daniel Rubin, "Comments on the Resolution," in Discussion Bulletin on the Draft Resolution on the Jewish Question, November 15, 1966, 12.

3. Ibid., 13.

4. Sid Resnick, "Can Radicals Support the Arab Terrorists? The Political Goals of Al Fatah Challenged by Progressives," *Jewish Currents* 23, no. 7 (July–August 1969): 5–7.

5. Ibid., 1, 10.

6. David P. Shuldiner, *Aging Political Activists: Personal Narratives from the Old Left* (Westport, CT: Praeger, 1995), 203, 214, 226.

7. I deal extensively with both left-wing and more conservative black attitudes toward the Arab-Israeli conflict in my *Black Power and Palestine: Transnational Countries of Color* (Stanford, CA: Stanford University Press, 2018). Accordingly, this study focuses on white leftists.

8. To give a few examples, the following treatments of the Movement during the "long sixties" make little or no mention of this issue at all: Terry Anderson's *The Movement and the Sixties: Protest in America from Greensboro to Wounded Knee* (New York: Oxford University Press, 1995); Todd Gitlin's *The Sixties: Years of Hope, Days of Rage* (New York: Bantam Books, 1987); David Farber's *The Age of Great Dreams: America in the 1960s* (New York: Hill & Wang, 1994); and Maurice Isserman and Michael Kazin's *America Divided: The Civil War of the 1960s*, 5th ed. (New York: Oxford University Press, 2015). Wider histories of the American Left and its decline give it no mention either: e.g., Stanley Aronowitz's *The Death and Rebirth of American Radicalism* (New York: Routledge, 1996); James Weinstein's *The Long Detour: The History and Future of the American Left* (Boulder, CO: Westview Press, 2003); Michael Kazin's *American Dreamers: How the Left Changed a Nation* (New York: Knopf, 2011); Paul Buhle's *Marxism in the United States: A History of the American Left*, 3rd ed. (New York: Verso, 2013). However, several authors have in fact dealt with the historic stances of the Left toward Israel and Zionism, although they have done so quite polemically and

almost exclusively through the lens of what they describe as a long history of left-wing anti-Semitism: Harvey Klehr, in *Far Left of Center: The American Radical Left Today* (Piscataway, NJ: Transaction Books: 1988); Robert S. Wistrich, in *From Ambivalence to Betrayal: The Left, the Jews, and Israel* (Lincoln: University of Nebraska Press, 2012); and Stephen H. Norwood, in *Anti-Semitism and the American Far Left* (New York: Cambridge University Press, 2013). By contrast, few books have explored other factors to explain how and why certain leftists in the 1960s and 1970s dealt with the Arab-Israeli conflict in the ways they did. Alex Lubin's *Geographies of Liberation: The Making of an Afro-American Political Imaginary* (Chapel Hill, NC: University of North Carolina Press, 2014) is one; it looks in part at black leftists in the 1960s. Keith P. Feldman's *A Shadow over Palestine: The Imperial Life of Race in America* (Minneapolis: University of Minnesota Press, 2015) sheds some light on how black and Jewish leftists, as well as some feminists, approached the question of Israel and the Palestinians in the 1960s and 1970s. Pamela E. Pennock's *The Rise of the Arab American Left: Activists, Allies, and Their Fight against Imperialism and Racism, 1960s–1980s* (Chapel Hill, NC: University of North Carolina Press, 2017) looks primarily at left-wing Arabs and Arab-Americans but does pay some attention to the white New Left. Finally, my *Black Power and Palestine*, also looks at black leftists such as those in the Student Nonviolent Coordinating Committee and the Black Panther Party.

9. Mark Rudd to the author, March 21, 2011.

10. Biographies of these and many other persons mentioned in this book can be found at https://folios.rmc.edu/michaelfischbach/biographies.

11. Bernardine Dohrn, "When Hope and History Rhyme," in *Sing a Battle Song: The Revolutionary Poetry, Statements, and Communiqués of the Weather Underground, 1970–1974*, ed. Dohrn, Bill Ayers, and Jeff Jones (New York: Seven Stories Press, 2006), 1.

## Chapter 1

1. The initial report that the Arabs had attacked first was in fact incorrect. Bob Feldman, "Sundial: Columbia SDS Memories. Chapter 10: The Viet Nam Summer of Love, 1967" (August 10, 2009), http://columbiasdsmemories.blogspot.com/2009/08/chapter-10-viet-nam-summer-of-love-1967.html.

2. For more on SNCC and the Palestinians, see my *Black Power and Palestine*.

3. Feldman, "Sundial: Columbia SDS Memories."

4. C. Wright Mills, "Letter to the New Left," *New Left Review* 1, no. 5 (September–October 1960): 18–23.

5. Davida Fineman, telephone interview by the author, April 17, 2018.

6. Few scholars have examined how the New Left approached the Arab-Israeli conflict, however. It is not mentioned, e.g., in Todd Gitlin, *The Whole World Is Watching: Mass Media in the Making and Unmaking of the New Left* (Berkeley: University of California Press, 1980); James Miller, *"Democracy is in the Streets": From Port Huron to the Siege of Chicago* (1987; Cambridge, MA: Harvard University Press, 1994); John McMillian and Paul Buhle, eds., *The New Left Revisited* (Philadelphia: Temple University Press, 2003); or Van Gosse, *Rethinking the New Left: An Interpretive History* (New

York: Palgrave Macmillan, 2005). One exception is Irwin Unger's *The Movement: A History of the American New Left, 1959–1972* (New York: Harper & Row, 1974).

7. Both events are detailed in my *Black Power and Palestine*.

8. As with studies of the New Left more generally, previous works on SDS largely have ignored the question of how the group understood the Arab-Israeli conflict and what, if any, impact this had on it. Kirkpatrick Sale's pioneering *SDS* (New York: Random House, 1973), e.g., makes no mention of the issue at all, nor does David Barber's *A Hard Rain Fell: SDS and Why It Failed* (Jackson: University Press of Mississippi, 2008). Alan Adelson's *SDS* (New York: Scribner, 1972) does mention how SDS wrestled with the issue but devotes only about two pages to it.

9. Roy Dahlberg, "Suggested Middle East Resolution Re: Arab-Israeli Reaction and Implications, Re: NIC Resolution," *New Left Notes*, June 19, 1967.

10. Judith Tucker, telephone interview by the author, July 17, 2012.

11. Dan Siegel, telephone interview by the author, February 9, 2012.

12. Much has been written, starting in the late 1960s and early 1970s themselves, about how and why Jewish youth were attracted to the New Left and highly represented in it, including Seymour Martin Lipset's "The Socialism of Fools: The Left, the Jews, and Israel," *Encounter*, December 1969, 24–35, and Nathan Glazer's "The New Left and the Jews," *Jewish Journal of Sociology* 11 (1969): 121–31. An entire conference on this topic was held in 1970 that led to *The New Left and the Jews*, ed. Mordecai S. Chertoff (New York: Pitman, 1971). Some of these analyses offered some fairly critical and hostile psychological explanations of what motivated Jewish leftists, as did Stanley Rothman and S. Robert Lichter's later work *Roots of Radicalism: Jews, Christians, and the New Left* (New York: Oxford University Press, 1982). Other writers analyzed this phenomenon more kindly, some of whom are discussed in this chapter and in chapter 4; their works are listed in the bibliography. A conference called "Jews and the Left" was held in New York in May 2012 by the YIVO Institute for Jewish Research and the American Jewish Historical Society. Some of the presentations at this conference were later published in Jack Jacobs, ed., *Jews and Leftist Politics: Jews, Israel, Anti-Semitism, and Gender* (New York: Cambridge University Press, 2017).

13. Robert J. Saks, a self-described Jewish member of the New Left, described the disconnect between New Leftists' generally warm feelings toward Israel with their unease with Israeli actions in his piece "Israel and the New Left," *Journal of Jewish Communal Service* 45, no. 2 (Winter 1968): 139–46.

14. Mark Rudd to the author, March 21, 2011.

15. David Gilbert to the author, March 1, 2012; Gilbert, *Love and Struggle: My Life in SDS, the Weather Underground, and Beyond* (Oakland, CA: PM Press, 2012), 29.

16. Bob Ross, telephone interview by the author, October 21, 2013.

17. Mike Klonsky, telephone interview by the author, October 7, 2013.

18. Bob Feldman, "From his '69 Awakening to the 'Wild-Animal' State and Lobby—Hilton Obenzinger on Israel." http://mondoweiss.net/2009/11/from-his-69-awakening-to-the-wild-animal-state-and-lobby-hilton-obenzinger-on-israel/; Hilton Obenzinger, telephone interview by the author, January 3, 2015.

19. Naomi Jaffe to the author, March 7, 2012.

20. Linda Charlton, "Jews Fear Anti-Zionism of New Left," *New York Times,* August 14, 1970.

21. Letter to the editor by "J.G." in *The Militant,* September 4, 1967, in *Israel and the Arabs: Militant Readers Debate the Middle East Conflict* (New York: Merit Publishers, 1969), 3.

22. *Students for a Democratic Society Papers, 1958–1970* (Glen Rock, NJ: Microfilming Corporation of America, 1977), reel 20, "Resolution on the Middle East," June 29, 1967. The report was written by Bob Weiland, Bob Speck, Henry Bucher, and Philip J. Hardy; the archival record is unclear as to whether or not the convention adopted it, but it does not appear that it was.

23. Larry Hochman, *Zionism and the Israeli State: An Analysis in the June War* (Ann Arbor, MI: Radical Education Project, 1967), 4, 14.

24. C. Wright Mills, *The Marxists* (New York: Dell, 1963).

25. Sale, *SDS,* 353.

26. Letters to the editor, "Support Al-Fatah," *New Left Notes,* March 20, 1969.

27. Susan Eanet, "History of the Middle East Liberation Struggle: Part 1," *New Left Notes,* February 28, 1969.

28. It may have been a reprint of a 1967 article by the same title written by the Marxist activist Tony Cliff. Jerome H. Bakst, "The Radical Left and al Fatah," *ADL Bulletin* 26, no. 7 (September 1969): 2.

29. They were the February 28, March 7, March 13, March 20, and April 17, 1969, issues.

30. Eanet, "History of the Middle East Struggle, Pt. 1."

31. Letters to the editor section, *New Left Notes,* March 20, 1969.

32. Adelson, *SDS,* 198.

33. Letter to the editor, "Foolish Socialism," *New Left Notes,* March 20, 1969.

34. Mordecai S. Chertoff, "The New Left and the Newer Leftists," in *New Left and the Jews,* ed. Chertoff, 194; Mel Galun, "The New Tone of Arab Propaganda on Campus" (New York: American Zionist Youth Federation, 1969).

35. Feldman, "Sundial: Columbia SDS Memories."

36. "Five Proposed Principles of SDS Unity," *Guardian,* July 5, 1969. Encyclopedia of Anti-Revisionism On-Line. Transcription, editing, and markup by Paul Saba. www.marxists.org/history/erol/ncm-1/sds-5.htm.

37. Wayne Price, telephone interview by the author, January 9, 2014.

38. Mark Rudd to the author, March 21, 2011; Bernardine Dohrn, telephone interview by the author, April 11, 2011.

39. Jerry Rubin, *We Are Everywhere. Written in Cook County Jail* (New York: Harper & Row, 1971), 75–76; Anita and Abbie Hoffman, *To America with Love: Letters from the Underground* (New York: Stonehill Publishing, 1976), 165.

40. Jerry Rubin, *Growing (Up) at 37* (New York: Warner Books, 1976), 75.

41. Ibid., 76; Charlton, "Jews Fear Anti-Zionism of New Left"; Rubin, *We Are Everywhere,* 75.

42. Pat Thomas, *Did It! From Yippie to Yuppie: Jerry Rubin, an American Revolutionary* (Seattle: Fantagraphics Books, 2017), 17.

43. Rubin, *We Are Everywhere*, 75–76.

44. Nancy Kurshan to the author, March 29, 2011.

45. Alan M. Dershowitz, *Taking the Stand: My Life in the Law* (New York: Crown Publishers, 2013), 435.

46. "The Liberation of Palestine and Israel," *New York Review*, July 1, 1971.

47. "Jewish Youth Seen and Heard at Dem Convention," Jewish Telegraphic Agency, July 12, 1972. www.jta.org/1972/07/12/archive/jewish-youth-seen-and-heard-at-dem-convention.

48. Hoffman and Hoffman, *To America with Love*, 130–31 (letter of October 13, 1974).

49. Ibid., 164–66 (letter of December 10, 1974).

50. Ibid.

51. "Jewish Aryanism in Israel," *The Realist* No. 1 (June–July 1958): 5.

52. Paul Krassner to the author, April 6, 2011.

53. Harry Ring, "The Govt. vs. Thorsten Krebs," *Militant*, October 19, 1964.

54. James Retherford, telephone interview by the author, April 1, 2011; see also Jim Retherford, "Remembering Stew Albert: the Yippies' Quiet Theorist." www.stewalbert/com/memorial.html.

55. Judy Gumbo Albert to the author, March 9, 2011; id., telephone interview by the author, April 1, 2011.

56. Nancy Kurshan to the author, March 29, 2011.

57. Jonah Raskin to the author, March 29, 2011.

58. James Retherford, telephone interview by the author, April 14, 2011.

59. FBI File 100–36217, report from Detroit office, June 12, 1970. https://archive.org/details/Yippies.

60. Pun Plamandon to the author, November 13, 2013.

61. Max Elbaum, *Revolution in the Air: Sixties Radicals Turn to Lenin, Mao, and Che* (New York: Verso, 2006), 41–42.

### Chapter 2

1. Yale University, Beinicke Rare Book and Manuscript Library, New Haven, CT, Leon F. Litwack Collection of Berkeley, California, Protest Literature (hereafter YULL), ser. 1: Files, box 2, folder 29, "Zionism, Western Imperialism, and the Liberation of Palestine."

2. Dan Siegel, telephone interview by the author, February 9, 2012. For a study of Arab student political activity in the United States during the 1960s and 1970s, see Pennock, *Rise of the Arab American Left*.

3. American Jewish Committee, *Arab Appeals to American Public Opinion* (New York: American Jewish Committee, Institute of Human Relations, 1969), 9.

4. For more about black groups and the conflict, see my *Black Power and Palestine*.

5. University of California at Berkeley, Bancroft Library, Social Protest Collection (hereafter SPC), ser. 6, Miscellaneous: 1954–82. carton 27, reel 100, folder 14: Arab-Israeli Conflict 1969–73, "Vietnam—Palestine: One Struggle."

6. Ibid., "The Real Enemy Is Now at the 'Front," "Blood for Arab Relief Is Needed *NOW!*"

7. Roxanne Dunbar-Ortiz, telephone interview by the author, February 3, 2012; id., *Outlaw Woman: A Memoir of the War Years, 1960–1975* (San Francisco: City Lights, 2001), 80–81.

8. Joel Aber, "The Role of the SWP in Supporting the Arab Revolution," *SWP Discussion Bulletin* 27, no. 12 (August 1969), 14.

9. Adelson, *SDS*, 127, 199; Steven M. Cohen, in Jeffrey K. Salkin, *A Dream of Zion: American Jews Reflect on Why Israel Matters to Them* (Woodstock, NY: Jewish Lights Publishing, 2007), 178.

10. University of Virginia, Albert and Shirley Small Library Special Collections Library, Student Council Appropriations Committee Archives. Records of the American Friends of Free Palestine 1970–74, Documents, Mannix to Ison, April 15, 1970; AFFP constitution; "Petition for Recognition as a University Organization, Academic Year 1970–71."

11. See Pennock, *Rise of the Arab American Left* for more details.

12. Nick Medvecky, "Revolution until Victory—Palestine al-Fatah," *South End*, January 8, 1969.

13. Nick Medvecky to the author, April 9, 2011.

14. American Jewish Historical Society, Philip Slomovitz (1896–1993), South End Collection, 1946–1974 (hereafter AJHSPS), ser. 1: Reactions to and Responses from *South End*, box 1, folder 1, Correspondence, Panush to Simons, January 8, 1969.

15. Ibid., Simons to Keast, January 24, 1969.

16. Ibid., Simons to Gubow, March 6, 1969; Miller to Tannenbaum, February 20, 1969; Miller to Brickner, February 20, 1969.

17. Hayim Hermesh, "Ha-Yehudim Shel al-Fateh [The Jews of al-Fateh]," *Ma'ariv,* February 28, 1969. The author would like thank Geremy Forman for translating the article.

18. February 2, 1969, radio interview with John Watson. AJHSPS, P-135, ser. 1, Reaction to and Responses from *South End*, n.d., 1969, 1971–73, box 1, folder 4, tape-recorded interview with John Watson, *South End* editor, February 2, 1969.

19. Ibid., February 2, 1969 radio interview with Robert J. Huber.

20. Wayne State University, Walter P. Reuther Library of Labor and Urban Affairs, Office of the President, William Rea Keast Collection (hereafter WRKC), box 36, folder 15, Kelley to Rose, April 9, 1969.

21. Nick Medvecky to the author, April 17, 2011.

22. Nick Medvecky to the author, June 4, 2015.

23. WRKC, box 36, folder 18 "The Situation at the *South End* as of January 22, 1969."

24. Ibid., Keast's draft letter. The author also received a copy of Keast's final letter from Nick Medvecky.

25. M. Jay Rosenberg, "To Uncle Tom and Other Such Jews," *Village Voice*, February 13, 1969.

26. M. Jay Rosenberg, "My Evolution as a Jew," *Midstream* 16, no. 7 (August–September 1970): 50–53; *Jerusalem Post* overseas edition, August 11, 1969; *Albany Student Press*, February 18, 1969; M. J. Rosenberg, telephone interview by the author, August 12, 2015.

27. *Albany Student Press*, February 18, 1969.

28. Ibid., February 11, 1969.

29. Michael J. Rosenberg, "Israel without Apology," in *The New Jews*, ed. James A. Sleeper and Alan L. Mintz (New York: Vintage Books, 1971), 82, 85.

30. Rosenberg, "My Evolution as a Jew," 52.

31. Jack Nusan Porter, "Jewish Student Activism: Northwestern University Leader Outlines Jewish New Left Development," *Jewish Currents* 24, no. 5 (May 1970): 33.

32. "Working Paper on the Orientation of the Jewish Liberation Project," July 1968. Copy in the author's possession.

33. American Jewish Historical Society, Jewish Student Organizations Collection, box 32, folder 10, Jewish Liberation Project, "Jewish Liberation Project Constitution."

34. An RZA poster bearing that slogan can be seen at www.palestineposterproject. org/poster/be-a-revolutionary-in-zion.

35. "Radical Zionist Manifesto," in Michael E. Staub, *The Jewish 1960s: an American Sourcebook* (Waltham, MA: Brandeis University Press, 2004), 247; New York University, Elmer Holmes Bobst Library, Tamiment Library and Robert F. Wagner Labor Archives, Printed Ephemera Collection on Subjects, box 8, Middle East, 1969–, Radical Zionist Alliance, "Socialism, Zionism, Liberation."

36. *Jerusalem Post*, May 27, 1969. For a general study of Zionist student groups in the 1960s, see Yisrael Ne'eman, "From the New Left to the Jewish Left: Zionist Student Activism in America from 1967–73" (MA thesis, University of Haifa, 2004).

37. *JTA Community News Reporter* 6, no. 46 (November 29, 1968).

38. "Appeal to Students to Counteract Anti-Israeli Influence," *Haaretz*, February 2, 1969, in *ISCAR*, no. 1 (May 1969): 3.

39. *Jerusalem Post*, June 4, 1969, and *Jerusalem Post* overseas edition, August 11, 1969.

40. Israel Shenker, "Mrs. Meir Aware of 'Image Crisis,'" *New York Times*, October 7, 1969.

41. Dan Vered, interview by the author, Tel Aviv, April 13, 2015.

42. Michael Lerner, "Jewish New Leftism at Berkeley," *Judaism* 18, no. 4 (Fall 1969): 478; Michael Lerner, telephone interview by the author, October 19, 2014.

43. Michael Lerner, telephone interview by the author, October 19, 2014.

44. Lerner, "Jewish New Leftism at Berkeley," 476–77.

45. The statement was signed by five people: Lerner, Savio, Susan Restone, Ann Marks, and Jerry Jackson. YULL, ser. 1, Files, box 2, folder 38, "Statement on the Middle East." The statement also can be found in *Judaism* 18 (Fall 1969): 483–87.

46. Committee for a Progressive Middle East, "Does Israel Have the Right to Exist?" Mimeographed leaflet in the author's possession.

47. Paul Jacobs, *Between the Rock and the Hard Place* (New York: Random House, 1970), 104–5; Peter Camejo, *Northstar: A Memoir* (Chicago: Haymarket Books, 2010), 81; Michael Lerner, telephone interview by the author, October 14, 2014.

48. SPC, ser. 6, Miscellaneous, 1954–82, carton 27, reel 100, folder 14, Arab-Israeli Conflict, 1969–73, flyer distributed by the Committee for Justice and Peace in the Middle East.

49. *Ba-Golah—In Exile* 1, no. 1 (1970).

### Chapter 3

1. Temple University, Paley Library, Special Collections, Liberation News Service Records, pt. II (LNS library collection) (hereafter LNSR), ser. 14, International, Mo.–Pa., box 3, folder 6, Palestine, dispatches no. 1. (n.d., but August 26, 1969) and no. 2 (August 27, 1969).

2. Nick Medvecky to the author, April 9, 2011 and April 12, 2011.

3. Jean Townes, telephone interview by the author, January 16, 2015.

4. Elizabeth Cobbs Hoffman, *All You Need is Love: The Peace Corps and the Spirit of the 1960s* (Cambridge, MA: Harvard University Press, 1998), 218.

5. They were Roger I. Tauss, Orville C. "Chris" Robinson Jr., Robert F. Firth, Joseph N. Center, Joseph A. Stork, Catherine B. Tackney, Jean W. Townes, Georgia K. Mattison, Joaquin E. "Gene" Guerrero Jr., Peewee "Rufus" Griffin, Mana Claire Zakaria, Randall E. Clarke, Marilyn N. Lowen, Nick Medvecky, Sharon Rose, Susan E. C. Teller, and Charles E. Simmons 3rd.

6. Gene Guerrero and Susie Teller, "Palestinian Report"; Susan Teller, "One Week in Lebanon Can Blow Your Mind"; Gene Guerrero, "How it Came About," all in *Great Speckled Bird*, October 4, 1970.

7. Sharon Rose, telephone interview by the author, February 3, 2011.

8. Ibid; Susan Teller Goodman, telephone interview by the author, June 3, 2011; Nick Medvecky to the author, April 26, 2011; CIA Operation CHAOS document of January 18, 1971. The document was obtained by Nick Medvecky, who kindly provided the author with a copy.

9. Nick Medvecky to the author, April 9, 2011 and April 26, 2011.

10. Gene Guerrero, telephone interview by the author, May 27, 2011; Susan Teller Goodman, telephone interview by the author, June 3, 2011; and Jean Whilden Townes, telephone interview by the author, January 16, 2015.

11. For more details about the experiences in the Ashbal camp and the medical clinic, see *From Refugees to Palestinians: The Birth of a Revolution* (Washington, DC: Middle East Research and Information Project, n.d.); the booklet is a copy of an article that appeared in *Liberated Guardian*, September 17, 1970.

12. Ibid.; "Al-Mu'tamarun fi Nadwat Filastin Yastankiruna Jara'im al-Salt [Conferees at the Palestine Seminar Denounce the Crimes in al-Salt]," *al-Fateh*, September 4, 1970.

13. "Revolutionary American Jews: Support the Palestinian Resistance," *Free Palestine* 2, no. 8 (December 1970): 3; "Al-Yahud al-Ahrar ma` al-Thawra al-Filastiniyya [Liberal Jews with the Palestinian Revolution]," *al-Fateh*, September 9, 1970.

14. Jean Townes, telephone interview by the author, January 16, 2015.

15. Susan Teller Goodman, telephone interview by the author, June 3, 2011.

16. Guerrero and Teller, "Palestinian Report" and Susan Teller, "One Week in Lebanon Can Blow Your Mind."

17. Susan Teller Goodman, telephone interview by the author, June 3, 2011.

18. Sharon Rose, telephone interview by the author, February 3, 2011.

19. Georgia Mattison, telephone interview by the author, November 22, 2013.

20. Ibid.

21. Guerrero and Teller, "Palestinian Report"; Guerrero, "How It Came About;" Gene Guerrero, telephone interview by the author, May 27, 2011.

22. Gene Guerrero, telephone interview by the author, May 27, 2011.

23. Joe Stork, telephone interview by the author, December 6, 2013.

24. LNSR, ser. 14, International, Mo.–Pa., box 4, folder 1, Palestine, Chris Robinson and Roger Tauss, "Palestine: They Say There is No Resistance," September 4, 1970.

25. Ibid., box 3, folder 7, Palestine, and box 4, folder 1, Palestine, Nick Medvecky's dispatch, September 12, 1970.

26. Judith Tucker, telephone interview by the author, July 17, 2012.

27. Ellen Siegel, "The Road to Jerusalem," *Freedomways* 23, no. 2 (1983): 90–92.

28. Ellen Siegel, telephone interview by the author, December 10, 2014.

29. Ibid.; Ellen Siegel and Nabil Ahmed, "Shared Memories," http://justworld-books.com/sabra-and-shatila-a-somber-anniversary.

30. Sherri Muzher, "Silenced No More: Jewish Supporters of Palestinian Rights Speak Out during Intifada," *Dissident Voice*, December 2, 2001, www.dissidentvoice.org/Articles/SherriSilenced.htm; Ellen Siegel, telephone interview by the author, December 10, 2014.

31. *Washington Post* syndicated news story, carried in, inter alia, *Tuscaloosa News*, September 28, 1970.

32. Abdeen Jabara to the author, April 28, 2014.

33. George Cavalletto, telephone interview by the author, January 18, 2013.

34. Ibid.; Blake Slonecker, "Living the Moment: Liberation News Service, Montague Farm, and the New Left, 1967–1981" (PhD diss., University of North Carolina, Chapel Hill, 2009), 226.

35. George Cavalletto, telephone interview by the author, January 18, 2013. The piece on Palestinian women appeared in, inter alia, *Rat: Subterranean News,* February 6–23, 1970. Copies of Liberation News Service packets have been archived online at www.lns-archive.org.

36. Sean Stewart, ed., *On the Ground: An Illustrated Anecdotal History of the Sixties Underground Press in the U.S.* (Oakland, CA: PM Press, 2011), 159–60; Jeff Blankfort, "Commentary," http://ifamericansknew.org/cur_sit/torture2.html.

37. Interview with Jeffrey Blankfort, http://sf.indymedia.org/news/2006/11/1733088. php. Ellipses in the original.

38. Peter Johnson and Joe Stork, "MERIP: The First Decade," *MERIP Reports,* nos. 100–101 (October–December 1981): 50–55.

39. For more on this, see my *Black Power and Palestine.*

40. Sami Shalom Chetrit, *Intra-Jewish Conflict in Israel: White Jews, Black Jews* (New York: Routledge, 2010), 109. There is a street in East Jerusalem named after Kies.

41. Reuven Avinoam, "The New Left in Israel" (July 1973), http://israeli-left-archive.org/greenstone/collect/zenglish/index/assoc/HASH64df.dir/doc.pdf.

42. Joel Beinin, telephone interview by the author, January 23, 2015.

43. Ibid.

44. Ibid.

45. He later changed his first name to Abdallah.

46. Given that the prominent Black Panther activists Bobby Seale and Huey Newton were from Oakland, the last two names were clearly pseudonyms.

47. NBC-TV "Nightly News," September 4, 1970. Recording obtained from the Vanderbilt University Television News Archive, http://tvnews.vanderbilt.edu/program.pl?ID=453454.

48. "Al Fatah Investigated," *Near East Report* 13, no. 10 (May 14, 1969).

49. "The Arab Propaganda Campaign on the Campus," *Near East Report* 13, no. 22 (October 29, 1969): 108; C. C. Aronsfeld, "New Left Germans and El Fatah," *Jewish Frontier,* October 1969: 21–23.

50. FBI, "The Fedayeen Impact—Middle East and United States" (June 1970), 51, www.governmentattic.org/2docs/FBI_Monograph_Fedayeen-Impact_1970.pdf.

51. FBI, "The Fedayeen Terrorist—A Profile" (June 1970), www.governmentattic.org/docs/FBI_Monograph_Fedayeen_Terrorist_June-1970.pdf. The document contained the man's name, but it was redacted out of the version that the FBI declassified in 2008.

52. CIA, Intelligence Report. "ESAU L: The Fedayeen (Annex to ESAU XLVIII: Fedayeen—"Men of Sacrifice") (January 1971), 25, www.scribd.com/document/46926781/CIA-1971-Origins-of-Fatah-Top-secret-A.

53. S. Marwan, "Tribute to Ghassan Kanafani," *al-Hadaf,* July 22, 1972, reprinted in *al-Awda,* June–July 2005, www.newjerseysolidarity.net/resources/kanafani/kanafani6.html. Kanafani was assassinated by Israeli agents in Beirut in July 1972.

54. Cited in Sarah Irving, *Leila Khaled: Icon of Palestinian Liberation* (London: Pluto Press, 2012), 50.

## Chapter 4

1. M. S. Arnoni, "Why the New Left Needs Israel," in *New Left and the Jews,* ed. Chertoff, 279, 284.

2. David Horowitz, "The Passion of the Jews," *Ramparts* 13, no. 3 (October 1974): 22.

3. Andrea Dworkin, *Life and Death: Unapologetic Writings on the Continuing War against Women* (London: Virago Press, 1997), 221–22.

4. Jonathan Kaufman, *Broken Alliance: The Turbulent Times between Blacks and Jews in America* (New York: Touchstone Press, 1995), 201.

5. Paul Jacobs, "A Time to Heal," *Ramparts* 6, 1 (July 1967): 3. A helpful study of American Jews' complicated and shifting relationship with Israel over the decades is Dov Waxman's *Trouble in the Tribe: The American Jewish Conflict over Israel* (Princeton, NJ: Princeton University Press, 2016).

6. Paul Jacobs, "The View from Tel Aviv and Beirut," *Ramparts* 11, no. 9 (March 1973): 63–64. Peled's comments appeared in the March 19, 1972, edition of the Israeli newspaper *Haaretz*; Weizman's appeared in the March 20, 1972, edition of the same paper. See Arie Bober, ed., *The Other Israel: The Radical Case against Israel* (Garden City, NY: Doubleday, Anchor Books, 1972), 85.

7. See the comments of former Defense Secretary Robert McNamara in *The 50 Years War: Israel and the Arabs*, a 1999 Public Broadcasting Service documentary film directed by Dai Richards and David Ash. The scholar of international law John Quigley has written an entire book on the legal questions surrounding Israel's decision to launch the 1967 war, with a detailed analysis of what various powers knew about the true state of affairs between Israel and the Arab world in the spring of 1967. John Quigley, *The Six-Day War and Israeli Self-Defense: Questioning the Legal Basis for Preventive War* (New York: Cambridge University Press, 2013).

8. M. S. Arnoni, "Rights and Wrongs in the Arab-Israeli Conflict (To the Anatomy of the Forces of Progress and Reaction in the Middle East)," *The Minority of One* 9, no. 9 (September 1967): 6–28.

9. Ibid., 23–24.

10. Arnoni, "Why the New Left Needs Israel," 284.

11. Ibid., 275; M. S. Arnoni, "Doing What Comes Unnatural," *Israel Magazine* 2, no. 2 (1969): 58.

12. New York University, Elmer Holmes Bobst Library, Tamiment Library and Robert F. Wagner Labor Archives, Edward S. Goldstein: Jewish Labor Committee Papers (hereafter JLCP), box 4, file 1, New Left and the Jewish Labor Committee, 1966–70, Tom Milstein, "The New Left: Areas of Jewish Concern: An Analysis." Milstein later published this as "The New Left: Areas of Jewish Concern" in *New Left and the Jews*, ed. Chertoff.

13. Linda Charlton, "Jews Fear Anti-Zionism of New Left," *New York Times*, August 14, 1970.

14. Sheldon Stern, "Support for Panthers Damned," *Ha-Orah—The Light* 2, no. 5 (January 30, 1970).

15. Decades later, some scholars still analyze left-wing hostility toward Israel and Zionism in the 1960s and 1970s from the perspective of anti-Semitism. See Stephen H. Norwood, *Antisemitism and the American Far Left* (New York: Cambridge University Press, 2013), and Robert S. Wistrich, *From Ambivalence to Betrayal: The Left, the Jews, and Israel* (Lincoln: University of Nebraska Press, 2012).

16. Michael Walzer and Martin Peretz, "Israel Is not Vietnam," *Ramparts* 6, no. 1 (July 1967): 11–14. Emphasis in the original.

17. Martin Peretz, "The American Left and Israel," *Commentary* 44, no. 5 (November 1967): 27–34.

18. Ibid. Italics in the original. The version of the article viewed online by the author did not contain individual page numbers.

19. Lipset, "'Socialism of Fools.'"

20. Ibid., 24, 28, 30.

21. "Arab *irrationality* appeals to them more than Israeli sobriety." Seymour Martin Lipset, "Jewish Interests and the New Left," in *New Left and the Jews*, ed. Chertoff, 159. Emphasis in the original.

22. Lipset, "'Socialism of Fools,'" 33.

23. *New Left and the Jews*, ed. Chertoff.

24. Tom Milstein, "The New Left: Areas of Jewish Concern," ibid., 304.

25. Chaim I. Waxman and William B. Helmreich, "Religious and Communal Elements of Ethnicity: American Jewish College Students and Israel," *Ethnicity* 4, no. 2 (June 1977): 122–32.

26. *Target USA: The Arab Propaganda Offensive* (n.p.: Anti-Defamation League of B'nai B'rith, 1975), 35.

27. Mike Marqusee, *If I Am Not for Myself: Journey of an Anti-Zionist Jew* (New York: Verso, 2008), 60.

28. Ibid., 60, 251.

29. Ibid., ix.

30. Paul Jacobs, *Between the Rock and the Hard Place* (New York: Random House, 1970), 33, 101.

31. Jacobs, "Time to Heal," 3–10.

32. Paul Jacobs, "No Peace in the Middle East," *Liberation* 14, no. 8 (November 1969): 33.

33. "The Liberation of Palestine and Israel," *New York Review*, July 1, 1971.

34. Jacobs, *Between the Rock and the Hard Place*, 151.

35. I. F. Stone, *Underground to Palestine* (New York: Boni & Gaer, 1946).

36. I. F. Stone, *I. F. Stone's Weekly*, December 5, 1966.

37. I. F. Stone, *I. F. Stone's Weekly*, June 12, 1967.

38. I. F. Stone, "The Future of Israel," *Ramparts* 6, no. 1 (July 1967): 41.

39. I. F. Stone, "Holy War," *New York Review*, August 3, 1967: 10–11.

40. It may have been the remains of Abu Zurayq village.

41. "Reflections on a Lifetime of Engagement with Zionism, the Palestine Question, and American Empire: An Interview with Noam Chomsky, Interviewed by Mouin Rabbani," *Journal of Palestine Studies* 41, no. 3 (Spring 2012): 92–120.

42. "Reflections on a National Conflict," in Noam Chomsky, *Middle East Illusions, Including Chomsky's Peace in the Middle East? Reflections on Justice and Nationhood* (Lanham, MD: Rowman & Littlefield, 2003), 99.

43. Noam Chomsky, "Nationalism and Conflict in Palestine," *New Outlook* 12, no. 9 (November–December 1969): 21–31. The article also appeared in *Liberation* 14, no. 8 (November 1969): 7–21, and was reprinted in at least two books by Chomsky, including *Middle East Illusions*.

44. Self-described Jewish New Leftist Robert Saks said much the same thing several years earlier in "Israel and the New Left," *Journal of Jewish Communal Service* 45, no. 2 (Winter 1968): 139–46.

45. Noam Chomsky, "Israel and the New Left," in *New Left and the Jews*, ed. Chertoff, 207, 213, 217, 227.

46. Noam Chomsky, "The Mideast: Dark at the End of the Tunnel," *Ramparts* 11, no. 7 (January 1973): 55.

47. Noam Chomsky, telephone interview by the author, September 4, 2012.

48. Noam Chomsky, "Israel and the American Intelligentsia," in C. P. Otero, ed., *Noam Chomsky: Radical Priorities* (Oakland, CA: AK Press, 2003), 89; Noam Chomsky, telephone interview by the author, September 4, 2012.

49. Chomsky, "Israel and the New Left," 211.

50. Barry Rubin, "How American Radicals See the Resistance Dilemma," *Journal of Palestine Studies* 1, no. 4 (Summer 1972): 25. Rubin soon, however, abandoned his left-wing, anti-Zionist politics.

51. David Horowitz, "The Passion of the Jews," *Ramparts* 13, no. 3 (October 1974): 58. Horowitz later abandoned the Left and moved right.

52. For a study of Waskow as an example of the "Jewish religious left," see Doug Rossinow, "'The 1900-Year Crisis': Arthur Waskow, the Question of Israel/Palestine, and the Effort to Form a Jewish Religious Left in America, 1967–1974," in *The Religious Left in Modern America: Doorkeepers of a Radical Faith*, ed. by Leilah Danielson, Marion Mollin, and Doug Rossinow (New York: Palgrave Macmillan, 2018), 233–54.

53. Arthur Waskow, "Draft of a Possible Position for Jewish Radicals in America, on 'The Diaspora, Zionism and Israel,'" *Sh'ma*, no. 4 (Fall 1970): 72–75.

54. Arthur Waskow, *The Bush Is Burning! Radical Judaism Faces the Pharaohs of the Modern Superstate* (New York: Macmillan, 1971), 76.

55. "The Liberation of Palestine and Israel," *New York Review*, July 1, 1971.

56. Waskow, *Bush*, 56–61, 66.

*Chapter 5*

1. "U.S. Is the Real Sponsor of Israel's Attack on the Arabs," *Workers World*, June 9, 1967.

2. Ibid.

3. "Workers World Party Statement on Mideast," *Workers World*, June 9, 1967.

4. "Aggressors and Oppressors," *Workers World*, June 24, 1967.

5. V. Copeland, "Israeli State; Not a Homeland but a Catspaw," *Workers World*, July 7, 1967.

6. On other occasions, it was called the Ad Hoc Conference Committee on the Middle East.

7. See the advertisement in *National Guardian*, June 11, 1967.

8. Deirdre Griswold, telephone interview by the author, November 14, 2013.

9. Bernard Lefkowitz, "View from the Left: A Meeting of Like Minds," *Village Voice*, June 29, 1967; "Group Plans Action against U.S.-Israel War," *Workers World*,

June 24, 1967; "Committee Calls Demonstration against U.S.-Israeli Aggression," *Workers World*, July 7, 1967.

10. Ad Hoc Conference Committee on the Middle East, "A Call to the Anti-War Movement: Don't Oppose Just *One* Case of U.S. Aggression" (reprint from a July 8, 1967 advertisement in *National Guardian*); "The U.S.-Israeli Aggression . . . In Whose Interest? The Jewish People—or U.S. Oil Monopolies?"(pamphlet). Emphasis in the original.

11. Mike Rubin, *An Israeli Worker's Answer to M. S. Arnoni* (New York: Ad Hoc Committee on the Middle East, 1968). For a full discussion of the anti-Israel resolution adopted at the conference, see my *Black Power and Palestine.*

12. Rita Freed, *War in the Mideast*, Committee to Support Middle East Liberation Pamphlet no. 5 (New York: World View Publications, 1972), 7.

13. Arabic transliteration: Qasid.

14. *The Black Panther*, November 3, 1973.

15. Fred Halstead and Barry Sheppard, "Special Interview: Palestine's Al Fatah," *Militant*, September 20, 1968. See also Barry Sheppard, *The Party: The Socialist Workers Party 1960–1988. Volume One: The Sixties. A Political Memoir* (Chippendale, Australia: Resistance Books, 2005), 211.

16. See, e.g., Ernest Mandel, "Draft Theses on the Jewish Question Today," *Fourth International* 9, no. 1 (January–February 1948): 18–24. Online document transcribed by Daniel Gaido and proofread by Scott Wilson, www.marxists.org/archive/mandel/1947/01/jewish.htm. For a scholarly analysis of these discussions, see Werner Cohn, "From Victim to Shylock and Oppressor: The New Image of the Jew in the Trotskyist Movement," *Journal of Communist Studies* [London] 7, no. 1 (March 1991): 46–68.

17. Karen Farsoun with Samih Farsoun and Alex Ajay. "Mid-East Perspectives from the American Left," *Journal of Palestine Studies* 4, no. 1 (Autumn 1974): 99–104.

18. "Arab Revolution Defense Urged by 4th International," *Militant*, July 16, 1967.

19. Dick Roberts, "The Egypt-Israeli Crisis," *Militant*, June 5, 1967.

20. "Israel and Socialism: Interview with Peter Buch," *Great Speckled Bird*, December 14, 1970.

21. Ibid.

22. *Zionism and the Arab Revolution: The Myth of a Progressive Israel* (New York: Young Socialist Alliance, 1967).

23. Ibid., 4, 7–8.

24. Les Evans, "The Arab Leaders and Imperialism," *Militant*, August 21, 1967.

25. Les Evans, "Palestine Arab Refugees Victims of Zionist Politics," *Militant*, June 19, 1967. Emphasis in the original.

26. Gary Collins and Leonard Gordon, "On the Mideast Conflict," *SWP Discussion Bulletin* 26, no. 8 (October 1967): 9–13.

27. *Israel and the Arabs: Militant Readers Debate the Mideast Conflict* (New York: Merit Publishers, 1969).

28. Joel Aber, "The Role of the SWP in Supporting the Arab Revolution," *SWP Discussion Bulletin* 27, no. 12 (August 1969): 13–15.

29. Sheppard, *Party,* 299.

30. The poster had been designed by Palestinian artist Kamal Boullata. The image can be seen in Gary Yanker, *Prop Art: Over 1000 Contemporary Political Posters* (New York: Darien House, 1972), 77, and online at www.palestineposterproject.org/poster/defend-the-arab-revolution.

31. "Israel and Socialism: Interview with Peter Buch."

32. Peter Buch, "Burning Issues of the Mideast Crisis," *International Socialist Review* 30, no. 2 (March–April 1969): 1–30; id., review of "Palestinian Liberation and Israel," ibid., no. 5 (September–October 1969): 56–64.

33. Gus Horowitz, telephone interview by the author, May 1, 2011.

34. Gus Horowitz, *Israel and the Arab Revolution: Fundamental Principles of Revolutionary Marxism* (New York: National Education Department of the Socialist Workers Party, 1973), 11, 18–20.

35. Ibid., 11–12, 20.

36. Ibid., "Counter Draft Resolution on Israel and the Arab Revolution: Resolution Rejected by the SWP Convention, August 1971, by Berta Langston, Bob Langston, and Jon Rothschild."

37. Stanford University, Hoover Institution. Socialist Workers Party Records, 1928–1990 (hereafter SWPR), International Assignments File, 1962–1987, Horowitz, Gus, folder 23: 1971–1973 (India, Sri Lanka, Middle East), Horowitz to Nicola, December 12, 1971; Havens to Horowitz, July 5, 1972; handwritten letter [by Gus Horowitz?], September 23, 1972; "Iraq," October 16, 1972; Horowitz to Jaber, December 27, 1974.

38. Tony Thomas, "Why Socialists Support the Arabs," *Militant,* November 2, 1973, in Dave Frankel, Dick Roberts, and Tony Thomas, *War in the Mideast: The Socialist View* (New York: Pathfinder Press, 1973), 21–22.

39. SWPR, International Assignments File, 1962–1987, Horowitz, Gus, folder 23, 1971–1973 (India, Sri Lanka, Middle East), Horowitz to Jaber, October 24, 1973; and December 27, 1974.

40. "Israel's Birth: Zionists Coldly Planned Terror," *Challenge,* July 1967; "Arabs Latest to Learn Lesson: Soviets Won't Fight Imperialism," *Challenge,* July 1967.

41. "Mid-East Swindle," *Challenge,* April 1969.

42. "Arabs Will Beat U.S.-Israel Imperialism AND Arab Nationalism," *Challenge,* August 1969.

43. *The First Arab-Israeli War, 1948–49,* Independent Socialist Clippingbooks Xerox Series No. X-2 (Berkeley: Independent Socialist Clippingbooks, 1967); *Zionism, Israel, & the Arabs: The Historical Background of the Middle East Tragedy,* Independent Socialist Clippingbooks No. 3 (Berkeley: Independent Socialist Clippingbooks, 1967).

44. Hal Draper, "The Origins of the Middle East Crisis," *New Politics* 6, no. 1 (Winter 1967): 13, 14, 18, 21, 22.

45. Wayne Price, telephone interview by the author, January 9, 2014.

46. Wayne Price, "Position Paper on the Mid East," August 1969 (unpublished document), 6. Author's collection.

47. *Spartacist* 11 (March–April 1968): 4–7.

## Chapter 6

1. For two examples of how the CPUSA party line analyzed these issues in the past, see Alexander Bittelman, *Program for Survival: The Communist Position on the Jewish Question* (New York: New Century Publishers, 1947); id., *To Secure Jewish Rights: The Communist Position* (New York: New Century Publishers, 1948).

2. Cited in the FBI document "The Fedayeen Impact—Middle East and the United States, June 1970, 49,www.governmentattic.org/2docs/FBI_Monograph_Fedayeen-Impact_1970.pdf.

3. Nathan Glazer, "The New Left and the Jews," *Jewish Journal of Sociology* 11 (1969): 129. The subject of the Jewish presence within the CPUSA has been a source of much study over the years. Some of these works are listed in the bibliography, including Gennday Estraikh's "Professing Leninist Yiddishkayt: The Decline of American Yiddish Communism," *American Jewish History* 96, no. 1 (March 2010): 33–60. A recent addition contribution to this literature is Harvey Klehr's "Jews and American Communism," in *Jews and Leftist Politics: Jews, Israel, Anti-Semitism, and Gender,* ed. Jack Jacobs (New York: Cambridge University Press, 2017).

4. Many continued to regard a Yiddish-speaking culture in the United States and elsewhere as a valid expression of Jewish identity.

5. Gus Hall, *For a Meaningful Alternative: Report to the June 10, 1967 Meeting of the National Committee of the Communist Party, U.S.A.* (New York: New Outlook Publishers, 1967), 3–4, 14.

6. Ibid., 14.

7. *Socialist Party of America Papers, 1919–1976, Addendum* (Glen Rock, NJ: Microfilming Corporation of America, 1977), microfilm, ser. A, National File—General Papers, 1919–1976, reel 6, 22–Jewish Labor Bund, Gus Hall, "Blueprint of a Mutual Declaration" (3/61).

8. Hyman Lumer, *The Middle East Crisis* (New York: New Outlook Publishers, 1967), 3, 6, 7, 15.

9. Other Yiddish papers leaned toward constituencies such as socialists, anarchists, and traditionalist Jews.

10. Estraikh, "Professing Leninist Yiddishkayt," 38–40.

11. "Time to Stop Calling 'Nazis,'" *Morgen Freiheit,* July 9, 1967.

12. New York University, Elmer Holmes Bobst Library, Tamiment Library and Robert F. Wagner Labor Archives, Communist Party USA Records (hereafter CPUSAR), ser. 1, National Administrative Records, 1913–2007, subser. B, National Bodies, 1929–2001, box 223, folder 25, Political Committee: Charges against Paul Novick, 1971, "To All Districts and National Committee Members, November 10, 1971," § "The Case of Paul Novick."

13. Ibid., § "Novick to members of the political committee, June 22, 1971."

14. "Jewish Communists in U.S. Strongly Oppose Kosygin's Stand on Israel," *Jewish Telegraphic Agency,* June 23, 1967, www.jta.org/1967/06/23/archive/jewish-communists-in-u-s-strongly-oppose-kosygins-stand-on-israel.

15. The two had split in 1965.

16. According to a report in the *New York Times*, the letter actually was written by Hyman Lumer. See Peter Kihss, "U.S. Reds Assail 2 Jewish Papers," *New York Times*, March 30, 1969. The letter can be found in CPUSAR, ser. III, Commissions and Departments, subser. E: Other Commissions, 1926–1999, box 215, folder 27, Jewish Commission: Discussion, Resolutions, "Letter to the Membership on the Jewish Question and Internationalism—From the National Committee, CPUSA" (n.d.).

17. Paul Novick, *The Character and Aims of the Morning Freiheit* (New York: Morgen Freiheit, n.d.).

18. Lawrence Bush, "Footprints: 'Pro-Israel, Non-Zionist'—and Arguing with the Left," http://jewishcurrents.org/tag/footprints.

19. Morris Schappes, *The Jewish Question and the Left—Old and New: A Challenge to the Left* (New York: Jewish Currents, 1970).

20. Ibid., 5–6, 18.

21. Ibid., various pages.

22. "Israel, What Now? An Editorial," *Jewish Currents* 25, no. 5 (May 1971): 3–4.

23. Sid Resnick, "Can Radicals Support the Arab Terrorists?," *Jewish Currents* 23, no. 7 (July–August 1969): 5–7.

24. Ibid., 1, 10.

25. Louis Harap, *The Zionist Movement Reconsidered* (New York: Jewish Currents, 1976), 30.

26. Ibid., 20, 30.

27. Ibid., 21–22.

28. CPUSAR, ser. III, Commissions and Departments, subser. E, Other Commissions, 1926–1999, box 215, folder 26, Jewish Commission: Conference Reports, 1968–80, "National Conference on Jewish Work, Communist Party, USA, New York City, September 7–8, 1968," 1–2, 8.

29. "For the Security of the State of Israel! For Peace in the Middle East!" *Jewish Currents* 23, no. 10 (November 1969): 3–6.

30. CPUSAR, "The Case of Paul Novick," and "Novick to members of the political committee, November 10, 1971."

31. FBI, "The Fedayeen Impact—Middle East and United States," www.governmentattic.org/2docs/FBI_Monograph_Fedayeen-Impact_1970.pdf.

32. Ibid., 50. For the number of informants, see FBI domestic intelligence inspection report, August 17–September 9, 1971, p. 94, https://archive.org/stream/foia_FBI_Domestic_Intelligence_Division-HQ-3/FBI_Domestic_Intelligence_Division-HQ-3#page/n105/mode/2up.

33. FBI File 100–56922 (Huey Percy Newton), SAC, New York to director, April 10, 1969, https://vault.fbi.gov/huey-percy-newton/Huey%20Percy%20Newton%20Part%2009%20of%2009/view, 134–37, 138–41. Two copies of the document are contained in the file, containing slightly different FBI redactions. *New York Times* journalists Peter Kihss and Irving Spiegel had written articles about dissension within the CPUSA in the two months prior to the date of the FBI document. The journalist whose name was edited out of the document when it was declassified may have been

Kihss. The blank spaces in the redacted document indicate that it was a short name. Moreover, another Marxist party called the Spartacist League claimed in the 1980s that the COINTELPRO program had sent letters to Kihss about other matters earlier in the 1960s. See "How the FBI Tried to Get us Kicked Out of the SWP: COINTEL-PRO 'Dirty Tricks,'" *Workers Vanguard*, January 11, 1985, 3, www.marxists.org/history/etol/newspape/workersvanguard/1985/0370_11_01_1985.pdf. For general information about COINTELPRO, see, among others, Nelson Blackstock, *COINTELPRO: The FBI's Secret War on Political Freedom* (New York: Pathfinder Press, 1988) and John Drabble, "Fighting Black Power–New Left Coalitions: Covert FBI Media Campaigns and American Cultural Discourse, 1967–1971, *European Journal of American Culture* 27, no. 2 (2008): 65–91.

34. CPUSAR, cited nn. 12–13 above, "The Case of Paul Novick" "Novick to members of the political committee, November 10, 1971," and "Novick to members of the national committee, November 10, 1971."

35. Ibid., "Lumer and Rubin to All Members of the Communist Party, U.S.A."; CPUSAR, ser. X, General Files, subser. A, Activities and Organizations Subject Files, box 87, folder 6: Morgen Freiheit. Document: "On the Expulsion of Paul Novick," April 13, 1973.

36. CPUSAR, ser. III, Commissions and Departments. subser. E, Other Commissions, 1926–1999, box 215, folder 26, Jewish Commission: Conference Reports 1968–80, "National Conference on Jewish Work, Communist Party, USA, New York City, September 7–8, 1968," 1–2, 8.

37. Estraikh, "Professing Leninist Yiddishkayt," 54.

38. Herbert Aptheker, *The Mid-East—Which Way to Peace?* (New York: Committee for a Just Peace in the Middle East, 1971).

39. Henry M. Winston, "Black Americans and the Middle East Conflict," *World Marxist Review* (November 1970): 19, 23. The CPUSA later reprinted an amended version of the article as a pamphlet. See Henry M. Winston, *Black Americans and the Middle East Conflict* (New York: New Outlook Publishers, 1970).

40. *Peoples World*, August 17, 1974.

41. "Viewpoint" section, *National Guardian*, June 3 and June 10, 1967.

42. Irving Beinin, "The Mideast War Solves No Problems," *National Guardian*, June 17, 1967; see also Beinin, "Tension 'Built Into' Mideast Setup," ibid., June 24, 1967.

43. Irving Beinin, "Discussion: The Mideast Dispute," *National Guardian*, July 29, 1967.

44. Ibid.

45. Letters to the editor, *National Guardian*, September 2, 1967.

46. Letters to the editor, *National Guardian*, September 16, 1967.

47. Abdullah Schleifer, "Arabs Weigh Liberation Fight." *National Guardian*, June 4, 1967.

48. Tabitha Petran, "Palestine Creates Own Liberation Force," *Guardian*, July 27, 1968.

49. James M. Davis, "Arabs Resist Israel's Occupation," *Guardian*, September 14, 1968.

50. "The Middle East," *Guardian*, February 1, 1969.

51. Leo Huberman, "Israel Is Not the Main Enemy," *Monthly Review* 19, no. 5 (October 1967): 8–9.

52. Paul M. Sweezy, "Israel and Imperialism," *Monthly Review* 19, no. 5 (October 1967): 2–6.

## Chapter 7

1. Carl Gershman, "Between War and Peace: The Issues in the Middle East Conflict," *Crossroads* 2, no. 6 (June 1971): 6, repr. by the Youth Committee for Peace and Democracy in the Middle East.

2. Stanford University, Hoover Institution, Carl Gershman Papers, 1962–84 (hereafter CGP), box 1, folder 34, "Israel and Vietnam—A Shaky Comparison" (n.d.).

3. One of the best treatments of the history of the SPA, and one that includes some discussion of its stances vis-à-vis Zionism and Israel, is Jack Ross's *The Socialist Party of America: A Complete History* (Lincoln, NE: Potomac Books, 2015).

4. *Socialist Party of America Papers, 1919–1976, Addendum* (Glen Rock, NJ: Microfilming Corporation of America, 1977) (hereafter SPAP), ser. A, National File—General Papers, 1919–1976, reel 4, § 16A–B, General, 1956–1974, "Arab-Israeli Crisis" (n.d., but 1967).

5. Yale University, Beinecke Rare Book and Manuscript Library, Leon F. Litwack Collection of Berkeley, California, Protest Literature, ser. 1, Files, file 12, "The Middle East—What Democratic Socialists Say" (n.d., but handwritten note indicating it was circulated on May 25, 1967).

6. David McReynolds, "The Destiny of Israel: a Minority View," *Village Voice*, June 29, 1967.

7. SPAP, ser. A, National File—General Papers, 1919–1976, reel 4, § 16A–B, General, 1956–1974, "Resolution on the Middle East as Endorsed by the National Committee" (n.d., but 1967). In addition to this document, the original Socialist International statement can be found in New York University, Elmer Holmes Bobst Library, Tamiment Library and Robert F. Wagner Labor Archives, Edward S. Goldstein, Jewish Labor Committee Papers, box 3, file 31, Middle East Crisis, 1967–68.

8. SPAP, cited ibid., "Draft Resolution on the Middle East Crisis" (n.d.).

9. Ibid., Bogdan Denitch, "Notes on a Socialist Foreign Policy" (n.d.). Emphasis in the original.

10. Ibid., "Resolution on the Middle East, Adopted by the Socialist Party National Committee" (n.d.); "Resolution on the Middle East, Adopted by the Socialist Party Convention—June 1970" (n.d.).

11. Ibid., "Resolution on the Middle East" (n.d., but apparently either 1969 or 1970).

12. Ibid., "Resolution on the Middle East, Adopted by the Socialist Party National Committee" (n.d.).

13. His sister-in-law Joan Suall (née Parnes), who was married to his brother Bert, later served in the same post from 1970 until 1972.

14. For more information about Rustin's activities among blacks on behalf of Israel, see my *Black Power and Palestine*.

15. CGP, box 1, folder 15, "Countering Anti-Israel Propaganda on the Campus" (January 1970); Carl Gershman, "Israel: The New Left Is Not the Enemy," *Sh'ma: A Journal of Jewish Responsibility* 1, no. 18 (October 22, 1971): 138.

16. SPAP, Series A: National File—General Papers, 1919–1976. Reel 4, Section § 16A-B: General 1956–1974. Document: "Draft Program, Section 3—International" (1970; draft written by Gershman).

17. Carl Gershman, "The New Face of Anti-Zionism," *The American Zionist* 62, no. 4 (December 1971): 16.

18. CGP, cited n. 15 above, "Countering Anti-Israel Propaganda"; Gershman, "Israel: The New Left Is Not the Enemy," 138.

19. *New York Times*, November 9, 1969.

20. Richard Nixon, *RN: The Memoirs of Richard Nixon* (New York: Grosset & Dunlap, 1978), 481, cited in Kathleen Christison, *Perceptions of Palestine: Their Influence on U.S. Middle East Policy* (Berkeley: University of California Press, 1999), 130.

21. Gershman, "New Face of Anti-Zionism," 17.

22. Gershman, "Between War and Peace," 12.

23. Ibid., 1.

24. Ibid., 6, 9.

25. Michael Harrington, "Oil and Blood Mix in the Middle East," *New America*, February 25, 1970, repr. by the Youth Committee for Peace and Democracy in the Middle East (n.d.); Harrington, "Imperialism in the Middle East," in *Israel, the Arabs and the Middle East*, ed. Irving Howe and Carl Gershman (New York: Quadrangle Books, 1972); Harrington, *The Long-Distance Runner: An Autobiography* (New York: Holt, 1988), 87.

26. Harrington, "Oil and Blood Mix in the Middle East," "Imperialism in the Middle East," and *Long-Distance Runner,* 87.

27. Michael Harrington, *Socialism* (New York: Bantam Books, 1972), 269.

28. David A. Hacker, "Social Democrats, USA: Learning from Our Past and Revived under New Leadership to Build for a Brighter Future for the United States of America and the World," 9, http://socialistcurrents.org/documents-public/Social_Democrats.pdf.

29. "DSOC Activists from Coast-to-Coast Say 'No' to NAM Merger Proposal," *Mainstream*, August 1980.

30. As quoted in Norman Podhoretz, "Now, Instant Zionism," *New York Times*, February 3, 1974.

31. Mitchell Cohen, "Democratic Socialism, Israel, and the Jews: An Interview with Michael Harrington," *Response* 9, no. 4 (Winter 1976): 36–37, www.bjpa.org/Publications/downloadFile.cfm?FileID=16496.

32. Ibid., 33–35.

33. "DSOC Activists from Coast-to-Coast Say 'No' to NAM Merger Proposal."

34. Max Elbaum, *Revolution in the Air: Sixties Radicals Turn to Lenin, Mao, and Che* (New York: Verso, 2006), 18–19; Stanley Aronowitz, "The New American

Movement and Why it Failed," *Works and Days.* 28, nos. 55–56 (2010): 21–33; Victor Cohen, "The New American Movement and the Los Angeles Socialist Community School," *Minnesota Review,* no. 69 (Fall–Winter 2007): 139.

35. "The Middle East Resolutions at the National Council: A Step Forward," in Karen Farsoun, with Samih Farsoun and Alex Ajay, "Mid-East Perspectives from the American Left," *Journal of Palestine Studies* 4, no. 1 (Autumn 1974): 116.

36. New American Movement, "Resolution on the Arab/Palestinian-Israeli Conflict" (n.d.), author's collection.

37. Wayne State University, Walter P. Reuther Library of Labor and Urban Affairs, Democratic Socialists of America Collection (hereafter DSAC), box 3, folder 16, Resolutions, "NAM Position on the Middle East" (n.d.).

38. "DSOC Activists from Coast-to-Coast Say 'No' to NAM Merger Proposal."

39. DSAC, box 3, folder 16, "Resolution on DSOC/Nam, Adopted at the DSOC National Executive Committee Meeting, March 22, 1981."

40. Ibid., "Proposed Points of Political Agreement between the DSOC an NAM Negotiating Committees, April, 1981."

41. Harrington, *Long-Distance Runner,* 65.

## Chapter 8

1. "Spring Mobilization to Discuss Mideast War at Next Meeting," *Workers World,* June 24, 1967.

2. Sharon Rose, combined review of *Liberation* 18, no. 6 (February 1974), and Arnold Forster and Benjamin R. Epstein, *The New Anti-Semitism* (New York: McGraw Hill, 1974), in *MERIP Reports,* no. 28 (May 1974): 28.

3. Fred Halstead does not even mention the issue in his 881-page tome about the Movement, *Out Now: A Participant's Account of the Movement in the United States against the Vietnam War* (New York: Pathfinder Press, 2001). Nor do scholars like Simon Hall in *Rethinking the American Anti-War Movement* (New York: Routledge, 2012); Gerald Nicosia in *Home to War: A History of the Vietnam Veterans' Movement* (New York: Crown Publishers, 2001); or Kenneth J. Heineman in *Campus Wars: The Peace Movement at American State Universities in the Vietnam Era* (New York: New York University Press, 1993). Adam Garfinkle does discuss it briefly in *Telltale Hearts: The Origins and Impacts of the Vietnam Anti-War Movement* (New York: St. Martin's Griffin, 1997), but not in terms of how it bedeviled the Movement of the 1960s.

4. "Spring Mobilization to Discuss Mideast War at Next Meeting."

5. Louis Proyect, telephone interview by the author, January 4, 2014.

6. "Spring Mobilization to Discuss Mideast War at Next Meeting"; Swarthmore College, Peace Collection, National Mobilization Committee to End the War in Vietnam Records (hereafter MOBER), ser. 1, box 1, Administrative Committee (May 5, 1967–December 1968), minutes of meeting, June 17, 1967.

7. The Mobe's official minutes of the meeting do not indicate that Dannenberg was present.

8. "Spring Mobilization Committee Gags Opponents of Mideast War," *Workers World,* July 20, 1967; MOBER, cited n. 5 above, minutes of meeting, July 8, 1967.

9. Advertisement in *National Guardian*, July 8, 1967.

10. Freed, *War in the Mideast*, introduction (no page number given), 114.

11. Arabs and Jews for a Democratic Palestine, "From Vietnam to Palestine" (n.d.), author's collection.

12. Milton Friedman, "New Left Jews Split on Mideast," *Jewish Week*, January 30, 1969.

13. FBI document online in Gale Cengage's "Archives Unbound" series, Vietnam Veterans against the War Collection (subscription required).

14. Socialist Workers Party, *Internal Information Bulletin*, November 1971, 8.

15. James T. Lafferty, "The Anti-War Movement & the Struggle for Palestinian Liberation," *Free Palestine*, August 1971, 4–5.

16. Wayne State University, Walter Reuther Library, James Lafferty Collection, Baum to Lipsky, October 26, 1971; "Statement of Rabbi Lelyveld, Dictated over Telephone Friday Morning, October 29, 1971"; "Statement of Dr. Joachim Prinz on November 6th Peace March" (dictated October 29, 1971); ADL press release, November 23, 1971.

17. New York University, Elmer Holmes Bobst Library, Tamiment Library and Robert F. Wagner Labor Archives, Jewish Labor Committee Papers, "Dear Friend" letter, March 24, 1972.

18. For a full account of King's attitude to the conflict, see my *Black Power and Palestine*.

19. Murray Friedman, with the assistance of Peter Binzen, *What Went Wrong? The Creation and Collapse of the Black-Jewish Alliance* (New York: Free Press, 1995), 250–51; August Meier and John H. Bracey Jr., gen. eds., *The Martin Luther King, Jr., FBI File. Part II: The King-Levison File* (microfilm) (Frederick, MD: University Publications of America, Inc., 1987), reel 7, 287, 290, conversation of June 6, 1967.

20. Ibid., reel 7, 274, conversation of May 31, 1967; reel 7, 291, conversation of June 6, 1967; reel 7, 295–99, conversation of June 8, 1967.

21. King Center archives, Atlanta, GA (hereafter KCA), "Issues and Answers, Sunday, June 18, 1967."

22. Both events are detailed in my *Black Power and Palestine*.

23. KCA, "Anti-Semitism, Israel, and SCLC: A Statement on Press Distortions" (1967).

24. "The Liberation of Palestine and Israel," *New York Review*, July 1, 1971.

25. Swarthmore College, Peace Collection, Women Strike for Peace Records, ser. A, 4, box 3, "Statement on the Middle East" (1967); Women Strike for Peace Southern California Council, "Statement on the Middle East Crisis," June 6, 1967; "N.Y. Women Strike for Peace Statement on the Middle East Crisis."

26. Ibid., Barbara Bick, "Toward Peace in the Middle East."

27. Ibid., Draft policy statement by Gladys Knobel. Emphasis in the original.

28. Abbie Hoffman, *Revolution for the Hell of It* (New York: Simon & Schuster, 1970), 40.

29. www.youtube.com/watch?time_continue=160&v=etwykxCFEkM.

30. Yale University, Beinecke Rare Book and Manuscript Library, Leon F. Litwack Collection of Berkeley, California, Protest Literature, ser. 1, Files, box 2, folder 29, "The Middle East—What Democratic Socialists Say."

31. Walzer and Peretz, "Israel Is not Vietnam," 11, 14.

32. Peretz, "American Left and Israel."

33. Pennock, *Rise of the Arab American Left*, 125. Ten days after making that statement, Robert Kennedy was shot by Sirhan Bishara Sirhan, a Palestinian whose family were made refugees by the 1948 Arab-Israeli war. Kennedy died the following day.

34. Roy Reed, "Critics on Vietnam Divided by Appeal on Israel," *New York Times*, June 12, 1967.

35. Swarthmore College, Peace Collection, Peter Weiss Collected Papers, box 1, Involvement with the Foreign Policy Council of New York Democrats, general, 1966–67, notes for "Israel and Vietnam: There Is a Difference" talk (n.d.); Foreign Policy Council of New York Democrats, "Israel & Vietnam" (n.d.; correspondence, 1967).

36. Wesley Pruden Jr., "Doves on Asia Turn to Hawks on Middle East," *National Observer*, June 15, 1970; Irving Spiegel, "7 Senators Urge Planes for Israel," *New York Times*, May 24, 1970.

37. "Playboy Interview: George McGovern—Candid Conversation," *Playboy* 18, no. 8 (August 1971): 62.

38. Harry Ring, "Doves into Hawks; a Lesson for the Peace Movement," *Militant*, June 12, 1967.

39. "File for the Record," *Near East Report* 12, no. 12 (June 11, 1968): 47.

40. McCarthy campaign pamphlet, www.4president.org/brochures/1972/mccarthy1972brochure.htm.

41. University of Utah, J. Willard Marriott Library, Special Collections and Archives, Utah Peace and Freedom Party Records, box 1, folder 3, "Utah Peace and Freedom Party, 1968 Platform."

42. Swarthmore College, Peace Collection, Vietnam Veterans against the War Records, National Office, 1971–73 (Chicago) file, Statement on Imperialism (n.d.).

43. "Middle East," VVAW/WSO *Newsletter*, October 1973.

44. "GIs: We Must Not Fight in the Middle East," *The Bond*, October 21, 1973. Emphasis in the original.

45. David Cortright, *Soldiers in Revolt: GI Resistance during the Vietnam War* (Chicago: Haymarket Books, 2005), 147–48.

## Chapter 9

1. Bill Ayers, *Fugitive Days: Memoirs of an Antiwar Activist* (Boston: Beacon Press, 2001), 241. Ayers employed pseudonyms in the book. In referring to Annie Stein, he used the name "Abby Stern." For information about Stein's life, see the book written by her grandson, Thai Jones: *A Radical Line: From the Labor Movement to the Weather Underground, One Family's Century of Conscience* (New York: Free Press, 2004), 27.

2. The first fifteen years of the twenty-first century saw an explosion of interest in the Weather Underground and a flurry of books about it, including memoirs by former members and collections of the group's writings. Many of these are listed below and in the bibliography. Some memoirs and analyses mention how the group dealt with the Arab-Israeli conflict, although not in any great detail.

3. For a comparative look at this phenomenon as it emerged both in the United States and Europe, see Jeremy Varon, *Bringing the War Home: The Weather Underground, the Red Army Faction, and Revolutionary Violence in the Sixties and Seventies* (Berkeley: University of California Press, 2004).

4. "Weather Letter," *Rat: Subterranean News,* July 15, 1970, in Harold Jacobs, ed., *Weatherman* (New York: Ramparts Press, 1970), 460–61.

5. Jacobs, ed., *Weatherman,* 440.

6. Gilbert, *Love and Struggle,* 29, 123.

7. Bernardine Dohrn, telephone interview by the author, March 30, 2011.

8. Mark Rudd, "Why Were There So Many Jews in SDS? (or, the Ordeal of Civility)," speech to the New Mexico Jewish Historical Society, November 2005. www.markrudd.com.

9. Howard Machtinger to the author, March 27, 2011.

10. Naomi Jaffe to the author, March 7, 2012.

11. David Gilbert to the author, March 1, 2012.

12. Eric Mann, "Radical Forum," *Guardian,* October 17, 1970. Others at the time interpreted Mann's comment "whatever action is decided to be appropriate" to mean possible attacks. See Lipset, "Socialism of Fools."; *New York Times,* January 3, 1971; *Ba-Golah—In Exile* 1, no. 1 (1970).

13. Laura Whitehorn, telephone interview by the author, March 8, 2012.

14. *Sing a Battle Song,* ed. Dohrn, Ayers and Jones, 337–38.

15. Ibid., 340–41, 342.

16. Diana Block, telephone interview by the author, January 3, 2013.

17. "Palestine Will Win!" *Breakthrough* 2, no. 1 (Spring 1978): 8–23.

18. Ibid., 9, 14, 22.

19. Ibid., 9–10, 14, 22, 23.

20. Ibid.

21. Hugh Hough, "Dohrn, Emerging after 10 Years, Is Still Critical of U.S.," *Washington Post,* December 4, 1980.

22. "Palestine Will Be Free! Zionism, White Supremacy and the Palestinian Revolution," *Breakthrough* 6, no. 1 (Spring 1982): 11.

23. Laura Whitehorn, telephone interview by the author, March 8, 2012.

24. Joe Tropea, "Laura Whitehorn: The Social-Justice Activist Talks about the Weather Underground, Black Panthers and the Double Standard of Violent Action in the U.S.," *Baltimore City Paper,* February 24, 2010, www2.citypaper.com/story.asp?id=19825.

25. www.usasurvival.org/docs/buck_indictment.pdf; United Press International news flash, April 5, 1984.

26. Bay Area Revolutionary Union, *Red Papers I,* Statement of Principles. Encyclopedia of Anti-Revisionism On-Line. Transcription, editing, and markup by Paul Saba. www.marxists.org/history/erol/ncm-1/red-papers-1/statement.htm.

27. See Max Elbaum, *Revolution in the Air: Sixties Radicals Turn to Lenin, Mao, and Che* (New York: Verso, 2006).

28. Ibid., 134, 136.

29. See FBI Domestic Intelligence Division inspection report, April 6, 1970, p. 61, https://archive.org/stream/foia_FBI_Domestic_Intelligence_Division-HQ-1/ FBI_Domestic_Intelligence_Division-HQ-1#page/n87/mode/2up/search/fatah.

30. Davida Fineman, telephone interview with the author, April 17, 2018.

31. Bill Nichols, "New from California Newsreel," *Jump Cut* 17 (April 1978): 10–13.

32. New York University, Elmer Holmes Bobst Library, Tamiment Library & Robert F. Wagner Labor Archives, Revolutionary Communist Party Records, box 1, folder 30, Middle East, document on the party's position on Zionism (n.d.).

33. Pennock, *Rise of the Arab American Left*, 101.

34. "Statement of the Political Unity of the October League." Transcription, editing, and markup by Paul Saba. www.marxists.org/history/erol/ncm-1/ ol-unity-statement-inter

35. "Documents from the Founding Congress of the Communist Party (Marxist-Leninist)," www.marxists.org/history/erol/ncm-3/cp-founding/section6.htm.

36. Communist Labor Party of the United States of America, *Congress Documents, September, 1974* (n.p.: Proletarian Publishers, 1974), 21–22.

37. "The Theory of Three Worlds and the Middle East Situation Today," *Workers' Press*, February–March 1978. Encyclopedia of Anti-Revisionism On-Line. Transcription, editing, and markup by Paul Saba. www.marxists.org/history/erol/ncm-1a/mlc-mid-east.htm.

38. Prior to 1974, the Democratic Front for the Liberation of Palestine was known as the Popular Democratic Front for the Liberation of Palestine.

39. US Senate, "Threats to the Peaceful Observance of the Bicentennial." *Hearing before the Senate's Committee of the Judiciary's Subcommittee to Investigate the Administration of the Internal Security Act and other International Security Laws, June 18, 1976* (Washington, DC: GPO, 1976), 17.

40. University of Utah, J. Willard Marriott Library, Special Collections, Fayez A. Sayegh Papers (hereafter FSP), box 93, folder 3, "Palestine Solidarity Committee, "Palestine! Funding Proposal: 1977."

41. Anne E. Geyer and Robert Y. Shapiro, "A Report: Human Rights," *Public Opinion Quarterly* 52, no. 3 (Autumn 1988): 391. Shaul Mitelpunkt details changing American attitudes toward Israel and the conflict in the 1970s in his *Israel in the American Mind: The Cultural Politics of US-Israeli Relations, 1958–1988* (New York: Cambridge University Press, 2018).

42. After 1977, the UN changed the date for the annual commemoration of International Day of Solidarity with the Palestinian People to November 29.

43. FSP, box 93, folder 3, "Palestine Solidarity Committee, "Palestine! Funding Proposal: 1977."

44. "Protest Rally in New York against Camp David," *Palestine: P.L.O. Information Bulletin* 4, no. 19 (November 1, 1978), www.newjerseysolidarity.net/plobulletin/ vol4no19nov1978/plobulletin_vol4no19nov1978.pdf.

45. Associated Press, June 3, 1979.

46. Elbaum, *Revolution in the Air*, 321ff. The author wishes to acknowledge other points raised by Elbaum in terms of the failures of the New Communist Movement..

## Chapter 10

1. Joshua Muravchik, "Comrades," *Commentary* 121, no. 1 (January 2006), www.commentarymagazine.com/article/comrades.

2. Duke University, Rare Book, Manuscript, and Special Collections Library, Social Democrats, USA Records (1937–1994) (hereafter SDUSAR), accession 96–104, box 15, Youth Institute for Peace in the Middle East (YIPME), Gershman to Sacher, October 14, 1976; "Program Proposal 1978–79"; "Funding Proposal" (n.d.).

3. Ben Wattenberg, "A Man Whose Ideas Helped Change the World," *Baltimore Sun*, April 22, 1992.

4. Wendy Rosenberg, "The Youth Institute for Peace in the Middle East: An Example of Youth Education in Action" (MA thesis, University of Pittsburgh, 1983), 5–6.

5. Robert I. Friedman, "The Enemy Within: How the Anti-Defamation League Turned the Notion of Human Rights on Its Head, Spying on Progressives and Funneling Information to Law Enforcement," *Village Voice*, May 11, 1993, 27–32.

6. These included Boston University, Clark University, the University of Massachusetts at Amherst, Tufts, New York University, Columbia, Cornell, Rutgers, Temple University, American University, George Washington University, Georgetown, Johns Hopkins University, University of Maryland, Wayne State University, Michigan, Michigan State, Indiana University at Bloomington, the University of Illinois, Chicago Circle, University of Georgia, UCLA, Stanford, Berkeley, the University of San Francisco, and many others.

7. SDUSAR, accession 96–104, box 15, Youth Institute for Peace in the Middle East (YIPME), Kopilow to Forster, October 1, 1975.

8. Ibid., "Youth Leaders Denounce Terror" (n.d., but late 1974); "Report on the Activities of the Youth Institute for Peace in the Middle East, Sept. 1974–June, 1975."

9. Ibid., "Youth Institute for Peace in the Middle East, Financial Report, July 1, 1976–June 30, 1977"; "Report to the Board of Directors of the Youth Institute for Peace in the Middle East from the Washington Office" (n.d., but November 1976).

10. Ibid., "Minutes of the Mid-Year Board Meeting, May 5, 1978, New York, New York"; Rustin to Moynihan, September 12, 1978.

11. Rosenberg, "Youth Institute for Peace in the Middle East," 28–34.

12. League for Industrial Democracy, *Special Report: The State of the Student Movement—1970* (New York: League for Industrial Democracy, n.d.).

13. *The American Challenge: A Social Democratic Program for the Seventies* (New York: Social Democrats, U.S.A. and the Young People's Socialist League, 1973), 55–56.

14. SDUSAR, box 1, Socialist Party National Committee Files, 1974–74, "Appeal to World Socialists: Support Israel" (November 10, 1973).

15. Ibid.

16. Stanford University, Hoover Institution, Albert Glotzer Papers (hereafter AGP), box 56, folder 1 (1973), Suall and Toth to SD and YPSL national and local leaders (October 12, 1973).

17. Ibid.

18. Ibid., November 2, 1973, press release.

19. *Report of the Socialist International Fact Finding Mission to the Middle East, Circular No. B 14/7* (London: Socialist International, 1977).

20. New York University, Elmer Holmes Bobst Library, Tamiment Library and Robert F. Wagner Labor Archives, Michael Harrington Papers, ser. III, Writings and Other Activities, box 7, folder 15, Confidential Memo from Gershman re: SI Bureau Meeting, 15–16 Oct '77, 17–19.

21. Harrington, *Long-Distance Runner,* 87.

22. Much has been written about Jewish neoconservatives; see, e.g., Murray Friedman, *The Neoconservative Revolution: Jewish Intellectuals and the Shaping of Public Policy* (Cambridge: Cambridge University Press, 2005). For the centrality of Israel in the neoconservative mind-set, see Daniel G. Hummel, "Israel and the Rise of the Neoconservatives, 1960–1976" (MA thesis, Colorado State University, 2010).

23. Norman Podhoretz, *Why Are Jews Liberals?* (New York: Vintage Books, 2010), 2.

24. Norman Podhoretz, "A Certain Anxiety," *Commentary* 52, no. 2 (August 1971): 4–10.

25. Gary Dorrien, *The Neoconservative Mind: Politics, Culture, and the War of Ideology* (Philadelphia: Temple University Press, 1993), 129.

26. Quoted in Norman Podhoretz, "Now, Instant Zionism," *New York Times*, February 3, 1974.

27. "'In the Long Run,' Revolutionary Left Zionism's Only True Ally, Says Ben-Aharon," Jewish Telegraphic Agency, August 2, 1972, www.jta.org/1972/08/02/archive/in-the-long-run-revolutionary-left-zionisms-only-true-ally-says-ben-aharon.

28. AGP, box 56, folder 1 (1973), November 2, 1973, press release.

29. Midge Decter, "A Look at Israel," *Commentary* 51, no. 5 (May 1971): 38–42.

30. SDUSAR, accession 96–104, box 15, Youth Institute for Peace in the Middle East (YIPME), list of YIPME board members on the masthead of various letters.

31. "Politics in America: An Interview with Carl Gershman," *Ba-Golah—In Exile* (Winter 5737/1977): 7.

32. Gershman, "New Face of Anti-Zionism," 17.

33. Norman Podhoretz, *Breaking Ranks: A Political Memoir* (New York: Harper & Row, 1979), 350–51.

34. AGP, box 56, folder 1 (1973), Suall and Toth to SD and YPSL national and local leaders (October 12, 173), attached "Dear Friend" document.

35. See Glazer's section in the article "McGovern and the Jews: A Debate," *Commentary* 54, no. 3 (September 1972): 43–51.

36. Decter, "Look at Israel," The online version of the article viewed by the author did not contain specific page numbers, www.commentarymagazine.com/articles/a-look-at-israel.

37. Peretz, "American Left and Israel." The online version of the article viewed by the author did not contain page numbers. It no longer appears online.

38. Lipset, "'Socialism of Fools.'"

39. Bernard Rosenberg and Irving Howe, "Are American Jews Turning to the Right?" in Lewis A. Coser and Irving Howe, eds., *The New Conservatives* (New York: Meridian Books, 1976), 77, 88.

40. Howard Sachar, *A History of Jews in America* (New York: Vintage Books, 1993), 824; "Jewish Vote Triples for Nixon; Jewish Majority Goes for McGovern," *Jewish Telegraphic Agency*, November 9, 1972, www.jta.org/1972/11/09/archive/jewish-vote-triples-for-nixon-jewish-majority-goes-for-mcgovern.

41. "U.S. Presidential Elections: Jewish Voting Record, 1916 through Present," www.jewishvirtuallibrary.org/jsource/US-Israel/jewvote.html.

42. Benjamin Balint, *Running Commentary: The Contentious Magazine That Transformed the Jewish Left into the Neoconservative Right* (New York: PublicAffairs, 2010), xi.

43. Peretz, "American Left and Israel," 27–34.

44. Peter Richardson, *A Bomb in Every Issue: How the Short, Unruly Life of Ramparts Magazine Changed America* (New York: New Press, 2009), 96.

45. American Jewish Committee, online archives, Salomon to Gold, October 28, 1975; "Notes for Confidential, Off-the-Record Report by Bert Gold to Board of Governors re AJD Activities on the 'Zionism/Racism'" issue (n.d.), www.ajcarchives.org/AJC_DATA/Files/751.PDF.

46. Nathan Abrams, *Norman Podhoretz and Commentary Magazine: The Rise and Fall of the Neocons* (New York: Continuum Books, 2010), 146.

## Chapter 11

1. Swarthmore College, Swarthmore College Peace Collection, War Resisters League Records (hereafter WRLR), ser. B, subser. II, box 1, Executive Committee meetings, 1974–74, January 16 and March 2–3, 1974; 1974 WRLR "Statement on the Middle East."

2. David McReynolds, "The Destiny of Israel: a Minority View," *Village Voice*, June 29, 1967.

3. Swarthmore College Peace Collection, Papers of David McReynolds, ser. 1, box 12, Business Correspondence, June 1967 (4), McReynolds to Wolf, June 23, 1967.

4. Ibid., McReynolds to Ostrer, June 20, 1967.

5. Shaul Mitelpunkt discusses these new American attitudes toward the Arab-Israeli conflict in the 1970s in *Israel in the American Mind*.

6. The committee consisted of McReynolds, Norma Lee Pleskin Becker, Jerry Coffin, and Allan Solomonow; Irma Zigas served as an ex-officio member. WRLR, ser. B, subser. II, box 1, Executive Committee meetings, 1974–74, January 16 and March 2–3, 1974; February 15–16, 1975.

7. Ibid., Executive Committee meetings, March 2–3, 1974; February 15–16, 1975.

8. Ibid., 1974 "Statement on the Middle East."

9. Ibid., Executive Committee meetings, December 4, 1974; February 15–16 and March 12, 1975.

10. Swarthmore College, Peace Collection, Fellowship of Reconciliation Records (hereafter FORR). § II, ser. D, box 7, Uri Avnery 1970 speaking tour; Brick to Paisley, September 28, 1970.

11. Ibid., Foxman to ADL regional offices, September 18, 1970. See also Balfour Brickner, "My Zionist Dilemmas," *Sh'ma* 1, no. 1 (November 9, 1970), cited in *The Jewish 1960s: A Sourcebook*, ed. Michael E. Staub (Waltham, MA: Brandeis University Press, 2004), 186; Waskow, *Bush*, 72–75.

12. American Jewish Historical Society, Jewish Peace Fellowship Records, box 7, folder, Uri Davis Controversy, Solomonow to "Danny," September 18, 1970; Robinson to members of the executive committee, September 9, 1970; "Israeli Pacifist to Tour U.S."; JPF Cancels Co-Sponsorship of Tour," Jewish Telegraphic Agency, November 20, 1970www.jta.org/1970/11/20/archive/israeli-pacifist-to-tour-u-s-jpf-cancels-co-sponsorship-of-tour.

13. Daniel Berrigan, "Responses to Settler Regimes," *American Report*, October 29, 1973, 5, 16–17. Berrigan was involved in several high-profile actions against the war in Vietnam, including helping to form Clergy and Laity Concerned about Vietnam in 1965 and burning military draft files in Catonsville, Maryland, in 1968, using homemade napalm. After going underground to avoid a prison sentence, Berrigan was captured and imprisoned from mid-1970 until early 1972.

14. Ibid.

15. Arthur Hertzberg, "Response to Daniel Berrigan on 'Settler Regimes,'" *American Report*, November 12, 1973, 7, 14.

16. Balfour Brickner, "'With Friends Like These . . . ,'" *American Report*, December 10, 1973, repr. in *The Great Berrigan Debate* (New York: Committee on New Alternatives in the Middle East, 1974), 16.

17. Noam Chomsky, "Daniel in the Lions' Den: Berrigan & His Critics," *Liberation* 18, no. 6 (February 1974): 15.

18. David Dellinger, "Bringing It All Back Home," *Liberation* 18, no. 6 (February 1974): 6–7, 25–29.

19. Paul Rogat Loeb, "Grand Illusion: American Jews and Israel," *Liberation* 18, no. 6 (February 1974): 30–31.

20. *New York Times*, December 16, 1973; United Press International story, *The Telegraph* (Nashua, NH), January 23, 1974.

21. Swarthmore College, Peace Collection, Manuscripts Collection, Committee on New Alternatives in the Middle East (hereafter, CONAMER), Allan Solomonow, "Dear Peace People" letter (n.d.).

22. Holt Labor Library, San Francisco, Berta Green Langston Papers (hereafter BGLP) ser. 5, Committee on New Alternatives in the Middle East, 1969–2005, carton 1, folder 37, Committee Sponsors and Arie Bober, Langston to Machover, November 7, 1969; Langston to Bober, November 7, 1969; Emmanuel Dror Farjoun to the author, January 19, 2018.

23. BGLP, carton 1, folder 34, Newspaper Clippings, Press Releases, Publicity and Marketing; folder 37, Committee Sponsors and Arie Bober, Langston to Leventhal, May 12, 1970.

24. CONAMER, Documents: "CONAIME *[sic]*—A Report to the Steering Committee," January 15, 1971.

25. Ibid., "Middle East Education Project."

26. Ibid., box 23, CONAME (2), Jim to several others, October 3, 1974; "Report to the CONAME Steering Committee," December 16, 1974; Hunter's memorandum, December 19, 1974.

27. Anne E. Geyer and Robert Y. Shapiro, "The Polls—A Report: Human Rights," *Public Opinion Quarterly* 52, no. 3 (Autumn 1988): 389–90.

28. Ibid., 393. The survey was done in May 1977.

29. For a detailed study of Arab student activism, see Pennock, *Rise of the Arab American Left.*

30. Association of Arab-American University Graduates, *The First Decade, 1967–1977* (Detroit: AAUG, 1977). For a thorough scholarly study of the AAUG, see Pennock, *Rise of the Arab American Left.*

31. Abdeen Jabara, "The AAUG: Aspirations and Failures," *Arab Studies Quarterly* 29, 3–4 (Fall 2007), www.thefreelibrary.com/Unfulfilled+expectations+the+genesis+and+demise+of+the+AAUG.-a0176372506.

32. For more on the Palestine Congress of North America, see Fawaz Turki, "The Passions of Exile: The Palestine Congress of North America," *Journal of Palestine Studies* 9, no. 4 (Summer 1980): 17–43.

33. Abdeen Jabara, "The American Left and the June Conflict," *Arab World* 14, nos. 10–11 (1967): 73–80.

34. Abdeen Jabara, "The Guild in Palestine: A History," *The Practitioner* 63, no. 4 (2006): 193.

35. National Lawyers Guild, *Treatment of Palestinians in Israeli-Occupied West Bank and Gaza: Report of the National Lawyers Guild 1977 Middle East Delegation* (New York: National Lawyers Guild, 1978), 139–41.

36. They were Howard Dickstein, Marsha Greenfield, Nancy Hormachea, Abdeen Jabara, Malea Kiblan, Garay Menicucci, Bill Montross, John Quigley, Matthew Ross, and Gunnar Sievert.

37. National Lawyers Guild, *Treatment of Palestinians in Israeli-Occupied West Bank and Gaza,* 142; Jabara, "Guild in Palestine," 194–95; Michael Steven Smith, *Lawyers for the Left: In the Courts, in the Streets, and on the Air* (New York: OR Books, 2019), 175–76

38. *Guild Notes,* April 1978; Jabara, "Guild in Palestine," 195.

39. See Morton Stavis in *Guild Notes,* July 1978.

40. Alan Dershowitz, "Can the Guild Survive Its Hypocrisy?" *American Lawyer,* August 11, 1978, 30–31; Smith, *Lawyers for the Left,* 175.

41. Abdeen Jabara, telephone interview by the author, May 23, 2012.

42. "Lawyers Divide on Israel," *Jewish Currents* 33, no. 2 (February 1979): 33.

43. Howard Dickstein, *Minority Report of the National Lawyers Guild on Treatment of Palestinians in Israeli Occupied Territories* (n.p., n.d.).

44. *Guild Notes,* April 1978; Jabara, "Guild in Palestine," 195; telephone interview with Abdeen Jabara, May 23, 2012.

45. Dickstein, *Minority Report*; Joseph Polakoff, "National Lawyers Guild Members Who Criticized Israel Admit Visiting Lebanon at Invitation of the PLO," Jewish Telegraphic Agency, December 1, 1978; "Lawyers Divide on Israel," 34.

46. FORRS II, ser. D, box 14, Palestine Human Rights Campaign, Zogby to Sponsor, August 14, 1978.

47. James Zogby and Jack O'Dell, eds., *Afro-Americans Stand Up for Middle East Peace* (Washington, DC: Palestine Human Rights Campaign, 1980), v–vi.

48. "Palestine Education Project Sept 81–May 82" (document in the author's possession); author's personal recollections.

49. From the author's many conversations with Wagner over the years.

50. FORR, § II, ser. D, box 14: Palestine Human Rights Campaign, "Draft: Call to a National Conference" (n.d.).

51. Geyer and Shapiro, "The Polls—A Report: Human Rights," 391.

52. Cavari, "Six Decades of Public Affection,"110.

## Chapter 12

1. Letty Cottin Pogrebin, "Anti-Semitism in the Women's Movement," *Ms.*, June 1982, 46, 62, 65. Italics in the original.

2. Women against Imperialism, "Taking Our Stand against Zionism and White Supremacy," *off our backs* (July 1982): 20.

3. For examples of how the women's movement was affected by opposing stances on the Arab-Israeli conflict, see Ellen Cantarow, "Zionism, Anti-Semitism and Jewish Identity in the Women's Movement," *Middle East Report*, no. 154 (September–October 1988): 38-43, 50: Feldman, *Shadow over Palestine*; Hanna Milstein, "The United Nations Women's Decade and Jewish Feminist Identity," *Ex Post Facto* 25 (Spring 2016): 199–222; and Brooke Lober, "Conflict and Alliance in the Struggle: Feminist Anti-Imperialism, Palestine Solidarity, and the Jewish Feminist Movement of the Late 20th Century" (PhD diss., University of Arizona, 2016).

4. See Judy Tzu-Chun Wu, *Radicals on the Road: Internationalism, Orientalism, and Feminism during the Vietnam Era* (Ithaca, NY: Cornell University Press, 2013), pt. III.

5. Sharon Rose and Cathy Tackney, *off our backs*, October 15, 1970, repr. by the Middle East Research and Information Project (MERIP).

6. *Grassroots Feminist Organizations. Part 1: Boston Area Second Wave Organizations, 1968–1998*. Primary Source Media. Christine Gauvreau, project editor (Woodbridge, CT: Gale Cengage Learning, 2008) (microfilm), Women's School Records. reel 38, folder 135, Courses [Summer]: Middle East, 1974, "Middle East: Women's Perspective" and Middle East Course Outline.

7. Women's Middle East Committee to Support the Palestinians, "Self-Determination for the Palestinian People. Solidarity with the Arab Masses" (n.p., n.d.).

8. Frances M. Beal, "Double Jeopardy: To be Black and Female," in *Sisterhood is Powerful: An Anthology of Writings from the Women's Liberation Movement*, ed. Robin Morgan (New York: Vintage Books, 1970), 340–53.

9. For more information, see my *Black Power and Palestine*.

10. For more on these two conferences, see Lober, "Conflict and Alliance in the Struggle."

11. United Nations, *Report of the World Conference of the International Women's Year, Mexico City, 19 June—2 July 1975*. UN Document E/CONF./66/34. (New York: United Nations, 1976), 3, 6. Emphasis in the original.

12. Letty Cottin Pogrebin, *Deborah, Golda, and Me: Being Female and Jewish in America* (New York: Crown Publishers, 1991), 154.

13. Suzanne Braun Levine and Mary Thom, eds., *Bella Abzug: How One Tough Broad from the Bronx Fought Jim Crow and Joe McCarthy, Pissed Off Jimmy Carter, Battled for the Rights of Women and Workers, Rallied against War and for the Planet, and Shook Up Politics along the Way* (New York: Farrar, Straus and Giroux, 2008), 6.

14. Merl Berwin and Jennifer Sartori, *Making Our Wilderness Bloom: Women Who Made American Jewish History*. Foreward *[sic]* by Ruth Bader Ginsberg (Brookline, MA: Jewish Women's Archive, 2004), 187.

15. Betty Friedan, *It Changed My Life: Writings on the Women's Movement* (Cambridge, MA: Harvard University Press, 1998), 448, 460.

16. Betty Friedan, *Life So Far: A Memoir* (New York: Simon & Schuster, 2006), 291.

17. US Department of State, *Report of the United States Delegation to the World Conference of the United Nations Decade for Women: Equality, Development and Peace. July 14–30, 1980, Copenhagen, Denmark* (n.p., n.d.).

18. Ibid., 14–15.

19. United Nations, *Report of the World Conference of the United Nations Decade for Women: Quality, Development and Peace. Copenhagen, 14 to 30 July 1980*. UN Document A/CONF.94/35. (New York: United Nations, 1980), 151–52.

20. Ibid., 152–53.

21. Nilüfer Çağatay and Ursula Funk, "Comments on Tinker's 'A Feminist View of Copenhagen,'" *Signs* 6, no. 4 (Summer 1981): 777.

22. Pogrebin, "Anti-Semitism in the Women's Movement," 46, 62, 69.

23. Ibid., 65.

24. Laura Whitehorn to the author, October 23, 2012.

25. Cantarow, "Zionism, Anti-Semitism and Jewish Identity in the Women's Movement," 42.

26. Diana Block, telephone interview by the author, January 3, 2013.

27. Judith Mirkinson, telephone interview by the author, December 14, 2012.

28. The woman asked not to be identified.

29. Toni Morrison, "What the Black Woman Thinks about Women's Lib," *New York Times Magazine*, August 22, 1971, 4; repr. in Toni Morrison, *What Moves at the Margin: Selected Nonfiction*, ed. Carolyn C. Denard (Jackson: University Press of Mississippi, 2008), 29.

30. "Letters Forum: Anti-Semitism," *Ms.*, February 1983, 13. Italics in the original. The ten women who signed the letter were Deborah Rosenfelt, Judith Stacey, Rayna Rapp, Temma Kaplan, Barbara Epstein, Jane Gurko, Judith Walkowitz, Bluma Goldstein, Diane Ehrensaft, and Ellen DuBois.

31. Ibid.

32. *Alliance against Women's Oppression: Our History and Our Political Line* (n.p., n.d.).

33. Five College Archives and Manuscript Collection, Smith College, Sophia Smith Collection. "Historical Note," http://asteria.fivecolleges.edu/findaids/sophia-smith/mnsss529_bioghist.html.

34. Alliance against Women's Oppression, *Zionism in the Women's Movement—Anti-Imperialist Politics Derailed,* Discussion Paper no. 4 (October 1983), 1–2, 10.

35. Ibid.

36. For more on WAI, see Lober, "Conflict and Alliance in the Struggle."

37. Women against Imperialism, *The Issue of Zionism in the Women's Movement* (San Francisco: Women against Imperialism, 1982).

38. Ibid., 2, 6, 7.

39. Ibid., 8.

40. Judith Mirkinson, telephone interview by the author, December 14, 2012.

41. Women against Imperialism, "Taking Our Stand against Zionism and White Supremacy," 20.

42. Di Vilde Chayes is Yiddish for "The Wild Beasts," with an English plural, from Yiddish English expression "[so-and-so] is a *vilde chaye*," said of someone who behaves in a wild or outrageous manner. The group included Evelyn Tornton Beck, Irena Klepfisz, Adrienne Rich, Melanie Kaye/Kantrowitz, Bernice Mennis, Gloria Z. Greenfield, and Nancy K. Bereano.

43. Di Vilde Chayes, "An Open Letter to the Women's Movement," *off our backs* 12, no. 6 (July 1982): 21. Emphasis in the original.

44. Freedom Archives, Women against Imperialism Records, box 5, folder 9, Palestine and Zionism, statement signed by nine Jewish women.

45. "We Are Lesbians," *Gay Flames,* September 11, 1970.

46. Janet Meyers, "Diaspora Takes a Queer Turn"; Alice Block, "Scenes from the Life of a Jewish Lesbian"; and Liza Cowan and Penny House, "Anti-Semitism in the Lesbian Movement"; all in *Dyke: A Quarterly,* no. 5 (Fall 1977): 17–19, 12–14, and 20–22.

47. Janet M. Gottler, letter in *Gay Community News,* June 19, 1982; Janet Gottler, telephone interview by the author, May 9, 2019.

48. "Jewish and Arab Women's Dialog," *off our backs* 13, no. 1 (January 1983): 6–7, 27.

49. Elly Bulkin, Minnie Bruce Pratt, and Barbara Smith, *Yours in Struggle: Three Feminist Perspectives on Anti-Semitism and Racism* (Brooklyn, NY: Long Haul Press, 1984).

50. Nawal El-Saadawi, "Reap What You Have Sown," *Al-Ahram Weekly Online,* May 31–June 6, 2001, http://wcckly.ahram.org.eg/Archive/2001/536/op5.htm.

51. See the biographical postscript about Nelson in the 1992 documentary film distributed by California Newsreel *Berkeley in the Sixties* (directed by Mark Kitchell) at https://studylib.net/doc/8134289/transcript---california-newsreel.

52. "Moving towards Home," in June Jordan, *Living Room: New Poems, 1980–1984* (New York: Thunder's Mouth Press, 1985), 132–24. Jordan's poems include "To Sing a Song of Palestine" and "Apologies to All the People in Lebanon," in *Directed by Desire: The Collected Poems of June Jordan* (Port Townsend, WA: Copper Canyon Press, 2007), 345 and 380–82. See also Feldman, *Shadow over Palestine,* 185.

53. Dworkin, *Life and Death,* 225.

## Epilogue

1. From the website of the Palestine National BDS Committee: "What is BDS?" at https://bdsmovement.net.

2. Eric Lee, "I Resign from Democratic Socialists of America," www.ericlee.info/blog/?p=1286.

3. See http://socialistcurrents.org/?page_id=621.

4. Personal correspondence with the Institute for Palestine Studies, December 21, 2015.

5. See the "playbook," www.juf.org/pdf/iec/IEC-playbook.pdf.

6. https://spme.org/boycotts-divestments-sanctions-bds/unmasking-bds-radical-roots-extremist-ends/19116/

7. On Canary Mission, see https://canarymission.org. Daniel Greenfield, *Students for Justice in Palestine: A Hate Group* (Sherman Oaks, CA: David Horowitz Freedom Center, 2015); Dan Diker, *Students for Justice in Palestine Unmasked: Terror Links, Violence, Bigotry, and Intimidation on US Campuses* (Jerusalem: Jerusalem Center for Public Affairs, 2018). The 200 figure is taken from the National Students for Justice in Palestine web page, www.nationalsjp.org.

8. Nathan Thrall, "How the Battle over Israel and Anti-Semitism Is Fracturing American Politics," *New York Times,* March 28, 2019.

# Bibliography

Primary Sources

*Archival Holdings*

American Jewish Committee Archives, New York. Bertram H. Gold Executive Papers.

American Jewish Committee Archives, New York. Interreligious Affairs Collection.

American Jewish Historical Society, New York. American Academic Association for Peace in the Middle East (N.Y.) Collection.

American Jewish Historical Society, New York. Jewish Peace Fellowship Records.

American Jewish Historical Society, New York. Jewish Student Organizations Collection.

American Jewish Historical Society, New York. Philip Slomovitz South End Collection.

American Jewish Historical Society, New York. Subject Files Collection.

Chicago History Museum, Chicago. Max Naiman Papers.

Columbia University, Columbia University Library Archives, New York. Central Files.

Columbia University, Columbia University Library Archives, New York. Historical Subject Files.

Columbia University, Columbia University Library Archives, New York. University Protest & Activist Collection.

Duke University, Rare Book, Manuscript, and Special Collections Library, Durham, NC. Social Democrats, USA Records.

Emory University, Robert W. Woodruff Library, Manuscripts, Archives, and Rare Book Library, Atlanta, GA. Harvey Klehr Papers.

Freedom Archives, San Francisco. Anti-Zionism Collection.

Freedom Archives, San Francisco. Colin Edwards Collection.

Freedom Archives, San Francisco. Palestine Collection.

Freedom Archives, San Francisco. Women against Imperialism Collection.

Holt Labor Library, San Francisco. Berta Green Langston Papers.

New York University, Elmer Holmes Bobst Library, Tamiment Library and Robert F. Wagner Labor Archives, New York. Alex Bittelman's "Things I Have Learned" Papers.

New York University, Elmer Holmes Bobst Library, Tamiment Library and Robert F. Wagner Labor Archives, New York. Communist Party, USA Records.

New York University, Elmer Holmes Bobst Library, Tamiment Library and Robert F. Wagner Labor Archives, New York. Democratic Socialists of America Records.

New York University, Elmer Holmes Bobst Library, Tamiment Library and Robert F. Wagner Labor Archives, New York. Edward S. Goldstein: Jewish Labor Committee Papers.

New York University, Elmer Holmes Bobst Library, Tamiment Library and Robert F. Wagner Labor Archives, New York. International Socialists Records.

New York University, Elmer Holmes Bobst Library, Tamiment Library and Robert F. Wagner Labor Archives, New York. Leslie Cagan Papers.

New York University, Elmer Holmes Bobst Library, Tamiment Library and Robert F. Wagner Labor Archives, New York. Max Shachtman Papers.

New York University, Elmer Holmes Bobst Library, Tamiment Library and Robert F. Wagner Labor Archives, New York. Michael Harrington Papers.

New York University, Elmer Holmes Bobst Library, Tamiment Library and Robert F. Wagner Labor Archives, New York. Morris Schappes Papers.

New York University, Elmer Holmes Bobst Library, Tamiment Library and Robert F. Wagner Labor Archives, New York. National Organization for Women, New York City Chapter Records.

New York University, Elmer Holmes Bobst Library, Tamiment Library and Robert F. Wagner Labor Archives, New York. New American Movement Papers.

New York University, Elmer Holmes Bobst Library, Tamiment Library and Robert F. Wagner Labor Archives, New York. Periodicals.

New York University, Elmer Holmes Bobst Library, Tamiment Library and Robert F. Wagner Labor Archives, New York. Printed Ephemera Collection on Organizations.

New York University, Elmer Holmes Bobst Library, Tamiment Library and Robert F. Wagner Labor Archives, New York. Printed Ephemera on Subjects.

New York University, Elmer Holmes Bobst Library, Tamiment Library and Robert F. Wagner Labor Archives, New York. Revolutionary Communist Party Records.

New York University, Elmer Holmes Bobst Library, Tamiment Library and Robert F. Wagner Labor Archives, New York. Socialist Workers Party Printed Ephemera Collection.

New York University, Elmer Holmes Bobst Library, Tamiment Library and Robert F. Wagner Labor Archives, New York. Students for a Democratic Society Printed Ephemera Collection.

Stanford University, Hoover Institution, Palo Alto, CA. Albert Glotzer Papers.

Stanford University, Hoover Institution, Palo Alto, CA. Carl Gershman Papers.

Stanford University, Hoover Institution, Palo Alto, CA. New Left Collection.

Stanford University, Hoover Institution, Palo Alto, CA. Social History Collection.

Stanford University, Hoover Institution, Palo Alto, CA. Socialist Workers Party Records.

Swarthmore College, Swarthmore College Peace Collection, Swarthmore, PA. Clergy and Laity Concerned Records.

Swarthmore College, Swarthmore College Peace Collection, Swarthmore, PA. Fellowship of Reconciliation Records.

Swarthmore College, Swarthmore College Peace Collection, Swarthmore, PA. Fifth Avenue Vietnam Peace Parade Committee.

Swarthmore College, Swarthmore College Peace Collection, Swarthmore, PA. Manuscripts Collection.

Swarthmore College, Swarthmore College Peace Collection, Swarthmore, PA. National Mobilization Committee to End the War in Vietnam Records.

Swarthmore College, Swarthmore College Peace Collection, Swarthmore, PA. National Peace Action Coalition.

Swarthmore College, Swarthmore College Peace Collection, Swarthmore, PA. Papers of David McReynolds.

Swarthmore College, Swarthmore College Peace Collection, Swarthmore, PA. Peter Weiss Collected Papers.

Swarthmore College, Swarthmore College Peace Collection, Swarthmore, PA. Vietnam Moratorium Committee.

Swarthmore College, Swarthmore College Peace Collection, Swarthmore, PA. Vietnam Veterans Against the War, Inc.

Swarthmore College, Swarthmore College Peace Collection, Swarthmore, PA. War Resisters League Records.

Swarthmore College, Swarthmore College Peace Collection, Swarthmore, PA. Women Strike for Peace Records.

University of Arkansas, University Libraries, Special Collections, Fayetteville, AR. Women's Library Collection.

University of California at Berkeley, Bancroft Library, Berkeley, CA. Social Protest-Collection.

University of California at Santa Barbara, David Library, Department of Special Collections. Santa Barbara, CA. Student Organizations Collection.

University of Chicago, University of Chicago Library, Special Collections Research Center, Chicago: Alan Sussman Collection.

University of Michigan, Bentley Historical Library, Ann Arbor, MI. Abdeen Jabara Papers.

University of Michigan, Bentley Historical Library, Ann Arbor, MI. Vice President for Student Affairs (Univ. of Michigan) Records.

University of Utah, J. Willard Marriott Library, Special Collections, Salt Lake City, UT. Fayez Sayegh Papers.

University of Utah, J. Willard Marriott Library, Special Collections, Salt Lake City, UT. Utah Peace and Freedom Party Records.

University of Virginia, Albert and Shirley Small Special Collections Library, Charlottesville, VA. Social Movements Collection.

University of Virginia, Albert and Shirley Small Special Collections Library, Charlottesville, VA. Student Council Appropriations Committee Archives.

Vanderbilt University, Television News Archive, Nashville, TN.

Wayne State University, Walter P. Reuther Library of Labor and Urban Affairs, Detroit. Detroit Revolutionary Movements Collection.

Wayne State University, Walter P. Reuther Library of Labor and Urban Affairs, Detroit. Dan Georgakas Collection.

Wayne State University, Walter P. Reuther Library of Labor and Urban Affairs, Detroit. James Lafferty Collection.

Wayne State University, Walter P. Reuther Library of Labor and Urban Affairs, Detroit. Office of the President, William Rea Keast Collection.

Yale University, Beinicke Rare Book and Manuscript Library, New Haven, CT. Leon F. Litwack Collection of Berkeley, California, Protest Literature.

### Archival Collections on Microfilms, CD-ROM, and/or Online

America in Protest: Records of Anti-Vietnam War Organizations. Part 1: Vietnam Veterans against the War. Primary Source Media. Woodbridge, CT: Gale Cengage, 2007.

America in Protest: Records of Anti-Vietnam War Organizations. Part 3: Student Mobilization Committee to End the War in Vietnam, 1966–1973. Primary Source Media. Woodbridge, CT: Gale Cengage, 2008.

American Jewish Committee, New York. Online archives. http://ajcarchives.org/main.php.

Five College Archives and Manuscript Collection, Smith College. Sophia Smith Collection. https://asteria.fivecolleges.edu/findaids/smitharchives/manosca4_main.html.

*Grassroots Feminist Organizations. Part 1: Boston Area Second Wave Organizations, 1968–1998.* Edited by Christine Gauvreau. Woodbridge, CT: Primary Source Media Series, Gale Cengage Learning, 2008.

The King Center, Atlanta, Georgia. Online archives. www.thekingcenter.org.

*The Martin Luther King, Jr., FBI File. Part II: The King-Levison File.* Edited by August Meier and John H. Bracey Jr. Frederick, MD: University Publications of America, Inc., 1987.

*Socialist Party of America Papers, 1919–1976, Addendum.* Glen Rock, NJ: Microfilming Corporation of America, 1977.

*Students for a Democratic Society Papers, 1958–1970.* Glen Rock, NJ: Microfilming Corporation of America, 1977.

United States, National Institutes of Health, National Library of Medicine. "Profiles in Science." The Christian B. Anfinsen Papers online collection. https://profiles.nlm.nih.gov/KK.

*Published, Microfilmed, and Online US Government Documents*

Central Intelligence Agency. "The Family Jewels." www.cia.gov/library/readingroom/docs/DOC_0001451843.pdf

————. Documents released in response to Freedom of Information Act requests: "Intelligence Report: ESAU L: The Fedayeen (Annex to ESAU XLVIII: Fedayeen—"Men of Sacrifice"), January 1971." www.theblackvault.com/documents/esau-49.pdf.

Federal Bureau of Investigation. Documents released in response to Freedom of Information Act requests: Subjects: Palestine Liberation Organization (New York Office); al-Fatah; "The Fedayeen Impact—Middle East and United States" (June 1970; www.governmentattic.org/2docs/FBI_Monograph_Fedayeen-Impact_1970.pdf); "The Fedayeen Terrorist—A Profile" (June 1970;https://archive.org/details/TheFeyadeenTerroristAnIntroductionJune1970).

————. "The FBI Files on the Weather Underground." Beverley Hills, CA: Paperless Archives, n.d.

————. https://vault.fbi.gov.

US Congress. House of Representatives. The Workers World Party and its Front Organizations. A Study Prepared by the Minority Staff of the Committee on Internal Security, House of Representatives, 93rd Cong., 1st sess. (April 1974). Washington, DC: GPO, 1974.

US Congress. Senate. Foreign and Military Intelligence, Book I. Final Report of the Select Committee to Investigate Governmental Operations with Respect to Intelligence Activities. Together with Additional, Supplemental, and Separate Views. Washington, DC: GPO, 1976.

————. "Threats to the Peaceful Observance of the Bicentennial." Hearing before the Senate's Committee of the Judiciary's Subcommittee to Investigate the Administration of the Internal Security Act and other International Security Laws. June 18, 1976. Washington, DC: GPO, 1976.

————. World Conference of the International Women's Year. Report to the Committee on Government Operations, United States Senate, by Senator Charles H. Percy, Illinois, United States Congressional Adviser to the World Conference of the International Women's Year, September 8, 1975. Washington, DC: GPO, 1975.

————. Extent of Subversion in Campus Disorders. Senate Committee on the Judiciary, Subcommittee to Investigate the Administration of the Internal Security Act and Other Internal Security Laws. Washington, DC: GPO, 1969.

US Department of State. Report of the United States Delegation to the World Conference of the United Nations Decade for Women: Equality, Development and Peace. July 14–30, 1980, Copenhagen, Denmark, 14–15. N.p., n.d.

*Interviews, Telephone Interviews, and Personal Communications*

Albert, Judy Gumbo

Al-Fattal, Randa Khalidi

Beck, Evelyn Tornton
Beinin, Joel
Block, Diana
Cantor, Aviva
Cavalletto, George
Chomsky, Noam
Dohrn, Bernardine
Dunbar-Ortiz, Roxanne
Farjoun, Emmanuel Dror
Feinstein, Mark
Feldman, Bob
Fineman, Davida
Gilbert, David
Goodman, Susan Teller
Gottler, Janet
Griswold, Deirdre
Guerrero, Gene
Guindon, Richard
Hayden, Tom
Horowitz, Gus
Hudson, Michael
Jabara, Abdeen
Jaffe, Naomi
Khaled, Leila
Klonsky, Mike
Krassner, Paul
Kurshan, Nancy
Lerner, Michael
Lowen, Marilyn
Lynd, Staughton
Machtinger, Howard
Mattison, Georgia
McReynolds, David
Medvecky, Nick
Menicucci, Garay
Mirkinson, Judith
Muskat, Hal
Obenzinger, Hilton
Plamandon, Pun
Porter, Thomas
Price, Wayne
Proyect, Louis
Quigley, John

Raskin, Jonah
Retherford, James
Rose, Sharon
Rosenberg, M. J.
Ross, Bob
Rudd, Mark
Siegel, Dan
Siegel, Ellen
Sokolow, Jeff
Stork, Joe
Townes, Jean Whilden
Tucker, Judith
Vered, Dan
Wagner, Donald
Whitehorn, Laura


## Unpublished Secondary Sources

Bernstein, Susan Croft. "Arab Propaganda in the United States, 1965–1970: A Case Study in International Communications." MA thesis, George Washington University, 1971.

Hummel, Daniel G. "Israel and the Rise of the Neoconservatives, 1960–1976." MA thesis, Colorado State University, 2010.

Lober, Brooke. "Conflict and Alliance in the Struggle: Feminist Anti-Imperialism, Palestine Solidarity, and the Jewish Feminist Movement of the Late 20th Century." PhD diss., University of Arizona, 2016.

Mitelpunkt, Shaul. "The Cultural Politics of US-Israeli Relations and the Rediscovery of American Empire, 1958–1986." PhD diss., University of Chicago, 2013.

Ne'eman, Yisrael. "From the New Left to the Jewish Left: Zionist Student Activism in America from 1967–73." MA thesis, University of Haifa, 2004.

Rosenberg, Wendy. "The Youth Institute for Peace in the Middle East: An Example of Youth Education in Action." MA thesis, University of Pittsburgh, 1983.

Slonecker, Blake. "Living the Moment: Liberation News Service, Montague Farm, and the New Left, 1967–1981." PhD diss., University of North Carolina at Chapel Hill, 2009.

Zamil, Abdulrahman Abdulla. "The Effectiveness and Credibility of Arab Propaganda in the United States." PhD diss., University of Southern California, 1973.


## Published Sources

Abdulhadi, Rabab Ibrahim. "Whose 1960s? Gender, Resistance, and Liberation in Palestine." In *New World Coming: The Sixties and the Shaping of Global Con-*

*sciousness,* ed. Karen Dubinsky, Catherine Krull, Susan Lord, Sean Mills, and Scott Rutherford. Toronto: Between the Lines, 2009.

Aber, Joel. "Atlanta Forum Report." *Party Builder: SWP Organizational Discussion Bulletin* 6, no. 2 (June 1970): 16.

———. "The Role of the SWP in Supporting the Arab Revolution." *SWP Discussion Bulletin* 27, no. 12 (August 1969): 13–15.

Abrams, Nathan. *Norman Podhoretz and Commentary Magazine: The Rise and Fall of the Neocons.* New York: Continuum Books, 2010.

Abu Rudeneh, Odeh. "The Jewish Factor in US Politics." *Journal of Palestine Studies* 1, no. 4 (Summer 1972): 92–107.

Adelson, Alan M. *SDS.* New York: Scribner, 1972.

Adler, Renata. *Toward a Radical Middle: Fourteen Pieces of Reporting and Criticism.* New York: Random House, 1969.

"Aggressors and Oppressors." *Workers World,* June 24, 1967.

Albert, Michael. *Remembering Tomorrow: From SDS to Life after Capitalism.* New York: Seven Stories Press, 2006.

al-Fateh. "Toward a Democratic State." Statement Issued at the 2nd World Conference on Palestine. N.p., 1970. Alliance against Women's Oppression. *Alliance against Women's Oppression: Our History and Our Political Line.* San Francisco: The Alliance, [1980].

———. *Zionism in the Women's Movement—Anti-Imperialist Politics Derailed.* Discussion Paper no. 4 (October 1983).

"Al-Yahud al-Ahrar ma` al-Thawra al-Filastiniyya [Liberal Jews with the Palestinian Revolution]." *al-Fateh,* September 9, 1970.

*The American Challenge: A Social Democratic Program for the Seventies.* New York: Social Democrats, U.S.A. and the Young People's Socialist League, 1973.

American Institute for Political Communication. *Domestic Communications Aspects of the Middle East Crisis.* N.p., 1967.

"Al Fatah Investigated." *Near East Report* 13, no. 10 (May 14, 1969).

American Jewish Committee. *Arab Appeals to American Public Opinion.* New York: American Jewish Committee, Institute of Human Relations, 1969.

*American Jewish Yearbook.* Vol. 69. New York: American Jewish Committee; Philadelphia: American Jewish Publication Society, 1968.

"Amman '71: Long Hot Summer." *MERIP* 1, no. 2 (August 1971): 1–2.

*The Anatomy of Peace in the Middle East.* Proceedings of the Annual Conference. New York: American Academic Association for Peace in the Middle East, 1969.

Anderson, Terry H. *The Movement and the Sixties: Protest in America from Greensboro to Wounded Knee.* New York: Oxford University Press, 1995.

*Answers and Questions: Information Points for Israelis Abroad, No. 1.* Jerusalem: Information Division of the Ministry of Foreign Affairs, 1970.

Aptheker, Herb. *The Mid-East—Which Way to Peace?* New York: Committee for a Just Peace in the Middle East, 1971.

"Arab-Israeli Conflict: Turn the Guns the Other Way." *Spartacist,* March–April 1968, 4–6.

"The Arab Propaganda Campaign on the Campus." *Near East Report* 13, no. 22 (October 29, 1969): 99–110.

"Arab Revolution Defense Urged by 4th International." *The Militant*, July 16, 1967.

"Arabs and Jews: An Editorial." *Ramparts* 6, no. 1 (July 1967): 2–3.

"Arabs Latest to Learn Lesson: Soviets Won't Fight Imperialism." *Challenge*, July 1967.

"Arabs Will Beat U.S.-Israel Imperialism AND Arab Nationalism." *Challenge*, August 1969.

Arnoni, Menahem S. "Doing What Comes Unnatural." *Israel Magazine* 2, no. 2 (1969): 57–59.

———. "Rights and Wrongs in the Arab-Israeli Conflict (To the Anatomy of the Forces of Progress and Reaction in the Middle East)." *The Minority of One* 9, no. 9 (September 1967): 6–28.

———. "Why the New Left Needs Israel." In *The New Left and the Jews*, ed. Mordecai S. Chertoff. New York: Pitman, 1971.

Aronowitz, Stanley. *The Death and Rebirth of American Radicalism*. New York: Routledge,1996.

———. "The New American Movement and Why It Failed." *Works and Days* 28, nos. 55–56 (2010): 21–33.

———. "Setting the Record Straight: Zionism from the Standpoint of Its Jewish Critics." *Logos* 3, no. 3 (Summer 2004). www.logosjournal.com/issue_3.3/aronowitz.htm.

Aronsfeld, C. C. "New Left Germans and El Fatah." *Jewish Frontier*, October 1969, 21–23.

Association of Arab-American University Graduates. *The First Decade, 1967–1977*. Detroit: AAUG, 1977.

Avineri, Shlomo. "Israel and the New Left." *Transaction* 7 (July–August 1970): 79–83.

Avinoam, Reuven. "The New Left in Israel" (July 1973). http://israeli-leftarchive.org/greenstone/collect/zenglish/index/assoc/HASH64df.dir/doc.pdf.

Ayers, Bill. *Fugitive Days: Memoirs of an Antiwar Activist*. With a new afterword by the author. Boston: Beacon Press, 2001.

Bakst, Jerome H. "The Radical Left and Al Fatah." *ADL Bulletin*, September 1969, 1–2, 8.

Balint, Benjamin. *Running* Commentary: *The Contentious Magazine That Transformed the Jewish Left into the Neoconservative Right*. New York: PublicAffairs, 2010.

Barber, David. *A Hard Rain Fell: SDS and Why it Failed*. Jackson, MS: University Press of Mississippi, 2008.

Bay Area Revolutionary Union. *Red Papers I*. Statement of Principles. Encyclopedia of Anti-Revisionism On-Line. Transcription, editing, and markup by Paul Saba. www.marxists.org/history/erol/ncm-1/red-papers-1/statement.htm.

Beal, Frances M. "Double Jeopardy: To be Black and Female." In *Sisterhood Is Powerful: An Anthology of Writings from the Women's Liberation Movement*, ed. Robin Morgan, 340–53. New York: Vintage Books, 1970.

Beinin, Irving. "Discussion: The Mideast Dispute." *National Guardian*, July 29, 1967.

———. "The Mideast War Solves No Problems." *National Guardian*, June 17, 1967.

Berger, Dan. *Outlaws of America: The Weather Underground and the Politics of Solidarity*. Oakland, CA: AK Press, 2006.

———, ed. *The Hidden 1970s: Histories of Radicalism*. New Brunswick, NJ: Rutgers University Press, 2010.

Berrigan, Daniel. "Responses to Settler Regimes." *American Report* 4, no. 2 (October 29, 1973):5, 16–17.

Berwin, Merl, and Jennifer Sartori. *Making Our Wilderness Bloom: Women Who Made American Jewish History*. Foreward *[sic]* by Ruth Bader Ginsberg. Brookline, MA: Jewish Women's Archive, 2004.

Bittelman, Alexander. *Program for Survival: The Communist Position on the Jewish Question*. New York: New Century Publishers, 1947.

———. *To Secure Jewish Rights: The Communist Position*. New York: New Century Publishers, 1948.

Blackstock, Nelson. *COINTELPRO: The FBI's Secret War on Political Freedom*. Introduction by Noam Chomsky. New York: Pathfinder Press, 1988.

Blankfort, Jeffrey. "Commentary." http://ifamericansknew.org/cur_sit/torture2.html.

Block, Alice. "Scenes from the Life of a Jewish Lesbian." *Dyke: A Quarterly*, no. 5 (Fall 1977): 17–19.

Block, Diana. *Arm the Spirit: A Woman's Underground Journey and Back*. Oakland, CA: AK Press, 2009.

Bober, Arie, ed., *The Other Israel: The Radical Case against Zionism*. Garden City, NY: Doubleday, Anchor Books, 1972.

Brickner, Balfour. "'With Friends Like These . . . '" *American Report*, December 10, 1973. Reprinted in *The Great Berrigan Debate* (New York: Committee on New Alternatives in the Middle East, 1974).

———. "My Zionist Dilemmas." In *The Jewish 1960s: A Sourcebook*, ed. Michael E. Staub. Waltham, MA: Brandeis University Press, 2004.

Brodek, Ted. "Fruits of Zionism." *Great Speckled Bird*, April 20, 1970.

"BS." "Palestine Plane Burnings." *Great Speckled Bird*, August 21, 1970.

Buch, Peter. "Burning Issues of the Mid-East Crisis." *International Socialist Review* 30, no. 2 (March–April 1969): 1–30.

———. "The Palestinian Revolution & Zionism." *International Socialist Review* 32, no. 1 (January 1971): 9–13, 24.

———. Review of "Palestinian Liberation and Israel." *International Socialist Review* 30, no. 5 (September–October 1969): 56–64.

Buhle, Paul. *Marxism in the United States: A History of the American Left*, 3rd ed. New York: Verso, 2013.

Bulkin, Elly. "Hard Ground: Jewish Identity, Racism, and Anti-Semitism." In *Yours in Struggle: Three Feminist Perspectives on Anti-Semitism and Racism*, ed. Elly Bulkin, Minnie Bruce Pratt, and Barbara Smith. Brooklyn, NY: Long Haul Press, 1984.

Burrough, Bryan. *Days of Rage: America's Radical Underground, the FBI, and the Forgotten Age of Revolutionary Violence.* New York: Penguin Press, 2015.

Bush, Lawrence. "Footprints: 'Pro-Israel, Non-Violence'—and Arguing with the Left." http://jewishcurrents.org/tag/footprints.

Çağatay, Nilüfer, and Ursula Funk. "Comments on Tinker's 'A Feminist View of Copenhagen.'" *Signs* 6, no. 4 (Summer 1981): 771–90.

Camejo, Peter. *North Star: A Memoir.* Chicago: Haymarket Books, 2010.

Cantarow, Ellen. "Zionism, Anti-Semitism and Jewish Identity in the Women's Movement." *Middle East Report,* no. 154 (September–October 1988): 38-43, 50.

Cavari, Amnon. "Six Decades of Public Affection: Trends in American Public Attitudes toward Israel." In *Israel and the United States: Six Decades of US-Israeli Relations,* ed. Robert O. Freedman. Boulder, CO: Westview Press, 2012.

*The Challenge of Change and Conflict in American Society.* New York: League for Industrial Democracy, 1975.

Chamberlin, Paul Thomas. *The Global Offensive: The United States, the Palestine Liberation Organization, and the Making of the Post-Cold War Order.* Oxford: Oxford University Press, 2012.

Charlton, Linda. "Jews Fear Anti-Zionism of New Left." *New York Times,* August 14, 1970.

Chertoff, Mordecai S. "The New Left and the Newer Leftists." In *The New Left and the Jews,* ed. Mordecai S. Chertoff. New York: Pitman, 1971.

Chetrit, Sami Shalom. *Intra-Jewish Conflict in Israel: White Jews, Black Jews.* New York: Routledge, 2010.

Chomsky, Noam. *Middle East Illusions, Including Chomsky's Peace in the Middle East? Reflections on Justice and Nationhood.* Lanham, MD: Rowman & Littlefield, 2003.

———. "Israel and the American Intelligentsia," in *Noam Chomsky: Radical Priorities.* Expanded 3rd ed., ed. C. P. Otero. Oakland, CA: AK Press, 2003.

———. "Israel and the Palestinians." *Socialist Revolution* 5, no. 2 (June 1975): 45–86, 133–41.

———. "Daniel in the Lions' Den: Berrigan & His Critics." *Liberation* 18, no. 6 (February 1974): 15–24.

———. "The Mideast: Dark at the End of the Tunnel." *Ramparts* 11, no. 7 (January 1973): 38–40, 53–55.

———. "Israel and the New Left." In *The New Left and the Jews,* ed. Mordecai S. Chertoff. New York: Pitman, 1971.

———. "Nationalism and Conflict in Palestine." *New Outlook* 12, no. 9 (November–December 1969): 21–31. Also published in *Liberation* 14, no. 8 (November 1969).

Christiansen, Samantha, and Zachary A. Scarlett, eds. *The Third World in the Global 1960s.* New York: Berghahn Books, 2013.

Christison, Kathleen. *Perceptions of Palestine: Their Influence on U.S. Middle East Policy.* Berkeley: University of California Press, 1999.

Cohen, Mitchell. "Democratic Socialism, Israel, and the Jews: An Interview with Michael Harrington." *Response* 9, no. 4 (Winter 1976): 33–39.

Cohen, Robert. *Freedom's Orator: Mario Savio and the Radical Legacy of the 1960s.* New York: Oxford University Press, 2009.

Cohen, Victor. "The New American Movement and the Los Angeles Socialist Community School." *Minnesota Review,* no. 69 (Fall–Winter 2007): 139–51.

Cohn, Werner. "From Victim to Shylock and Oppressor: The New Image of the Jew in the Trotskyist Movement." *Journal of Communist Studies* 7, no. 1 (March 1991): 46–68.

Collins, Gary, and Leonard Gordon. "On the Mideast Conflict." *SWP Discussion Bulletin* 26, no. 8 (October 1967): 9–13.

Communist Labor Party of the United States. *Congress Documents. September 1974.* N.p.: Proletarian Publishers, 1974.

Copeland, V[incent]. "Israeli State; Not a Homeland but a Catspaw." *Workers World,* July 7, 1967.

Cortright, David. *Soldiers in Revolt: GI Resistance during the Vietnam War.* New introduction by Howard Zinn. Chicago: Haymarket Books, 2005.

Cowan, Liza, and Penny House. "Anti-Semitism in the Lesbian Movement." *Dyke: A Quarterly,* no. 5 (Fall 1977): 20–22.

Curtis, Michael, ed. *People and Politics in the Middle East. Proceedings of the Annual Conference of the American Academic Association for Peace in the Middle East.* New Brunswick, NJ: Transaction Books, 1971.

Dahlberg, Roy. "Suggested Middle East Resolution Re: Arab-Israeli Reaction and Implications, Re: NIC Resolution." *New Left Notes,* June 19, 1967.

Davis, James M. "Arabs Resist Israel's Occupation." *Guardian,* September 14, 1968.

Davis, Uri. "Journey Out of Zionism: The Radicalization of an Israeli Pacifist." *Journal of Palestine Studies* 1, no. 4 (Summer 1972): 59–72.

Davis, Uri, and Norton Mezvinsky, eds. *Documents from Israel, 1967–1973: Readings for a Critique of Zionism.* London: Ithaca Press, 1975.

DeBenedetti, Charles, with Charles Chatfield, assisting author. *An American Ordeal: The Antiwar Movement of the Vietnam Era.* Syracuse, NY: Syracuse University Press, 1990.

Decter, Midge. "A Look at Israel." *Commentary* 51, no. 5 (May 1971): 38–42.

Dellinger, David. "Bringing It All Back Home." *Liberation* 18, no. 6 (February 1974): 6–7, 25–29.

Dershowitz, Alan M. *Taking the Stand: My Life in the Law.* New York: Crown Publishers, 2013.

———. "Can the Guild Survive Its Hypocrisy?" *American Lawyer,* August 11, 1978, 30–31.

Diker, Dan. *Students for Justice in Palestine Unmasked: Terror Links, Violence, Bigotry, and Intimidation on US Campuses.* Jerusalem: Jerusalem Center for Public Affairs, 2018.

Di Vilde Chayes [Jewish lesbian feminist collective]. "An Open Letter to the Women's Movement." *off our backs* 12, no. 6 (July 1982): 21.

"Documents from the Founding Congress of the Communist Party (Marxist-Leninist)." http://marxists.anu.edu.au/history/erol/ncm-3/cp-founding/intro.htm.

Dohrn, Bernardine. "When Hope and History Rhyme." In *Sing a Battle Song: The Revolutionary Poetry, Statements, and Communiqués of the Weather Underground, 1970–1974*, ed. Dohrn, Bill Ayers, and Jeff Jones. New York: Seven Stories Press, 2006.

Dohrn, Bernardine, with Bill Ayers and Jeff Jones, eds. *Sing a Battle Song: The Revolutionary Poetry, Statements, and Communiqués of the Weather Underground, 1970–1974*. New York: Seven Stories Press, 2006.

Dorrien, Gary. *The Neoconservative Mind: Politics, Culture, and the War of Ideology.* Philadelphia: Temple University Press, 1993.

"Dr. Timothy Leary (Weather Underground Statement)." In *Sing a Battle Song: The Revolutionary Poetry, Statements, and Communiqués of the Weather Underground, 1970–1974*, ed. Bernadine Dohrn, Bill Ayers, and Jeff Jones; 153–55. New York: Seven Stories Press, 2006.

Drabble, John. "Fighting Black Power–New Left Coalitions: Covert FBI Media Campaigns and American Cultural Discourse, 1967–1971. *European Journal of American Culture* 27, no. 2 (2008): 65–91.

Draper, Hal. "Anatomy of the Pro-Zionist Apologist." *New Politics* 6, no. 4 (Fall 1967): 56–70.

———. "A Brief Tour of Social-Chauvinism." *New Politics* 6, no. 2 (Spring 1967): 83–90.

———. "The Origins of the Middle East Crisis." *New Politics* 6, no. 1 (Winter 1967): 13–22.

———, ed. *The First Arab-Israeli War, 1948–49.* Independent Socialist Clippingbooks Xerox Series No. X-2. Berkeley: Independent Socialist Clippingbooks, 1967.

———, ed. *Israel: The First Decade.* Xeroxcopy Series No. X-3. Berkeley: Independent Socialist Clipping Books, 1967.

———, ed. *Zionism, Israel, & the Arabs: The Historical Background of the Middle East Tragedy.* Independent Socialist Clippingbooks No. 3. Berkeley: Independent Socialist Clippingbooks, 1967.

"DSOC Activists from Coast-to-Coast Say 'No' to NAM Merger Proposal." *Mainstream*, August 1980.

Duberman, Martin. *A Saving Remnant: The Radical Lives of Barbara Deming and David McReynolds.* New York: New Press, 2011.

Dunbar-Ortiz, Roxanne. *Outlaw Woman: A Memoir of the War Years, 1960–1975.* San Francisco: City Lights, 2001.

Dworkin, Andrea. *Life and Death: Unapologetic Writings on the Continuing War against Women.* London: Virago Press, 1997.

Eanet, Susan. "Arab Women Fight." *New Left Notes*, March 7, 1969.

———. "History of the Middle East Liberation Struggle: Part 1." *New Left Notes*, February 28, 1969.

Edelsberg, Herman. *Whose Fight in the Middle East? An Analysis of America's National Interest.* Washington, DC: B'nai B'rith International Council, 1970.

Ehrman, John. *The Rise of Neoconservatism: Intellectuals and Foreign Affairs, 1945– 1994.* New Haven, CT: Yale University Press, 1995.

Elbaum, Max. *Revolution in the Air: Sixties Radicals Turn to Lenin, Mao, and Che.* New York: Verso, 2006.

Ellerin, Milton, and Abraham S. Karlikov. *Zionism, Israel and the New Left.* New York: American Jewish Committee, 1971.

El Saadawi, Nawal. "Reap What You Have Sown." *Al-Ahram Weekly Online*, May 31– June 6, 2001. http://weekly.ahram.org.eg/Archive/2001/536/op5.htm.

Ende, Gabriel. "Leaving All This Behind: Reflections on a Matured Zionist Commitment." In *The New Jews*, ed. James A. Sleeper and Alan L. Mintz. New York: Vintage Books, 1971.

Estraikh, Gennady. "Professing Leninist Yiddishkayt: The Decline of American Yiddish Communism." *American Jewish History* 96, no. 1 (March 2010): 33–60.

———. *Yiddish in the Cold War.* Studies in Yiddish No. 7. A Legenda Book. London: Modern Humanities Research Association and Maney Publishing, 2008.

Evans, Les. "The Arab Leaders and Imperialism." *The Militant*, August 21, 1967.

———. "Palestine Arab Refugees Victims of Zionist Politics." *The Militant*, June 19, 1967.

Farber, David. *The Age of Great Dreams: America in the 1960s.* New York: Hill & Wang, 1994.

Farber, David, and Beth Bailey. *The Columbia Guide to America in the 1960s.* New York: Columbia University Press, 2001.

Farjoun, Emmanuel. "Zionism after the June 1967 War." *New Politics* 8, no. 4 (Fall 1970): 64–71.

Farsoun, Karen, with Samih Farsoun and Alex Ajay. "Mid-East Perspectives from the AmericanLeft." *Journal of Palestine Studies* 4, no. 1 (Autumn 1974): 94–119.

Fein, Leonard J. "The New Left and Israel." In *The New Left and the Jews*, ed. Mordecai S. Chertoff. New York: Pitman, 1971.

Feitelson, Rose, and George Salomon. *The Many Faces of Anti-Semitism.* Foreword by Nathan Glazer. N.p.: American Jewish Committee, 1967.

Feldman, Bob. "Sundial: Columbia SDS Memories. Chapter 10: The Viet Nam Summer of Love, 1967." http://columbiasdsmemories.blogspot.com/2009/08/chapter-10-viet-nam-summer-of-love-1967.html.

———. "From His '69 Awakening to the 'Wild-Animal' State and Lobby—Hilton Obenzinger on Israel." http://mondoweiss.net/2009/11/from-his-69-awakening-to-the-wild-animal-state-and-lobby-hilton-obenzinger-on-israel/.

Feldman, Keith P. *A Shadow over Palestine: The Imperial Life of Race in America.* Minneapolis: University of Minnesota Press, 2015.

"File for the Record." *Near East Report* 12, no. 12 (June 11, 1968): 47.

Findley, Paul. *They Dare to Speak Out: People and Institutions Confront Israel's Lobby.* Westport, CT: Lawrence Hill, 1985.

Finkelstein, Norman G. *Knowing Too Much: Why the American Jewish Romance with Israel Is Coming to an End.* New York: OR Books, 2012.

Fischbach, Michael R. *Black Power and Palestine: Transnational Countries of Color.* Stanford, CA: Stanford University Press, 2018.

"Five Proposed Principles of SDS Unity." *Guardian,* July 5, 1969. Encyclopedia of Anti-Revisionism On-Line. Transcription, editing, and markup by Paul Saba. www.marxists.org/history/erol/ncm-1/sds-5.htm.

Foley, Tom. "How Trotskyites Support War Aims of Tel Aviv Hawks," "The Kind of State Trotskyites Would Set up in Mideast," and "Self-Determination for the Palestinians." In *Self-Determination in the Mideast: A Debate from the Pages of The Militant and Daily World. Dave Frankel versus Tom Foley.* New York: Pathfinder Press, 1974.

"For a Secure Israel! For a Secure Peace in the Middle East! Statement of Leaders of Progressive Jewish Organizations and Institutions in the USA, Issued Dec. 1, 1970." *Jewish Currents* 25, no. 1 (January 1971): 6.

"For the Security of the State of Israel! For Peace in the Middle East!" *Jewish Currents* 23, no. 10 (November 1969): 3–6.

Forster, Arnold, and Benjamin R. Epstein. *The New Anti-Semitism.* New York: McGraw-Hill, 1974.

Frankel, Dave, Dick Roberts, and Tony Thomas. *War in the Middle East: A Socialist View.* New York: Pathfinder Press, 1973.

Freed, Rita. *War in the Mideast.* Committee to Support Middle East Liberation Pamphlet No. 5. New York: World View Publishers, 1972.

———. *The War in the Mideast, June 1967: What Were the Forces Behind It?* New York: Ad Hoc Committee on the Mideast, 1967.

Friedan, Betty. *Life So Far: A Memoir.* New York: Simon & Schuster, 2006.

———. *It Changed My Life: Writings on the Women's Movement.* Cambridge, MA: Harvard University Press, 1998.

Friedman, Milton. "New Left Jews Split on Mideast." *Jewish Week,* January 30, 1969.

Friedman, Murray. *The Neoconservative Revolution: Jewish Intellectuals and the Shaping of Public Policy.* Cambridge: Cambridge University Press, 2005.

Friedman, Robert I. "The Enemy Within: How the Anti-Defamation League Turned the Notion of Human Rights on Its Head, Spying on Progressives and Funneling Information to Law Enforcement." *Village Voice,* May 11, 1993: 27–32.

*From Refugees to Palestinians: The Birth of a Revolution.* Washington, DC: Middle East Research and Information Project, n.d.

Fruchter, Norman. "Arendt's Eichmann and Jewish Identity." In *For a New America: Essays in History and Politics from Studies on the Left, 1959–1967,* ed. James Weinstein and David W. Eakins. New York: Random House, 1970.

Gal, Allon, ed. *Envisioning Israel: The Changing Ideals and Images of North American*

*Jews.* Jerusalem: Magnes Press, Hebrew University; Detroit: Wayne State University Press, 1996.

Galun, Mel. *The New Tone of Arab Propaganda on Campus.* New York: American Zionist Youth Foundation, 1969.

Garfinkle, Adam. *Telltale Hearts: The Origins and Impacts of the Vietnam Anti-War Movement.* New York: St. Martin's Griffin, 1997.

General Union of Palestine Students. *Toward a Democratic Palestine. Second World Conference on Palestine,* n.d.

Georgakas, Dan, and Marvin Surkin. *Detroit: I Do Mind Dying.* 1975. 2nd ed. Cambridge, MA: South End Press, 1998.

Gershman, Carl. "The Andrew Young Affair." *Commentary* 68, no. 5 (November 1, 1979). www.commentarymagazine.com/article/the-andrew-young-affair.

———. "Between War and Peace: The Issues in the Middle East Conflict." *Crossroads* 2, no. 6 (June 1971). Reprinted by the Youth Committee for Peace and Democracy in the Middle East (n.p., n.d.).

———. "Ethnicity as a Social Force." In *The Challenge of Change and Conflict in American Society.* New York: League for Industrial Democracy, 1975.

———. "Israel: The New Left Is Not the Enemy." *Sh'ma: A Journal of Jewish Responsibility* 1, no. 18 (October 22, 1971): 137–38.

———. "Matzpen and Its Sponsors." *Commentary* 50, no. 2 (August 1970): 52–53.

———. "The New Face of Anti-Zionism." *American Zionist* 62, no. 4 (December 1971): 15–17.

———. "The New Left, Israel, and Jewish Youth." *The Call* 40, no. 4 (July 1971): 3–5.

Geyer, Anne E., and Robert Y. Shapiro. "The Polls—A Report: Human Rights." *Public Opinion Quarterly* 52, no. 3 (Autumn 1988): 386–98.

Gilbert, David. *Love and Struggle: My Life in SDS, the Weather Underground, and Beyond.* With an Appreciation by Boots Riley. Oakland, CA: PM Press, 2012.

———. *SDS/WUO: Students for a Democratic Society and Weather Underground Organisation.* Toronto: Arm the Spirit; Montreal: Abraham Guillen Press, 2002.

Ginsberg, Allen. "Thoughts & Recurrent Musings on Israeli Arguments." *Liberation* 18, no. 6 (February 1974): 14.

Ginsberg, Benjamin. *The Fatal Embrace: Jews and the State.* Chicago: University of Chicago Press, 1993.

"GIs: We Must Not Fight in the Middle East." *The Bond,* October 21, 1973.

Gitlin, Todd. *The Sixties: Years of Hope, Days of Rage.* New York: Bantam Books, 1987.

———. *The Whole World Is Watching: Mass Media in the Making & Unmaking of the New Left.* Berkeley: University of California Press, 1980.

Glazer, Nathan. "The New Left and the Jews." *Jewish Journal of Sociology* 11 (1969): 121–31.

Goldstein, Eric L. *The Price of Whiteness: Jews, Race, and American Identity.* Princeton and Oxford: Princeton University Press, 2006.

Gorny, Yosef. *The State of Israel in Jewish Public Thought: The Quest for Collective Identity.* Foreword by Michael A. Meyer. New York: New York University Press, 1994.

Gosse, Van. *Rethinking the New Left: An Interpretive History.* New York: Palgrave Macmillan, 2005.

*The Great Berrigan Debate.* New York: Committee on New Alternatives in the Middle East, 1974.

Greenfield, Daniel. *Students for Justice in Palestine: A Hate Group.* Sherman Oaks, CA: David Horowitz Freedom Center, 2015.

Guerrero, Gene. "How It Came About." *Great Speckled Bird*, October 4, 1970.

Guerrero, Gene, and Susie Teller. "Palestinian Report." *Great Speckled Bird*, October 4, 1970.

Hacker, David A. "Social Democrats, USA: Learning from Our Past and Revived under New Leadership to Build for a Brighter Future for the United States of America and the World." http://socialistcurrents.org/documents-public/Social_Democrats.pdf.

———. "Jewish Currents—A History." www.geocities.ws/stuart323__99/JewishCurrent.htm.

Hall, Gus. *For a Meaningful Alternative: Report to the June 10, 1967 Meeting of the National Committee of the Communist Party, U.S.A.* New York: New Outlook Publishers, 1967.

Hall, Simon. *Rethinking the American Anti-War Movement.* New York: Routledge, 2012.

Halstead, Fred. *Out Now: A Participant's Account of the Movement in the United States against the Vietnam War.* New York: Pathfinder Press, 2001.

Halstead, Fred, and Barry Sheppard. "Special Interview: Palestine's Al Fatah." *The Militant*, September 20, 1968.

Harap, Louis. *The Zionist Movement Reconsidered.* New York: Jewish Currents, 1976.

Harrington, Michael. "Are Socialist Leaders Compromising with Terrorism? The P.L.O. and the Democratic Left." *Commonweal* 107, no. 1 (January 1980): 10–13.

———. "Imperialism in the Middle East." In *Israel, the Arabs and the Middle East,* ed. Irving Howe and Carl Gershman. New York: Quadrangle Books, 1972.

———. *The Long-Distance Runner: An Autobiography.* New York: Holt, 1988.

———. "Oil and Blood Mix in the Middle East." *New America*, February 25, 1970. Reprinted by the Youth Committee for Peace and Democracy in the Middle East (n.p., n.d.).

———. *Socialism.* New York: Bantam Books, 1972.

Hayden, Tom. *Rebel: A Personal History of the 1960s.* Los Angeles: Red Hen Press, 2003.

———. *The American Future: New Visions beyond Old Frontiers.* Boston: South End Press, 1980.

Heineman, Kenneth J. *Campus Wars: The Peace Movement at American State Universities in the Vietnam Era.* New York: New York University Press, 1993.

Hermesh, Hayim. "Ha-Yehudim Shel al-Fateh [The Jews of al-Fateh]." *Ma'ariv*, February 28, 1969.

Hertzberg, Arthur. "Reply to Daniel Berrigan." *American Report* 4, no. 3 (November 12, 1973): 7, 14.

Hochman, Larry. "Israel and the Arab Revolution." *Arab World* 15, no. 6 (June 1969): 14–17.

———. *Zionism and the Israeli State: An Analysis in the June War.* Ann Arbor, MI: Radical Education Project, 1967.

Hoffman, Abbie. *The Autobiography of Abbie Hoffman.* Introduction by Norman Mailer. With a new afterword by Howard Zinn. New York: Four Walls Eight Windows, 1980.

———. *Soon to Be a Major Motion Picture.* Introduction by Norman Mailer. New York: Putnam, 1980.

———. *Revolution for the Hell of It.* New York: Simon & Schuster, 1970.

Hoffman, Anita, and Abbie Hoffman. *To America with Love: Letters from the Underground.* New York: Stonehill Publishing, 1976.

Hoffman, Elizabeth Cobbs. *All You Need Is Love: The Peace Corps and the Spirit of the 1960s.* Cambridge, MA: Harvard University Press, 1998.

Horowitz, David. "The Passion of the Jews." *Ramparts* 13, no. 3 (October 1974): 21–28.

Horowitz, Gus. *Israel and the Arab Revolution: Fundamental Principles of Revolutionary Marxism.* Education for Socialists. New York: National Education Department of the Socialist Workers Party, 1973.

Hough, Hugh. "Dohrn, Emerging after 10 Years, Is Still Critical of U.S." *Washington Post*, December 4, 1980.

House, Penny, and Liza Cowan. "Anti-Semitism in the Lesbian Movement." *Dyke: A Quarterly*, no. 5 (Fall 1977): 20–22.

"How American Radicals See the Resistance Dilemma." *Journal of Palestine Studies* 1, no. 4 (Summer 1972): 8–26.

"How the FBI Tried to Get Us Kicked Out of the SWP: COINTELPRO 'Dirty Tricks,'" *Workers Vanguard*, January 11, 1985. www.marxists.org/history/etol/newspape/ workersvanguard/1985/0370_11_01_1985.pdf.

Howe, Irving. "The Campus Left and Israel." In *Israel, the Arabs and the Middle East*, ed. Irving Howe and Carl Gershman. New York: Quadrangle Books, 1972.

———. "Political Terrorism: Hysteria on the Left." In *The New Left and the Jews*, ed. Mordecai S. Chertoff. New York: Pitman, 1971.

Huberman, Leo. "Israel Is Not the Main Enemy." *Monthly Review* 19, no. 5 (October 1967): 8–10.

Hudson, Michael C., and Willard G. Oxtoby. *America and the Middle East.* N.p.: New Haven Committee on the Middle East Crisis, 1968.

Interview with Jeffrey Blankfort. http://sf.indymedia.org/news/2006/11/1733088.php.

Irving, Sarah. *Leila Khaled: Icon of Palestinian Liberation.* London: Pluto Press, 2012.

"Israel and Socialism: Interview with Peter Buch." *Great Speckled Bird*, December 14, 1970.

*Israel and the Arabs: Militant Readers Debate the Middle East Conflict.* New York: Merit Publishers, 1969.

"Israel Report." *MERIP* 1, no. 4 (November 1971): 1, 12.

"Israel, What Now? An Editorial." *Jewish Currents* 25, no. 5 (May 1971): 3.

"Israel's Birth: Zionists Coldly Planned Terror." *Challenge*, July 1967.

Isserman, Maurice. *If I Had a Hammer . . . : The Death of the Old Left and the Birth of the New Left.* New York: Basic Books, 1987.

———.*The Other American: The Life of Michael Harrington.* New York: Public Affairs, 2000.

Isserman, Maurice, and Michael Kazin. *America Divided: The Civil War of the 1960s.* 4th ed. New York: Oxford University Press, 2012.

Jabara, Abdeen. "The AAUG: Aspirations and Failures." *Arab Studies Quarterly* 29, 3–4 (Fall 2007): 15–19.

———. "The American Left and the June Conflict." *Arab World* 14, nos. 10–11 (1967): 73–80.

———. "The Guild in Palestine: A History." *The Practitioner* 63, no. 4 (2006): 193–99.

Jacobs, Harold, ed. *Weatherman.* New York: Ramparts Press, 1970.

Jacobs, Jack, ed. *Jews and Leftist Politics: Jews, Israel, Anti-Semitism, and Gender.* New York: Cambridge University Press, 2017.

Jacobs, Paul. *Between the Rock and the Hard Place.* New York: Random House, 1970.

———. "No Peace in the Middle East." *Liberation* 14, no. 8 (November 1969): 22–33.

———. "A Time to Heal." *Ramparts* 6, no. 1 (July 1967): 3–10.

———. "Some of His Best Friends Were . . . " *Ramparts* 12, no. 9 (April 1974): 10–13.

———. "The View from Tel Aviv and Beirut." *Ramparts* 11, no. 9 (March 1973): 36–40, 58–59.

Jacobs, Ron. *Daydream Sunset: The 60s Counterculture in the 70s.* Petrolia, CA: CounterPunch Books, 2015.

———. *The Way the Wind Blew: A History of the Weather Underground.* New York: Verso, 1997.

"Jewish and Arab Women's Dialog." *off our backs* 13, no. 1 (January 1983): 6–7, 27.

"Jewish Aryanism in Israel." *The Realist*, no. 1 (June–July 1958): 5.

Jewish Liberation Project and Committee to Support Middle East Liberation. *Arab-Israeli Debate: Toward a Socialist Solution.* New York: Times Change Press, 1970.

*The Jewish Question and the Left—Old and New: A Challenge to the Left.* New York: Jewish Currents, 1970.

"Jews and the Left." *Journal of Palestine Studies* 4, no. 3 (Spring 1975): 154–60.

Jezer, Marty. *Abbie Hoffman: American Rebel.* Piscataway, NJ: Rutgers University Press, 1993.

Johnson, Peter, and Joe Stork. "MERIP: The First Decade." *Middle East Report,* nos. 100–101 (October–December 1981): 50–54.

Jones, Thai. *A Radical Line: From the Labor Movement to the Weather Underground, One Family's Century of Conscience.* New York: Free Press, 2004.

Jordan, June. *Directed by Desire: The Collected Poems of June Jordan.* Port Townsend, WA: Copper Canyon Press, 2007.

———. *Living Room: New Poems, 1980–1984.* New York: Thunder's Mouth Press, 1985.

Joseph, Ben. "Lumer on the Middle East: A Refutation of His Analysis of the Arab-Israeli War." *Jewish Currents* 21, no. 9 (October 1967): 9–13, 38.

Kaufman, Jonathan. *Broken Alliance: The Turbulent Times between Blacks and Jews in America.* New York: Touchstone Press, 1995.

Kazin, Michael. *American Dreamers: How the Left Changed a Nation.* New York: Knopf, 2011.

Kenan, Amos. "New Left Go Home." In *The New Left and the Jews*, ed. Mordecai S. Chertoff. New York: Pitman, 1971.

———. "Who Are the Defeatists?" *Liberation* 14, no. 8 (November 1969): 7–39.

Khaled, Leila. *My People Shall Live: The Autobiography of a Revolutionary*, ed. George Hajjar. London: Hodder & Stoughton, 1973.

Kihss, Peter. "U.S. Reds Assail 2 Jewish Papers." *New York Times*, March 30, 1969.

Klehr, Harvey. *Far Left of Center: The American Radical Left Today.* Piscataway, NJ: Transaction Books, 1988.

———. "Jews and American Communism." In *Jews and Leftist Politics: Jews, Israel, Anti-Semitism, and Gender*, ed. Jack Jacobs. New York: Cambridge University Press, 2017.

Klinghoffer, Judith A. *Vietnam, Jews and the Middle East: Unintended Consequences.* New York: St. Martin's Press, 1999.

Kurlansky, Mark. *1968: The Year That Rocked the World.* New York: Ballantine Books, 2004.

Lafferty, James T. "The Anti-War Movement & the Struggle for Palestinian Liberation." *Free Palestine*, August 1971.

Laqueur, Walter. "Revolutionism & the Jews: 1—New York and Jerusalem." *Commentary* 51, no. 2 (February 1971): 38–46.

———, ed., and Judith Tydor Baumer, assoc. ed. *The Holocaust Encyclopedia.* New Haven, CT: Yale University Press, 2001.

"Lawyers Divide on Israel." *Jewish Currents* 33, no. 2 (February 1979): 33–34.

League for Industrial Democracy. *Special Report: The State of the Student Movement—1970.* New York: League for Industrial Democracy, n.d.

Lee, Eric. "I Resign from Democratic Socialists of America." www.ericlee.info/blog/?p=1286.

———. *Saigon to Jerusalem: Conversations with U.S. Veterans of the Vietnam War Who Emigrated to Israel.* Jefferson, NC: McFarland, 1992.

Lefkowitz, Bernard. "View from the Left: A Meeting of Like Minds." *Village Voice*, June 29, 1967.

Leonard, Aaron J., and Conor A. Gallagher. *Heavy Radicals: The FBI's Secret War on America's Maoists. The Revolutionary Union/Revolutionary Communist Party, 1968–1980.* Washington, DC: Zero Books, 2014.

Lerner, Michael P. *Healing Israel/Palestine: A Path to Peace and Reconciliation.* Berkeley: North Atlantic Books, 2003.

———. "Jewish New Leftism at Berkeley." *Judaism* 18, no. 4 (Fall 1969): 473–78.

———. "Respectable Bigotry." *American Scholar* 38 (Autumn 1969): 606–17.

———. *The Socialism of Fools: Anti-Semitism on the Left.* Oakland, CA: Tikkun, 1992.

Levine, Suzanne Braun, and Mary Thom, eds. *Bella Abzug: How One Tough Broad from the Bronx Fought Jim Crow and Joe McCarthy, Pissed Off Jimmy Carter, Battled for the Rights of Women and Workers, Rallied against War and for the Planet, and Shook Up Politics along the Way.* New York: Farrar, Straus and Giroux, 2008.

"The Liberation of Palestine and Israel." *New York Review,* July 1, 1971.

Liebman, Charles S. *Pressure without Sanctions: The Influence of World Jewry on Israeli Policy.* Madison, NJ: Farleigh Dickenson University Press, 1977.

Lipset, Seymour Martin. "Jewish Interests and the New Left." In *The New Left and the Jews,* ed. Mordecai S. Chertoff. New York: Pitman, 1971.

———. "The Socialism of Fools: The Left, the Jews, and Israel." *Encounter,* December 1969, 24–35.

Loeb, Paul Rogat. "Grand Illusion: American Jews and Israel." *Liberation* 18, no. 6 (February 1974): 30–31.

Lubin, Alex. *Geographies of Liberation: The Making of an Afro-American Political Imaginary.* Chapel Hill, NC: University of North Carolina Press, 2014.

Lumer, Hyman. "The Middle East and the Intellectuals." *Commentary* 50, no. 4 (October 1970).

———. *The Middle East Crisis.* New York: New Outlook Publishers, 1967.

Lumer, Hyman, and Meir Vilner. *Zionism: Is It Racist? Two Statements on the UN Resolution.* New York: Committee for a Just Peace in the Middle East, n.d.

Lynn, Frank. "New Left Hits Israel, Viet War, Draft," *Newsday,* September 5, 1967.

Magil, A. B. *Crisis in the Middle East: Which Way Israel?* New York: New Century Publishers, 1956.

Mandel, William. "Israel—'Republic of Victims of Fascism.'" *The Movement* 3, no. 11 (November 1967): 10, 15.

Mann, Eric. "Radical Forum." *Guardian,* October 17, 1970.

Marqusee, Mike. *If I Am Not for Myself: Journey of an Anti-Zionist Jew.* New York: Verso, 2008.

McAlister, Melani. *Epic Encounters: Culture, Media, and U.S. Interests in the Middle East, 1945–2000.* Berkeley: University of California Press, 2001.

"McGovern and the Jews: A Debate." *Commentary* 54, no. 3 (September 1972).

McMillian, John. *Smoking Typewriters: The Sixties Underground Press and the Rise of an Alternative Media in America.* New York: Oxford University Press, 2011.

McReynolds, David. "The Destiny of Israel: A Minority View." *Village Voice,* June 29, 1967.

McReynolds, David, and Abraham Friend. "Two Views on the Middle East Crisis." *New Politics* 8, no. 3 (Summer 1970): 5–12.

Medoff, Rafael. *Jewish Americans & Political Participation: A Reference Handbook.* Santa Barbara, CA: ABD-CLIO, 2002.

Medvecky, Nick. "Revolution until Victory—Palestine al-Fatah." *Inner City Voice,* November 1969.

Meyers, Janet. "Diaspora Takes a Queer Turn." *Dyke: A Quarterly,* no. 5 (Fall 1977): 12–14.

"The Middle East." *Guardian,* February 1, 1969.

"Middle East." VVAW/WSO *Newsletter*, October 1973.

"Middle East." *Winter Soldier* 5, no. 2 (February 1975).

"The Middle East Conflict: A Socialist Labor Party Statement" (1978). www.slp.org.

Middle East Research and Information Project. *From Refugees to Palestinians: The Birth of a Revolution*. Washington, DC.: The Project, n.d. [1970?].

"The Mideast Conflict: Viewpoint." *Guardian*, June 10, 1967.

"Mid-East Swindle." *Challenge*, April 1969.

Miller, James. *"Democracy Is in the Streets": From Port Huron to the Siege of Chicago*. 1987. Cambridge, MA: Harvard University Press, 1994.

Mills, C. Wright. "Letter to the New Left," *New Left Review* 1, no. 5 (September–October 1960): 18–23.

———. *The Marxists*. New York: Dell, 1963.

Milstein, Hanna. "The United Nations Women's Decade and Jewish Feminist Identity." *Ex Post Facto* 25 (Spring 2016): 199–222.

Milstein, Tom. "The New Left: Areas of Jewish Concern." In *The New Left and the Jews*, ed. Mordecai S. Chertoff. New York: Pitman, 1971.

Mitelpunkt, Shaul. *Israel in the American Mind: The Cultural Politics of US-Israeli Relations, 1958–1988*. New York: Cambridge University Press, 2018.

Morgan, Bill, ed. *The Letters of Allen Ginsberg*. Philadelphia: Da Capo Press, 2008.

Morgan, Robin, ed. *Sisterhood is Powerful*. New York: Vintage Books, 1970.

Morrison, Toni. *What Moves at the Margin: Selected Nonfiction*. Edited and with an introduction by Carolyn C. Denard. Jackson: University Press of Mississippi, 2008.

Mungo, Ray. *Famous Long Ago: My Life and Hard Times with Liberation News Service*. New York: Citadel Press, 1990.

Muravchik, Joshua. "Comrades." *Commentary* 121, no. 1 (January 2006). www.commentarymagazine.com/article/comrades.

"Al-Mu'tamarun fi Nadwat Filastin Yastankiruna Jara'im al-Salt [Conferees at the Palestine Seminar Denounce the Crimes in al-Salt]." *al-Fateh*, September 4, 1970.

Muzher, Sherri. "Silenced No More: Jewish Supporters of Palestinian Rights Speak Out during Intifada," *Dissident Voice*, December 2, 2001. www.dissidentvoice.org/Articles/SherriSilenced.htm.

Nes, David G. *The June War in the Middle East*. Boulder, CO: American Committee for Justice in the Middle East, n.d.

New American Movement. "Resolution on the Arab/Palestinian-Israeli Conflict." N.p., 1979.

"A Nice Jewish Girl" [by Sharon Rose]. *Great Speckled Bird*, October 26, 1970.

Neyer, Joseph. *"A State Like Any Other State"?* New York: Youth Committee for Peace and Democracy in the Middle East, 1969.

Nichols, Bill. "New from California Newsreel," *Jump Cut* 17 (April 1978): 10–13.

Nicosia, Gerald. *Home to War: A History of the Vietnam Veterans' Movement*. New York: Crown Publishers, 2001.

"NLN Talks to Abu Ammar: An Interview with a leader of Al-Fateh." *New Left Notes*, April 17, 1969.

Norwood, Stephen H. *Antisemitism and the American Far Left*. New York: Cambridge University Press, 2013.

Novak, William. "Nine Lies about Israel." *Genesis 2* (December 1973) Reprinted in *The Great Berrigan Debate* (New York: Committee on New Alternatives in the Middle East, 1974).

Novick, Paul. *The Character and Aims of the Morning Freiheit*. New York: Morgen Freiheit, n.d.

"OAS Leans Left." *Near East Report* 13, no. 18 (September 3, 1969): 84.

Oglesby, Carl. *Ravens in the Sun: A Personal History of the 1960s Antiwar Movement*. New York: Scribner, 2008.

O'Neil, William L. *The New Left: A History*. Wheeling, IL: Harlan Davidson, 2001.

Otero, C. P., ed., *Noam Chomsky: Radical Priorities*. Expanded 3rd ed. Oakland, CA: AK Press, 2003.

"Palestine." *MERIP* 1, no. 4 (November 1971): 1, 12.

Palestine Book Project. *Our Roots Are Still Alive: The Story of the Palestinian People*. San Francisco: People's Press, 1977.

"Palestine: PLO Wins Major Victory." *Winter Soldier* 4, no. 12 (December 1974).

"Palestine Will Be Free! Zionism, White Supremacy and the Palestinian Revolution." *Breakthrough* 6, no. 1 (Spring 1982): 8–16.

"Palestine Will Win!" *Breakthrough* 2, no. 1 (Spring 1978): 8–23.

Pennock, Pamela E. *The Rise of the Arab American Left: Activists, Allies, and Their Fight against Imperialism and Racism, 1960s–1980s*. Chapel Hill, NC: University of North Carolina Press, 2017.

Peretz, Martin. "The American Left and Israel." *Commentary* 44, no. 5 (November 1967): 27–34.

Petran, Tabitha. "Palestine Creates Own Liberation Force." *Guardian*, July 27, 1968.

———. *Zionism: A Political Critique*. Somerville, MA: New England Free Press, [1968?].

"Playboy Interview: George McGovern—Candid Conversation." *Playboy* 18, no. 8 (August 1971): 55–70, 190–93.

Podhoretz, Norman. *Breaking Ranks: A Political Memoir*. New York: Harper & Row, 1979.

———. "A Certain Anxiety." *Commentary* 52, no. 2 (August 1971).

———. *Ex-Friends: Falling Out with Allen Ginsberg, Lionel & Diana Trilling, Lillian Hellman, Hannah Arendt, and Norman Mailer*. New York: Free Press, 1999.

———. *Making It*. New York: Random House, 1967.

———. "Now, Instant Zionism." *New York Times*, February 3, 1974.

———. *Why Are Jews Liberals?* New York: Vintage Books, 2010.

Pogrebin, Letty Cottin. "Anti-Semitism in the Women's Movement." *Ms.*, June 1982: 45–48, 62–72.

———. *Deborah, Golda, and Me: Being Female and Jewish in America.* New York: Crown Publishers, 1991.

"Politics in America: An Interview with Carl Gershman." *Ba-Golah—In Exile,* Winter 5737/1977.

Pollack, Herman. "Observations in Israel: Before and during the 'Yom ha-Din' War." *Jewish Currents* 28, no. 7 (July–August 1974): 4–7.

Porter, Jack Nusan. "Jewish Student Activism: Northwestern University Leader Outlines Jewish New Left Development." *Jewish Currents* 24, no. 5 (May 1970): 23–34.

Porter, Jack Nusan, and Peter Dreier, eds. *Jewish Radicalism: A Selected Anthology.* New York: Grove Press, 1973.

Price, Wayne. "Position Paper on the Mid East." Unpublished document. August 1969.

Progressive Labor Party. *Revolution Today: U.S.A. A Look at the Progressive Labor Movement and the Progressive Labor Party.* An Exposition-Banner Book. New York: Exposition Press, 1970.

"Progressive Labor Party Says: U.S. Imperialist Decline = Mid-East Genocide. Arab and Israeli Workers Must Unite to Kill All the Oil Bosses." *Challenge,* November 2, 1973.

"Protest Rally in New York against Camp David." *Palestine: P.L.O. Information Bulletin* 4, no. 19 (November 1, 1978). www.newjerseysolidarity.net/plobulletin/vol4no19nov1978/plobulletin_vol4no19nov1978.pdf.

Pruden, Wesley, Jr. "Doves on Asia Turn [in]to Hawks on Middle East." *National Observer,* June 15, 1970.

Raab, Earl. "The Deadly Innocences of American Jews." *Commentary* 50, no. 6 (December 1970).

"Randa Khalidi on Palestinians, Black Panthers, and Dramaturgy." *Daily Star,* February 16, 2013. www.dailystar.com.lb/Culture/Performance/2013/Feb-16/206682-randa-khalidi-on-palestinians-black-panthers-and-dramaturgy.ashx;

Raskin, Jonah. *For the Hell of It: The Life and Times of Abbie Hoffman.* Berkeley: University of California Press, 1996.

———. *Out of the Whale: Growing Up in the American Left.* New York: Links Books, 1974.

Reed, Roy. "Critics on Vietnam Divided by Appeal on Israel." *New York Times,* June 12, 1967.

"Reflections on a Lifetime of Engagement with Zionism, the Palestine Question, and American Empire: An Interview with Noam Chomsky, Interviewed by Mouin Rabbani." *Journal of Palestine Studies* 41, no. 3 (Spring 2012): 92–120.

*Report of the Socialist International Fact Finding Mission to the Middle East, Circular No. B 14/7.* Introduction by Bruno Kreisky. London: Socialist International, 1977.

Resnick, Sid. "Can Radicals Support the Arab Terrorists? The Political Goals of Al Fatah Challenged by Progressives." *Jewish Currents* 23, no. 7 (July–August 1969): 1–10.

———. "Is a Jewish State a Racist State: Israel as a National State Compared with European Socialist States." *Jewish Currents* 25, no. 5 (May 1971): 5–10.

Retherford, Jim. "Remembering Stew Albert: the Yippies' Quiet Theorist." www.stewalbert/com/memorial.html.

"Revolutionaries Must Fight Nationalism: An Editorial, June 1969." *PL Magazine*, August 1969.

"Revolutionary American Jews: Support the Palestinian Resistance." *Free Palestine* 2, no. 8 (December 1970): 3.

"Revolutionary Student Brigade Calling for April 19th Demos around War." *VVAW/ WSO Newsletter*, March 23, 1975.

Richards, Dai, and David Ash, directors. *The 50 Years War: Israel and the Arabs*. 1999.

Richardson, Peter. *A Bomb in Every Issue: How the Short, Unruly Life of Ramparts Magazine Changed America*. New York: New Press, 2009.

Ring, Harry. "Doves into Hawks; a Lesson for the Peace Movement." *The Militant*, June 12, 1967.

———. "The Govt. vs. Thorsten Krebs." *The Militant*, October 19, 1964.

Roberts, Dick. "The Egypt-Israeli Crisis." *The Militant*, June 5, 1967.

Rodrick, Stephen. "Martin Peretz Is Not Sorry. About Anything." *New York Times Magazine*, January 30, 2011.

Rose, Sharon. Combined review of *Liberation* 18, no. 6 (February 1974) and Arnold Forster and Benjamin R. Epstein, *The New Anti-Semitism* (New York: McGraw Hill, 1974), in *MERIP Reports*, no. 28 (May 1974): 28–30.

———. "Zionism in the Mid-East." *Win* 6 (June 15, 1970): 8–9.

Rose, Sharon, and Cathy Tackney. *off our backs* 1, no. 11 (October 25, 1970). Reprinted by the Middle East Research and Information Project (MERIP).

Rosen, Bernard K. "Socialist Policy for the Middle East." *New Politics* 6, no. 2 (Spring 1967): 74–83.

Rosen, Stephen J., and Yosef L. Abramowitz. *How Americans Feel about Israel*. AIPAC Papers on U.S.-Israel Relations, 10. [Washington, DC]: American Israel Public Affairs Committee, 1984.

Rosenberg, Michael Jay. "Israel without Apology." In *The New Jews*, ed. James A. Sleeper and Alan L. Mintz. New York: Vintage Books, 1971.

———."My Evolution as a Jew." *Midstream: A Monthly Jewish Review*, August–September 1970.

———. "To Uncle Tom & Other Such Jews." *Village Voice*, February 13, 1969.

Ross, Jack. *The Socialist Party of America: A Complete History*. Lincoln, NE: Potomac Books, 2015.

Rossinow, Doug. "'The 1900-Year Crisis': Arthur Waskow, the Question of Israel/Palestine, and the Effort to Form a Jewish Religious Left in America, 1967–1974." In *The Religious Left in Modern America: Doorkeepers of a Radical Faith*, ed.

Leilah Danielson, Marion Mollin, and Doug Rossinow, 233–54. New York: Palgrave Macmillan, 2018.

Roth, Benita. *Separate Roads to Feminism: Black, Chicana, and White Feminist Movements in America's Second Wave.* New York: Cambridge University Press, 2004.

Rothman, Stanley, and S. Robert Lichter. *Roots of Radicalism: Jews, Christians, and the New Left.* New York: Oxford University Press, 1982.

Rubin, Jerry. *Do It! Scenarios of the Revolution.* Introduction by Eldridge Cleaver. New York: Simon & Schuster, 1970.

———. *Growing (Up) at 37.* New York: Warner Books, 1976.

———. "Notes from a Yippizolean Era." Youth International Party article written for the underground press, n.d.

———. *We Are Everywhere. Written in Cook County Jail.* New York: Harper & Row, 1971.

Rubin, Mike. *An Israeli Worker's Answer to M. S. Arnoni.* New York: Ad Hoc Committee on the Middle East, 1968.

Rudd, Mark. *Underground: My Life with SDS and the Weathermen.* New York: Harper, 2009.

———. "Why Were so Many Jews in SDS? (Or, the Ordeal of Civility)." Talk delivered at the New Mexico Jewish Historical Society, November 2005. www.markrudd.com.

Ryan, Maria. *Neoconservatism and the New American Century.* New York: Palgrave Macmillan, 2010.

Sabin, Albert B., with David S. Landes, Allen Pollack, and Herbert Stroup. *The Arabs Need and Want Peace, but—Impressions and Conclusions of the Mission of American Professors for Peace in the Middle East to Jordan and the United Arab Republic, June 24 to July 5, 1968.* New York: American Professors for Peace in the Middle East, 1968.

Sachar, Howard. *A History of Jews in America.* New York: Vintage Books, 1993.

Saks, Robert J. "Israel and the New Left." *Journal of Jewish Communal Service* 45, no. 2 (Winter 1968): 139–46.

Sale, Kirkpatrick. *SDS.* New York: Random House, 1973.

Salkin, Jeffrey K. *A Dream of Zion: American Jews Reflect on Why Israel Matters to Them.* Woodstock, NY: Jewish Lights Publishing, 2007.

Schappes, Morris U. *The Jewish Question and the Left—Old and New: A Challenge to the New Left.* A Jewish Currents Reprint. New York: Jewish Currents, 1970.

Scheer, Robert. "Oil and the Arabs. The Nasser Thesis: Part II." *Ramparts* 6, no. 6 (January 1968): 36–42.

———. "A Nasser Thesis." *Ramparts* 6, no. 4 (November 1967): 84–98.

Schleifer, Abdullah *[sic]. The Fall of Jerusalem.* New York: Monthly Review Press, 1972.

———. "Arabs Weigh Liberation Fight." *National Guardian,* June 4, 1967.

"The Security of the State of Israel." *War and Peace in the Middle East.* New York: Morgen Freiheit, 1967.

Selfa, Lance, ed. *The Struggle for Palestine*. Chicago: Haymarket Books, 2002.

*Self-Determination in the Mideast: A Debate from the Pages of "The Militant" and "Daily World." Dave Frankel versus Tom Foley*. New York: Pathfinder Press, 1974.

Seliger, Ralph. "Muravchik, 90, Socialist and Jewish Labor Committee Leader." *Jewish Daily Forward*, January 12, 2007. http://forward.com/articles/9826/muravchik—socialist-and-jewish-labor-committe/.

Selzer, Michael. *Israel as a Factor in Jewish-Gentile Relations in America*: *Observations in the Aftermath of the June, 1967 War*. With an Introduction by Rabbi Elmer Berger. New York: American Council for Judaism, 1968.

Shenker, Israel. "Mrs. Meir Aware of 'Image Crisis.'" *New York Times*, October 7, 1969.

Sheppard, Barry. *The Party: The Socialist Workers Party, 1960–1988. Volume One: The Sixties. A Political Memoir*. Chippendale, Australia: Resistance Books, 2005.

Shuldiner, David P. *Aging Political Activists: Personal Narratives from the Old Left*. Westport, CT: Praeger, 1995.

Siegel, Ellen, and Nabil Ahmed. "Shared Memories." Just World Books. http://justworldbooks.com/sabra-and-shatila-a-somber-anniversary.

———. "The Road to Jerusalem." *Freedomways* 23, no. 2 (1983): 90–98.

Sklar, Martin J., and James Weinstein. "Socialism and the New Left." In *For a New America: Essays in History and Politics from Studies on the Left 1959–1967*, ed. David Weinstein and David W. Eakins. New York: Random House, 1970.

Sleeper, James A., and Alan L. Mintz. *The New Jews*. New York: Vintage Books, 1971.

Slonecker, Blake. *A New Dawn for the New Left: Liberation News Service, Montague Farm, and the Long Sixties*. New York: Palgrave Macmillan, 2012.

Smith, Michael Steven. *Lawyers for the Left: In the Courts, in the Streets, and on the Air*. New York: OR Books, 2019.

Socialist Labor Party. "The Middle East Conflict." A Socialist Labor Party Statement. 1978.

Socialist Workers Party. *Internal Information Bulletin*, November 1971.

———. *SWP Discussion Bulletin* 26, no. 8 (October 1967).

Spiegel, Irving. "7 Senators Urge Planes for Israel." *New York Times*, May 24, 1970.

"Spring Mobilization Committee Gags Opponents of Mideast War." *Workers World*, July 20, 1967.

"Spring Mobilization to Discuss Mideast War at Next Meeting." *Workers World*, June 24, 1967.

"The State of Righteousness: Liberal Zionists Speak Out." Huff Post Religion, April 24, 2012. www.huffingtonpost.com/michael-walzer/liberal-zionists-speak-out-state-of-righteousness_b_1447261.html.

"Statement on the Middle East." *Judaism* 18 (Fall 1969): 483–87.

"Statement of the Political Unity of the October League." Transcription, editing, and mark-up by Paul Saba.www.marxists.org/history/erol/ncm-1/ol-unity-statement-inter.

Staub, Michael E. *The Jewish 1960s: An American Sourcebook*. Waltham, MA: Brandeis University Press, 2004.

———. *Torn at the Roots: The Crisis of Jewish Liberalism in Postwar America*. New York: Columbia University Press, 2002.

Staudenmaier, Michael. *Truth and Revolution: A History of the Sojourner Truth Organization, 1969–1986*. Oakland, CA: AK Press, 2012.

Stern, Sheldon. "Support for Panthers Damned." *Ha-Orah—The Light*, January 30, 1970.

Stern, Sol. "American Jews and Israel: A Symposium." *Commentary* 85, no. 2 (February 1988).

———. "I. F. Stone: The Journalist as Pamphleteer." *Ramparts* 6, no. 7 (February 1968): 53–55.

———. "Israel without Apology." *City Journal*, Summer 2003. www.city-journal.org/html/13_3_israel.html.

———. "My Jewish Problem—and Ours: Israel, the Left, and the Jewish Establishment." *Ramparts* 10, no. 2 (August 1971). Reprinted in *Jewish Radicalism: A Selected Anthology*, ed. Jack Nusan Porter and Peter Dreier (New York: Grove Press, 1973).

———. "The Left and Israel: 'My Jewish Problem and Ours' Part II." *Ha-Yom*, October 1971.

———. "The *Ramparts* I Watched." *City Journal*, Winter 2010. www.city-journal.org/2010/20_1_ramparts.html.

Stone, I. F. "The Future of Israel." *Ramparts* 6, no. 1 (July 1967).

———. "Holy War." *New York Review of Books*, August 3, 1967.

———. *Underground to Palestine*. New York: Boni & Gaer, 1946.

Stork, Joe. "The American New Left and Palestine." *Journal of Palestine Studies* 2, no. 1 (Autumn 1972): 64–69.

Stork, Joe, and Sharon Rose. "Zionism and American Jews." *MERIP Reports* 29 (June 1974): 3–13, 26.

Sweezy, Paul M. "Israel and Imperialism." *Monthly Review* 19, no. 5 (October 1967): 1–8.

*Target USA: The Arab Propaganda Offensive*. N.p.: Anti-Defamation League of B'nai B'rith, 1975.

Teller, Susan. "One Week in Lebanon Can Blow Your Mind." *Great Speckled Bird*, October 4, 1970.

"Tension 'Built Into' Mideast Setup." *National Guardian*, June 24, 1967.

"The Theory of Three Worlds and the Middle East Situation Today." *Workers' Press*, February–March 1978. Encyclopedia of Anti-Revisionism On-Line. Transcription, editing, and markup by Paul Saba.www.marxists.org/history/erol/ncm-1a/mlc-mid-east.htm.

Thomas, Michael. *American Policy toward Israel: The Power and Limits of Beliefs*. New York: Routledge, 2007.

Thomas, Pat. *Did It! From Yippie to Yuppie: Jerry Rubin, an American Revolutionary*. Seattle: Fantagraphics Books, 2017.

Thrall, Nathan. "How the Battle over Israel and Anti-Semitism Is Fracturing American Politics." *New York Times*, March 28, 2019.

"Time to Stop Calling 'Nazis.'" *Morgen Freiheit*, July 9, 1967.

Trabulsi, Fawwaz. "The Palestine Problem: Zionism and Imperialism in the Middle East." *New Left Review* 1, no. 57 (September–October 1969): 53–90.

Tropea, Joe. "Laura Whitehorn: The Social-Justice Activist Talks about the Weather Underground, Black Panthers and the Double Standard of Violent Action in the U.S." *Baltimore City Paper*, February 24, 2010. www2.citypaper.com/story. asp?id=19825.

"Two Views on the Middle East Crisis." *New Politics* 8, no. 3 (Summer 1970): 5–6.

Turki, Fawaz. "The Passions of Exile: The Palestine Congress of North America." *Journal of Palestine Studies* 9, no. 4 (Summer 1980): 17–43.

———. "Thoughts of a Palestinian Exile." *Ramparts* 11, no. 3 (September 1972): 42–46.

Unger, Irwin. *The Movement: A History of the American New Left 1959–1972*. New York: Harper & Row, 1974.

United Nations. *Report of the World Conference of the International Women's Year, Mexico City, 19 June–2 July 1975*. UN Document E/CONF./66/34. New York: United Nations, 1976.

———. *Report of the World Conference of the United Nations Decade for Women: Quality, Development and Peace. Copenhagen, 14 to 30 July 1980*. UN Document A/CONF.94/35. New York: United Nations, 1980.

"U.S. Is the Real Sponsor of Israel's Attack on the Arabs." *Workers World*, June 9, 1967.

Varon, Jeremy. *Bringing the War Home: The Weather Underground, the Red Army Faction, and Revolutionary Violence in the Sixties and Seventies*. Berkeley: University of California Press, 2004.

Walzer, Michael, and Martin Peretz. "Israel Is not Vietnam." *Ramparts* 6, no. 1 (July 1967): 11–14.

War Resisters League. *Statement on the Middle East*. N.p.: 1974.

———. "Draft of a Possible Position for Jewish Radicals in American, on 'The Diaspora, Zion, and Israel.'" *Response: A Contemporary Jewish Review* 4 (Fall 1970): 72–75.

Waskow, Arthur. *The Bush Is Burning! Radical Judaism Faces the Pharaohs of the Modern Superstate*. New York: Macmillan, 1971.

———. "Draft of a Possible Position for Jewish Radicals in America, on 'The Diaspora, Zionism and Israel.'" *Sh'ma* No. 4 (Fall 1970): 72–75.

Watkins, Rychetta. *Black Power, Yellow Power, and the Making of Revolutionary Identities*. Jackson, MS: University of Mississippi Press, 2012.

Wattenberg, Ben. "A Man Whose Ideas Helped Change the World." *Baltimore Sun*, April 22, 1992.

Waxman, Chaim I., and William B. Helmreich. "Religious and Communal Elements of Ethnicity: American Jewish College Students and Israel." *Ethnicity* 4, no. 2 (June 1977): 122–32.

Waxman, Dov. *Trouble in the Tribe: The American Jewish Conflict over Israel*. Princeton, NJ: Princeton University Press, 2016.

"We Are Lesbians." *Gay Flames*, September 11, 1970.

Weinstein, James. *Ambiguous Legacy: The Left in American Politics*. New York: New Viewpoints, 1975.

———. *The Long Detour: The History and Future of the American Left*. Boulder, CO: Westview Press, 2003.

Weinstein, James, and David W. Eakins, eds. *For a New America: Essays in History and Politics from* Studies on the Left, *1959–1967*. New York: Random House, 1970.

Weinstock, Nathan, and Jon Rothschild. *The Truth about Israel and Zionism*. New York: Pathfinder Press, 1973.

Werthheimer, Jack. "Breaking the Taboo: Critics of Israel and the American Jewish Establishment." In *Envisioning Israel: The Changing Ideals and Images of North American Jews*, ed. Alon Gal. Detroit: Wayne State University Press; Jerusalem: Magnes Press, 1996.

"What Are 'Palestinian Legitimate Rights': An Editorial." *Jewish Currents* 28, no. 7 (July–August 1974): 3.

"When Extremes Meet." *Near East Report* 12, no. 19 (September 17, 1968): 76.

"Why We Are Youth for Stalin." In *The Role of the Dictatorship of the Proletariat in the International Marxist-Leninist Movement. The October Revolution vs. the "Cultural Revolution"* (April 1968). Encyclopedia of Anti-Revisionism Online. Transcription, editing, mark up by Paul Saba.www.marxists.org/history/erol/1960-1970/youthforstalin.htm.

Winston, Henry M. "Black Americans and the Middle East Conflict." *World Marxist Review* (November 1970): 18–23.

———. *Black Americans and the Middle East Conflict*. New York: New Outlook Publishers, 1970.

Wistrich, Robert S. *From Ambivalence to Betrayal: The Left, the Jews, and Israel*. Lincoln: University of Nebraska Press, 2012.

Women against Imperialism. *The Issue of Zionism in the Women's Movement*. San Francisco. Women against Imperialism, 1982.

———. "Taking Our Stand against Zionism and White Supremacy." *off our backs* 12, no. 7 (July 1982).

"Women: Your Place Is with the Commandos, Not Only with Your Children." *Rat: Subterranean News*, February 6–23, 1970.

"Workers World Party Statement on Mideast." *Workers World*, June 9, 1967.

Wu, Judy Tzu-Chun. *Radicals on the Road: Internationalism, Orientalism, and Feminism during the Vietnam Era*. Ithaca, NY: Cornell University Press, 2013.

Yanker, Gary. *Prop Art: Over 1000 Contemporary Political Posters*. New York: Darien House,1972.

Young, Cynthia A. *Soul Power: Culture, Radicalism, and the Making of a U.S. Third World Left*. Durham, NC: Duke University Press, 2006.

Young Socialist Alliance. *Zionism and the Arab Revolution: The Myth of a Progressive Israel*. New York: Young Socialist Alliance, 1967.

"Zionism Is Racism." *Osawatomie* 2, no. 1 (April–May 1976): 22–23.

# Index

Mann, Eric, 141

Mao Zedong, 15, 146

Maoism. *See* Marxism

MAPAI Party, 35–36, 53, 83, 109

MAPAM Party, 35–36, 53, 54

Marcy, Sam, 75, 121–22

Marks, Ann, 216n45

Marquette University, 181

Marqusee, Mike, 65–66

Marxism: Albanian, 148; Maoism, 87, 146, 149; revisionism, 76; Students for a Democratic Society moves toward, 15

Marxist-Leninist Collective, 148

Massachusetts Institute of Technology, 34, 68, 174; Arab Club, 69

Mattison, Georgia, 46, 52, 217n5

Matzpen, 16, 83, 174

May 19th Communist Organization, 144, 192

MC5, 23

McCarthy, Eugene, 131

McCarty, Joseph, 28

McGovern, George, 77, 130–31, 159, 162; Jewish vote, 165

McReynolds, David, 109–10, 168–69, 237n6

Media, 54, 110, 126

Medvecky, Nick: student journalism, 29–31; travels in Middle East, 40–42, 43–44, 47, 217n5

Meir, Golda, 35, 79, 80, 159

Melkite (Greek) Catholics, 183

Mellen, Jim, 15

Menicucci, Garay, 239n36

Mennis, Bernice, 242n42

Mennonites, 182

Methodist Federation for Social Action, 180–81

Mexico City, 187, 188, 190

Meyers, Janet, 197

Michigan: attorney general, 30–31; state legislature, 30

Michigan State University, 235n6

Middle East Council of Churches, 182

*The Middle East Crisis. See* Hyman Lumer

Middle East Information Project (MERIP), 47, 48, 52, 72; *MERIP Reports*, 52

Middle East Peace Coalition, 180–81

*Mid-East Probe*, 173

*Militant, The. See* Socialist Workers Party

Mills, C. Wright, 10, 15

Milstein, Tom, 65

Milwaukee, Wisconsin, Pfister Hotel, 78–79

*Minority of One*, 61–62

Mirkinson, Judith, 192, 195–96

Mitchell, Charlene, 103

Mizrachi Women's Organization of America, 131

Mobe, The. *See* Spring Mobilization Committee to End the War in Vietnam

*Monthly Review*, 105–06

Montreal, Canada, 55

Montross, Bill, 239n36

Morgan, Robin, 188

*Morgen Freiheit*, 91, 94–97, 99–101

Morgenthau, Hans, 154

Morrison, Toni, 193

Morrock, Richard, 16–17

Mossadegh, Mohammad, 46

*Mother Jones*, 66

Movement, The: definition, 3

Moynihan, Daniel P., 156, 157, 166

Mozambique, 11, 133, 197

*Ms.*, 184, 191, 193

Munich (1938), 159, 160

Munich Olympic Games Massacre, 48, 140, 142

Muravchik, Joshua: socialist movement, 112; Young People's Socialist League, 153, 154, 157;

Zionism is racism, 147, 166, 188, 189. *See also* women's movement
United Press International, 145
United States: arms sales to Israel, 6, 109, 110, 130, 131; Central Intelligence Agency (CIA): 43, 54, 60, 155; CIA's Operation MH/CHAOS, 43; congress, 159; conscription ended, 137; defense department, 60; Emergency Aid Bill for Israel, 159; Federal Bureau of Investigation (FBI), 55, 93, 100; FBI's COINTELPRO, 100, 226–27n33; house of representatives, 204; justice department, 55; Middle East policy, 112, 114, 148; military personnel protest, 134; military strength, 70, 114, 162–63, 165; Palestine Liberation Organization, 118; presidential elections (1968), 80, 105, 130–32, 165; presidential elections (1972), 130–31, 165; presidential elections (1976), 175; presidential elections (1980), 165; pre-war assessment of 1967 Arab-Israeli war, 60; rapprochement with China, 152; state department, 37, 155, 189; UN Human Rights Commission, 166; UN mission, 76, 78; voting age lowered, 137. *See also* Arab-Israeli peace process
United States Youth Council, 155
University of California at Berkeley, 11, 88, 198; 235n6; Arab Students' Association, 27; Arab-Israeli student activism, 25–27, 36–38, 84, 109; Committee for a Progressive Middle East, 36–38; Free Speech Movement, 36, 101, 145; *Jewish Radical*, 33; Radical Student Union, 38; Sproul Plaza, 25, 38, 109, 129
University of California at Los Angeles, 27, 56, 82
University of Chicago, 28

University of Georgia, 235n6
University of Illinois at Chicago Circle, 235n6
University of Iowa, 181
University of Maryland, 28, 235n6
University of Massachusetts at Amherst, 235n6
University of Miami at Coral Gables, 35
University of Michigan, 12, 136, 177, 235n6
University of Pennsylvania, 69, 84
University of San Francisco, 235n6
University of Virginia, 28
University of Washington, Radical Jewish Student Union, 33
University of Wisconsin at Madison, 28
University of Wisconsin at Milwaukee, 28

Vancouver, Canada, 185
Vered, Dan, 35–36
Viet Cong, 22, 23, 24, 26, 37, 123, 146, 197
Vietnam, 13, 139, 197; North Vietnam, 39, 101, 102, 185; revolutionaries, 4, 133; South Vietnam, 185
Vietnam Veterans Against the War, 132
Vietnam Veterans Against the War/ Winter Soldier Organization, 132–33
Vietnam War: American forces leave, 135, 168, 187; American war crimes, 77; bombing, 102; Israel-Vietnam comparison, 63, 66, 77, 78, 102, 121, 123, 124–25, 130, 131; veterans groups, 132–34. *See also* anti-Vietnam War movement
*Village Voice*, 31–32, 109–10, 169

Wagner, Donald E., 181, 182–83
Walkowitz, Judith, 241n30
Walzer, Michael, 63, 66, 129
*War in the Mideast, June 1967: What Were the Forces Behind It? See* Rita Freed